INVESTIGATING PHENOMENAL CONSCIOUSNESS

ADVANCES IN CONSCIOUSNESS RESEARCH

ADVANCES IN CONSCIOUSNESS RESEARCH provides a forum for scholars from different scientific disciplines and fields of knowledge who study consciousness in its multifaceted aspects. Thus the Series will include (but not be limited to) the various areas of cognitive science, including cognitive psychology, linguistics, brain science and philosophy. The orientation of the Series is toward developing new interdisciplinary and integrative approaches for the investigation, description and theory of consciousness, as well as the practical consequences of this research for the individual and society.

Series A: Theory and Method. Contributions on the development of theory and method in the study of consciousness.

Volume 13

Max Velmans (ed.)

Investigating Phenomenal Consciousness
New methodologies and maps

INVESTIGATING PHENOMENAL CONSCIOUSNESS

NEW METHODOLOGIES AND MAPS

Edited by

MAX VELMANS
University of London

JOHN BENJAMINS PUBLISHING COMPANY
AMSTERDAM/PHILADELPHIA

TM The paper used in this publication meets the minimum requirements of American National Standard for Information Sciences — Permanence of Paper for Printed Library Materials, ANSI z39.48–1984.

Library of Congress Cataloging-in-Publication Data

Investigation phenomenal consciousness : new methodologies and maps / edited by Max Velmans
    p.   cm. -- (Advances in consciousness research, ISSN 1381-589X ; v. 13)
    Includes bibliographical references and index.
    1. Phenomenological psychology. 2. Consciousness. I. Velmans, Max, 1942- II. Series
BF204.5.I58   2000
153--dc21   00-039749
ISBN 90 272 5133 9 (Eur.) / 1 55619 193 6 (US) (Pb only; alk. paper)

John Benjamins Publishing Co. • P.O.Box 75577 • 1070 AN Amsterdam • The Netherlands
John Benjamins North America • P.O.Box 27519 • Philadelphia PA 19118-0519 • USA

Table of Contents

Acknowledgements

The theme of this book originated in an International Symposium on "Methodologies for the Study of Consciousness", organised by Max Velmans, Janet Richardson, and Arthur Zajonc, funded and hosted by the *Fetzer Institute*, Michigan, USA, in September 1996. The intensive four days of presentations and discussions were published in the symposium proceedings *Methodologies for the Study of Consciousness: A New Synthesis* (eds. J. Richardson and M. Velmans), The Fetzer Institute, 1997. Some of the chapters in this book have been developed from the proceedings; others are entirely new. I would like to thank the original participants David Abram, Bernard Baars, Ron Brady, John Crook, Peter Fenwick, David Fontana, Brian Goodwin, Guven Guzeldere, Rom Harré, Ivan Havel, Jane Henry, Elizabeth McCormick, Millar Mair, John Pickering, Peter Reason, Janet Richardson, Marilyn Schlitz, Alwyn Scott, Gregory Simpson, Richard Stevens, Charles Tart, Frances Vaughan, and Arthur Zajonc for their inspiration and wisdom, and The Fetzer Institute, particularly Arthur Zajonc and Chuck Willis, for their encouragement and continued support. My special thanks are also due to my partner Janet Richardson who helped to formulate and plan this project.

Max Velmans, December 1999

Contributors

Natalie Depraz, College Internationale de Philosophie, 1 rue Descartes, 75005 Paris, France.

Peter Fenwick, Institute of Psychiatry, London. Home address: 42 Herne Hill, London, SE4 9QP, UK.

David Fontana, School of Social Sciences, University of Cardiff, Glamorgan Building, King Edward VII Avenue, Cardiff CF10 3WT, UK.

Rom Harré, Linacre College, Oxford University. Home address: 111 Church Way, Iffley Village, Oxford, OX4 4EG, UK.

Jane Henry, Experiential Research Group, Crowther N Wing, Open University, Walton Hall, Milton Keynes MK7 6AA, UK.

John Pickering, Psychology Department, Warwick University, Coventry, CV4 7AL, UK.

Janet Richardson, Florence Nightingale School of Nursing and Midwifery, King's College London, James Clerk Maxwell Building, 57 Waterloo Road, London SE1 8WA, UK.

Alwyn Scott, Department of Mathematics, University of Arizona, Tucson, AZ 85721 USA.

Howard Shevrin, University of Michigan Medical Centre. Home address: 2021 Vinewood Blvd., Ann Arbor, MI 48104, USA.

Mark Solms, Academic Department of Neurosurgery, St Bartholomew's & Royal London Hospital, Whitechapel, London E1 1BB.

Richard Stevens, Department of Psychology, Open University, Walton Hall, Milton Keynes MK7 6AA, UK.

Charles T. Tart, Institute of Transpersonal Psychology, 744 San Antonio Road, Palo Alto, California 94303, USA.

Francisco J. Varela, LENA, Neurosciences Cognitives et Imagerie Cérébrale, CNRS UPR 640, Hôpital de la Salpètriere, 47 Blvd. de l'Hôpital, 75651 Paris Cedex 13, France.

Max Velmans, Department of Psychology, Goldsmiths, University of London, New Cross, London SE14 6NW, UK.

Pierre Vermersch, GREX, 38 rue Nollet, Paris 75017, France.

Roger Walsh, Department of Psychiatry, University of California Medical School, Irvine, CA. 92697-1675, USA.

Ken Wilber, 6183 Red Hill Rd., Boulder, CO 80302, USA.

CHAPTER *1*

An Introduction to Investigating Phenomenal Consciousness

Max Velmans

The study of consciousness predates the founding of modern experimental psychology, and was its original focus of interest. Psychology's original method, "experimental introspection" (developed by Wundt) was intended to be a form of 'chemistry of the mind' in which compound experiences were to be analysed into their constituent elements; early psychologists also attempted to chart the manner in which variations in the elements of consciousness depend on variations in stimulus conditions (psychophysics). However, experimental introspectionism, in its early forms, did not provide a firm foundation for the growth of a science of consciousness, let alone a science of psychology.

Different laboratories produced widely differing estimates of the number of component elements of consciousness, and used different categorical systems. There were differences of opinion over what was an elemental as opposed to a compound experience. Crucially, there was no agreed method for settling disagreements. Psychologists also became increasingly uncomfortable with the need to couch all their investigations in terms of how things are experienced. Watson (1913) for example, argued that it was fruitless to speculate on how non-human animals experience the world, and that this blocked the development of a study of behaviour which could be applied both to humans and to non-human animals. Refocusing psychology on the study of behaviour would also provide it with a public, "objective" database, commensurate with other areas of science.

Although introspective methods continued to be used in clinical fields, for example in psychoanalysis and psychotherapy, with the ascendance of Behaviourism the study of consciousness came to be regarded as bad scientific practice. Even in psychophysics, where it persisted, the language used to describe the methodology avoided all reference to consciousness. Verbal reports (of perceived stimulus dimensions) were regarded as "verbal behaviour," or verbal reports were avoided altogether by requiring subjects to respond to stimuli with some non-verbal motor response (such as pressing a button). These developments in psychology were reflected in the attitudes of the wider scientific community, and for much of the 20th Century consciousness has been thought to be beyond scientific investigation.

At the present time, we are in a period of transition. While some of the scientific community remains cautious, the resurgence of interest in consciousness in recent years is becoming intense.

The reasons for this are diverse:

1. Culturally, there is increasing dissatisfaction with a worldview in which consciousness in its many forms has no natural place. For the science of psychology this 'loss of consciousness' is acute — a psychology that investigates brain states and behaviour but not how humans *experience* the world, cannot be complete.

2. In recent theorising about the relation of mind to body it is becoming recognised that consciousness poses not just one problem, but many. Some of the problems lend themselves to investigation by existing scientific means, some require the development of new methodologies, and some require theoretical advance. But these problems are increasingly being thought of as problems for science (rather than for philosophy).

The newly emerging science of consciousness is correspondingly diverse. Much of the research is taking place within psychology and the related biological sciences (see readings in Velmans, 1996; Cohen & Schooler, 1997 and reviews by Crick and Koch, 1998; Frith, Perry and Lumer, 1999). Cognitive psychologists, for example, focus largely on the contrasts between conscious and nonconscious processes and seek to fit consciousness into some functional model of the mind/brain. Social psychologists increasingly view consciousness as embedded in social context and culture, and have turned to qualitative methodologies to illuminate such relationships. Neuropsychologists have uncovered many dissociations within consciousness and between conscious and nonconscious states. They are also beginning to isolate some of the neural conditions for consciousness. In the clinical domain there is a reawakening interest in psychosomatic interactions, for example, in the influence of imagery, meditation, biofeedback, hypnosis, and placebo treatments on bodily states.

The broad field of "consciousness studies" also includes input from many other disciplines ranging from the natural sciences to the social sciences. Efforts to establish a more complete model of mind have also received input from disciplines such as parapsychology and the study of spiritual practices, currently thought (by many) to be at the edge of or outside of the prevailing scientific paradigm.

Methodologies

Within experimental psychology and the related biological sciences, the focus has largely been on relating given states of consciousness to given states of the brain, defined either in structural or functional terms. While subjective reports of conscious experience enter into such studies, they remain minimal, for example requiring subjects to report on whether they can detect, identify or notice changes in relatively simple stimuli. *The purpose of such reports is mainly to provide information about the processes antecedent to consciousness rather than about consciousness as such.* Although the use of subjective reports is widespread in experimental psychology, they are still regarded by some researchers with suspicion, even as reliable indicators of whether a stimulus is conscious or not.[1] This suspicion is fostered by the prevailing tendency towards reductionism in philosophy and science, along with a reliance only on what can be observed from a "third-person perspective."

Although this re-awakened interest in consciousness and its relation to psychological processes is a welcome development there is increasing doubt about whether a science of consciousness can be properly carried out only from a third-person perspective. For example, many of the presuppositions which ground the third- versus first-person distinction are currently under challenge (see Chapter 15, and Velmans, 1993, 1999b, 2000). Equally, the traditional *separation of the observer from the observed* is difficult to sustain when consciousness is the focus of interest (particularly in subjective reports or other forms of self-examination), suggesting the need, at least in some contexts for a *participative science*. States of consciousness are also embedded in, and partly determined by social and ecological contexts, requiring a more holistic approach to analysis (see Harman, 1994, and readings in Harman & Clark, 1994). More generally, traditional studies of psychological processes do not in themselves address the complexities of human life *as experienced*, nor in any broad sense, the difficulties these present (see Claxton 1991). The understanding and transformation of human experience requires different methodologies.

In response to this, the broad field of consciousness studies employs and is continuing to develop a wide range of methodologies (both ancient and modern) appropriate to the different questions one can ask about consciousness, and the different approaches appropriate to its fuller understanding. Unfortunately, this diversity is also leading to considerable compartmentalisation and fragmentation. For example, there is little understanding of how traditional studies of psychological processing relate to more introspective first-person investigations, and uncertainty about how to translate the findings derived from first-person methods into a systematic, intersubjective science. Nor is there a clear understanding of what the practical applications of such a science might be. The issues are ontological and epistemological as well as methodological. The purpose of this book is to introduce some of the creative ways in which first-person methods can be used and to re-assess their limitations. Suggestions are also made about how to heal the fragmentation in consciousness studies, by placing different approaches to the study of consciousness into a broader context, establishing their domain of applicability and providing some bases for synthesis.

The book

PART 1: METHODOLOGIES is not intended to be an exhaustive survey of the many techniques for studying consciousness. Rather it samples from a range of methods that give first-person phenomenology a central place, although many approaches also stress the value of triangulating first-person findings with traditional third-person measures, or stress the dependence of first-person investigations on establishing intersubjectivity (second-person relationships) within a social context.

Part 1A: Chapters 2, 3 and 4 exemplify different ways of relating conscious and unconscious mental states to processing in the brain:

Peter Fenwick (Chapter 2) provides an introduction to the range of neuro-imaging techniques that are currently available for investigating brain activities that accompany conscious experience, giving a brief overview of their advantages and limitations. These include magnetic resonance imaging and functional magnetic resonance imaging (MRI, fMRI), MRI spectroscopy, positron emission tomography (PET), single photon emission tomography (SPET), magnetoencephalography (MEG), and electroencephalography (EEG). Experiences whose correlates have been investigated with such techniques range from externally generated ones such as visual input, to those where the subjective response to stimuli is more important than the representation of external stimuli as such, for example, orgasm, and the response to psychotropic drugs. Experiences that rely largely on endogenous processing have also been studied, including imagined (rather than real) movements, emotions such as fear anger and disgust, and the cognitive activity accompanying a "theory of mind." With these techniques, the brain can be partitioned into numerous functional areas whose relationship to consciousness can be studied in detail. However, Fenwick warns that such imaging techniques do not reveal consciousness itself and do not allow one to study it as it is in itself. The metaphysical assumptions implicit in this largely third-person approach also exclude any understanding of how neuronal activity becomes "subjective experience."

Howard Shevrin (Chapter 3) illustrates how findings based on first- and third-person investigations can complement each other by providing mutual support for inferences about mental processing. This can apply to both conscious and unconscious mental states. In the research that he reviews, first-person information (patients' accounts and understanding of their symptoms) is combined with third-person cognitive and neurophysiological measures to provide evidence for "unconscious conflict" — an inference about unconscious processing initially derived from psychodynamic theory. He also provides evidence that unconscious affective processing is active and controlled rather than merely dispositional or automatic. Unconscious processes also appear to be highly individual and subject to the influences of personality and the vicissitudes of individual history, unlike the nomothetic models of such processes typically derived from purely third-person investigative techniques.

Mark Solms (Chapter 4) examines clinical situations in which the interpretations suggested by first- and third-person evidence conflict. It is often taken for
granted that third-person accounts are to be preferred in such instances. Solms,
however, advocates a more neutral stance. As he notes, traditional "subjective"
and "objective" research traditions in psychology provide different perspectives on a common underlying reality (the mind itself). Consequently, differences between these can be utilised to correct viewpoint-dependent
observational errors and theoretical interpretations, whether they are first- or
third-person. To illustrate, he provides detailed case histories of the "right
hemisphere syndrome" (a combination of anosognosia, neglect, and defective
spatial cognition) for which there are three standard interpretations in behavioural neuroscience. Surprisingly, first-person data obtained via psychoanalytic
investigations suggest a fourth account of this syndrome that provides a fuller
understanding that is consistent with *all* the data.

Part 1B: Chapters 5 and 6 re-examine the scope and limits of first-person
methods as such:

Richard Stevens (Chapter 5) suggests that phenomenology should be the
central discipline in consciousness studies but argues that this requires procedures for mapping phenomenal consciousness just as there are for neurophysiological mapping. He re-examines the history of phenomenological methods in
Western psychological science, from the early work of Wundt and James to the
more recent work of Jaynes, Romanyshyn, Donaldson and Csikszentmihalyi,
and notes that in none of these is there a clear statement of methods for
phenomenological mapping. The eidetic analysis of phenomenological psychologists working in the tradition of Husserl does appear to be systematic.
However these methods arguably elicit abstractions rather than providing an
account of what is actually being experienced. Stevens asks "what is it about
consciousness that makes it so resistant to investigation?" His answer is that
conscious experience is in itself essentially sensory though it is underpinned by
implicit meaning systems. To make progress one needs to distinguish between
these. Only the former allows for sufficient intersubjective agreement to
provide a consistent mapping onto neurophysiology. The latter requires hermeneutic reconstruction that varies according to the assumptions and methods of
the researcher. A further feature of consciousness is its capacity to construct as
it represents, which may pose the need for a third epistemology that Stevens
terms "transformational."

Natalie Depraz, Francisco Varela and Pierre Vermersch (Chapter 6), by contrast, describe a recently developed phenomenological method of investigation that is not restricted to abstractions. As with other methods in the tradition of Husserl, this has at its heart the so-called phenomenological reduction or *épochè*, which can also be described as "a reflective act", "becoming aware", or "mindfulness". In essence, this requires a *suspension* of habitual thought and judgement, a *conversion* of attention from "the exterior" to "the interior" and *letting-go* — a state of receptivity towards the experience. Based on their work in Paris, the temporal dynamics of these phases are described in careful detail. The authors point out that for the purposes of communication and the establishment of intersubjectively shared, systematic knowledge, such investigations need to be accompanied by two further phases involving engagement with others: *expression* and *validation* (a transition from a first- to a communally shared second-person perspective). They also indicate how aspects of this methodology relate to classical Buddhist investigative techniques.

Part 1C: Chapters 7, 8 and 9 focus on methods for *changing* experience rather than describing it and analysing it:

Jane Henry (Chapter 7) surveys the methodologies used to transform experience in clinical practice and the growing field of personal and professional development. She begins by contrasting the diverse theoretical positions of the key schools, but goes on to suggest that there is more commonality in practice, and outlines some of the critical, common factors identified by outcome research. She then goes on to question the wisdom of some of the principles that are widely assumed to be necessary to transform consciousness in clinical and applied psychology. The standard clinical orientation focuses on pathology rather than positive potential. Privileged strategies tend to stress rational routes to insight and to assume a need for emotional discharge. This has led to the neglect of other strategies that research on well-being suggests may be more critical, such as the importance of social interaction and active involvement in challenging but achievable tasks.

Janet Richardson (Chapter 8) presents a case for applying an "intersubjective science" to the study and development of the "therapeutic relationship" in clinical settings. Combining theoretical analyses of intersubjectivity drawn from psychology and nursing, she illustrates the effects of establishing genuine intersubjectivity or 'shared consciousness' both on what is revealed in diagnostic procedures and on therapeutic outcomes. 'Objective' measures are needed to diagnose and treat disease. But intersubjectivity is required to understand the *experience* of illness, for example through attention to patients' stories, and by the development of empathy in clinical practice. Openness and 'presence' within a therapeutic encounter can also have non-specific healing effects that are often regarded as "placebo effects" in the evaluation of conventional and complementary medicine. However these effects can be harnessed rather than dismissed. In research, qualitative methods such as ethnography, grounded theory and phenomenology are particularly well suited to an open-ended exploration of the individual, social and cultural factors that might facilitate such effects, although quantitative methods are needed to test their efficacy. Once the healing factors are understood it may, to some extent, be possible to train practitioners to develop the appropriate skills.

David Fontana (Chapter 9) gives a detailed account of how methods for examining consciousness have been used as a means to change it in diverse cultures for nearly 3000 years. Irrespective of cultural differences, similar features emerge. These include the view that normal consciousness is only one of many potential conscious states, that some states can be categorised as being at higher "levels," and that it is possible to realise human potential by entering into progressively higher states. He then summarises one of the clearest models of these states, the Advaita model of Vedantic Hinduism, and shows how many of the "oppositions" in Western thought (materialism versus idealism, self versus no-self) are not necessarily opposed in Eastern thought or in Western mystical traditions. Rather, seeming opposites translate into how things appear at different "levels of realisation." Of the many techniques suggested to change conscious experience, Fontana picks out disidentification (with ordinary conscious contents) and mindfulness (clear and focused attention) as central. How do we assess these practices and these claims? Fontana suggests that investigators need to examine their effects both on others and themselves. One can also note the cultural impact of such practices on social cohesion, education, philosophy, literature and the arts.

PART 2: MAPS provides six different overviews of the consciousness studies terrain.

Alwyn Scott (Chapter 10) presents an applied mathematician's view of consciousness research and presents a case for consciousness being a property of nonlinear biological systems that emerged at the point that organisms developed the ability to make choices. However, he stresses that present day physical science is far from achieving even a qualitative understanding of an object as intricate as the human brain embodied in a biological substrate and embedded in culture. Given this, such simplifying notions as reductive materialism, genetic determinism, and computer functionalism appear to be more the beliefs of certain scientists than necessary conclusions of physical science. According to Scott, formulations at least as general as those of philosophers Karl Popper and Ken Wilber will be required to encompass the nature of mind. He also offers several suggestions for modifications in the nature of scientific research in specific fields of activity that may be appropriate during the coming century. The chapter closes with an observation first advanced by ethnologist Ruth Benedict that a fundamental understanding of the nature of human consciousness may require the re-emergence of a complementary relationship between the sciences and the humanities.

Rom Harré (Chapter 11) provides an example of how the consciousness studies terrain might be charted from the perspective of linguistic philosophy. Following Wittgenstein, he suggests that by analysing the rules for the application of a word we can gain insight into its domain of application. The term "consciousness" for example has a relational component (consciousness of) and involves "perceptual centredness" (exemplified by the use of first-person expressions). He suggests that common sense psychology currently seems to include four classes of being — souls, persons, organisms and molecules — and that each of these is described with its own characteristic "grammar." For example, unlike organisms and molecules, the soul and the person can be said to have moral responsibility. The distinction between tasks, and the tools used to carry out the tasks may be a useful way to relate these "grammars." Soul and person grammars, for example, are used to describe tasks while organism and molecule grammars describe the tools to carry them out. Such considerations may have consequences for the forms that consciousness takes in different societies. Linguistic and other symbolic forms provide means by which experience is made available to someone in an act of cognition. In so far as these symbolic forms are local to a given society, they may contribute to a local, socially constructed field of awareness.

Charles Tart (Chapter 12) approaches the problems of consciousness from the point of view of one who has devoted many years to investigating altered states of consciousness (ASCs). He warns against reductionism, which does not take into account the wider effects of the phenomena of consciousness on personal life, values, culture, and on science itself. Rather, the phenomena have to be studied in their own right, and this applies especially to the effects of ASCs. The *essential* methods of science (observation, theorizing, prediction, communication and consensual validation) also have to be distinguished from the particular methodologies one might apply in a given field. He proposes that the essential methods of science can be applied from *within* various ASCs, using the state-specific perceptions and forms of thought which characterise these states to form a variety of state-specific, complementary sciences that will expand our understanding of both consciousness and world. Prospects for the development of such state-specific sciences are also discussed.

John Pickering (Chapter 13) suggests that first- and third-person investigations of consciousness can proceed in a spirit of mutual co-operation and points out that some of the seeming difficulties have to do with the *ethos* of third-person science to which much of psychology subscribes. Third-person methods usually employ impressive machinery which carry the badge of "big science" — with funding and other implications for psychology as a discipline within the *realpolitik* of the academy. However psychology suffers from a degree of rigidity as a consequence. For example, the stress on experimental control and conformity to norms (implicit in the use of statistics) tends to marginalise individual differences. Exclusive reliance on mechanistic, computational models overlooks more organic, systems views of cognition. The treatment of first-person accounts as unreliable folk-psychology, opens the way to consciousness being thought of as nothing more than a state of the brain. Because subjectivity cannot be encompassed within such approaches, this over-extension of reductionist thought will leave psychology at an *impasse*. As an alternative, Pickering advocates a post-modern pluralism, in which multiple perspectives are an intrinsic condition of knowing anything. These would include phenomenological as well as cognitive and neurological methods. Systematic qualitative methods also need to supplement quantitative ones, allowing for new forms of triangulation and theory development (this has happened in recent investigations of the experience of "time" and investigation of Eastern practices such as meditation). Such developments will mean a broadening of the psychology curriculum and recognition that methods carry values — which opens the way to a more complete, inclusive science of mental life.

Ken Wilber and Richard Walsh (Chapter 14) provide a very broad map of consciousness studies that incorporates nearly all current disciplines that might be directly or indirectly relevant to its understanding. They begin by comparing the major schools of thought, including cognitive science, introspectionism, neuropsychology, psychotherapy, social and developmental psychology, psychiatry, psychosomatic medicine, studies of altered states, Eastern and contemplative traditions, quantum approaches, research into "subtle energy", and evolutionary psychology. They then fit the complementary features of the world that these disciplines study into an elegant map defined by two dimensions: the individual versus the collective, and the interior versus the exterior. Different forms of existence are also arranged on the map in terms of their evolutionary development, ranging from primitive forms in the origin or centre of the map to more complex forms as one moves from the centre to the periphery. This defines "four quadrants" in which evolution can take place: evolution can be individual and interior (forms of consciousness), collective and interior (forms of cultural life), individual/ exterior (physical forms), and collective/exterior (individuals forming into progressively larger groups). Each quadrant has an appropriate descriptive language — an "I", "we" or "it" language (corresponding to having a first, second or third-person perspective). It also has domain-appropriate validity claims: for example the truthfulness of a claim about subjective experience versus the accuracy of a claim about an "objective" state of affairs. However all forms of valid knowing have something in common: an injunction, an apprehension, and a confirmation. In short, follow a given procedure, apprehend the evidence, and confirm the claim. Given that each quadrant is a part of the whole, Wilber & Walsh suggest that consciousness actually exists distributed across all four quadrants with all of their various levels and dimensions. The subjective is embedded in the intersubjective, the objective and the interobjective. In their view reductionism is doomed to fail, nor can the explanatory gap between the "subjective" and the "objective" be bridged by formal thought. Rather all quadrants are mutually supporting and need to be simultaneously explored — an "all level, all quadrant" approach to consciousness studies.

My own final map (**Velmans, Chapter 15**) approaches consciousness studies with the traditional concerns of an experimental psychologist. It stresses the need for a phenomenology of consciousness and begins with an outline of the various ways in which conventional third-person studies of body and brain can be complementary to first-person studies of experience. It then comes to grips with some of the enduring problems: How can one study "subjective" experiences "objectively"? What methodological problems peculiar to the study of experience need to be resolved? What are the appropriate ways to deal with "observer effects" which become acute with introspective methods where the observer *is* the observed. I suggest that the "subjective" versus "objective" distinction is largely artefactual and rooted in a misleading description of the contents of consciousness that dualists and reductionists share. The everyday 3-dimensional physical world that we experience is *part-of* the contents of consciousness not *apart-from* it — and the evidence of physics relies on the observations/experiences of scientists much as the evidence of consciousness studies relies on the observations/experiences of scientists and subjects. This requires a more careful analysis of scientific "objectivity". Scientists can be objective in the sense of being "dispassionate," scientific method can also be "objective" in the sense that it follows well-specified, repeatable procedures, observations can be "objective" in the sense of *inter-subjective*, but no observations are objective in the sense of being *observer-free*. The consequences for "repeatability" and the "empirical method" in science are then worked out. In essence, the empirical method is: *if you follow these procedures you will observe or experience these results.* The chapter then gives a brief survey of methodological problems that are peculiar to consciousness studies. Unlike the phenomena studied in/physics, there are asymmetries of access to individual experiences. Phenomena in consciousness studies also differ in terms of their relative permanence, stability, measurability, controllability, describability, complexity, variability, and their dependence on the observational arrangements. While domain-specific methodologies have been developed to cope with some of these problems, much remains to be done. For example, "observer effects" can be particularly strong in consciousness studies either when the observed is another human being or oneself. If one's aim is to study a given conscious state one can attempt to minimise such effects. Alternatively, if one's aim is to change a given conscious state, one can harness such effects. Close observer — observed engagements for example foster the creation of intersubjectivity (a joint "second-person perspective"). Some techniques for observing one's own conscious states can also, potentially, transform them. *How* different forms of engagement with others or oneself might facilitate such change is an important topic for research.

Overview of the Maps

Close study of the maps reveals broad areas of commonality. However, there are major differences of emphasis and, occasionally, areas of disagreement. All the maps agree for example that there are different aspects of consciousness studies that may need to be described by different "languages" — for example a first-person "I" language versus a third-person "it" language, and that the *relationships* between entities, events or processes so described need to be understood. However, Harré argues that while first-person words can express feelings, they do not describe them — a view not generally shared by other authors in the book. Harré also suggests that an analysis of the use of language *as such* will clarify the problems of consciousness, and Tart suggests that there may be a variety of "logics" or forms of thought that are specific to given (altered) states of consciousness. These claims go beyond the general support for a multidisciplinary approach expressed, for example, in the chapters by Scott, and Pickering, and elaborated on by Wilber & Walsh. To take another example, Scott treats consciousness as a property of complex, nonlinar systems that emerged only once organisms were able to make *choices*, while Wilber and Walsh prefer Teilhard de Chardin's suggestion that "Refracted rearwards along the course of evolution, consciousness displays itself qualitatively as a spectrum of shifting shades whose lower terms are lost in the night."[2] Another interesting point of difference concerns the ultimate limitations of consciousness studies: Wilber & Walsh, for example, despair of ever being able to cross the explanatory gap from the "subjective" to the "objective" by the use of formal thought. However, in my own map I suggest that the "gap" exists only because the conventional point of departure is wrong. *All* observations in science are ultimately "subjective" although they can become "objective" in being *intersubjective*.

It should be stressed that none of these maps is intended to be definitive and all the maps are open to development and change. However, taken together, they begin to define some of the rough contours of this complex, interdisciplinary field. Fundamental differences between the maps should not be ignored, as they are invitations to further debate and investigation. At the same time, the differences should not be allowed to obscure areas of emerging consensus. There is consensus for example, that consciousness cannot be fully understood from an external, third-person perspective. The third-person investigation of brain structures and functions that support conscious experiences remains important, but this needs to be supplemented by systematic first-person study of what it is like to be in given conscious states. The nature of such states is also heavily influenced by the way they are embedded in social contexts. How "I" view matters is influenced by the way "we" view matters — which requires systematic study of the complex interchange between first-, second-, and third-person perspectives. It is also interesting to note that Tart, Wilber & Walsh, and I independently arrive at an identical conclusion about what might be *essential* to consciousness studies. At the heart of the study of consciousness is an injunction, which in essence is, "do this and you will experience this," or, "if you follow these procedures you will observe or experience these results." The study of consciousness, like the rest of science, relies on the *empirical method*.

Notes

1.   See for example the attacks on introspective reports in target articles by Holender (1986), Shanks & St. John (1994) (with accompanying open peer reviews) and the subsequent critiques of these attacks by Kihlstrom (1996), Velmans (1991, 1999a).

2.   I discuss the relative merits of such "continuity theories" versus emergent, "discontinuity theories" in Velmans (2000) Chapter 12.

References

Claxton, G. 1991. "Psychosophy: Are we ready for a science of self-knowledge?" *Psychologist* 4: 249–252.

Cohen, J.D. and Schooler, J.W. (eds) 1997. *Scientific Approaches to Consciousness*. Mahwah, N.J.: Lawrence Erlbaum Associates.

Crick, F. and Koch, C. (1998) "Consciousness and neuroscience", *Cerebral Cortex* 8: 97–107.

Frith, C., Perry, R. and Lumer, E. 1999. "The neural correlates of conscious experience: And experimental framework." *Trends in Cognitive Sciences* 3, 105–114.

Harman, W. 1994. "The scientific exploration of consciousness: Towards an adequate epistemology." *Journal of Consciousness Studies* 1(1): 140–148.

Harman, W. and Clark, J. (eds) 1993. *The New Metaphysical Foundations of Modern Science*. Sausilito, California: Institute of Noetic Sciences.

Holender, D. 1986. "Semantic activation without conscious identification in dichotic listening, parafoveal vision, and visual masking." *Behavioral and Brain Sciences* 9:1–66.

Kihlstrom, J.F. 1996. "Perception without awareness of what is perceived, learning without awareness of what is learned." In M. Velmans (ed.) *The Science of Consciousness: Psychological, Neuropsychological, and Clinical Reviews*, London: Routledge.

Shanks, D.R. & St.John, M.F. 1994. "Characteristics of dissociable human learning systems." *Behavioral and Brain Sciences* 17(3): 367–447.

Velmans, M. 1991. "Is human information processing conscious?" *Behavioral and Brain Sciences* 14(4): 651–726.

Velmans, M. 1993. "A reflexive science of consciousness." In *Experimental and Theoretical Studies of Consciousness: Ciba Foundation Symposium 174*, Chichester: Wiley.

Velmans, M. (ed.) 1996. *The Science of Consciousness: Psychological, Neuropsychological and Clinical Reviews*. London: Routledge.

Velmans, M. 1999a. "When perception becomes conscious." *British Journal of Psychology* 90(4), 543–566.

Velmans, M. 1999b. "Intersubjective science." *Journal of Consciousness Studies* 6(2/3): 299–306.

Velmans, M. 2000. *Understanding Consciousness*. London: Routledge.

Watson, J. B. 1913. "Psychology as the behaviorist views it." *The Psychological Review* XX: 158–177.

PART 1A

Combining First- and Third-Person Methods

CHAPTER 2

Currrent Methods of Investigation in Neuroscience

Peter Fenwick

Science yet again seems poised to understand how the brain works. In the time of Galen it was the ventricles of the brain that were thought to be important. The flow of humours throughout the body from these ventricles circulated the characteristics of the individual. In the 1700s mechanical models of the brain and mind were very fashionable. The nerves were seen as strings pulling open various valves within the brain which instigated brain function. The telephone switchboard analogy of the early part of this century was more complex and had a greater range of explanation. The current explanatory models use the analogy of computers and artificial intelligence theories: this 'hardware' and 'software' is used to model brain function.

Neuroscience deals predominantly with mechanism

Western neuroscience depends on the metaphysical assumptions of science which were formulated in the 17th century. These assumptions state that there is an objective external world which is independent of subjective experience and which contains no subjective qualities. These assumptions were well formulated by Galileo when he described the primary and secondary qualities of the world. Primary qualities were those which would exist without the presence of an experiencer. Such qualities as weight, mathematical form, velocity etc are all primary qualities. Secondary qualities such as subjective experience, smell, taste, vision etc, were not the subject of science. These assumptions have resulted in a very powerful neuroscience because they have allowed us to study the brain as mechanism and to come to a thorough understanding of its structure and functioning. The weak point of this view is that consciousness and subjective experience are excluded by definition, leaving only an objective third-person view of the brain. This has led many neuroscientists to suggest that mind and consciousness are nothing more than functions of the brain, rather than to acknowledge that this view is contaminated by its metaphysical limitations.

These assumptions are seldom questioned and remain covert and underpin every discussion in neuroscience. Unless it is clearly understood that they limit in a significant way the questions that can be asked and the answers that it is reasonable to give, then the limited range of explanations which flow from these assumptions will be taken as the total range of explanations that science can give. Consciousness and subjective experience will thus always remain excluded by definition (alternative definitions of consciousness that do not exclude its phenomenology are given by Farthing 1992, ch. 1; Velmans 1996).

It has always been assumed that consciousness would somehow magically appear if our scientific understanding increased to the point where we had a comprehensive map of how the brain worked. In order to test this theory I will review the latest neuro-imaging and functional techniques to see whether or not the assumption that consciousness can be understood from a third-person perspective is correct.

Neuroimaging

Magnetic resonance imaging (MRI)

The 1990s were designated the decade of the brain. This was the time when MRI examination moved out of the research laboratories and became available in most district hospitals, where it is now a standard method of determining brain structure and of how structure is affected by organic cerebral disease. The theory behind MRI is that it is possible to reverse the spin axis of protons in brain tissue by subjecting the patient to a very high magnetic field gradient and radio-frequency pulses. When the spin axis is changed, energy is absorbed, and when the pulse is removed and the spin axis returns, energy is released. A pattern is built up of energy absorption and release and this is the data of the MRI scan. Computer imaging then forms a three-dimensional image from this data. As proton density is highest in the water of the brain, a very good resolution is obtained between water-rich and water-poor structures, or between the white matter of the brain, the grey matter, and the cerebro-spinal fluid. The resolution of the imaging depends on several factors, the most important of which is the strength of the background field. Early machines had helium cooled super-conducting magnets of 0.5 tessla; modern diagnostic machines producing excellent images are 1.5 tessla and the new research machines go up to 4 tessla. A structural resolution of between half and one mm is now easily obtainable. There are a number of protocols that can be run on the machines which show the proton density, proton spin recovery, relaxation times etc. Each protocol shows brain structure in a different way. Automated procedures for dividing up the brain into regions of interest have now been devised. This can be done both in adults and children (Kates et al. 1999).

The use of the MRI as a psychophysiological tool is restricted by the physical characteristics of the machine when acquiring data. Firstly, the patient has to be slid into a narrow tube which many patients find unsettling, particularly if they are frightened of closed spaces. Secondly, during the acquisition of data the machine makes a loud thumping, banging noise that is very disturbing, and finally, because of the constricted space, it is very difficult to deliver stimuli adequately.

Functional MRI

Functional MRI (fMRI) is one of the most exciting advances in functional brain imaging. The concept behind it is a simple one, and depends on the difference between oxyhaemoglobin and carboxyhaemoglobin. Brain that is functioning has a higher oxygen uptake rate than resting brain. Thus the ratio of oxy- to carboxyhaemoglobin in the active area is different to that in the surrounding brain. It is therefore possible to measure increases in functional activity over baseline by use of functional MRI with a very high spatial resolution, within 1–2 mm. There are three major disadvantages that limit this technique. The first is the vascular reflex, which is the time that it takes small arterioles to dilate and increase blood flow to areas that change their metabolic activity. This is in the order of 2–3 seconds and thus significantly limits the temporal resolution of any psychophysiological changes that can be investigated. There are new mathematical methods which project the change backwards in time so as to estimate when the change started, but these methods are subject to error and thus short time resolutions are unreliable. Secondly, the time it takes to record an MRI slice, is limited to about 300 msecs, or about 3 slices per second although this is shorter in some machines. Finally, the patient has to remain still throughout the experiment as change is detected by a difference method and thus any small movements will significantly blur the result, particularly as the changes are in the range of 1–2% only. As important as stillness is the paradigm in which the stimulus is delivered. Usually a box-car design is used, one minute stimulus on and one minute stimulus off over a number of trials. All the stimulus on trials are then averaged, as are the stimulus off trials. The difference scans are then studied and statistics applied to the changes. Again it must be emphasised that all the time the experiment is going on the machine is banging and crashing as it takes the scans (Ogawa et al. 1990).

MRI spectroscopy (^{1}H-MRS)
Another sensitive technique is MRI spectroscopy (^{1}H-MRS). In this technique the absorption spectra of various chemicals, usually NAA (N-Acetyl aspartate), CHO (choline-containing compounds) and CR (creatinine-phosphocreatinine) can be measured (Kegeles et al. 1998). This is usually done over a large volume of tissue, about two cm^3, although in the new machines the volumes are significantly reduced to about a quarter of this. The NAA/CR and CHO/CR ratios are measured and differences between populations of subjects are compared. Again, information about pathology as well as information about change in response to function can be obtained. For example, NAA/CR ratios have been shown to be lower in the temporal lobe in schizophrenic patients than in healthy subjects. (Cecil et al. 1999).

Positron emission tomography (PET)
Positron emission tomography is now an old and well known technique from the 1980s. It depends on the principle of the decay of radioactive atoms, usually oxygen or glucose. As the radioactive atoms decay two positrons are emitted 180 deg. in opposite directions. A number of counters are fixed in a circle surrounding the head so the difference in the time of flight of these two particles can be measured. This then allows the precise location within the

brain of the decaying atoms to be measured. From the map of radioactivity an image of brain slices can be built up. PET scan spatial resolution is extremely good, with differences down to below 1mm. The most common metabolic brain scans are those using either radioactive oxygen or glucose (^{18}F) 2-fluoro-2-deoxy-D-glucose. Areas of higher metabolic activity will have an increased blood flow and therefore an increased density of radioactive material. It is the difference in radioactive activity between the background radiation in the no-task condition and the change in radiation in the task condition which show the metabolic hot spots in the brain slice. These differences are calculated by the use of statistics. (Friston et al. 1991).

The limitation of this method is the time that it takes to record a scan, usually about ten seconds, although modern scanners can go down to three or four and below. But more important than the scan time is the vascular reflex time mentioned above in fMRI. This reflex again takes up to 3 seconds before sufficient blood, and thus radiation, can be taken to the metabolically active area. However, with its excellent spatial resolution, PET has proved to be invaluable in studying brain functional topography.

Single photon emission tomography

Single photon emission tomography is a method that is very similar to PET, except that photons are measured rather than positrons, and SPET scanners are less intimidating than those of PET. SPET gives lower definition than PET but has the advantage that a radioactive ligand, usually HMPAO can be injected at the time of maximum activity where it is taken up by brain substance according to blood flow and thus shows the area of maximum metabolic activity. This cannot be done so easily with PET as the patient has to remain in the scanner all the time. The fact that the radioactivity is fixed in the brain after injection makes the SPET technique very flexible when comparing a functional with a non-functional state. For example, to find out the location of a seizure focus the ligand can be injected as soon as the seizure starts while the patient is still on the ward, and then the patient taken to the scanner a few minutes after injection to have the radioactive distribution within the brain measured. The hot spot indicates the likely focus of seizure activity.

PET has the advantage that receptor ligands can be radioactively tagged and then injected so as to show receptor binding sites. This can also be done by SPET. Much new information has been derived on how neurotransmitter molecules bind to the brain and the precise sites where they are active. A comparison between PET and SPET, looking at the quantification of benzodiazepine receptor binding has been carried out by Bremner et al. (1999).

Magnetoencephalography

Magnetoencephalography (MEG) measures the small brain magnetic fields beyond the scalp. These fields are a million times smaller than the earth's magnetic field, so the measurements have to take place in a magnetically shielded room, using very sensitive magnetometers. The measurement is based on SQUID technology (Super-conducting quantum interference devices) and the sensors are immersed in liquid helium. The latest machines are capable of recording more than 150 channels of information from different parts of the scalp. The subject places their head in a helmet and has to remain completely still during the collection of the data. New powerful software then allows the magnetic sources within the brain to be calculated and the active areas of interest defined.

Why MEG is so interesting is that magnetic waves pass through the brain, skull and scalp with little attenuation, and thus give an accurate picture of brain activity. The traditional methods of recording brain electrical activity are by the EEG, which looks at the electrical potentials on the scalp surface, the ECoG, which measures electrical activity directly from the cortex, and stereo EEG which records the activity from implanted electrodes in the depth of the brain. Although in theory it is possible to get the same information from the EEG as it is from the MEG, in practice it is very difficult to attach 150 EEG channels to the scalp and the electrical information gained is subject to degradation by the brain, skull and scalp. Modern analysis techniques show MEG to be superior with resolutions down to two or three mm. It is customary to derive MRI structural images and co-register these with the electro-magnetic data to show the areas of brain which are functionally active.

The main advantage of electrical and magnetic methods of brain function analysis is the very high temporal resolution. The temporal resolution is totally dependent on the sampling rate, which can go up to thousands of Hertz if necessary. The main disadvantage, certainly of EEG but possibly not of MEG, is that the signal to noise ratio is very low for some interesting EEG waveforms. Thus when studying the arrival and spread at the cortex of activity from peripheral receptors, averaging has to be carried out. Averaging is a method for increasing the signal to noise ratio, but it has the disadvantage that the variance between trials is lost. Thus important information about the spread of activity within the cortex can only be seen in a coarse-grained way. Recent work has shown that individual trials can be resolved using MEG. Some exciting new work shows the magnetic flux changes over milliseconds in different brain areas, and how the auditory cortex prepares itself to hear an expected auditory stimulus (Ioannides et al. 1994).

Summary of analysis methods

It is clear that all methods of analysis have drawbacks. PET, SPET and MRI functional imaging suffer from a very poor time resolution — seconds, but have a high spatial resolution — 1 mm. EEG and MEG have an excellent time resolution of fractions of milliseconds, with a poor spatial resolution. It is now customary to combine data from more than one method so that the high spatial resolution of MRI is co-registered with the high time resolution of MEG or EEG. This combination is extremely effective in analysing brain events.

Localising the brain response to external input (objective reality)

Excellent studies have produced clear functional data which indicate the localisation of the primary receiving areas of the five senses. Stimulation studies of the cerebral cortex have demarcated the primary motor cortex, the primary sensory cortex, the primary auditory cortex, and the primary visual cortex. The primary receiving areas of the brain respond to micro-electrode stimulation with simple sensory responses — buzzes in the auditory cortex, simple phosphenes or points of light in the visual cortex, and simple sensations of touch or tingling from the parietal cortex. (Halgren et al. 1978). More complex sensations are produced if the secondary receiving areas are stimulated. The visual system is probably best understood: the area V1 of the visual cortex is concerned with registering the map of the stimulation of the retina, area V2 with stereo vision, V3 with depth and distance, V4 colour vision, V5 motion, and V6 calculates an object's position in real space rather than in relation to other objects. The information from all these areas combines to make the visual world (Sillitoe 1987).

Thus detailed data exist on the way information is taken into the brain and the main stages of sensory processing have now been outlined. Stimulation studies of the parietal cortex have shown that from the time the stimulus is applied to the cerebral cortex about 300 msecs must elapse before the stimulus can enter consciousness. (Libet 1999). From this it is possible to calculate the number of neuronal synapses that must be involved before a conscious experience arises. Very good models exist of the flow of current and chemical change within the sensory cortex after stimulation, but little can so far be said about how these changes transform into subjective experiences.

Mapping the brain's response to subjective and objective stimuli

In the studies mentioned above there is a clear correlation between activity in a particular area of the cortex and the subjective responses when this area is stimulated. Even though there is a correlation with subjective experience, detailed knowledge of brain areas, neuronal structure and chemistry do not lead to an explanation of consciousness or subjectivity. It will be useful now to consider studies in which the subjective component is primary and the external input is secondary. Perhaps then the correlates of consciousness may be found more precisely within the brain.

One experiment is the perception and recognition of facial expression. A recent study looked at the recognition of threatening and non-threatening facial expressions in paranoid and non-paranoid schizophrenics using functional magnetic resonance imaging (fMRI). Each subject viewed black and white photographs of facial expressions of either fear, anger or disgust. These were contrasted with expressions of mild happiness. All the patients were less accurate in identifying these expressions and showed less activation to these stimuli than normals. Non-paranoids performed poorly, whereas paranoids were more accurate in recognising different facial expressions. In normals, facial expressions of fear and disgust activate the amygdala and visual cortex, and in response to disgust, these regions, together with the striatum. Facial expression of anger in normals produce activation in the inferior frontal cortex, anterior cingulate gyrus, striatum, superior temporal gyrus, and visual cortex. In the schizophrenics, the insular was activated in response to facial expressions of disgust, but fearful facial expressions failed to activate the amygdala and angry facial expressions failed to activate any area (Philips 1999).

Another example is masturbating to orgasm. Orgasm is a subjective sensation, although it does of course have its objective correlates. Tiihonen et al. (1994) carried out a study using rCBF on 8 males, asking them to mastur- bate to orgasm. At the time the orgasm was occurring the subjects were scanned. During orgasm there was a decrease in cerebral blood flow in most cortical areas except the right pre-frontal cortex, where cerebral blood flow increased. The authors argued that the right prefrontal cortex is an important structure for responses concerning the male orgasm. The decrease in cortical blood flow is seen when strongly emotionally valenced events occur.

In both these studies, even though a subjective component is correlated with the objective stimulus, there is still no clear evidence of how the specific sensations of sexual climax or perceptions of emotion come into conscious- ness. One can only say that a specific area of brain 'lights up' when a particular subjective sensation accompanies a physical input. This seems to be true however fine the subjective differentiation of the physical input, or however fine the resolution of brain function.

Mapping subjective experience

If one could map subjective experiences that arise only internally, would this further our understanding of the nature of conscious experience? A very good review of this area is given in the *Journal of Consciousness Studies* Vol. 6, 1999, *The view from within*. A number of studies have examined this question. The first cerebral blood flow study to compare imagined movements with real movements was that of Ingvar and Philipson (1977). This study showed that there is a clear difference in the areas of brain involved. Real movements involve the motor cortex, whereas imagined movements involve the pre- frontal cortical regions. Subsequent studies have shown that other areas are also involved. Dorso-lateral pre-frontal cortex is activated when imagined movements are chosen. There is also some suggestion that this may be asymmetrical, with the left frontal cortex being more involved, although this does depend on the actual task imagined. It is thus possible to draw up a difference map between imagined and actual movements and to define the brain structures that are involved only with imagination. Excellent reviews in this area are those of Ingvar (1999) and Spence and Frith (1999).

Another PET study looked at imagined sexual activity or imagined competitive arousal and mapped the areas in the brain that were involved. Firstly, "each subject was asked to provide a written description of specific autobiographical events characterised by maximally pleasant sexual arousal, and another characterised by maximally pleasant competitive arousal in the context of athletic success, e.g. a specific game-winning play such as scoring an important goal in ice-hockey." These were compared to two neutral descriptions without emotion. During the study the scenarios were read back to the subject and he was instructed to "close his eyes, listen carefully to the scripts, and imagine the event portrayed as vividly as possible and maintain this state until the end of each scan." After 60 seconds of vivid imagination, PET data were acquired using ^{15}O-CO_2 administration. The results showed increased activity in specific anterior paralimbic territories in the ventral globus pallidus, as well as decreased activity in widespread heteromodal association areas. These results provide further evidence for a generalised role of anterior temporal and anterior cingulate cortex in emotionally relevant information processing (Rauch et al. 1999). These authors go on to point out that a previous study of transiently induced happiness in women found widespread rCBF decreases in heteromodal association areas. They also suggest that the failure to find rCBF changes in the amygdala may be because the amygdala principally responds to external stimuli (Reiman et al. 1997), hence imagery driven states such as those induced in the current study might not produce detectable amygdala activation.

In recent years there has been considerable interest in a "Theory of mind" area of the brain which allows us to intuit the functioning of other minds and also recognise that we too have a mind. This ability is reduced or absent in autism. In order to investigate whether the theory of mind area is functioning, the subject is told several stories and then asked their meaning. Some of these stories relate to ordinary simple situations, such as a man going into a shop and buying a newspaper; these are the control conditions. The theory of mind stories relate to a man going into a shop, taking something, and then feeling guilty when spoken to by a policeman. The subjects have to understand that the man in the story in a certain situation will feel guilty and they will only do this if they are able to recognise that the man would have feelings similar to their own in a similar situation — ie that he too has a mind (Frith 1997).

The results of these studies show that there is a brain area in the left medial pre-frontal cortex that changes its metabolism when it extracts the meaning from these stories. If the subject has autism, and is unable to extract the meaning, then a slightly different area of brain below that area in the pre-frontal cortex changes its metabolism. Once again, although the experiences are totally subjective, one is still left after detailed analysis with the correlation between reported subjective data and functional brain areas. There is no clear explanation as to why or how these subjective experiences come into consciousness. As Schwartz (1999) has commented,

> "The predominant explanation for the orchestrated demeaning of first person investigations during recent decades is rooted in the elevated role that the materialistic perspective has ascended to in Western science....The notion that what is essential to any valid explanation of naturally occurring phenomena is that it is based on data immediately derivable from the five senses. To those committed to the systematic investigation of inner experience, this raises the not insignificant problem of validating within the context of a predominant cultural norm explanations using data which, while as immediate and as vivid as externally based five-sense data, do not fit into the somewhat arbitrarily drawn boundaries that materialist science accepts as consensually verifiable."

Brain function correlation with alteration in conscious states

Since the 1950s when Dement and co-workers first defined and measured the different changes in brain activity which occur in sleep, there have been numerous studies correlating different EEG changes with altered states of consciousness. It has been clearly demonstrated that arousal and anxiety increase the EEG frequency, whereas relaxation leads to an alpha dominant state, and sleep onset is characterised by theta activity. Within this overall pattern, there are differences that correlate with different subjective states. Now brain imaging methods have expanded the picture. PET studies have shown changes in brain metabolism related both to the level of sleep and to the phase of sleep. For example, in dreaming sleep there are increases in radioactive glucose uptake in the anterior mesial limbic and paralimbic structures. These structures are thought to be involved in the modulation of emotional and motivational behaviour, selective attention, learning and memory, and the coordination of hypothalamic function (Braun et al. 1997).

Vollenweider, in Zurich, gave a number of subjects psychotropic drugs, (amongst them psilocybin and cannabis), studied the changes in metabolism within the brain and correlated these with the global changes in subjective experience which occur in some drug-induced altered states of consciousness. He notes that there are essentially three different types of experience, those containing oceanic feelings, those with hallucinations, and those in which the subject feels that they are disintegrating. Oceanic feelings correlate with changes in metabolism in mainly the frontal and temporal areas. The hallucinogenic experiences show change in activity in the sensory cortical areas, whereas the feelings of ego disintegration show increased metabolic activity in the thalamus and markedly reduced activity in the cortex.

As with the earlier examples, a direct correlation between brain function and a conscious state can be found in such studies. However, as before, there is as yet little understanding of *how* experiences arise from brain functioning or are altered with changes in brain function.

Overview

It is clear from the above review that our understanding of brain function and the way the different areas of cortex become active under different conditions has enormously expanded during the last decade. The strengths of the techniques described above are that complex paradigms may be set up to test aspects of neural wiring and cognitive structures. Receptor contribution to mental states and behaviour can be characterised. The brain can be partitioned into numerous more elementary functional areas that can be studied in detail.

The major building blocks of brain function now seem to be in place, although there is much in the detail that still needs to be worked out. Our Newtonian science has been extremely effective in coming to an understanding of cerebral structure and function. The major gap is moving from this to subjectivity. This is the so-called 'hard problem' of Chalmers (1996). However clever the experimental paradigm the answer is always in terms of cerebral activation or inhibition. The very wide variance between people, e.g. brain to brain, makes it difficult to attribute consciousness to any specific brain area although the systems involved are becoming clearer. The current limitation of PET, SPET and fMRI is that they depend on blood flow reflexes which are very slow (1–2 secs) although their spatial accuracy is high. On the other hand, MEG and EEG, which have a good time resolution, are poor spatially. Clearly it is studies which combine a mixture of techniques which are most likely to provide us with a detailed picture of the brain at work.

However, these methods cannot look at consciousness (subjectivity) directly, but only at its reflection through cerebral structures. No matter how fine the resolution and however detailed the information that we get, we will always be left with the question of how neuronal activity becomes subjective, i.e. comes into consciousness. What our neuroscience will do is to define more and more closely the conditions under which consciousness arises, but the arising of conscious subjectivity will always be outside the frame from which we are asking the question. There is no way round this using our current metaphysical assumptions, which see subjectivity as a bolt-on extra goody that suddenly arises magically.

References

Braun, A., Balkin, T., Wesenten, N., Carson, R., Varga, M., Baldwin, P., Selbie, S., Belenky, G., Herscovitch, P. 1997. "Regional cerebral blood flow throughout the sleep/wake cycle. An H_2(15)O PET study." *Brain* 120: 1173–1197.

Bremner, J., Baldwin, R., Horti, A., Staib, L., Ng, C., Tan, P., Ponce, Y., Zoghbi, S., Zseibyl, J. Soufer, R., Charney, D., Innes, R. 1999. "Quantitation of benzodiazepine receptor binding with PET ([11C)iomazenil and SPECT ([123I)iomazenil: preliminary results of a direct comparison in healthy human subjects." *Psychiatry Research Neuro-imaging* 91: 71–91.

Cecil, K., Lenkinski, R., Gur, R.E., Gur, R.C., 1999. "Proton magnetic resonance spectroscopy in the frontal and temporal lobes of neuroleptic naïve patients with schizophrenia." *Neuropsychopharmacology* 20: 131–140.

Chalmers, D. 1996. *The Conscious Mind: In Search of a Fundamental Theory*, New York and Oxford: Oxford University Press.

Farthing, J.W. 1992. *The Psychology of Consciousness*, Englewood Cliffs, NJ: Prentice-Hall.

Friston, K., Frith, C. Liddle, P., Frackowiak R. 1991. "Comparing functional (PET) images. The assessment of significant change." *Journal of Cerebral Blood Flow and Metabolism.* 11. 690–699.

Frith, U. 1997. Autism. *Scientific American* April. 92–101.

Halgren, E., Walter, R., Cherlow D., Crandall, P. 1978. "Mental phenomena evoked by electrical stimulation of the human hippocampal formation and amygdala." *Brain* 101: 83–117.

Ingvar, D. 1999. On volition. *Journal of Consciousness Studies 6: 1–10.*

Ioannides, A.A., Fenwick, P.B.C., Lumsden, J., Liu, M.J., Bamidis, P.D., Squires, K.C.,

Lawson, D., and Fenton, G.W. 1994. "Activation sequence of discrete brain areas during cognitive processes: results from magnetic field tomography." *J. Electroencephalography and clinical Neurophysiology.* 91: 399–402.

Kates, W., Warsofsky, I., Patwardihan, A., Abrams, M., Liu, A., Naidu, S., Kaufmann, W., Reis, A. 1999. "Automated talairich atlas-based parcellation and measurement of cerebral lobes in children." *Psychiatry Research Neuroimaging* 91: 11–30.

Kegeles, L., Humaran, T., Mann, J. 1998. "In vivo neurochemistry of the brain in schizophrenia as revealed by magnetic resonance spectroscopy." *Biological Psychiatry* 44: 382–398

Libet, B. 1999. "Do we have free will?" *Journal of Consciousness Studies* 6: 47–57

Ogawa, S., Lee, T., Kay, A., Tank, D. 1990. "Brain magnetic resonance imaging with contrast dependent blood oxygenation." *Proc. of the National Academy of Science, USA* 87 (24), 8868–8872.

Philips, M., Williams, L., Senior, C., Bulmore, E., Bremmer, M., Andrew, C., Williams, S., David, A. 1999. "A differential neural response to threatening and non-threatening negative facial expressions in paranoid and non-paranoid schizophrenics." *Psychiatry Research Neuroimaging* 92: 11–31

Rauch, S. Shin, L. Dougherty, D., Alpert, N. Orr, S. Lasko, M. Macklin, M. Fischman, A., Pitman, R. 1999. "Neural activation during sexual and competitive arousal in healthy men." *Psychiatry Research Neuroimaging* 91: p1–10.

Reiman, E., Lane, R., Aherne, G., Schwartz, G., Davidson, R., Friston, K., Yun, L., Chen, K. 1997. "Neuroanatomical correlates of externally and internally generated human emotion." *American Journal of Psychiatry* 154: 918–925

Schwartz, J. 1999. "Mental force and the advertence of bare attention." *Journal of Consciousness Studies* 6: 293–296.

Sillitoe, A., 1987. "The visual system." *The Oxford Companion to the Mind* Ed. Gregory, R. pp 796- 803. OUP.

Spence, S., Frith, C. 1999. "Towards a functional anatomy of volition." *Journal of Consciousness Studies* 6: 11–29.

Tiihonen, J., Kuikka, J., Kupila, J. 1994. "Increase in cerebral blood flow of right prefrontal cortex in man during orgasm." *Neuroscience Letters* 170, 241–243

Velmans, M. 1996. "An introduction to the science of consciousness." In M. Velmans ed. *The Science of Consciousness: Psychological, Neuropsychological and Clinical Reviews*, London: Routledge.

CHAPTER 3

The Experimental Investigation of Unconscious Conflict, Unconscious Affect, and Unconscious Signal Anxiety

Howard Shevrin

In this paper I will address two questions, one directed to cognitive psychologists, and the other to psychoanalysts. The answers to these questions will take the form primarily of experimental results, but will also incorporate a number of theoretical implications which it is hoped will provide conceptual bridges across which both cognitive psychologists and psychoanalysts can cross over to each other's side of the theoretical divide and feel more at home with each other's views than is currently the case.

This is the question addressed to cognitive psychologists: Given the recent increased interest in unconscious perception, memory, and implicit learning, what theoretical place does the unconscious have in how cognitive psychologists conceive of the mind? True to its British empiricist tradition, leavened with a good deal of Watson and Skinner, cognitive psychologists generally talk as if they are only interested in findings and how to replicate findings which requires careful attention to experimental design, method and procedure — all significant virtues. But one finds very little comprehensive theory, or much theory at all.

Perhaps a good example of this nose to the empirical grindstone approach is to be found in otherwise invaluable work of Greenwald and his collaborators (1995). On the basis of a particularly well-executed experiment involving literally thousands of subjects, Greenwald concluded that unconscious perception exists, but that it is at best ephemeral, its effects lasting at most 100 msec. True, in his experiment this interpretation may be warranted. But in order to offer it as a theoretical generalization Greenwald had to ignore numerous other studies demonstrating that unconscious effects can last for days, let alone hours, minutes or even seconds (e.g., Snodgrass, Shevrin, Kopka, 1993). No theoretician would make this mistake.

For these and other reasons the pages of cognitive psychology journals are chockfull of findings and a preoccupation with methodological precision, but shockingly devoid of comprehensive theory. By comprehensive I mean a theory that explains more than the immediate set of findings at hand, and one that can generate an explanation of findings at a conceptual and phenomenological distance from the original ground on which the theory was based. For example, the Shiffrin and Schneider (1977) equation of consciousness with controlled processes and the unconscious with automatic processes, has not only run into problems on its own home ground (see Allport, 1989), but has proven to be remarkably ungenerative; at best it is the modern heir of the 19th century distinction between voluntary action and habit which did not exactly win the theoretical sweepstakes back then. Finally, what often parades as theory in cognitive psychology is little more than empirical generalizations emerging from one or several experiments. This is a take no chances approach to science.

Psychoanalysis, on the other hand, has the opposite problem. Freud, as a representative figure of continental science, had no problem in proposing grand sweeping theories in which the same underlying principles would explain neurotic symptoms, psychotic disorders, dreams, humor, development, broad cultural currents, and the evolution of civilization. Moreover, this conceptually all-engulfing gamut of theory was based on a handful of case studies presented in high literary style, but still entirely anecdotal in nature — no experimental design, no controls, no well defined measures. There is no way that Freud could have survived a review in any contemporary psychological journal. Nevertheless his theory has proven to be remarkably generative. Indeed, the very focus of this volume on unconscious processes bears witness to the influence of his theory, although he might have been impatient with what he would consider the methodological nitpicking of much experimental work.

And there is the rub. By and large, psychoanalysis has not developed a systematic, investigative, research-oriented dimension to its science; it has remained with a few significant exceptions a clinical science, its major interest and investment devoted to the treatment of patients and the training of clinicians. If it has a research interest it is in research aimed at proving the effectiveness of psychoanalytic treatment and in studying the nature of the analytic process.

The question I would direct to psychoanalysts is the following: What is the place in psychoanalysis of experimental research directed at investigating its underlying basic principles so that the theory can be exposed to falsification? On this point it is interesting to note that Grunbaum (1984), a persistent critic of psychoanalysis, takes issue with Popper, who denied that psychoanalytic principles can be falsified. Grunbaum believes that they can, but that it has not been done primarily because efforts to do so have mainly been pursued in the clinical situation itself which, according to his critique, is methodologically vitiated by suggestion. The research described below is experimental in method and design and thus avoids Grunbaum's pitfall.

Three experiments

As a theory of mind as well as a method of treatment, psychoanalysis makes certain fundamental assumptions which perforce cannot be tested in the psychoanalytic situation (Rapaport, 1967/1949; Shevrin, 1973; Edelson, 1988). There are two such fundamental assumptions which Freud (1915) referred to as the "pillars" of the psychoanalytic method and theory: (1) the existence of a psychological causative unconscious, and (2) the way in which this unconscious makes itself known is indirect, taking the form of displacements, condensations and symbols which require certain rules of inference. Freud himself was aware that these two assumptions needed confirmation independent of the psychoanalytic situation for which he turned to post-hypnotic suggestion. As Freud recognized, other methods must be used in order to address the need for independent evidence to support these two crucial assumptions (which have been under attack from the very beginning of psychoanalysis). William James (1890) referred to the concept of an unconscious in the course of his ten arguments against the unconscious as sheer "whimsy". In the absence of a canon of clinical inference (Rapaport, 1967/1949), the application of the rules of inference is largely intuitive in nature and it has proven difficult to investigate with other methods, although we have begun to develop such methods in our laboratory (Brakel, Kleinsorge, Snodgrass, Shevrin, in press; Snodgrass, Shevrin, Brakel & Medin, 1995).

In any case, it is the assumption of a psychological causative unconscious which merits prior attention. I will describe three experiments, one which deals with unconscious conflict, a second with unconscious affect, and a third with signal anxiety. Each of these experiments addresses a fundamental issue in psychoanalytic theory which points to a considerable theoretical gap in cognitive psychology. At the same time each of the experiments draws upon the well-developed tradition of methodological rigor which is the crowning achievement of cognitive psychology. The evidence brought forward is not anecdotal, but emerges from reasonably well-designed, controlled experiments.

I will start with the experiment on unconscious affect because I will need to use it as a way of introducing a method which has proven to be of great usefulness in our work: the event-related potential, or ERP, which is derived from the electroencephalographic (EEG) record. As I will try to show, the ERP method gives us a non-psychological marker for unconscious processes independent of the other psychological methods used.

The ERP is based on John Stewart Mill's principle of concomitant variation. When events are repeated the one aspect that is constant will emerge as stronger or more evident and those that vary randomly will cancel out. If one applies this principle to brain responses it becomes possible to obtain a brain response to a particular stimulus characterized, on the one hand, by constant factors that vary only little from response to response and, on the other, by random factors unrelated to the stimulus which will in effect cancel each other out over a number of stimulus repetitions as illustrated in Figure 1.

In Figure 1 the EEG segment (the top three curves), obtained immediately following a given repeated stimulus, appear to vary in their fluctuations. However, if you add them up algebraically you obtain an average curve (bottom curve) in which there is one large excursion followed by random fluctuations. The large excursion, or voltage amplitude component, is one part of the brain's response to the stimulus. Countless ERP studies have shown that these constant amplitude components are related to such psychological processes as attention, perception, and memory (see Coles and Rugg, 1995 for a review of this evidence). The great strength of the ERP method is that it captures the stimulus-related brain events in real time, in milliseconds, and is thus in effect concomitant with the stimulus; the major limitation of the ERP is that it tells you very little about the source of the brain activity; for that you need the newly developing neuroimaging methods. In previous research my colleagues and I had demonstrated that ERPs could be used to discriminate

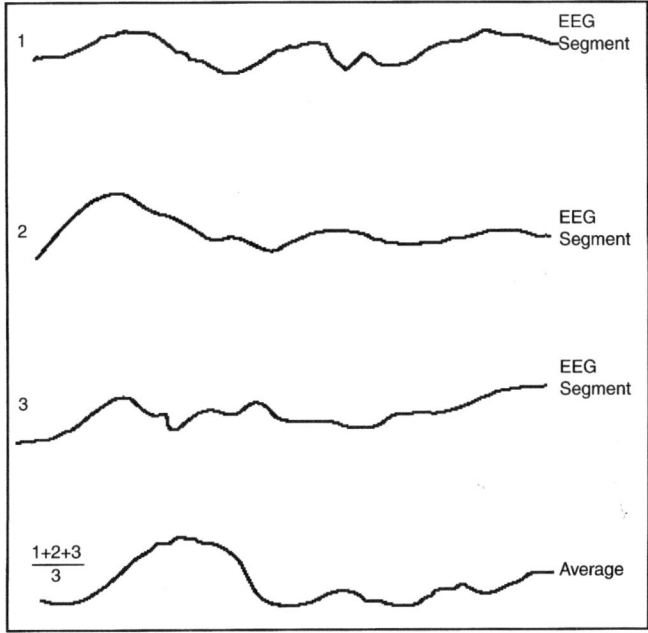

Figure 1. How ERP's are derived from the EEG

between two subliminal stimuli (Shevrin and Rennick, 1967; Shevrin and Fritzler, 1968; Shevrin, 1973).

First experiment: Unconscious affect

It is notable that Freud, who dared to assert to skeptical scientists that ideas can be unconscious, became cautious when it came to emotion. In the late 19th century, at the very beginnings of psychology as a science, the early pioneers, Wundt, James, Titchener and others defined psychology as quintessentially the science of consciousness. The concept of an idea defined what consciousness was about. Thus the thought that an idea could be unconscious was unthinkable. Yet Freud asserted otherwise and not only psychoanalysts but nowadays psychologists and neuroscientists are coming round to the same belief, that a cognition (the contemporary term for an idea) can in fact be unconscious in some phase of its activity. But Freud drew the line on affect. In his paper on the unconscious, Freud asserted that while "...unconscious ideas continue to exist after repression as actual structures in the system unconscious, all that corresponds in that system to unconscious affects is a potential beginning which is prevented from developing" (Freud, 1957/1915, p.178). He insisted that affect was intrinsically a conscious phenomenon. In this respect he sounded like the early psychologists who rejected out of hand the notion that an idea could be unconscious. But he had a problem with the clinical evidence for unconscious guilt, especially in obsessive patients. He sought to solve this problem by hypothesizing that there was a *disposition* to experience guilt (consciously) under certain circumstances, and that it was this disposition that was unconscious. This was a dangerous conceptual path to follow, for if this were true of affects, why not of ideas, including memories and motivations? The dynamic unconscious then ceases to be concurrently active, and in important respects, independent of conscious processes, and instead becomes the repository of latent possibilities linked to conscious activations. One could also relate Freud's dispositional concept of affect to the notion of a personality trait which would not implicate the unconscious either as active or dispositional. It thus is of some theoretical importance to see if one could demonstrate that affects can in fact be unconscious.

In cognitive psychology very little attention is given to affect. Bower (1987) has attempted to incorporate affect into a connectionist theory by positing that an affect, or mood, is simply another network node which can be activated along with other nodes; the issue of consciousness as such is not addressed. In social cognitive research, Zajonc (1993) and Bargh (1989), replicating earlier work of psychoanalytical investigators Smith, Spence and Klein (1959), have demonstrated that affectively charged facial expressions presented subliminally will influence how a supraliminal stimulus is judged. In more recent neuroscience research, LeDoux (1995) has hypothesized on the basis of his work on decorticate rats that, insofar as the cortex is absent and aversive conditioning can occur largely dependent on the amygdala, the aversive affect must be unconscious. In none of these studies is the status of unconscious affect addressed with respect to whether it is dispositional or active.

In the experiment now to be reported, conducted by Bernat as part of his doctoral dissertation (Bernat, Bunce, & Shevrin, in press), subjects were exposed subliminally and supraliminally to twenty words having either positive or negative emotional meaning, or valence (see Table 1). These emotional meanings were determined by having subjects rate the words on the Evaluative (E) scales developed by Osgood, May, & Miron (1975).

Table 1: Bernat, Bunce, Shevrin, in press
Osgood Evaluative means for 17 Ss in this study and 111 Ss in questionaire only replication.

(17 Ss)		(111 Ss)		
Word Stimulus	Osgood Evaluative Mean	Word Stimulus	Osgood Evaluative Mean	
hostile	−2.48	hostile	−2.29	
angry	−2.24	angry	−2.08	
jealous	−2.12	depressed	−1.94	
unhappy	−2.09	jealous	−1.85	
distressed	−2.09	unhappy	−1.62	Negative
depressed	−1.99	envious	−1.55	Valence
envious	−1.67	agitated	−1.50	
sad	−1.65	distressed	−1.48	
agitated	−1.48	fearful	−1.38	
fearful	−1.39	sad	−1.31	
tense	−1.38	lonely	−1.25	
lonely	−1.07	tense	−1.16	
nervous	−1.07	worried	−1.09	
jittery	− .87	sluggish	− .94	
sluggish	− .79	nervous	− .79	
worried	− .75	jittery	− .60	
anxious	− .51	anxious	− .55	
drowsy	− .31	drowsy	− .18	
wild	.29	wild	.03	
still	.91	still	− .74	
quiet	.98	quiet	− .99	
aroused	1.29	excited	−1.21	
enthusiastic	1.60	aroused	1.37	
calm	1.64	at rest	1.39	
at rest	1.66	enthusiastic	1.52	
tranquil	1.74	elated	1.57	
excited	1.75	calm	1.79	Positive
relaxed	1.75	tranquil	1.85	Valence
elated	2.12	relaxed	2.03	
affectionate	2.40	affectionate	2.20	
warm-hearted	2.60	loving	2.48	
loving	2.66	warm-hearted	2.51	

Note: Means for 17 Ss and 111 Ss were strongly correlated (.99, p<.001). The top brackets identify the ten most negative valence words, and the bottom brackets identify the ten most positive valence words.

In Figure 2 the plots illustrate what the supraliminal and subliminal ERPs look like when all responses, to negative as well as positive words, are averaged together. You will note in the upper part of the figure that the supraliminal curve looks like what an ERP curve should look like with prominent amplitude excursions, while the subliminal curve looks almost like a straight line. However, if you multiply the subliminal curve by a factor of four you will see that it has almost the same amplitude structure as the supraliminal curve (lower two curves in the figure). In fact the correlations between the two curves are substantial across a number of electrodes (see legend for Figure 2).[1] This mathematical transformation is only intended for

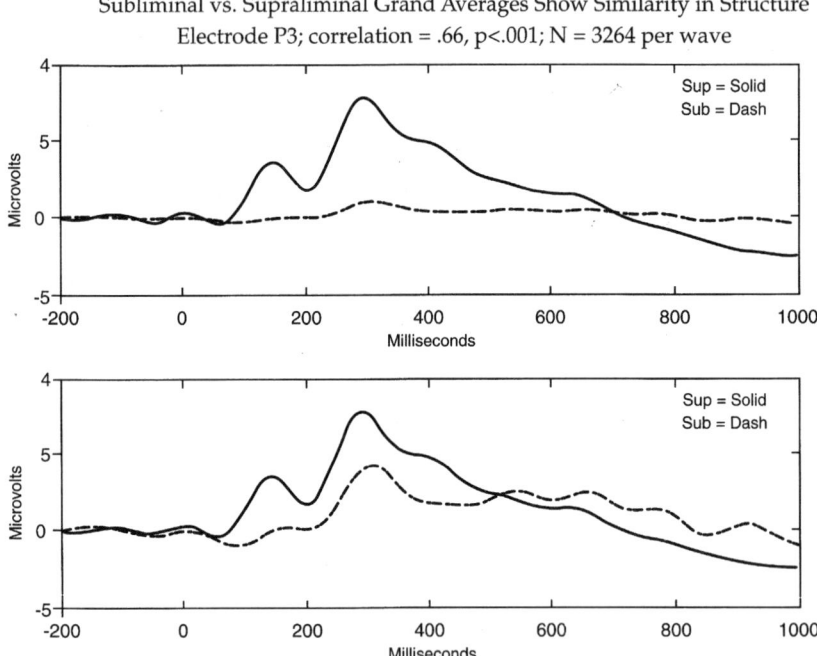

Subliminal vs. Supraliminal Grand Averages Show Similarity in Structure
Electrode P3; correlation = .66, p<.001; N = 3264 per wave

Correlation for other electrodes - F3=.91; F4=.91; CzPz=.85; P3=.66; P4=.80; Oz=.48

Figure 2. Bernat, Bunce, Shevrin, in press

1. In all figures in which electrodes are mentioned the following designations apply: F3 = left frontal, F4 = right frontal, P3 = left parietal, P4 = right parietal, Oz = midline occipital, CzPz = one third of distance from midline vertex to midline parietal.

illustrative purposes; the actual statistical analyses are based on the untrans-
formed curves.

Now if we divide the averages for the total ERPs into those for the
positive and negative affect words, we obtain the plots, one for supraliminal
and one for subliminal presentations, illustrated in Figure 3 and Figure 4.
Consistently the ERPs to the negative emotional words are more positive in
voltage than those to the positive emotional words (positive is in the upward
direction). Also note that there is a brain lateralization effect for the subliminal
ERPs; the difference between negative and positive emotion words is greater
on the left side than the right which is not the case supraliminally. All
differences cited in these curves are highly significant statistically.

On the basis of these results one can say that affect meaning is registered
unconsciously. The brain differentiates between positive and negative meanings entirely without benefit of consciousness.

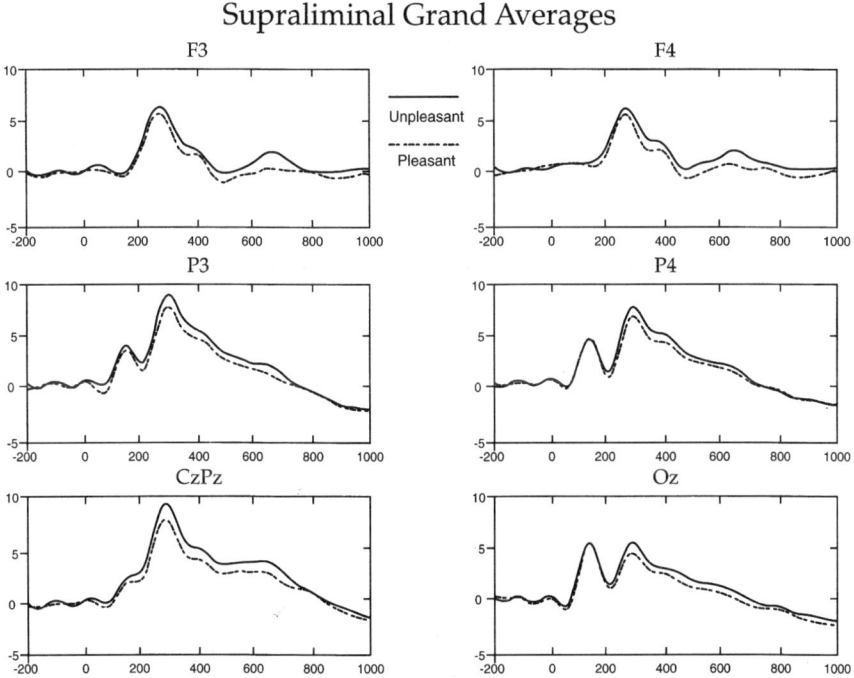

Supraliminal Grand Averages

Figure 3. Bernat, Bunce, Shevrin, in press

Subliminal Grand Averages

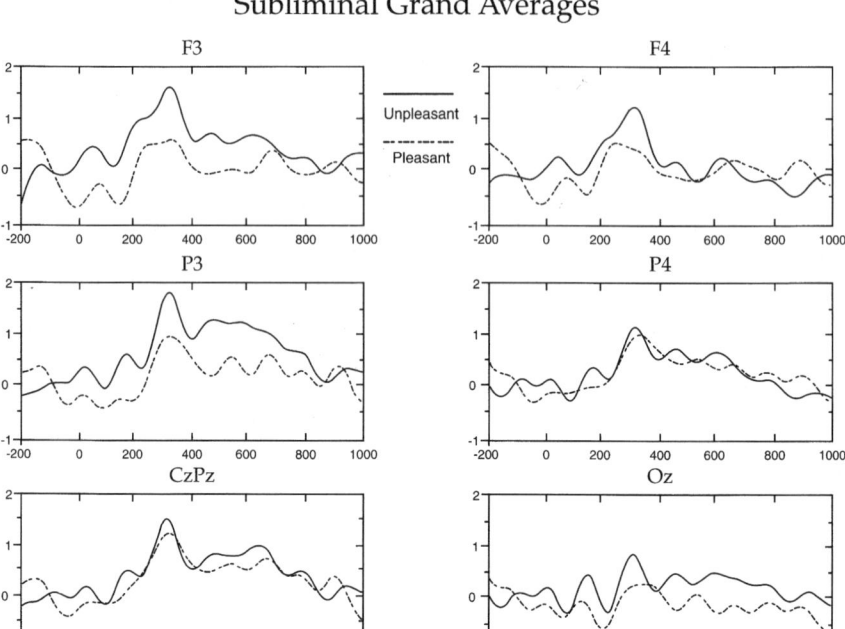

Figure 4. Bernat, Bunce, Shevrin, in press

But affect is more than the meaning of words; affect has expressive and physiological dimensions as well. Is there evidence for expressive and physiological concomitants of subliminal affective stimuli? In fact there is. In our laboratory Bunce, Bernat, Hibbard and Shevrin (1999) have shown that a schematic face aversively conditioned subliminally elicits greater tension in the corrugator muscle above the eyes which is indicative of a negative emotional expression as in a frown. In other research which I will refer to later in greater detail, Wong, Shevrin, and Williams (1994) have shown that an angry face conditioned to a mild aversive shock supraliminally will elicit an elevated skin conductance response when the conditioned stimulus, the angry face, is presented subliminally. The skin conductance response is an indicator of sympathetic nervous system activation associated with flight reactions. Other research by Ohman and colleagues (1995) have also shown skin conductance elevation for phobic stimuli presented out of consciousness. Finally, research such as that of LeDoux (1995) has demonstrated the neuroanatomical local-ization of negative affects in the amygdala which LeDoux has argued is the non-conscious phase of these emotions.

Thus there is evidence for the processing of emotional meaning, the elicitation of expressive signs of emotion, and the activation of physiological responses entirely unconsciously. The only thing lacking is consciousness. This is exactly the status of unconscious ideas. Unconscious affect exists and is not simply dispositional, or a personality trait. From a psychoanalytic standpoint, in my judgment, it makes better sense clinically to accept that affects are actively unconscious; indeed I believe we are constantly respond-ing to unconsciously activated expressive signs all the time in gesture, facial musculature, and tone of voice of which both the one having the experience and the one perceiving these signs are unaware. The dynamic unconscious is an active, ongoing process and not dispositional for affect any more than for ideas. The experiment I have just described contributes to that demonstration in a way that clinical experience cannot.

At the same time, the results raise a theoretical issue for cognitive and social cognitive psychologists concerning the nature of affect experience. Unconscious processes are not dispositional in nature or repositories of per-sonality traits, but are highly interactive processes that can go on indepen-dently of conscious experience and influence behavior without any conscious awareness of this influence.

Second experiment: Unconscious conflict

I described the unconscious affect study first in order to introduce you to the role that ERP brain responses can play in the investigation of unconscious processes, and to demonstrate that experiment can contribute to settling a theoretical issue relevant to clinical practice and to cognitive theory. The experiment I will now describe is much more complex and aims much higher (Shevrin, Bond, Brakel, Hertel & Williams, 1996). It is offered as a first effort at integrating psychodynamic, cognitive, and neurophysiological methods into one comprehensive method directed at investigating the role that uncon-scious conflict plays in symptom formation, a key psychoanalytic hypothesis based on the presupposition of a psychological causative unconscious. To my knowledge these three methods have never been combined in this way.

To the extent that the experiment succeeds it calls into question narrowly cognitive and social cognitive conceptions of the unconscious and takes us far beyond Greenwald's interpretation that unconscious influences last no longer than 100 msec. Positive results would also undermine further the equation of conscious with controlled and the unconscious with automatic. At the very least the results demonstrate that control can be unconscious. First the three separate methods as employed in the experiment will be described.

Psychodynamic method

Every experiment is based on some act of abstraction, just as every case report has to be selective, and every systematic psychotherapy research chooses some variables rather than others. The trick is to make the right abstraction. In point of fact if Galileo had dropped the cannon ball and feather from the top of the leaning tower of Pisa, as the apocraphyl story has it, he would not have demonstrated the principle of uniform acceleration; the feather would have fallen much slower than the cannon ball for obvious reasons of wind and air currents. Instead Galileo abstracted from the complex physical reality the inclined plane with which he elegantly demonstrated the principle a thousand feathers and cannonballs would have failed to support.

What is the abstraction on which our experiment is based? It is in how the psychoanalytic clinical method has been adapted (abstracted, if you will) for the purposes of the research. First and foremost it was essential that the clinician, as the ultimate judge of the clinical material, be central to the effort. The clinician would be encouraged to deal with the clinical material in the same manner as with any case encountered in daily practice; there would be no directing the clinician to use rating scales or attend to some variables more than others. Yet clearly we could not use an entire analysis, nor did I feel that sampling hours from a longer treatment would do because sampling in my judgment violated the organic integrity of a treatment. An evaluation for diagnostic purposes, however, has a natural time course and is complete in itself so that it is not simply an arbitrary sampling of hours and it is much briefer than a treatment. Yet, if properly conducted, rich material can be elicited. Each evaluation conducted in the research observed three essential aspects of the psychoanalytic clinical method: (1) a series of in-depth, unstructured interviews were carried out in which both content and process were addressed; (2) an account of the complaint and relevant history were obtained,

with attention paid to the manner in which the patient engaged in the evaluation; (3) initial transferential and resistance issues were noted and, where
indicated, addressed as a further source of diagnostic information. Thus the
essentials of the psychoanalytic clinical method were employed for diagnostic
but not therapeutic purposes.

In addition to a series of interviews, generally four in number, we also
administered a battery of psychological tests, the WAIS-R, Rorschach, and
TAT. We were emboldened to include tests because of the experience of
Appelbaum, Siegel, and Rosen (1977) in employing tests in the Menninger
Foundation psychotherapy project. They reported that the tests predicted
outcome and status at follow-up better than predictions made on the basis of
interviews. The main finding was that the tests made possible a more valid
assessment of ego strength which figured prominently in the outcome of
treatment and in the stability of findings at follow-up. Used appropriately,
tests provide an in depth picture of the more invariant features of personality
organization and are thus not as subject to the often adventitious circumstances of interviews. Together, interviews and tests offer a workable picture
of personality organization in depth, making inferences possible about the
nature of the unconscious conflict underlying a specific symptom.

On the basis of the interviews and tests, which were audio-recorded and
transcribed, each clinician arrived at a psychodynamic formulation which
included the patient's account of the presenting symptom, the patient's understanding of the symptom, and hypotheses concerning the unconscious conflict
underlying the symptom.

Finally, the clinician was asked to perform a function derived from the
task of inferring the unconscious conflict from the patient's communications:
to select words or brief phrases used by the patient that were related in some
way or derived from the hypothesized unconscious conflict. In addition, the
clinician was asked to select words or brief phrases used by the patient which
captured the nature of the symptomatic experience, a much easier task.

What I have just described constituted the psychodynamic method
adapted, or if you will, abstracted from its use in a psychoanalytic treatment
for purposes of the research. As already indicated, words were selected that
were related to the unconscious conflict as agreed upon by four clinical judges
who studied the transcripts. Words were also selected which captured the
patients' conscious experiences of their symptoms. Of the eleven subjects in
the study, nine suffered from social phobias and two from pathological grief

reactions. Two other groups of words were drawn from the end points of the Osgood Evaluation scale (Osgood, May, and Miron, 1975), a group of quite negative words judged as unrelated either to the unconscious conflict or conscious symptom words and a group of highly positive words again judged to be unrelated to the two key categories. There were eight words in each category. The four categories were balanced for length, and to the extent possible, for parts of speech, as well as for frequency of usage as determined by tables based on psychotherapy protocols (Dahl, 1979). An example of the words selected for one subject is given in Table 2 along with a precis of the psychodynamic formulation of the underlying unconscious conflict agreed upon by the judges.

Cognitive subliminal method

Instead of the affect words used in the previous affect study, the words selected by the clinicians, plus two groups of control words (illustrated previously) were flashed in the tachistoscope subliminally at 1 msec and in a

Table 2. Shevrin, Bond, Brakel, Hertel, Williams, 1996

Conscious symptom words (C)	Unconscious conflict words (U)	Osgood unpleasant words (E–)	Osgood pleasant words (E+)
Shorter Breaths	Massasing Muscles	Air Pollution	Pocket Radios
Heart Faster	Ripped Apart	Non-Believer	Space Travel
Rotten Fish	Parents' Bed	Atomic Bomb	Cleanliness
Swallowing	Men Hugging	Poor People	Right Hand
Cafeteria	On My Back	Cheating	Pleasant
Headache	Stab Me	Cancer	Kindness
Nauseous	John	Lying	Quality
Tense Up	Evil	Debt	Bath

Note: Stimulus words of subject 7, a 20-year-old male suffering from a public eating phobia. The conscious symptom (C) words were all drawn from his answers to interview questions about his experiences while eating in public. The unconscious conflict (U) words were drawn from the subject's interviews and test responses which, in the clinician's diagnostic judgment, reflect an underlying unconscious conflict with men over dominance and submission that was hypothesized to be related to his phobia. The E – and E + words were drawn from the end points of the Osgood evaluative dimension and have been judged to be unrelated to the C and U words. The four word categories were balanced for length and frequency of usage.

second supraliminal condition, at 40 msec. Luminance was set at 10 foot/ lamberts, the same as the surrounding light so that dark adaptation was not necessary at any point in the experiment. Each of the eight words making up each category was presented six times in randomized order. At exposure conditions of 1 msec at 10 foot lamberts we have good reason to believe on the basis of much research in our laboratory (Snodgrass, Shevrin and Kopka, 1993) and elsewhere (Van Selst and Merikle, 1993) that each conscious symptom and unconscious conflict word registered unconsciously. In point of fact, as I will argue later in my discussion, all the words initially register preconsciously, but a different fate befalls them depending on whether they are conscious symptom or unconscious conflict words as reflected in the ERP brain responses.

Neurophysiological method

The brain responses are obtained in the same way as described in the first experiment on unconscious affect. But the method of analysis had to take a different turn because of one important difference. In the experiment on unconscious affect the same words were presented to each subject so that there was uniformity from subject to subject; in this experiment the key words were different from subject to subject introducing a substantial degree of variability which would make it hard to identify amplitude components reliably across subjects. An innovative method of biosignal analysis was developed by Williams & Jeong (1992) which made possible a much more subtle identification of the brain responses associated with the tachistoscopically presented words and which was not affected by the subject by subject individuality of the words selected. The Williams-Jeong method, known as a time-frequency feature analysis, enabled us to identify a brain frequency in the ERPs every 4 msec. Through a number of statistical manipulations it was possible to select a series of five such time-frequency features which discriminated between the word categories of interest. In effect these series of five time-frequency features are brief "brain melodies" if we bear in mind that melody is also a succession of time-frequency features, and it may be more than a coincidence that this parallel exists.

The results of our analysis were encouraging. The conscious symptom, unconscious conflict, and ordinary unpleasant categories were each compared with the ordinary pleasant category, which served as a placebo control. On the basis of a discriminant analysis, sequences made up of five time-frequency features were used to discriminate between the categories in each comparison. We found that the unconscious conflict words were better discriminated from the pleasant words subliminally than supraliminally; the opposite was found for the conscious symptom words. No differences were found for the ordinary unpleasant words. (See Shevrin, Bond, Brakel, Hertel, and Williams, 1996, pp. 133–147, for a detailed description of statistical methods and results.) The time-frequency feature analysis demonstrated that as long as the unconscious conflict words were unconscious, they were differentiated from the pleasant words; once they were presented consciously, the brain "acted" as if they were no different from the pleasant words. It is not difficult to take the next step and infer that some inhibitory process was at work to keep the "togetherness" found subliminally from occurring consciously. Nor would it seem a fool-hardy leap to believe that this inhibitory process was defensive in nature. This interpretation was supported by two other convergent findings:1) There was a significant positive correlation (.77, p<.05) between the experimental effect (the extent to which subliminal correct classification was greater than supral-iminal correct classification) and scores on the Hysteroid-Obsessoid Ques-tionnaire (Caine and Hawkins, 1963); the more hysterical subjects (typically more repressive than obsessional patients) showed the greater experimental effect, 2) When asked to sort the 32 words subjects had been shown into as many categories as they wished, subjects sorted the unconscious conflict words into significantly more categories than the conscious symptom words, paralleling the absence of a differentiated category for the unconscious con-flict words as determined by the brain response findings for the supraliminal condition. Taken together these two additional findings lend support to the inference that an inhibitory, repressive process was at work.

The results suggest that it is possible to take a construct like unconscious conflict and with suitable methods find support for its probable existence and in the course of which to support independent of the clinical context the presupposition of a psychological causative unconscious. From a methodologi-cal standpoint the clinicians not only formulated their view of the unconscious conflict *in advance,* but on the basis of a series of ratings, selected the words so that they were unrelated to the conscious symptom words. The one character-istic differentiating the unconscious conflict words from the others was their relationship to the hypothesized conflict underlying the symptom. Other pos-sible factors such as word length and frequency of usage, customary control variables, were taken into account. Moreover, the ERPs provide strong evidence that there are brain processes that instantiate the activity of unconscious conflict and associated defenses. Finally, the evidence that highly selective and organizing processes subject to particular motivations are going on unconsciously calls into question the automaticity of unconscious processes.

Third experiment: Unconscious signal anxiety

The concept of signal anxiety is at the heart of the psychoanalytic theory of defense and consequently of the avoidance of psychic danger. It is a perfect example of a theoretical construct necessitated by the requirements of a theory. On the basis of this theory signal anxiety must be inferred to operate prior to the activation of any defense. It is when signal anxiety fails to function for whatever reason that traumatic anxiety may take over. There is some controversy as to whether signal anxiety is a tamed form of anxiety, or a small amount of it, and is thus an affect, or whether it is a purely cognitive indicator. In the latter instance, it would not be an affect at all, but an unconscious cognition. The experiment I will now describe speaks to this issue, as well as providing empirical support for the concept of signal anxiety.

The experiment is based on a classical Pavlovian aversive conditioning paradigm. What Wong, Shevrin, & Williams (1994) did was to condition in consciousness a schematic representation of an angry face to a mild electric shock (the control was a schematic representation of a happy face). To establish conscious aversive conditioning is not at all difficult; it has been done hundreds if not thousands of times. In fact, it has been contended that conditioning can only take place consciously, a contention that another one of Wong's experiments refutes (Wong, Bernat, Bunce and Shevrin, 1997).

Prior to the conscious creation of an aversive conditioning to the angry face, a baseline series was administered in which both faces were presented subliminally. The critical phase of the experiment occurred following the supraliminal conditioning phase. In this last phase the two faces were again presented subliminally. In each of the three phases of the experiment — baseline subliminal, conditioning supraliminal, post-conditioning subliminal — ERP brain responses were obtained.

The mild electric shock was administered in the supraliminal conditioning series three seconds after the angry face was presented. In the post-

HOWARD SHEVRIN

conditioning subliminal phase the electric shock would have occurred at that
same point, but it did not. Nevertheless at about 500 msec. prior to that point
an interesting ERP fluctuation occurred following the conditioned face. It was
a negative (downward) voltage excursion which gradually returned to baseline before the three-second end point at which the shock would have occurred. In a considerable number of entirely supraliminal studies this wave is
found just prior to the point at which the subject anticipates some experimental
signal to appear. For example, the subject might be told that once a green light
comes on to be prepared to respond to a red light. In that interval of time the
ERP will show this same negative voltage excursion and for that reason it is
called an expectancy, or e-wave.

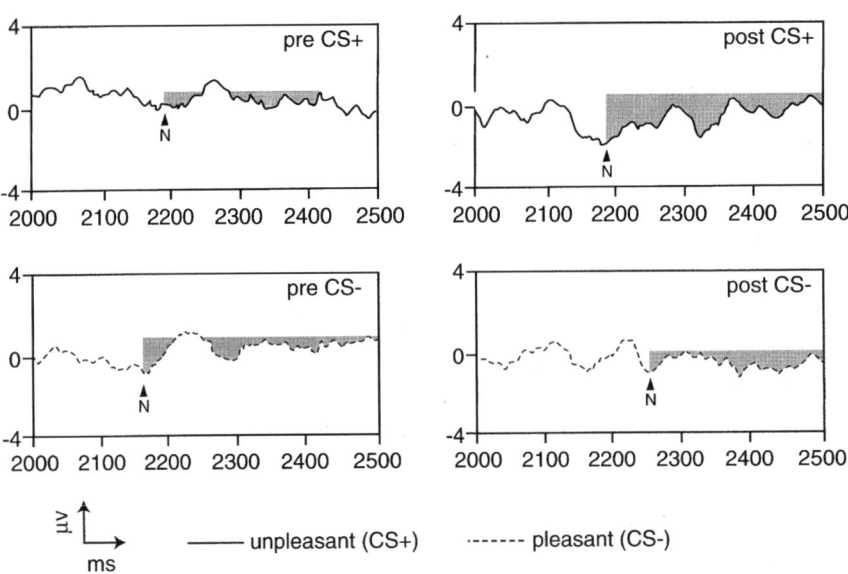

Figure 5. Wong, Shevrin, Williams, 1994. All plots are for P3. Pre and Post refer to the
subliminal conditions before and after supraliminal conditioning. N with arrow above
indicates maximum negative voltage excursion from baseline within 500 msec prior to
when shock event occurred in the conditioning series. Shaded region denotes total area of
expectancy wave from maximum negative voltage excursion to return to baseline and thus
provides a measure of the extent of the expectancy wave. This area is significantly greater
for the post CS+condition (see text).

Similarly, in our experiment an expectancy wave occurred after the conditioned face had been flashed and just prior to when the shock would have been administered, but in our experiment both the conditioned stimulus and the expectation were entirely unconscious. It is again not a great leap to infer that the unconscious e-wave was a signal for the anticipated aversive event (see Figure 5).

In this same experiment there was also evidence for skin conductance changes to the conditioned stimulus occurring in the third post-conditioning subliminal phase. As an indicator of sympathetic activation it adds the unconscious affective component to the cognitive component provided by the e-wave. Taken together these two findings support a view of signal anxiety as being comprised of both a cognitive and affective component. The time course of these two components are somewhat different: the e-wave, a central nervous system brain event, starts to occur at about 2500 msec after the subliminal stimulus is flashed and is over by 3000 msec.; the skin conductance response generally starts at about the same time but lasts anywhere from two to four seconds longer. It is possible to surmise that if the e-wave signal is not attended to that the sympathetic activation reflected in the skin conductance might grow longer and stronger and finally break into consciousness in the form of overt anxiety. This hypothesis is eminently testable in future experiments.

But is the e-wave an indicator of signal anxiety in the full psychoanalytic meaning of the term? What is that full meaning? To begin with, some wish or impulse needs first to be aroused unconsciously whose fulfillment would lead to a psychic danger. The unconscious activation of that wish is sufficient to trigger signal anxiety, leading to instituting defenses which would keep the wish from becoming conscious or influencing action. Can any claim be made that an unconscious wish or impulse was involved in the conditioning experiment? The answer is probably not. Nor is the danger involved great or traumatic; it is simply the anticipation of a mild physical pain. What can be claimed is that the analogous situation set up in the experiment must draw upon the same mechanism as the clinical situation. The signal capacity is there to be used whether the danger is from within or from without, great or small, and it functions unconsciously (see Wong, 1999 for a fuller discussion of these issues).

Discussion

In this discussion I will address three questions. The first will return to the question posed at the beginning of this paper and concerns the role of research in psychoanalysis and in particular the role of research on unconscious processes. The second question returns to the question posed to cognitive psychologists concerning the implications of research on unconscious processes for a broader cognitive theory. The third question deals with the relations between mind and brain and should be of interest both to psychoanalysts and cognitive psychologists. Following the discussion of these three questions, the discussion will end with an overview of where matters stand at this point concerning research on unconscious processes. These are the three questions:

1. Do the findings from the three experiments described bear on what psychoanalysts deal with in the clinical situation?
2. What implications do the findings have for our understanding of the relationship between conscious and unconscious processes?
3. Do the findings point the way for possible bridges between mental and neurophysiological processes?

The first question

Psychoanalysts worry that efforts to resort to experimentation to investigate concepts and theories important to the conduct of treatment will so simplify these concepts and theories that the finding will have no bearing on them, even though the experimenters may well believe that they do. So we must ask ourselves whether the three experiments reported here have avoided that pitfall.

In the first experiment the question addressed concerned the status of unconscious affect. Are we dealing with affect dispositions or with true ongoing affect states differing from conscious affects only by virtue of being unconscious, much as is the case with unconscious ideas, fantasies and motivations. A worrisome theoretical implication emerged if we were to consider unconscious affects as dispositions only, as Freud and others have proposed. If that were so, why not dispositional ideas, fantasies, and motivations? Where and on what basis could one draw the line at affect? From Freud to the present day clinicians treat unconscious guilt, for example, as if it were an active unconscious process resulting in otherwise inexplicable self-punitive acts. And if guilt can be dynamically, as opposed to dispositionally, unconscious, why not other affects?

Now we can proceed to consider if the means used in the experiment are suitable to answering the question. Or put another way, is the necessary experimental abstraction a valid representation of the clinical and theoretical issues? At first glance one is struck by the triviality of the means compared to the serious issues at stake. The stimuli are ordinary words carrying degrees of affective meaning for anybody; they are not conflict-related or personally meaningful as in the instance of unconscious guilt. Let us first take up the matter that the stimuli are simply words. In real life (i.e., outside the laboratory) feelings are evoked by other people, the analyst for example, and not by words alone. But is this always the case? Literature, to name one important exception, depends entirely on our capacity to respond emotionally to words. In any good story or novel, however, words are not presented in isolation from each other, but are used skillfully to depict a meaningful human encounter. As I will comment on later, there is also a human encounter in our experiment in which the isolated words take on meaning.

With these considerations in mind, let me return to the results which do indicate that not only are the emotional meanings responded to differently unconsciously, but that these seemingly innocuous words elicit unconscious sympathetic arousal and facial expressive changes. For all the world they appear to elicit an affect albeit without any conscious experience.

Thus it does not appear to be necessary to rely on powerful, personally meaningful excitants in order to demonstrate that an affect can be unconscious. We can use much paler versions as long as they belong to the class of affect arousers. And in the experimental context we need not rely on clinical inference based on the presupposition of a psychological causative unconscious. We have operationalized the unconscious by way of the subliminal procedure. The subject in the experiment is simply unaware, and cannot be aware, of the stimulus to which the affective response is being made.

But there are other dimensions of the clinical situation psychoanalysts believe to be critical to the emergence of a particular experience at a particular time which do not appear to be taken into account in the experiment. I refer primarily to the status of the transference and countertransference. This is a most important point and can easily be overlooked. In the three experiments as I have described them I made no reference to transferential issues; it was as if the subjects were tested in an interpersonal vacuum, the ideal goal of most cognitive experimenters. The mind in most cognitive experiments (not ours as I will show later) is suspended for study in a sanitized experimental booth, sound-proofed, electronically-proofed, and person-proofed. The experimental procedure is run off a computer to which the vacuum-suspended mind responds on cue. Each mind is considered to be an exemplar of all minds, and the more completely the experimental procedure is automated (rid of the experimenter's presence) and routinized, the firmer the basis for generalizing from a few minds to all minds.

So runs the logic of much current experimentation. Except that it is not so. Recently a blue ribbon panel appointed by the American Psychological Society, the main organization of cognitive psychologists in the United States, issued a report on the status of research in cognitive psychology (Brewer and Luce, 1998). The panel came to two important conclusions and recommendations. The first was that cognitive research has failed to take individual differences into account and has thus been limiting the generalizability of its findings. There are different minds suspended in that vacuum, not just instances of one general mind. Future research should take individual differences into account. The second conclusion was that cognitive research should take context into account. The panel put it in strictly cognitive terms, pointing out that the fact that stimuli need to be repeated in experiments does not mean that the second stimulus presentation is really the same as the first presentation, the assumption made by all cognitive researchers. The second presentation is different by virtue of its being the second and not the first! In this quite concrete way the panel was pointing out that the specific context was a vital part of the experiment. And how one defines context becomes a matter of importance. If one puts together these two conclusions- keeping in mind individual differences and differences in individual context- we begin to lessen the distance between the consulting room and the laboratory. Transference and countertransference are the reactions of two unique individuals in a very special context which changes from time to time. It would seem to be the very antithesis of a general mind suspended in an interpersonal vacuum.

Once we take these considerations into account have we not invalidated the experiments I have offered as having anything to say about the clinical situation? Are they not about generalized minds suspended in an interpersonal vacuum? The answer is that they cannot possibly be that because no such circumstance exists. And this is precisely the point made by the blue ribbon panel. They were unmasking a myth and offering corrective recommendations that would acknowledge the reality of individual differences and individual contexts.

What is necessary to clarify is how transference and countertransference enter into the experimental situation. There is in fact tacit recognition that they do. It is expected as a default condition that subjects will have the necessary interest and willingness to cooperate so that the experimental instructions are listened to and followed. If a subject gives any indication at any point of not abiding by this default condition he or she is eliminated from the experiment. Only willing, cooperative subjects, those with positive transferences (perhaps because most are undergraduate students being tested by faculty or graduate students) remain in the experiment. The rebellious, defiant, ill at ease for whatever reason, those in other words with negative transference, are dismissed.

Countertransference issues are again tacitly recognized and dealt with through sanitizing. It is expected that if the experimenter who devised the experiment and formulated the hypotheses were to administer the experiment he or she would manage somehow to influence the subject's behavior so that the results would support the hypotheses. And there is a body of research confirming this expectation. One can imagine an eager experimenter invested in his or her hypotheses, yet committed to the rigors of the scientific method, attempting to interact with a willing, cooperative subject by strictly adhering to the letter of the instructions, but somehow managing to bias the subject's responses in favor of the hypotheses. This is not unheard of in the clinical situation. The corrective response in cognitive experimentation has been to remove the experimenter from the experiment. For the subjects the experimenter, lurking somewhere behind the computer, becomes a "blank screen" onto which they will project their individual ideas as to what the experiment is about, or what it means to the experimenter- helping him get tenure, a publication, etc. These individual responses must work to increase variability and thus, in statistical terms, the error variance is magnified making positive results less likely.

In all our experiments we make sure that the experimenter is in touch with the subjects throughout the experimental procedure. The aim is to assure that the subject remains involved, attentive and alert, drawing as much as possible on the subject's positive transference and curiosity. Any sign of fatigue or disinterest is immediately responded to by offering a rest period, or inquiring after how the subject is doing. In experiments in which the EEG is used we can tell immediately if the subject is becoming fatigued or uninvolved by the appearance of the alpha rhythm in the record; if the subject is becoming tense, irritated, upset these are usually reflected in an increase in muscle activity easily identified in the EEG record by high frequency waves. But it is mainly the experimenter in the booth who is in touch with the subject and undertakes to maintain an even level of positive involvement and execution of the task. These essentially clinical interventions are impossible if the procedure is entirely automated.

By the same token the experimenter usually experiences a positive countertransference toward the subject, eager to have the subject fulfill the requirements of the procedure and complete the experiment so that the goals of the research can be achieved. Although the experimenter shares in the programmatic goals of the research, in any given experiment the experimenter is unaware of the way in which the design of the experiment is being executed, whether for example a positive or negative emotional word is being presented, so that the experimenter cannot bias the outcome of the experiment by any prior knowledge.

As in the clinical situation transference and countertransferance serve to elicit the phenomena of interest, whether it is the patient's recall or enactment of childhood memories in the patient-analyst relationship, or the subject's readiness to submit to a procedure in which most of the time nothing is to be seen, but attention and alertness are still requested. The distance in these respects between the consulting room and the laboratory is one of degree and not one of kind. We cannot choose but be human in either setting. And thus I submit we can generalize from the laboratory to the consulting room.

The second question

Before addressing this second question, there is one objection from a psychoanalytic standpoint to the subliminal method itself as a means of investigating the unconscious which needs reply. The objection is straightforward: Granted that the subliminal method operationalizes the means to investigate unconscious processes, is it really the same unconscious as psychoanalysis has conceptualized? Perhaps it is some purely cognitive unconscious having to do with perception or attention, but of little pertinence to the unconscious whose influences are investigated in psychoanalysis.

As a start in answering this objection, I can do no better than to quote Freud. He was commenting on the then novel experiments of Otto Poetzl in which the recovery in dreams of subliminal content was first demonstrated. Freud observed:

> "An important contribution to the part played by recent material in the construction of dreams has been made by Poetzl in a paper which carried a wealth of implications...The questions raised by Poetzl's experiment go far beyond the sphere of dream interpretation as dealt with in this volume...it is worth remarking on the contrast between this new method of studying the formation of dreams experimentally and the earlier, crude technique for introducing into the dream stimuli which interrupted the subject's sleep" (Freud, 1953/1900, fn. pp. 180–181).

Apparently Freud, the originator of the psychoanalytic view of the unconscious and a presumed critic of experimental approaches to psychoanalytic concepts, perceived that this particular experimental approach based on subliminal stimulation carried a "wealth of implications" for understanding better the crown of his achievements- the unconscious work of dream formation. I could let the case rest there, but there is more that can be said. It would be a mistake for psychoanalysts to separate off any portion of the unconscious and consider it non-psychoanalytic. I submit it would be very hard to know where to draw the line between what is the non-psychoanalytic and the psychoanalytic unconscious. As I will return to later, the preconscious, defined in psychoanalysis as what can be immediately and voluntarily retrieved, emerges as a much more important part of the unconscious as a result of subliminal experiments, and links the cognitive and the dynamic.

Assuming now that we are dealing with the same unconscious in subliminal experiments as in the consulting room, do we learn anything new about the relationship between conscious and unconscious processes from the three experiments? To begin with, I have tried to convince you that the first experiment, along with a number of others, supports the view that affects can be unconscious in much the same way as ideas, fantasies, and motivations. The notion of a dispositional unconscious is inimical to the concept of a dynamic unconscious and misconstrues entirely the active and interactive nature of all unconscious processes.

In the second experiment on unconscious conflict we have shown that clinicians' judgments as to what belongs to unconscious conflict and what to conscious symptom experience is supported by totally independent and objective measures. The evidence is at the very least consistent with the explanation that an inhibitory, defensive process is at work when the unconscious conflict words enter consciousness.

But there is one aspect of the findings which bears closer scrutiny. I refer to the important role played by preconscious as distinct from dynamic or repressed unconscious processes. It was Charles Fisher (1957), the pioneer in subliminal research, who called attention to this implication of the subliminal method. He suggested that it made sense to assume that all stimuli, supraliminal as well as subliminal, registered preconsciously. This point of view has also been advanced more recently by Velmans (1991). Let me underscore the presumption in this proposition that supraliminal as well as subliminal stimuli are initially registered preconsciously. Cognitive psychologists would not contest this point. For example the activation of semantic networks is considered to take place automatically, that is, unconsciously. We are not aware of this activation.

However, cognitive psychologists might balk at the further implications of Fisher's position. He hypothesized that it was in the preconscious that the first transferences took place. By transference here I mean the first opportunity for the past to influence the present, which is the generic meaning of transference. As all cognitive psychologists would agree, although they would not use this terminology, all recognition takes place preconsciously, that is, a current perception of a familiar person is matched with a memory so that we recognize someone rather than cognize them. In the generic sense of the word, a transference has taken place, albeit one that contains a minimum of distortion and it is a psychological process that goes on without benefit of consciousness.

But other transferences may take place preconsciously as well, those in which the activated past and the motives involved may transform the perceptual registration beyond recognition, or invest them with such powerful conflictual significance that to become conscious of them would be anxiety arousing. From this standpoint the preconscious serves as a crucial way station determining what can become veridically conscious, what is displaced and distorted before becoming conscious, and what is kept from consciousness.

There is also another important consideration that emerges from subliminal experiments generally — a condition determining consciousness itself. It is apparently the case that in order for a stimulus to become conscious it must last for a certain minimum duration, or be of sufficient intensity. This of course has been known to psychophysicists for well over a hundred years. But what they did not know is that stimuli below the conscious threshold can undergo different fates depending on their relationship to conflict. In our experiment it would appear that the unconscious conflict words are categorized by the brain's response as belonging together, suggesting that a transference has taken place so that they are now part of the dynamic unconscious. The words are experienced unconsciously as related to each other on the basis of conflict. The fact that their relationship to each other is unconscious is further supported by the finding that when presented supraliminally the brain responses no longer place them in the same category. The supraliminal words are still cognized- they are after all simply words- but it is the significant relationship they bear to each other that is disrupted and no longer cognized. Subject RH (see Table 2) could not allow himself to realize consciously that his friend John was the target of intensely ambivalent feelings captured by words from a dream about John revealed during the interviews that had to do with evil and being stabbed, on the one hand, and men hugging and massaging muscles, on the other. Consciously John was a close friend, unconsciously he was a dangerous competitor who had alternately to be defeated and placated.

An issue to be taken up later but which deserves mention at this point, is the personal and individual nature of unconscious processes. In other research in our laboratory (Snodgrass, Shevrin, and Kopka, 1992; Snodgrass and Shevrin, 1999), we have shown that the unconscious processing of quite neutral words, with little apparent relevance to unconscious conflict, is very much affected by personality factors. The extent to which access to consciousness of subliminally registered stimuli is in part determined by a range of personality factors, confirming the Brewer and Luce (1998) report that individual differences must be taken into account in cognitive investigations.

Over and above these considerations, it is evident from the three experiments that the relationship between conscious and unconscious processes cannot be described solely in terms of the controlled/automatic distinction. Velmans (1991) provides an excellent evaluation of a wide range of research demonstrating how unconscious processes are controlled and conscious processes may be automatic. The relationship between conscious and unconscious processes is best characterized as being constituted of complex interacting forces, (1) involving transferences, or the range of influences the past can have on the present, (2) defenses, or the effort to forestall conscious anxiety, (3) motivations, which may or may not be in conflict, (4) the influence of personality dispositions, and finally, (5) the intensity and duration of the stimulus. What becomes conscious at any given time and in what form is largely determined by these factors. It would, for example, follow from this formulation that under certain circumstances a stimulus that is of sufficient intensity and duration to ordinarily become conscious may not if these other factors are strong enough. Although rare, this phenomenon does occur and takes the form of negative hallucinations (Brakel, 1989). No current theory in cognitive psychology can account for this phenomenon.

The third question

In some respects answering this third question is likely to prove the most tendentious and difficult of the three, but perhaps the most challenging. Granting for the sake of argument that the ERP brain responses are markers for something like unconscious processes, what do they tell us if anything about what is actually going on in the brain? And more to the point can we go beyond correlations between psychological and neurophysiological events to identify true bridging concepts?

There is one possible bridging concept suggested by our research which derives from the Williams' time-frequency feature biosignal analysis and Gerald Edelman's neural Darwinian theory of brain evolution and development (Edelman, 1987). In Edelman's theory the brain is conceived of as a highly complex dynamic system, constantly developing and changing its functional organization as the individual interacts with the world. The best way to illustrate this is to demonstrate that a particular action, like lifting a glass, can be accomplished in almost an infinitely varied number of ways, each different motion requiring a somewhat different organization of neuronal systems in order for the act to be accomplished. The context at the time, something I have referred to earlier, determines how the brain will shift its organization to accomplish a given act. This context is in part external, the shape and position of the glass, and in part internal, what else one is doing at the time or what purpose lifting the glass is intended to serve. What is invariant is the overall functional organization, rather than any fixed set or number of neurons. Just as these considerations hold true for intra-individual variability in brain functioning, they also hold true for inter-individual differences developing over the life of an individual. The same acts may be accomplished by different neuronal organizations in different individuals depending on the vicissitudes of their encounters with the world; in fact the functional brain organizations of identical twins may be different for this very reason.

Edelman's theory takes into account individuality and context, the two principles advocated by the blue ribbon panel appointed by the American Psychological Society. These two principles are central to the psychoanalytic conception of the mind, and I have tried to show that this conception must also be incorporated into a cognitive account of unconscious processes as well. These two principles of individuality and context are also embodied in the time-frequency feature analysis used in the study of unconscious conflict. The words selected were different from subject to subject; unlike the other two studies the stimuli were unique to each subject's own life experiences and individuality. The name John would have meant something entirely different to someone other than RH. The time-frequency features selected were also different from subject to subject; what they did share was the functional capacity to discriminate one class of words from another. The classes of words in turn bore a functional relationship to complex mental organizations.

What might be one functional property of these different organizations, mental and neurophysiological, which they both share, and could thus serve as a bridging concept? I believe one real possibility is what we call rhythm in mental organization, an essential property of all forms of art, for example, and frequency in brain organization. In recent years, the role of brain frequencies as the means through which superordinate functional organizations are formed has been receiving close attention. The work of Singer (1996), for example, on vision in the cat has shown that the various visual subsystems of which there are some thirty are integrated, or 'bound' together by resonating frequencies. In our own time-frequency feature analyses these little brain melodies may be serving a similar role but at the level of affect organization. I have attempted to find out if these brain melodies might in fact be carrying affect information. I transformed the sequences of time-frequency features into the audible range by simply multiplying the brain frequencies and the brief time intervals between them by suitable factors. I then had judges listen to the now audible brain melodies and to rate them on degrees of unpleasantness. To my surprise the melodies associated with the supraliminally presented unconscious con-flict words were rated as quite unpleasant. On closer inspection it seemed to be due to the relationship between the fourth and fifth features. The fifth, and last, feature appeared to leap in frequency so that it came across literally as a jarring

note. Is it possible that the same process occurs internally? The time-frequency series ends with an unconscious negative affective signal eliciting
inhibitory defenses. It may in fact be that this negative affective signal is
related to the unconscious expectancy wave Wong, Shevrin and Williams
(1994) found in their aversive conditioning experiment.

It is also possible to imagine that these brain melodies, sequences of time-
frequency features, on one level are the means through which regions of the
brain are integrated into a functional unit instantiating, for example, unconscious conflict, just as synchronous firing across many visual systems results
in the "binding" required for the unitary perception of an object; on another
level these same sequences of time-frequency features may isomorphically
organize affect and motor systems resulting in the outward manifestation of
these internal patterns. These initially internal frequency patterns would be
manifested in perceptible rhythmic organizations which would find expression in the conscious experience of an affect, the tonalities of speech, expressive gesture, and in all of the various mediums artist have discovered through
which to convey affect states. I believe these possibilities were envisioned by
Susanne Langer in her work, Feeling and Form (1953). Brain frequencies and
rhythmic patterns may be different aspects of the same organization and in this
respect might serve as a concept bridging the distance between complex
conscious and unconscious mental events, on the one hand, and brain processes, on the other.

Conclusions and implications

Psychological and neuroscientific investigations of unconscious processes
have an important role to play in expanding our knowledge of the relationship
between mind and brain, and conscious and unconscious processes. The
findings in the three experiments reported in this paper raise challenging
questions for cognitive psychologists who have an overly-limited view of the
nature of unconscious processes. Affect, conflict, unconscious expectancies
and anxieties are not given any consideration in cognitive research and thus
the tendency is for the theories of the unconscious to be overly narrow and
purely cognitive in nature. On the other hand, as these experiments also show,
it is possible to conduct controlled experimental investigations of these factors
and not rely solely on anecdotal clinical evidence or highly speculative

theories. Psychoanalysts who tend to dismiss the need for experimentation must take into consideration the value of experimentation in providing independent support for their clinical experience and theories.

By providing assurance to cognitive psychologists that the findings are based on sound experimental methodology and to psychoanalysts that the methods employed do justice to their concepts and theories, it becomes possible to imagine that the research offers a bridge across which both disciplines can find the way to each other's side. Let us avoid the situation described by Kihlstrom (1996) when he noted that research in subliminal perception would have died in the 1960s if not for the efforts of a small group of psychoanalytic investigators (of which I was one) whose research did not reach beyond a small circle despite the fact, states Khilstrom, that the studies met "reasonably stringent methodological standards" (p.26). Khilstrom explains this disinterest on the part of experimental psychologists as caused by their "distrust...towards anything smacking of psychoanalytic theory" (p.26). Given the present surge of interest in unconscious processes in cognitive psychology and neuroscience, perhaps experimental psychologists can overcome their distrust and judge psychoanalytic theory on its merits, and given the recent developments in subliminal methodology described in this paper, perhaps psychoanalysts can overcome their distrust of experimental findings and we can at last take advantage of both worlds.

References

Allport, A. 1989. Visual attention. In M.I. Posner (ed.), *Foundations of Cognitive Science*, 631–682. Cambridge, MA: MIT Press.

Applebaum, S.A., Siegal, R.S., & Rosen, I.C. 1977. *Anatomy of Change*. New York: Plenum Press.

Bargh, J.A. 1989. "Conditional automaticity: Varieties of autonomic influence on social perception and cognition." In J.S. Uleman & J.A. Bargh (eds), *Unintended Thought*, 3–51. New York: Guilford.

Bernat, E., Bunce, S.C., & Shevrin. 1999. Event-related brain potentials differentiate positive and negative mood adjectives during both supraliminal andsubliminal processing. International Journal of Psychophysiology (in press).

Bower, G.H. 1987. "Mood and memory." *American Psychologist,* 36, (2), 129–48.

Brakel, L.A.W. 1989. "Negative hallucinations, other irretrievable experiences, and two functions of consciousness." *The International Journal of Psychoanalysis,* 70, Part 3, 461–479.

Brakel, L., Kleinsorge, S., Snodgrass, M., & Shevrin, H. 1995. Attributional versus relational similarity as a function of subliminal versus supraliminal duration in judgments about geometric figures. International Journal of Psychoanalysis (in press).

Brewer, M.B., & Luce, R.D. 1998. "Basic research in psychological science." American Psychological Society *Observer*. Report 6, 3–39.

Bunce, S.C., Bernat, E., Wong, P.S., & Shevrin, H. (In press) "Further evidence for unconscious learning: Preliminary support for the conditioning of facial EMG to subliminal stimuli." *Journal of Psychiatric Research*.

Coles, M.G.H., & Rugg, M.D. 1995. "Event-related brain potentials: An introduction." In M.D. Rugg & M.G.H. Coles (eds), *Electrophysiology of Mind. Event-Related Brain Potentials and Cognition*, 1–26. New York: Oxford University Press.

Dahl, H. 1979. *Word Frequencies of Spoken English*. Detroit, MI: Verbatim Books.

Edelman, G.M. 1987. *Language and Interpretation in Psychoanalysis*. New Haven, CT: Yale University Press.

Edelson, M. 1988. *Psychoanalysis: A Theory in Crisis*. Chicago: University of Chicago Press.

Fisher, C. 1957. "A study of the preliminary stages of the construction of dreams and images." *Journal of the American Psychoanalytic Association*, 5, 60–67.

Freud, S. 1957. "The unconscious." In J. Strachey (ed. & trans.), *The Standard Edition of the Complete Psychological Works of Sigmund Freud, 14*, 159–216. London: Hogarth Press. [Original work published 1915.]

Greenwald, A., Klinger, M., & Schuh, E.S. 1995. "Activation by marginally perceptible "subliminal") stimuli: Dissociation of unconscious from conscious cognition." *Journal of Experimental Psychology: General, 124*(1), 22–42.

Grunbaum, A. 1984. *The Foundations of Psychoanalysis*. Berkeley, CA: University of California Press.

James, W. 1890. *Principles of Psychology*. New York: Holt.

Kihlstrom, John F. 1996. "Perception without awareness of what is perceived, learning wihtout awareness of what is learned." In M. Velmans (ed.), *The Science of Consciousness: Psychological, Neuropsychological and Clinical Reviews*, 23–46. London: Routledge.

Langer, S.K. 1953. *Feeling and Form*. New York: Charles Scribner's Sons.

LeDoux, J.E. 1995. "Emotion: Clues from the brain." *Annual Review of Psychology, 46*, 209–35.

Murphy, S., Zajonc, R.B. 1993. "Affect, cognition, and awareness: Affective priming with optimal and suboptimal stimulus exposures." *Journal of Personality and Social Psychology*, 64(5), 723–739.

Ohman, A., Esteves, F., Soares, J. 1995. "Preparedness and pre-attentive associative learning: Electrodermal conditioning to masked stimuli." *Journal of Psychophysiology*, 9, 99–108.

Osgood, C.E., May, W.H., & Miron, M.S. 1975. *Cross-Cultural Universals of Affective Meaning*. Urbana: University of Illinois Press.

Rapaport, D. 1967. "The scientific methodology of psychoanalysis." In M.M. Gill (ed.), *The Collected Papers of David Rapaport*, 165–220. New York: Basic Books.

Shevrin, H. 1973. "Brain wave correlates of subliminal stimulation unconscious attention, primary- and secondary-process thinking and repressiveness." *Psychological Issues, Monograph 30,* 8(2), 56–87.

Shevrin, H. 1998. The experimental investigation of unconscious conflict, unconscious affect, and signal anxiety. Paper presented at Yale University, November 21, 1998.

Shevrin, H., & Fritzler, D. 1968. "Visual evoked response correlates of unconscious mental processes." *Science,* 161, 295–298.

Shevrin, H., & Rennick, P. 1967. "Cortical response to a tactile stimulus during attention, mental arithmetic and free associations." *Psychophysiology,* 3, 381–388.

Shevrin, H., Bond, J.A., Brakel, L.A.W., Hertel, R.K., Williams, W.J. 1996. *Conscious and Unconscious Processes.* New York: The Guilford Press.

Shiffrin, R.M., & Schneider, W. 1977. "Controlled and automatic information processing. II Perceptual learning, automatic attending, a general theory." *Psychological Review,* 84, 127–190.

Singer, W. 1996. "Neuronal synchronization: A solution to the binding problem?" In R. Llinas & P.S. Churchland (eds.), *Sensory Processes: The Mind-Brain Continuum,* 101–130. Cambridge, MA: MIT Press.

Smith, G., Spence, D., & Klein, G. 1959. "Subliminal effects of verbal stimuli." *Journal of Abnormal and Social Psychology,* 59, 167–176.

Snodgrass, M., Shevrin, H., & Kopka, M. 1993. "The mediation of intentional judgments by unconscious perceptions: The influences of task strategy, task preference, word meaning, and motivation." *Consciousness and Cognition,* 2, 169–193.

Snodgrass, M., Shevrin, H., Brakel, L., & Medin, D. 1995. Evidence for qualitative differences in the principles of organization for conscious and unconscious categorization. Poster presented at the 7th Annual Meeting of the American Psychological Society.

Snodgrass, M. & Shevrin, H. Unconscious inhibition at the objective threshold: A replicable and qualitatively different unconscious perceptual effect. (Submitted for publication).

Van Selst, H., & Merikle, P.M. 1993. "Perception below the objective threshold?" *Consciousness and Cognition,* 2, 194–203.

Velmans, M. 1991. "Is human information processing conscious?" *Behavioral and Brain Sciences,* 14 (4), 651–726.

Williams, W.J., & Jeong, J. 1992. "Reduced interference time-frequency distributions." In Boashash (ed.), *Time-Frequency Signal Analysis: Methods and Applications.* Melbourne, Australia: Longman Chesire-Wiley.

Wong, P.S. 1999. "Anxiety, signal anxiety, and unconscious anticipation: Neuroscientific evidence for an unconscious signal function in humans." *Journal of the American Psychoanalytic Association,* 47, 3, 817–841.

Wong, P.S., Shevrin, H., & Williams, W. 1994. "Conscious and unconscious processes: An ERP index of an anticipatory response in a conditioning paradigm using visually masked stimuli." *Psychophysiology,* 1, 87–101.

Wong, P.S., Bernat, E., Bunce, S., & Shevrin, H. 1997. "Brain indices of nonconscious associative learning." *Consciousness and Cognition,* 6, 519–544.

CHAPTER 4

A Psychoanalytic Contribution to Contemporary Neuroscience

Mark Solms

St. Bartholomeus and Royal London School of Medicine

Introduction

The psychoanalytic method was designed to systematically explore *subjective experience* in a standard, naturalistic setting, with the aim of drawing scientific inferences about the functional organisation of the apparatus that generates experience (the human mind). When psychoanalysis was born (1895–1900) there was little prospect of learning anything useful about the functional organisation of the human mind from the vantage point of neuroscience. Neuroscience was restricted essentially to the study of anatomical preparations. At that time, a systematic study of the determinants of subjective experience was more likely to yield useful insights into the functional organisation of the mind than any neuroscientific approach. Today, however, the situation has reversed itself. Due to dramatic technological advances, the functional architecture of the mind is being probed to great benefit by a variety of neuroscientific techniques; and psychoanalytic methods have been all but abandoned.

This does not mean that psychoanalytic methods no longer have anything to contribute to mental science. Indeed, psychoanalysts and neuroscientists are ultimately studying the *same thing* (viz., the functional organisation of the human mind) from two different points of view. If that is true — and it is difficult to argue that it is not — then it seems reasonable to expect that these two observational perspectives should complement one another. That is, psychoanalytic and neuroscientific (introspective and extrospective) data *combined* should provide a better and more secure basis for inferences about the functional organisation of the mind than either viewpoint on its own.

In this chapter I want to demonstrate that — even today — scientific understanding of the mind is enhanced when neurological methods of investigation are supplemented by psychoanalytic methods. I will describe a concrete example: a neuropsychological syndrome that is currently understood in terms of theories derived primarily from neurobehavioral methods of investigation. These theories seem questionable in the light of the evidence that psychoanalytic research brings to light. I hope this example will convince readers that it would be a mistake to discard the psychoanalytic method completely, even if only for the reason that the systematic exploration of subjective experience remains a useful source of data (and theory) about the mind.

The mental sequelae of right middle cerebral artery stroke

Description of the syndrome

Right middle cerebral artery strokes are associated with a distinctive neurobehavioural syndrome, loosely described as the 'right hemisphere syndrome'. This syndrome consists of three interrelated symptoms. The first of these is *anosognosia*. In its extreme form, anosognosia presents as denial of illness in the face of patently contradictory evidence. In Babinski's (1914) classical description, hemiplegic patients insisted they could walk, and in Anton's (1899) study cortically blind patients claimed they could see. In less extreme cases this symptom presents as *anosodiaphoria*, in which patients do not openly deny that they are disabled but they assume an emotionally indifferent attitude to their disabilities.

The second cardinal element of the right hemisphere syndrome is *neglect*. Patients with neglect ignore the left-hand side of space, including the left-hand side of the own body, despite intact sensory capacity to perceive it. There is also a motor form of neglect, known as *hemiakinesia*, in which the patient fails to use the left limbs despite preserved instrumental capacity.

It is not uncommon for these patients, when their own paralysed limbs are presented to them in such a way that they are forced to acknowledge their existence, to claim that the limbs do not belong to them. They are more willing to accept that they belong to the examiner (even though this would imply that the examiner has more than four limbs) than to accept that the paralysed arm or leg is attached to their own body. This combination of neglect and anosognosia is called *somatoparaphrenic delusion*.

Patients with neglect have been reported who feel disgust when they are compelled to attend to the left-hand side of their own bodies (using mirrors, for example). This sense of revulsion is sometimes organised into a near psychotic hatred of the left arm or leg — a condition known as *misoplegia*. This is a paradoxical form of neglect, in which the patient becomes obsessed by the left-hand side of the body, rather than ignores it.

The third complex of symptoms that comprise the right hemisphere syndrome are classified as *disorders of spatial perception and cognition*. These take various forms: constructional apraxia, dressing apraxia, topographical disorientation, defective face recognition, imperception of facial emotion, inadequate judgement of line orientation, and so on.

Current theories of right perisylvian function

The last-mentioned symptoms provide the general basis for almost all contemporary neuropsychological theories of right perisylvian function. According to these theories, the right hemisphere convexity is specialised for *spatial perception and cognition*. This conception is so well established in contemporary neuropsychology that it hardly needs restating here (see DeRenzi, 1982, for a review).

Recently, this general theory has been supplemented by a number of special theories which attempt to account specifically for those emotional symptoms of anosognosia and neglect (and somatoparaphrenic delusions) which cannot be explained in purely spatial terms.

The first of these is the theory that the right cerebral hemisphere is dominant for *attentional arousal* (Heilman, Watson & Valenstein 1993; Mesulam 1981). According to this theory the right perisylvian region is part of an attention arousal loop (which also includes frontal, anterior limbic, thalamic and core brainstem structures). This loop privileges the right cerebral hemisphere with regard to the arousal and distribution of attention. Both spatial hemifields are thought to be under the purview of the right hemisphere, whereas the left hemisphere attends only to the right hand side of space. Consequently, when the left hemisphere is damaged the right hemisphere remains capable of maintaining full attentional focus in both spatial fields, whereas when the right hemisphere is damaged attention is restricted to the right hemispatial field of the intact left hemisphere. This accounts for neglect, and for some of the cardinal features of anosognosia.

The second theory asserts that the right cerebral hemisphere is dominant for *negative emotions* (while the left hemisphere is dominant for positive emotions). This theory explains anosognosia and anosodiaphoria in the following way: when the right hemisphere is damaged the patient has access only to the intact positive emotions of the left hemisphere, therefore they feel inappropriately positive about their condition (see Gainotti, 1997, for a review).

The third theory was proposed by Damasio (1994). It has two components. The first is a modified version of the James-Lange paradigm, which states that emotions are *perceptions of the current state of one's own body.* Damasio adds that the brain also contains mnemic representations of previous body states, with the result that what Damasio calls 'as if' emotions can be generated when current perceptions activate somatic memory dispositions, thereby bypassing the current state of the body. Secondly, Damasio suggests that the right hemisphere is dominant for the perceptual representation of the body, and therefore for monitoring its current somatic and visceral state. He concludes that damage to the right hemisphere will result in an inordinate reliance on 'as if' emotions, based on the pre-morbid state of the body. This mechanism accounts for the symptoms of anosognosia and anosodiaphoria, and presumably also accounts for impoverishment of emotionality in general — which is a feature of the right hemisphere syndrome that is frequently remarked upon, and which has led to the view in some quarters that the right hemisphere is dominant not only for negative emotions, but in fact for all emotions — that it is the 'emotional' hemisphere.

All of these theories — derived primarily from neurobehavioral observation — do not go far beyond the directly observable (extrospective) data. Right hemisphere lesions produce disorders of spatial perception and cognition; therefore the right hemisphere must be specialised for spatial perception and cognition. Right hemisphere lesions produce unilateral disorders of attention; therefore the right hemisphere must be responsible for the bilateral distribution of attention. Right hemisphere lesions are associated with emotional indifference and unconcern; therefore the right hemisphere must be specialised for negative emotions. Right hemisphere lesions result in impoverished emotionality and defective somatic awareness; therefore the right hemisphere must be responsible for monitoring the somatic basis of normal emotionality.

There is nothing wrong with simple theories which stay close to observable data; indeed, such theories — being easily operationalized — are highly valued in science. But psychoanalysts have reason to be cautious in this regard. We have learned when investigating the underlying mechanisms of mental disorders that these disorders are far more complex than they superficially appear to be, and that the essential mechanisms underlying them are often quite remote from the manifest behaviours. Sometimes we find that the underlying causes of a disorder are the very opposite of what behavioural observation would suggest. This obscurity of the underlying mechanism is attributed to the clinical phenomenon of 'resistance' — which we explain by a mechanism called 'defence' — which results in motivated distortion, obscuration and obliteration of distressing thoughts and perceptions.

First clinical example

Mr C was a 59-year-old civil engineer who underwent an endartorectomy of the right common carotid artery following a transient ischaemic attack, which presented as left-sided hemiparesis. A pre-operative angiogram induced complete hemiplegia, and the endartorectomy was performed as an emergency procedure. After the operation, however, dense left hemiplegia persisted, together with equally dense hemianopia on the left side and a mild somatosensory deficit. An MRI scan demonstrated a large area of infarction in the right temporo-parietal region, which was interpreted as a thrombosis of the inferior branch of the right mid-cerebral artery.

The neuropsychological assessment was conducted five weeks postinsult. It demonstrated a severe right hemisphere syndrome. Mr C made no attempt to compensate for his hemianopia (in other words, he *neglected* it), and he was inattentive to stimuli arising from the left hand side in the other sensory modalities too. He even ignored questions that were asked of him when the examiner sat on his left. In addition, he was *anosodiaphoric*. Although he did not openly deny that his left arm was paralysed, he tended to ignore, minimise and rationalise the paralysis, saying for example that 'it *was* like a dead piece of meat, but *now* its just a little bit lame and lazy'. In addition, his visual-spatial judgement was poor, which was a serious deficit, considering the fact that, as a civil engineer, his livelihood depended largely on this skill. He retained abstract knowledge of topographical relationships, but his constructional performances were apraxic. He displayed the 'closing-in phenomenon', often seen in right parietal patients, in which the construction seems to collapse in on the model. He was moderately disoriented in concrete space. This was complicated further by his neglect. There was severe acalculia (of the spatial type). This deficit, too, was a blow to his capacity to function as an engineer. He reported a complete cessation of dreaming, but his visual imagery seemed to be intact. Memory was essentially normal. Formal spoken and written language skills were preserved but speech was aprosodic (monotonous or lacking in expressive intonation) and was punctuated by inappropriate pauses. All higher motor functions were preserved in the non-paralysed limb. Verbal regulation of executive performances, too, was intact. Complex logical problems were solved with ease.

Shortly after his neuropsychological assessment, Mr C began a rehabilitation programme. However, the therapists reported that he was unwilling to co-operate with them. This occurs quite often with anosognosic patients in rehabilitation settings. They don't co-operate with the therapists because they fail to see why they should; they believe that they have no need for rehabilitation.

In the psychoanalytic setting Mr C presented in an aloof, imperious and egocentric fashion. He was oblivious to the world around him, except insofar as it affected his own well-being and needs, and he was quite unable to see things from another person's point of view. This included an eschewing of social convention. For example, he openly picked his nose during his sessions and wiped the products on the knee of his trousers. He frequently sat blankly staring into space for long periods of time, seldom taking social initiative except when he wished to express a complaint or make an urgent request. He responded to direct questions with a minimum of effort, in clipped monosyllabic tones, and not infrequently with manifest irritation. He took little in and he showed no gratitude. It was as if he had withdrawn into a cocoon of self-sufficiency, and yet he was simultaneously needy and demanding.

Despite his tendency to minimise and rationalise his major deficits, such as his hemiplegia and hemianopia, Mr C was hypochondriacal in regard to minor ailments, such as a sore back and difficulty in sleeping. He was equally intolerant of frustrations of any kind. This was expressed most clearly in relation to the nursing staff, whom he treated as if they were combined into one big mother whose only function was to meet his personal needs, and moreover to do so immediately. His intolerance of frustration and delay was also expressed in relation to the inevitable limitations that were imposed on him by his physical and mental handicaps, by the hospital milieu, and by the demands of his rehabilitation regime. Most important of all, he expected — indeed demanded — to make an immediate and total recovery, so that he could return to work forthwith, as well as to his previous respected position in society. His demeanour conveyed an intense (unacknowledged) need to regress — that is, to be looked after and cared for — and yet he consciously abhorred dependence and vulnerability of any kind and he wanted to be treated as if he were the chairman of a public company. Thus, while he made constant, whining demands of the staff, he simultaneously insisted on doing everything for himself. In sum, he closely resembled the proverbial 'his majesty the baby'.

This patient's subjective attitude to his deficits, as it was revealed in the psychoanalytic situation, was extremely interesting. He spoke of the left side of his body in just the same way as he did of the nursing staff, as if it was merely another piece of external reality that was refusing to do his bidding. It was a source of irritation and annoyance to him, but also something that he did not feel any great interest in or concern about. It was as if it had nothing to do with him personally. From the subjective viewpoint, it appeared that he had single-handedly redrawn the boundaries of his physical self, so that he now only recognised his torso and his right sided limbs as truly belonging to him. The left-hand side was there to serve him, but it was not making a terribly good job of it, and he did not really want to be associated with it. Accordingly, he seemed to experience his deficits as if they were impingements which emanated from the outside world, rather than from his own beloved self. For example, he spoke of his left hand as something that 'offended' him or 'inconvenienced' him, as one might speak of a rude guest or an unwelcome visitor. On one occasion he described his hand as 'not obeying the orders that I am sending it'. It was like an inefficient servant or a disobedient employee, whose behaviour he was not prepared to tolerate for much longer, while he also did not want to become too personally involved with them.

Despite this apparent detachment from his deficits, Mr C was forever clutching at straws of improvement and drawing his analyst's attention to them. Please notice this tendency to withdraw from the external world, and for the subjective boundaries of the self to retreat from the left side of the body (which nevertheless remains part of the objective self); I shall have much to say about it later.

Now I would like to focus on something specific about Mr C's presentation, which I have held back until now. This begins to reveal something of the subjective mechanisms underlying his anosodiaphoria. I have said that Mr C presented in a detached, aloof, even imperious fashion. Nevertheless, every now and then, for no obvious reason, *his face would suddenly crumple, and he would either burst into tears for a brief moment or he would look as if he was about to burst into tears*, before rapidly finding his composure again. The whole episode would be over in a flash, forming a curiously incongruous contrast to his more pervasive attitude of invulnerable superiority.

If one gave this patient the Minnesota Multiphasic Personality Inventory, or the Beck Depression Inventory, or any other such behavioural questionnaire, these episodes would be overlooked completely. Mr C himself was only too happy to forget them. This form of data collection (which is used in most neuropsychological research in this area) would therefore produce a somewhat misleading picture of his emotional state. But in the analytic situation it was impossible to miss these episodes; and the analyst was able to explore their immediate precipitants and form an impression as to what was causing them. In doing so it became evident to her[1] that they were directly associated with thoughts and feelings of the kind that were most conspicuously absent in his more pervasive, anosodiaphoric state. I have space to illustrate this by means of just one example. I hope the reader will accept that all of these episodes followed a similar basic pattern.

The physiotherapist reported to the analyst that she had been trying to teach Mr C to walk again, but she had made little headway for the reason that Mr C seemed totally indifferent to the errors that he was making, and he simply ignored her when she pointed them out to him. This was a typically anosognosic response, and the physiotherapist interpreted it as such. Yet, on the following day, in the privacy of the analytic situation, Mr C described what had happened, clearly indicating that he *was* partly aware of the deficits that the physiotherapist had tried in vain to point out to him the day before. The session proceeded as follows, according to the analyst's verbatim account:

> At first he sat silently, in his typical detached state. After a few minutes, I asked what he was thinking about. He said that the physiotherapists were teaching him to walk, and he added in a confessional tone (looking a bit ashamed) that the physiotherapist had told him that he had made a few

mistakes. [Here he was apparently attributing to the physiotherapist his own perception of his mistakes, which he was simultaneously minimizing, as he was very far indeed from being able to walk normally.] Then he said (with the same confessional, embarrassed tone) that the occupational therapist had also assigned a task to him, which involved the use of blocks, and he hadn't managed it. I said in reply that it was difficult for him to acknowledge the problems his stroke had left him with, but it seemed that he was now more able to see them. Mr C carried on as if I had not spoken. He said that his physiotherapy was 'okay', but that his arm had not progressed to the degree that he required. Then, at this point, he suddenly withdrew from conversing with me and began to exercise his left hand and arm with his right one. I commented that it seemed as if he could not bear the wait, and wanted his arm to be completely better immediately. 'No', he said, momentarily reverting to his rationalizations, 'I just don't want my left arm to get weak from non-use'. I replied that it was perhaps too painful for him to acknowledge what he was on the verge of recognizing a moment earlier — namely that his arm really was completely paralysed — and that the question of whether it would recover or not was largely beyond his control. This comment provoked an instantaneous crumpling of his face and a burst of painful emotion accompanied by pre-tearfulness. Turning to me, he said in desperation, 'but *look* at my arm (pointing to his left arm) — what am I going to *do* if it doesn't recover?'. (This was his most reflective comment to date, which involved a full recognition of his plight — a truly defenceless moment.) Then Mr C was silent for a long while, whereafter he reverted to his usual apparently indifferent state.

This vignette, which was typical of these episodes, illustrates that the sudden moments of tearfulness and pre-tearfulness in this case were easily understood within their subjective context. They represented breakthroughs of apparently suppressed feelings about the deficits which he had previously denied; and in this instance, these feelings applied to deficits which he had been minimising and rationalising away just moments before the anxiety and concern broke through. In short, the analyst's carefully timed and tactfully worded interventions in the analytic situation momentarily overcame the patient's resistances, and enabled him to face squarely the facts that he had up until then been strongly disinclined to acknowledge. This begins to suggest that Mr C's whole aloof, detached, narcissistic persona might have served — at least in part — to divert his attention (and ours) away from the painful underlying facts of his newly dependent and vulnerable position. This is what I meant earlier when I said that psychoanalysis sometimes reveals that the underlying mechanism of a mental disorder — the mechanism behind the resistances — is the very opposite of what it appears to be.

If readers are not yet convinced of this, then at least, at this stage, I hope they will accept that the psychoanalytic evidence casts doubt on the claim that these patients simply lack negative emotions, or that they are simply unaware of the current state of their bodies, or that they are simply unable to attend to their deficits on the left hand side. It suggests that the underlying psychological situation is more complex than that. These patients evidently are continuously encoding information about their defective bodies, and at some level they do indeed have knowledge about their handicaps, and the emotional implications thereof. All that they lack is the capacity — or, perhaps, the *inclination* — to attend to this knowledge, to enable it to enter conscious awareness.

In case readers think that the phenomenon I have just described was idiosyncratic to the one case, and that it cannot be demonstrated in other cases of anosognosia or anosodiaphoria, I will briefly describe a second case.

Second clinical example

Mrs B was a 55-year old woman who had suffered a stroke 18 years ago, in the final trimester of her third pregnancy. Clinical investigations at the time revealed that there had been a thrombosis of the right middle cerebral artery, affecting primarily the posterior cortical region and underlying white matter. Mrs B was left with a dense left hemiplegia, affecting her face, arm and leg. A CT scan taken six years after the stroke confirmed this diagnosis and localisation, and revealed a large area of low density in the right parietal lobe, extending subcortically into the internal capsule. The medical notes stated only that she was anosodiaphoric and 'aloof' at the time of her stroke, and that she had been completely anosognosic in the acute post-stroke period, but it appears that no formal neuropsychological assessment was conducted. Eighteen years later, when she was referred for psychoanalytic therapy, she was still significantly hemiparetic, but she walked with the aid of a stick, and was even able to drive a modified car. By this time, there were no manifest cognitive deficits.

In evaluating Mrs B's personality, we are in the extremely fortunate position of being able to compare our own clinical observations with detailed premorbid observations which were recorded by a psychoanalytic psychotherapist who had treated her for two years immediately prior to her stroke. I cannot go into all the details here. I would like to emphasise only that there was no evidence in the premorbid notes of depressive illness or episodes, and certainly no mention at all of the curious symptom that her present analyst observed; namely the fact that Mrs B — just like Mr C — was prone to sudden breakthroughs of tearfulness in the context of an otherwise rather distant, brittle and affectless presentation. In sharp contrast to these moments of really quite uncontrollable tearfulness, Mrs B described herself as a 'coper', and as someone who 'never wore her heart on her sleeve'.

Mrs B described these episodes as involving sad feelings, in relation to which she felt considerable distance, and yet she was simultaneously unable to inhibit them. When asked what the sad feelings were about, she said that she did not know. Yet when describing the episodes, it was readily apparent to the analyst that they were intimately related to the physical handicaps that had marred her life after her stroke. For example, in her first analytic session, Mrs B reported an episode involving a young man who had recently joined the Stroke Aid Society (a voluntary support group for stroke patients). The young man was describing his experience of his handicaps and weeping, when Mrs B, too, began to cry uncontrollably. At this point the analyst made the rather obvious remark that Mrs B was crying in identification with the young man, about her *own* handicaps. However, surprisingly, Mrs B did not agree with this remark. She said that she was a 'coper', whom others turned to for help. When the analyst suggested that she might be coping on the outside but sad on the inside, Mrs B again totally rejected the notion, and insisted that she really was coping; she reminded the analyst that her stoke had happened a long time ago, and she repeated that she had fully come to terms with it.

Here is a second episode. Mrs B commented that she was more emotional than she used to be before her stroke, although, as already described, she also felt as if her emotions were not really her own any more. She then elaborated:

> She had noticed that these uncontrollable feelings — notably weeping which she couldn't stop — were always set off by a specific external event. For example, they erupted when she saw 'Fiddler on the Roof' [this patient was Jewish, and of Eastern European descent]. Then she corrected herself; 'no', she said, 'there are times that I am continually tearful, regardless of the external context'. The tearfulness seems to come from nowhere. She went on to describe an example of her lack of resistance to crying. She said that the other day she had read one sentence in a book, and she immediately started crying uncontrollably. I asked what the sentence was about, but she couldn't remember it. She knew that it involved a husband and wife and a court case, about which they were talking, but that was all. [She did remember the sentence in a subsequent session, as will be seen in a moment.] She agreed

that there might have been personal associations that she was not aware of. Once again, she described vividly how cut off from, and yet simultaneously overwhelmed by, such feelings she had become since her stroke.

One week later, Mrs B returned to this issue:

> She said that she had looked up the 'forgotten' sentence, in the book which had made her cry. She described the episode again, this time making it clear how severe the crying was; she said that she had been unable to stop sobbing for over an hour. The sentence referred to *a court case surrounding a thalidomide child.* She said that this episode was typical of how she would start crying and would then be unable to stop until the overwhelming feeling had spent itself. I asked her what the image of a thalidomide child made her think of. She said she had first heard of thalidomide children about six years after her stroke. Her associations were to practical issues; for example, she was preoccupied with how a victim of the drug would grow up and cope in life, without limbs. She thought that physiotherapy might help, as it had always helped her, and still did. Then she was silent. I said that it seemed likely that she identified herself with the thalidomide children, and that her overwhelming feelings in response to reading about them showed that she was still holding back powerful feelings about her own physical disability. In response to this comment, Mrs B became defensive, and subtly changed the subject. First she said that she and her whole family had always been open about physical matters, including her disability. Then she said that her family of origin, too, had always been very liberal about 'those matters' — there was no excessive modesty around bathtimes, and so on.

I hope my point is clear: this anosodiaphoric patient with a right perisylvian stroke, just like Mr C, was apparently suppressing distressing feelings associated with her physical handicaps. She consciously denied or avoided or rationalised these feelings away, but unconsciously they were always imminent, and under favourable intersubjective circumstances the underlying, repressed feelings broke through into consciousness, in the form of uncontrollable tearfulness. It should be equally clear that the feelings in question were *depressive* in nature, and directly related to the painful losses that this patient had suffered as a result of her stroke. Further psychoanalytic investigation of her defences against these feelings (which I do not have space to describe here) suggested that their primary function was to shore up a fragile and damaged self-esteem; in other words to shore up what we in psychoanalysis would call her *narcissism*.

Preliminary theoretical remarks

I do not know how prevalent these eruptions of tearfulness and pre-tearfulness are in the anosognosic and anosodiaphoric population in general. No doubt there are cases — again I do not know how many — in which there are no such episodes. However, the fact that a subgroup does exist in which depressive affects break through in this way, suggests that even in the cases where negative emotions are more pervasively absent, this may be due to repression. That is, depressive affects may be totally absent in these other cases because in them they are *successfully* kept away from consciousness, not because they are truly absent in the sense implied by the theory which claims that the right cerebral hemisphere is a repository for negative emotions. By similar reasoning, the existence of these cases suggests that even in those cases where such breakthroughs of emotional awareness do not occur, these patients might be unaware of or unconcerned about their deficits, not because they *cannot* direct attention to them in the sense that the attentional arousal theory implies, but rather because their attention is actively *diverted away* from them. The same applies to the somatic monitoring theory. The case of Mr C, in particular, showed that these patients *are* unconsciously aware of the damaged state of their bodies. They evidently know perfectly well what has happened to their bodies, but they do not *want* to know.

This suggests that a fundamental mechanism underlying the inattentional, hypoemotional and somatoparaphrenic symptoms of the right hemisphere syndrome is the mechanism of *repression*. This raises numerous further questions, and most specifically this one: why do *right* perisylvian patients in particular suffer from repressions, whereas other patients (*left* perisylvian patients, for example) do not? In other words, what is it about the functions of the right perisylvian region that make patients with lesions just there so intolerant of depressive emotions and the associated thoughts about loss and dependency? I will attempt to address this question in due course. But first, I want to describe some further cases with right perisylvian lesions who presented in very different ways to Mr C and Mrs B. These are right hemisphere cases in which the defence against depression apparently failed more or less *completely*.

Third clinical example

Mrs A was a 61-year old Austrian woman who was treated psychoanalytically ten months after she suffered massive damage in the right perisylvian region of her brain as the result of a middle cerebral artery subarachnoid haemorrhage. Her lesion predominantly affected the right temporo-parietal region, but it also extended anteriorly into the frontal convexity, and medially down to the depth of the thalamus. This stroke left her with a dense left hemiplegia and hemianopia, and she was wheelchair-bound. Neuropsychologically, she presented with a severe right hemisphere syndrome, characterised by dense left *hemineglect*, *anosognosia* for her hemiplegia and hemianopia, *constructional apraxia*, *topographical amnesia*, and other gross impairments of visuospatial behaviour and cognition. In other words she was severely impaired, both motorically and visuospatially, but she was consciously *unaware* of these impairments.

This was the first case of right hemisphere syndrome that I studied psychoanalytically, so I was interested to see what we could learn about the deep psychology of neglect and anosognosia, and I was keen to begin to take my initial bearings for a psychoanalytic perspective on the functions of the right perisylvian region. However, in one crucial respect Mrs A was an atypical case of this syndrome, because, notwithstanding her anosognosia and neglect (that is to say, her apparent unawareness of the physical consequences of her stroke) she was *clinically depressed*. Indeed, that is why she was referred to me in the first place.

According to two letters I received, including one from her GP (who was a compatriot of hers and a life-long friend), Mrs A had never suffered from depressions premorbidly. However, one of the most conspicuous symptoms of her stroke was a severe mood disorder, which presented with all the clinical hallmarks of a full-blown melancholia. She was almost constantly in tears, she believed that she was an enormous burden to the world and that everybody hated her, and she had twice attempted to kill herself — once by trying to jump out of a window and once by throwing herself down a flight of stairs. The only reason she did not succeed in these attempts was because she was too motorically and spatially impaired to manage the logistics of what she wanted to do.

So here we have a patient with a massive right perisylvian lesion, with apparently normal lateralization and a full-blown right hemisphere syndrome, who was simultaneously severely depressed. This fact alone demonstrates one of the main points I am trying to make, namely that these patients are indeed capable of experiencing profoundly negative emotions. This is difficult to reconcile with the idea that the usual hypoemotionality of these cases is due to a literal deficiency of negative affect. It is more compatible with the view that their hypoemotionality is only *apparent*; that negative emotions are not *absent* in these cases, rather they are unconsciously imminent but repressed.

I have up until now been using the term 'repression' in a loose sense, more or less synonymously with the broader term 'defence'. Actually, in psychoanalysis we distinguish between many different varieties of defence. Although all defences serve the same fundamental purpose (namely keeping distressing thoughts, feelings or perceptions away from consciousness) they do this in many different ways. In Mrs A's case, as will presently be seen, the form of defence that she used was *introjection*. It is no coincidence that this mechanism, like the defences used by Mr C and Mrs B, is a *narcissistic* form of defence.

In one of her first analytic sessions Mrs A explained that the reason why she was so depressed was simple: it was because the staff all hated her, especially the cleaning and kitchen staff, and because she kept on losing things, or rather, because people kept stealing things from her. With this explanation, she burst into tears, and said that she would never be able to repay the rehabilitation team for everything that we were doing for her. She sobbed deeply for a good few minutes. Between sobs, she repeated her complaint about being hated; adding that not only did the staff all hate her, her fellow patients hated her too. So these were *her* explanations of her depression: 'I keep losing things' and 'everybody hates me'.

She recounted her life history in rather official tones, speaking in a somewhat distant way, as if she was sketching the anamnesis of a patient to a colleague. At one moment during this quasi-clinical monologue, however, her distant, professional tone faltered, and she began to cry quietly. This was at the point when she mentioned that her father had died when she was still a child. I drew her attention to this, and said that the memory of the loss of her father was still very painful for her. She responded by saying that she was feeling upset at the thought of her *loss of independence* since her stroke. She then quickly pulled herself together, and continued with her earlier, official-sounding presentation of her history.

This leads us to an interesting question. How could it be that Mrs A was suicidally depressed about the loss of her independence (as she called it) and yet, simultaneously, *she was consciously unaware of the concrete basis of that loss*? For let us not forget that although it seems self-evident to *the external observer* what she meant when she said that she had lost her independence, subjectively Mrs A was unaware of the fact that she was hemiplegic, and hemianopic, and so on. We are thus faced with a paradoxical situation, in which Mrs A was depressed about the very events that she simultaneously denied had ever happened in the first place.

Here, as was the case for the first two patients, the concept of unconscious knowledge is indispensable to us. This concept allows us to say that Mrs A's depression was a reaction to a loss of which she was *unconsciously* aware; it was a reaction to knowledge which she was defending herself against. Moreover, the fact that this knowledge was unacceptable to her *is what made it* impossible for her to mourn the loss in a healthy way. If you cannot admit to yourself that you have lost something, how can you undertake the painful process of gradually detaching yourself from it? This is what had happened to Mrs A's neglected body-half, and this was the emotional basis of her anosognosia. She could not mourn the loss of her independence because she could not consciously admit what had happened to her.

But this does not explain the full clinical picture. It is apparent — as it was in cases B and C — how the defensive denial of a loss can result in neglect and anosognosia, the *negative* symptoms; but why should it result in *positive* melancholic symptomatology? Why, in this case, did it result in self-directed hatred and culminate in the wish to commit suicide? And why did Mrs A feel that everybody hated her? These symptoms cannot be attributed to simple denial.

Anyone who has worked analytically with clinically depressed patients will see what I am leading up to. Mrs A's melancholic reaction to the loss of her bodily integrity was a product of the fact that she had denied that loss in a very particular way. This is something that we are very familiar with from classical psychoanalytic studies of melancholia (Freud 1917).

These patients feel that everybody hates them because they hate themselves. Both the source *and* the object of their hatred is themselves. That much is obvious; and it was obvious in Mrs A's case too. She positively despised herself — or, at least, she positively despised herself as she was *now*, all crippled and dependent, following her stroke. But *this was precisely the image of herself that she denied.* This reveals the specific mechanism of defence that Mrs A used to suppress that image of herself. She suppressed it by means of an *introjection.* This defence mechanism is absolutely typical of melancholia. These patients cannot bear to acknowledge the loss of a loved object, so they deny that loss *by introjecting the lost object* — by taking it into themselves (in their unconscious imagination) and making it a part of themselves. They thereby subjectively retain the lost object inside of themselves, in the form of an unconscious introject. They deny the loss of the object by *becoming* the lost object.

So, in Mrs A's case, she ignored the paralysed left arm that was attached to her real external body, because, for her, subjectively, *the original, intact arm was still preserved safely inside of her* (in the unconscious part of her ego). Thereby the paralysed arm was neglected and the disability was denied. This was the *subjective* basis of her neglect and anosognosia.

But what about the self-directed hatred? It seems that this was directed toward another, very different image of herself, of which she *also* had unconscious knowledge. This is due to the fact that, when Mrs A introjected the image of her own intact body, which she now idealised, in order to preserve it safely inside of her, she simultaneously introjected the damaged image of her handicapped body, which had let her down so terribly, and which she hated with the vengeance of a lover scorned. This is because *in reality* these two images are inextricable from each other. An idealised picture of reality necessarily co-exists with a split-off repository for the information that does not square with the idealisation but nevertheless exists. Thus every idealised introject is coupled with a hated opposite. Here, then, was the subjective basis of Mrs A's self-hatred, and therefore of her melancholia. She identified herself with an idealized image of herself, which hated a (split off) denigrated image of herself.

Please note that the process of introjection is not a *normal* reaction to object loss; it is a *pathological* (narcissistic) reaction. The healthy reaction is the reaction of normal *mourning*. In normal mourning one recognises that the object never was under one's omnipotent control; that even though you needed it so much it was always something separate from you, and that it is now gone forever. This recognition triggers a long and painful process, in which one gradually detaches oneself from the object.

But Mrs A reaction was the pathological one; and this was the cause of her self-directed hatred. When she said consciously that everybody hated her, what she meant unconsciously was that *she* hated *herself*, that she hated the part of herself that she could no longer depend on and that no longer cared for her, the part that was outside the sphere of her omnipotent control. Ultimately, therefore, she hated reality itself. But the *most* hated aspect of reality, the part of it that she had always depended on so absolutely, and which had now let her down so terribly, was inextricable from the very part that was introjected into her own beloved self. That is why her self-hatred was such an extremely dangerous situation, liable to end in suicide.

Provisional theoretical conclusions

Before moving on to the final two cases, I will re-cap my argument so far. Using the psychoanalytic method of investigation, we have found that unconsciously, right hemisphere patients with neglect and anosognosia are far from being unaware of and indifferent to their tragic situations. A small amount of analytic work quickly brings the underlying potential for profound depression to the subjective surface. Thus a patient who appears bland and unconcerned about his or her incapacities the one minute, will after a not very deep or elaborate psychoanalytic interpretation, suddenly be fending off floods of tears the next minute. Observations of this sort, in the first two cases that I summarised, led us to conclude that in these cases their manifest symptoms of anosodiaphoria were in part *defensive* — more specifically, that they were a narcissistic defence against awareness of the loss of a loved object. In the third case, which I have just discussed, we saw what happens when these defensive manoeuvres fail completely. The third patient, who, like the other two, suffered a stroke in the region of the right middle cerebral artery, was overcome by a full-blown clinical depression, the psychoanalysis of which revealed the typical mechanism of melancholia that Freud (1917) first elucidated — that is, she suffered the consequences of a narcissistic introjection of a lost object, which culminated in intense hatred toward that object being diverted inwards, towards the patient's own self.

These three cases combined lead me to formulate the following hypothesis: behind the cardinal clinical manifestations of the right hemisphere syndrome (when they are considered subjectively) there lies *a failure of the process of mourning*. Rather than mourn the loss of their healthy bodies in the normal way (as *left* hemisphere patients do) these patients institute massive defensive measures which are designed to protect themselves against any awareness of their loss. In short, the cardinal manifestations of the right hemisphere syndrome are revealed by psychoanalytic research to be, at least in part, narcissistic defences against a recognition of loss and the associated depressive affects.

Although this explanation of the subjective phenomenology of the right hemisphere syndrome contradicts the simplistic notion that the right hemisphere is specialised for negative affects, I do not think that it altogether contradicts the attention-arousal hypothesis of Heilman et al. (1993) and Mesulam (1981). Nor is it entirely incompatible with the somatic-monitoring hypothesis of Damasio (1994). The psychoanalytic perspective merely *adds* something to those hypotheses. In the case of the attention-arousal hypothesis, it points to the fact that *the distribution of attention in the mental apparatus is not an unmotivated function*. Although it may well be true that attention is not appropriately aroused and distributed in these cases, this is not attributable simply to a damaged attention-arousal module; rather, it is the result of a *motivated* process designed to protect the subject against awareness of an intolerable aspect of reality. Likewise, in the case of the somatic monitoring hypothesis, I do not think that these patients are emotionally indifferent because they have *lost* bodily awareness; rather, they are indifferent because they are *defending themselves against* their awareness of a subjectively intolerable body image.

Whether these formulations are accepted or not, the essential point remains that the clinical psychoanalytic observations on which they are based — that is to say, the presence of significant depressive affects in right perisylvian patients, which are usually suppressed, and which are linked directly with perceptions of and ideas about their physical handicaps — suggests that we need to revise (or at the least *add* something to) the prevailing cognitive theories of anosognosia, anosodiaphoria and neglect.

Before I end with a consideration of what light all of this might cast on the *normal* psychological functions of the right cerebral hemisphere, I would like to report briefly on two further patients with right perisylvian strokes, who presented in the psychoanalytic situation in ways that also cannot easily be accounted for by the prevailing cognitive theories, but which can be explained if the cognitive theories are supplemented by the psychoanalytic theory of narcissism.

Fourth clinical example

Mr D was an Irishman living, until recently, in London. He was 34 years old at the time that he was seen by an analyst. At the age of 32, two-and-a-half years before he was admitted to our rehabilitation unit, he had suffered a subarachnoid haemorrhage. Investigations at that time had revealed a posterior communicating artery aneurysm. The bleed was associated with significant spasm in the distribution of the right anterior cerebral and middle cerebral arteries, causing a large, continuous area of infarction in the right frontal, temporal and parietal lobes. The aneurysm was clipped by a neurosurgeon attached to our unit.

Considering the extent of his lesion, Mr D was fortunate indeed to have made an excellent physical recovery, and he was able to return to work, albeit at a lower level of employment than before. Whereas he had been working as an estate agent at the time of his stroke, he was now employed as a boiler operator.

Although he had initially suffered from the typical neuropsychological sequelae of a right hemisphere stroke, namely neglect, anosognosia and spatial disorders, these were recovering, and by the time that the analyst saw him he was considered to be cognitively nearly normal. His physical deficit, too, was limited to a mild left-sided hemiparesis, which presented essentially as weakness and clumsiness of the left hand. In addition, this hand was subject to paroxysms of clonic twitching.

However, Mr D was absolutely obsessed by this left hand, which he hated passionately and refused to use (even though the neurosurgeon felt that the hand was capable of a good degree of further functional recovery — an opinion with which the physiotherapists concurred). This was, therefore, a case of *misoplegia*. A man with a massive right hemisphere lesion of the type that frequently leads to profound neglect and anosognosia, but who was now presenting clinically with the very *opposite* symptoms; that is an absolute *obsession* with his left hand and with his physical deficits.

On admission to our unit, Mr D underwent a routine neuropsychological assessment. This revealed a mild degree of left hemispatial neglect, which was evident on formal testing, but not in his ordinary behaviour. Also, there was considerable left-sided hemiakinesia, that is, unilateral *motor* neglect. This resulted in a failure to use his hand in situations in which it certainly could have been functionally useful. In addition, this patient reported a total cessation of dreaming, the onset of which he dated to his stroke. Apart from this, and a moderate degree of affective disinhibition, other localising symptoms and signs could not be demonstrated.

The neuropsychologist noted in his report that Mr D displayed a peculiarly aggressive and negative attitude towards him. In addition, he noted that he seemed hypervigilant, and he remarked on the fact that he was extremely possessive of his own medical notes. For example, when the neuropsychologist paged through the various scans in the envelope which was at the end of his bed, Mr D leapt up and took them away from him. He would only allow him to look at the images one at a time, and on condition that he returned each scan to the envelope before looking at the next one. He showed the same suspicious and controlling attitude toward the reading of the written notes in his clinical file. Other staff members reported similar behaviours. They also reported that Mr D was verbally aggressive, toward the staff in particular, and that he tended to pace up and down the corridors of the hospital. He himself described this as 'letting off steam', which was an interesting way of putting it, considering the fact that, since his stroke, he was employed as a boiler operator.

I want to quote just one clinical vignette from the psychoanalytical treatment of this patient, to illustrate his cardinal emotional symptom — that is, his hatred of his paretic hand: his misoplegia. This is an extract from his seventh session:

> As he sat down in my consulting room, Mr D told me that he had had a good weekend and he asked me — in the form of an accusation — why I had not attended the previous ward round. He said that at the ward round the neuro-surgeon asked him if he was seeing her, 'that's all' — he added — 'and then he said that my brain scan was fine'. Now Mr D exploded with a malignant rage. First he reported, as usual, how disgusting the hospital food was, to the extent that all he had ever enjoyed was his cigarette after each meal. Then he said, 'I've spoken to the matron *and* the head sister about it — other patients keep quiet but I speak my mind.' He also informed me that he was discharging himself later that week, no matter what — 'they can bring the *whole* British Army to hold me here, but I'm *not* staying. And *apart* from this place being a *dump*, not *one* bit of improvement have I seen. I'm supposed to get fine movements back in my hand, but *look* at this; would you think *this* bloody thing is doing anything? — it's useless!' Then, suddenly, Mr D hit his left hand, hard, with his other hand. 'I've had *not* more than *one* hour of individual attention since I came here — I *could* have *paid* someone myself, to treat me at home. Those OT's — they're useless — *useless* — I'm going to *smash* — start *smashing* all the furniture in OT up. They don't know *what* they're doing — they will say I'm improving just to save their *own* bloody skins.' I intervened, and said, 'you're not sure whether it is us or your hand you hate. The problem is that your hand is part of yourself, and hating a part of your own self is an impossible situation to be in.' For an instant he calmed down, and then he said, 'well, I can see the hospital's predicament, having so many patients … but my old individual physiotherapist helped me such a lot with my arm and leg … but I left Belfast before she could work on my hand.'

After this he became extremely angry again, and he continued the tirade. 'But even when I went for the brain scan the doctor wasn't a medic's backside — he was just a vet ... a *vet*, I'm telling you!' I commented at greater length now, saying much the same thing as before, in different words, and adding that he felt humiliated by all these doctors lording it over him, and he wanted to be treated like a man again, rather than a little boy. While I spoke Mr D sat still and listened. Then there was a long silence, after which he said: 'And I haven't seen the Professor *once* — I saw him in December and *he* suggested that I come here; and I haven't seen him *once* since then.' Suddenly Mr D jumped up and said, 'I *can't* live like this. I *knew* when the surgeon mentioned brain damage, it was the end of my life. I'm lucky I didn't have another bleed, and although this one was very serious, I *wish* I had! I'm going to commit suicide — that's why I've bought a shotgun!', and he put his finger in his mouth, then at his temple, and he said, 'here ... or here. I would rather be *dead* — six foot under — I've had a *guts-full!*' While he said this he paced around the room, and I felt that he was trying to stop himself from attacking me, or his hand. (I feared for my safety.) Then he said, 'I'll *smash* this hand into a *million* pieces and post the pieces to the surgeon, in envelopes, one by one'. Then he mimed the action of smashing it on the radiator. 'Like *this* — I would do *this* if you weren't here.' I said, 'you want to punish him for damaging you, and you want to damage him back; so you're not sure anymore whether your hand is part of him or part of you.' Again he calmed down a bit, and he alternated between pacing around and sitting down. 'I'm giving my hand six months and if it has *not* improved, I will come back and ask for an artificial claw.' He kept saying, 'I can't live like this; I'm going to have it amputated.' He also seemed to be slipping into a delusional state, and he said, 'when I *first* came into this hospital I *bit* my hand and *spat* the pieces of meat out, because I *can't* stand it!' This certainly never happened in reality. I wanted to reinstate his contact with reality, and started saying 'the only way of *knowing* if you would improve was to test things out ...' but he interrupted me, and said, '*that's* it — bad luck *again*, it always happens with me! I'd rather *know* where I stand than go through this.' He was extremely angry and distressed, and his larynx was moving rapidly up and down. I said, again, that he needed to take control of the situation; he needed to show he was still in charge.

I hope this vignette provides an adequate impression of this man's subjective state. The clinical picture in his case was dominated by aggressive outbursts, directed towards (1) the hospital staff and everything associated with it, and (2) his own mildly paretic left hand. The analytic sessions usually began with an outpouring of complaints and threats, directed towards either of these objects. Moreover, the two objects of his hostility appeared to be quite interchangeable. That is, subjectively, the hospital and the paretic hand appeared to mean the same thing to Mr D. The left hand was therefore treated *as if it were a part of external reality* rather than a part of his own self. At one point Mr D actually stated that the hand felt as if it did not belong to him. The hand thus represented some part of his own self that he had both *lost* and *disowned*. An analysis of his attitudes in this regard suggested that, in fact, he was trying to turn the *passive* experience of losing it into an *active* experience of disowning it. The complex of painful feelings and ideas associated with the dysfunctional hand involved recognition by the patient of the fact that he was not omnipotent, that he was unable to control reality (even those aspects of reality with which his ego was narcissistically merged, such as his own hand, and the internalised caring mother that it stood for), that he was therefore subject to experiences of loss, including the loss of his adult status, and above all, that he was therefore dependent on others for help in some important aspects of his life. In other words, the fact of the paretic hand represented a *narcissistic injury* which was intolerable to him. This seemed to represent the crux of the psychological symptom complex. At one point in his sessions, Mr D recognised consciously his intolerance of these feelings, when he described his situation as 'utterly degrading.'

Note that Mr D's reaction to this narcissistic injury was to *expel* the hand — and all the bad feelings associated with it — out of the sphere of his beloved omnipotent self and into the hated external reality, to which it now so obviously belonged. There, it was attacked ruthlessly and relentlessly, sometimes by actual physical violence, sometimes in fantasy bordering on delusion (e.g. biting the hand to bits and spitting out the pieces, or chopping it up and posting it to the surgeon). It was noteworthy that these attacks always involved a 'disowning' or expulsive aspect.

A *paranoid* configuration is evident in this psychical configuration based on *projection*. In psychoanalysis, we class paranoia together with melancholia as a *narcissistic* neurosis. The world was split rigidly into good and bad, and all the bad was projected outward, including the unwanted parts of his self. Equally, the few 'good' objects that Mr D recognised (such as his 'unlucky' father) were idealised and blurred with his own self. The analyst, too, was sometimes idealised and sometimes denigrated, depending on whether Mr D was able to maintain the fantasy that she was entirely available and understanding. Any indication of her separateness (for example, when she did not attend the wardround) precipitated a shift from the one to the other extreme of his ambivalence.

The obsessive wish to have the hand amputated and replaced by an artificial one or a metal 'claw' apparently constituted an attempt by the patient to force external reality to coincide with his internal (omnipotent) fantasy, that is, to have the offending hand *actually* split off from his beloved body and replaced by something that was 'not me'. In this way, too, he could conquer his traumatic loss, by turning passive into active.

The externalisation or projection of the hand accounted for its interchangeability with the hospital and everything associated with it. For Mr D, his hand represented something external to himself which was constantly failing him; so he sat, full of hatred, bitterness and complaints, impatiently waiting for it to be made better. Any recognition of personal involvement in his current imperfect, damaged and dependent state was intolerable. He did not reflect consciously upon the fact that a sub-arachnoid haemorrhage (caused by a constitutional weakness of his own body) was the source of his illness, nor that improvement in his symptoms would require active co-operation and effort from him personally. Instead, he blamed the surgeon and the rehabilitation staff alternately, either for damaging him or otherwise for failing to make him better.

Rather than recognise that he was, psychologically speaking, a 'baby' (patient) heavily dependent on the love and care of a good enough 'mother' (the medical staff) for his survival, Mr D treated the hospital as a neglectful mother, giving him disgusting food and useless medications; constantly letting him down in innumerable ways, and never devoting herself properly and exclusively to him. He actively controlled and rejected the mother-hospital, he gave ultimatums and made threats of all types, and eventually he withdrew from her care completely, rather than passively experience the pain of his dependency, imperfection, and loss.

The suicidal aspect of the presentation is also germane. (It was as if Mr D was saying, 'If you don't give me the breast exclusively, immediately and exactly as I want it, then I won't take it at all; I won't take anything in — I will bite, spit and expel it and smash everything up into bits, including myself, and it will all be your fault, and *that* will teach you a lesson!') However the self that was killed in the suicidal aspect of this fantasy represented something other than his own beloved self; it represented sharing, imperfection, loss, etc., attributes which had been transformed in fantasy into a part of the outside world. This was recognisable in the interchangeability of his threats of suicide, his threats towards his hand, and his threats towards others. In his mind, these were *all* externally directed threats. In other words, Mr D's worst fear was that the paretic hand, which was perceived as part of the bad, hated external reality, would become permanently attached to him, and thereby contaminate his omnipotent, perfect, and beloved self. If this narcissistically intolerable situation came about his only defence would have been to kill the hand, and the internal object that it represented, and therefore, to kill himself.

Thus, in summary, in this case, we see a patient struggling with the fact that a piece of the object world to which he was attached, namely his own hand (which was associated unconsciously with his early maternal care), abandoned him, let him down, started to behave independently, refused to do his bidding, and so on — in short, revealed itself to be not really under his omnipotent control after all.

This narcissistic insult resulted in a regression in the level of the attachment, from object love to narcissism, with the consequent defusion of ambivalence, resulting in massive release of destructive impulses and a splitting of the object (and therefore the ego) into absolutely 'good' and 'bad' parts. This created a positively life-threatening situation, similar to what we saw in Mrs A — where an object which the patient regarded with feelings of murderous hate was experienced *subjectively* as being internal to the self. Whereas in Mrs A's case this took the form of an *introjection* of the bad lost object, and therefore resulted psychopathologically in a suicidal melancholia, and cognitively in anosognosic neglect of the introjected limb; in Mr D's case, there was a further, *projective* aspect to the defensive process, in which he made desperate attempts to *expel* the internalized bad object, and therefore the bad part of his ambivalent self-image, into the hated, indifferent external reality to which it now so obviously belonged. This resulted psychopathologically in an aggressive paranoia, and cognitively in *the very opposite of neglect and anosognosia*. In this way, Mr D managed to keep melancholia, that is to say, self-directed hatred consequent upon object loss, at bay; instead, he experienced the bad object as coming at him from the *outside* world, in the form of incompetent, neglectful and disgusting surgeons, hospitals and mothers, who were constantly trying to imprison him, subjugate him, and force their useless care upon him. In this way, despite the great price he had to pay in terms of his mental health, Mr D was able to avoid the painful work of normal mourning, which was absolutely intolerable for him.

Hopefully it is clear why I feel that this case of right perisylvian damage, like the other three I have discussed, supports my contention that the emotional abnormalities associated with damage to this part of the brain are attributable to *a failure of the process of mourning*. I hope also that it is apparent why I feel that the attention-arousal, somatic-monitoring and negative-affect hypotheses cannot account for the full range and complexity of right perisylvian clinical presentations as they unfold in the psychoanalytic situation.

I do not see how one can account for a case like that of Mr D in terms of the prevailing cognitive theories; he presented in almost every way with the very opposite emotional symptoms to what these theories would predict. He did not neglect or fail to attend to his left-hand side; he was positively obsessed by it. Likewise, he did not ignore or fail to notice his hemiparesis; he was unable to get it out of his mind. And he most certainly was not deficient in respect of negative affectivity; he was a seething cauldron of aggression and hatred. A case that presents in this way is difficult to explain within the framework of the prevailing cognitive theories. By contrast, the psychoanalytic theory of defence — the idea that there are positive symptoms which are actively inhibited in the standard form of the right hemisphere syndrome — is readily able to account for the fact that *the same lesion can produce two diametrically opposite emotional symptoms.*

Final clinical example

Due to limitations of space, I will skim over the fifth case, and then move directly to my conclusions regarding the normal psychological functions of the right perisylvian region. This last case in the series, *Mr E*, was a 30-year-old man with a right parietal AVM draining from the midcerebral artery to the sagittal sinus. The AVM was surgically resected, leaving him with a large avascular area of infarcted brain in the right fronto-parietal region. This left him with a variety of physical handicaps about which he, like Mr D, felt anything but unconcerned and indifferent. The analytic investigation revealed that this right perisylvian patient, like all the others we have studied, defended himself against full awareness of his loss by means of a narcissistic organisation. He tried to keep depressive affects at bay by identifying himself with the therapeutic staff, rather than with the other patients. He, too, became a provider of help rather than a recipient of it (in subjective fantasy at least), and in this way he fended off the necessary work of mourning. However, this defence proved highly unsuccessful, and suicidal depressions frequently broke through, which he then secondarily re-defended himself against by means of violent rages against the surgeons, the therapeutic staff, and the hospital, in much the same way as Mr D did. In this way, he — like Mr D — was able to direct the narcissistic rage outwards, rather than have to kill himself.

The two major ways in which the defences of all five patients broke down, therefore, coincided with two great risks that a regression to narcissism always carries with it. For, according to the psychoanalytic theory of narcissism, the withdrawal of object love back into the ego is always accompanied by a defusion of ambivalence, resulting in a splitting of the (now introjected) object. The ambivalence that lies buried deeply within all object relationships (that is to say, our mixed feelings toward all objects; our recognition that they possess both good and bad attributes) — that ambivalence unravels whenever our attachments to the object world regress to narcissism. When this happens, the real object is split (subjectively) into loved and hated parts, which are treated as if they really are two separate things. Herein lies the slippery slope to suicidal melancholia — which arises from the *introjection* of the hated component of the object — and to aggressive paranoia — which arises from a secondary *projection* of it.

Final theoretical conclusions

What does all of this reveal about the functions of the right perisylvian convexity? In a theoretical nutshell, what we have seen in all of these cases is a diminution in whole object relationships[2] (and therefore in object love), and a corresponding *regression to narcissism* (self love, with the splitting of the object that entails, and the resultant primitive defences). On this basis, I would advance the following theoretical formulation. The right perisylvian convexity is a crucial component of the *neuroanatomical substrate of whole object representation*, and therefore a *neurophysiological vehicle for whole object attachments* and the capacity for *mature object relations*. Destruction of these whole object representations, caused by right perisylvian damage, therefore results in a loss of the ability to bind our fundamentally ambivalent attitude toward the real object world, with all of its inherent frustrations and privations, and therefore to an inability to relate to objects in a mature, balanced and realistic way.

Right perisylvian damage therefore radically undermines the *means* by which we normally transform infantile narcissistic modes of relating into mature and realistic ones. This is the specific factor in the right hemisphere syndrome that distinguishes it emotionally from the various syndromes that are associated with equivalent lesions in the association cortex of the *left* cerebral hemisphere — where objects are represented not concretely but

rather symbolically, as words rather than things — and where damage therefore typically results in states of normal mourning. (For psychoanalytic studies of four left perisylvian cases, see Kaplan-Solms & Solms 2000.)

The merit of a psychoanalytic account of the normal emotional functions
of the right hemisphere convexity is that, unlike the prevailing neuropsychological theories, it is able to accommodate the full range and complexity of the
subjective symptoms of anosognosia and neglect in these cases. It is also
consistent with what we know about the *spatial* functions of the right hemisphere convexity, which sit uneasily with the existing theories of anosognosia
and neglect. We have always known — and today it is beyond dispute — that
the right hemisphere convexity is specialised for the perception and cognition
of our relations with concrete, external space. What our psychoanalytic observations (and the psychoanalytic theory of narcissism) provide is a link between these spatial aspects of right hemisphere functioning and the emotional
aspects of its functioning.

In short, what appears to happen in these patients — and what I hope I
have adequately illustrated with the brief clinical vignettes I have cited — is
that their external object attachments are withdrawn, with the result that their
emotional relations with the outside world regress quite pervasively back to
the narcissistic level. In short, *external objects collapse into the self*, resulting
subjectively in a veritable collapse of external space and, with that, in an
abandonment to varying degrees of recognition of the independent existence
of external things — of their allocentric, lawful nature. Henceforth *space is
treated narcissistically*, as if it were arranged as the patient *wished* it to be,
rather than how it actually *is*.

If I am not being too laconic, I hope it is apparent how a psychoanalytical
approach to this syndrome reveals the underlying unity of the hemineglect,
anosognosia *and* spatial disorders in a way that the conventional cognitive
theories do not. However, whether the reader accepts these psychoanalytic
theoretical formulations or not, I hope that I have at least demonstrated that the
psychoanalytic *method* generates observations which reveal significant shortcomings with the existing neuropsychological theories of the anosognosia-
neglect syndrome.

Oliver Sacks once remarked — in a very apt turn of phrase — that
'neuropsychology is admirable, but it excludes the psyche.' He elaborated:

> Neuropsychology, like classical neurology, aims to be entirely objective, and
> its great power, its advances, come from just this. But a living creature, and

especially a human being, is first and last … a subject, not an object. It is precisely the subject, the living 'I', which is excluded [from neuropsychology]. (Sacks 1984, p. 164)

I hope I have been able to show that the combined use of neuropsychological and psychoanalytical methods goes some way towards redressing this imbalance.

Notes

1. The analyst in four of the five cases reported in this chapter was Karen Kaplan-Solms. Some demographic details have been changed to protect patients' confidentiality.

2. The term 'whole object relationships' refers to a mature mode of relating to objects, in which things are treated emotionally *as they actually are in reality* (with both good and bad attributes). Whole object relationships are contrasted with primitive object relationships in which the object is treated narcissistically, in which case the object is *split* according to the feelings that it evokes (into a good object and a bad object). The narcissist typically attempts to merge with the good object and expel the bad, but invariably fails, for the reason that the split is purely subjective and does not coincide with reality.

References

Anton, G. 1899. "Über die Selbstwahrnehmung der Herderkrankungen des Gehirns durch den Kranken bein Rindenblindheit und Rindentaubheit." *Arch. Psychiatr.*, 32: 86–127.

Babinski, J. 1914. "Contribution à l'étude des troubles mantaux dans l'hémiplégie organique cérébrale (anosognosie)." *Rev. Neurol.*, 27: 845–8.

Damasio, A. 1994. *Descartes' Error: Emotion, Reason and the Human brain.* New York: Grosset/Putnam.

DeRenzi, E. 1982. *Disorders of Space Exploration and Cognition.* Chichester: Wiley.

Freud, S. 1917. "Mourning and melancholia." *Standard Edition*, 14: 243–58.

Gainotti, G. 1997. "Emotional disorders in relation to unilateral brain damage." In T. Feinberg & M. Farah (eds). *Behavioral Neurology and Neuropsychology.* New York: McGraw Hill.

Heilman, K., Watson, R. & Valenstein, E. 1993. "Neglect and related disorders." In K. Heilman & E. Valenstein (eds), *Clinical Neuropsychology.* Oxford: Oxford University Press.

Kaplan-Solms, K. & Solms, M. (2000). *Clinical Studies in Neuro-Psychoanalysis.* Madison: International Universities Press/ London: Karnac Books.

Mesulam, M. 1981. "A cortical network for directed attention." *Ann. Neurol.*, 4: 309–25.

Sacks, O. 1984. *A Leg to Stand On.* London: Picador.

PART 1B

Re-examining the Scope and Limits of First-Person Methods

CHAPTER 5

Phenomenological Approaches to the Study of Conscious Awareness

Richard Stevens
The Open University

Introduction: The crucial role of phenomenological methods

I use the term *phenomenological methods* to refer to any techniques designed to access, conceptualize, and represent what is going on in phenomenal consciousness. Much of contemporary interest in consciousness revolves around the hope of exploring the precise relationships between specific conscious experiences and the neurophysiological processes which relate to them. However, in experimental studies which try to do this (using brain imaging, for example, see Fenwick, this volume), while the information about what is going on neurophysiologically may be specific and precise, the phenomenal or experiential side of the equation is not directly accessed but almost invariably *assumed* (e.g. a subject is instructed to look at a given figure and this is then taken to be the phenomenal stimulus) or *inferred* in fairly elementary and crude fashion from a simple verbal report (e.g. when the subject reports seeing a bright light). More sophisticated phenomenological methods which plot and represent the content and form of specific experiences might thus be expected to provide crucial information in helping us establish the relationship between neurophysiological processes and conscious awareness.

Like consciousness, *phenomenology* is a word used in many different and often elusive ways. Except where otherwise indicated, I shall use the term in this chapter in a broad sense to refer to the study of phenomenal consciousness, i.e. of what we are consciously experiencing or are aware of. For the reasons given above, phenomenology in this sense should be a central discipline in the field of consciousness studies. My task here will be to explore some of the very different ways in which phenomenologically-oriented psychologists have gone about studying their subject matter — subjective experience.

Neurophysiological methods depend on advances in technology and their application to access particular processes under investigation. There is relatively little dispute about what are the most useful methods for particular tasks. Methodological advances are quickly taken up by researchers in the area. This can hardly be said to be the case with phenomenological methods. As we shall see, these come in varied forms. All have limitations in terms of what they can do. Each is embedded in a set of methodological and ontological assumptions. While each approach may have its adherents, no one set of methods have achieved the status of being generally accepted techniques for accessing conscious experience. Why not? What are the problems and limitations involved? What can and should we expect phenomenological methods to contribute to the study of consciousness? The chapter will attempt to explore such issues. I shall suggest that to begin to elucidate them will require us to turn our attention to the nature of conscious experience itself and the epistemological problems this creates.

I will begin by adopting a broadly historical context and then review some of the very different forms that phenomenological approaches may take. I will go on to examine more closely some specific exemplars of phenomenological research before concluding with a discussion about how the conclusions from this review of phenomenological methods relate to the nature of conscious experience itself. Note that throughout this chapter what we are looking for is an effective method or set of methods that will allow us to access and represent what is going on in phenomenal consciousness.

The phenomenological orientation of early psychology

One of the most ambitious and extensive projects to explore the content and nature of phenomenological experience was the experimental phenomenology of Wilhelm Wundt. The express purpose of what is generally considered the first psychological laboratory — the Institute for Experimental Psychology set up in Leipzig in 1875 was to apply systematic, scientific method (the 'methods of physiology') to exploring and understanding the nature of the mind (the 'problems of philosophy'). As a core part of that enterprise, Wundt pioneered the use of observers (usually graduate students or co-researchers) trained to report as consistently and precisely as possible on their own sensory experience. These introspective studies were supplemented by those involving inference from the performance of subjects on tasks (the different response times taken, for example, when different aspects of a choice or stimulus-response task were systematically varied). Wundt established his own journal, *Philosophische Studien,* to report the results of the many studies conducted in his laboratory. For him, however, the results were not so much of interest in themselves as for what they indicated about the mental processes underlying experience.[1] Wundt used groups of subjects and quite often subjected his results to statistical analysis. The outcome was a systematic analysis of the dimensions of conscious experience. Sensory perceptions, for example, could be analysed in terms of mode, quality, intensity and duration, and feelings in terms of three dimensions, pleasant — unpleasant, tension — relaxation, and active — passive. It is interesting that the latter account based on introspective studies is, like much of Wundt's work, in close accord with later work, in this case the factor analytic based studies of feeling judgements by Osgood et al. (1957).

Only a small proportion of the immensely prolific works of Wundt (more than 500 papers and books, totalling more than 60,000 pages) has been translated into English. So knowledge of Wundt in the English-speaking world is often through secondary accounts. More recent re-evaluations (e.g. Blumenthal 1975; Danziger 1990) show that traditional accounts of Wundt's work (e.g. Boring 1950) which tend to focus almost entirely on his work in experimental phenomenology and on the elementarism of his approach, greatly underestimate the sophistication of his accounts of mental phenomena. Wundt's approach was elementarist both in the sense that his subjects were required to break down their perceptions into sensory and feeling components, and in that he was concerned to distil out the specific processes underlying conscious experience. But he also directed much of his energy into exploring how these 'elements' interrelated and combined. For him, somewhat akin to the Gestalt psychologists after him (and in contradistinction to his traditional image), the whole was very much more than the sum of its parts. He made a key distinction between perception and what he termed apperception. Apper-

ception refers to the constructive processes involved in selective attention —
the creative synthesis which involves flexible attributions of meaning (albeit
unconsciously) to percepts which are in the focus of attention.

Wundt was also clear that his method of experimental phenomenology
could be applied only to immediate sensory perception. The study of higher
order attributions of meaning involved in language required, he claimed, a
fundamentally different approach that involved an understanding of history
and culture. This was the subject matter of the as yet untranslated volumes of
his later *Völkerpsychologie*. A core notion here is that of 'general impression'
(*Gesamtvorstellung*). The apperception of a 'general impression' of the concept or thought underlies and is distinct from our ability to use language to
articulate it. This is why we can be aware that what we say does or does not
effectively express what we mean. Similar distinctions between sensory
awareness, linguistic symbols and implicit meanings will be returned to in the
final discussion section of this chapter and it will be argued that they have
crucial implications for phenomenological methodology.

One of the many American visitors to Wundt's laboratory was William
James, subsequently to become as much a figure of influence in the development of psychology in the USA as Wundt was in Germany. Although James'
approach was inherently eclectic and pragmatic, incorporating results and
ideas from both physiological and psychological research, his starting point
was phenomenological experience, both his own and that of others. He
explored, for example, the phenomenology of religious experiences, will, the
experience of self and, most notably, conscious experience itself. James
acknowledged that his main work, *The Principles of Psychology* (1890) had
been partly inspired by Wundt and occasionally drew (albeit sometimes
critically) from his ideas. However, while both men accepted the centrality of
the need to explore phenomenological experience, the manner in which they
engaged in this was quite different. An exemplar of James's method of
phenomenological analysis is given in Chapter 9 of *The Stream of Thought*.
Here, presumably (though not explicitly) working from the basis of his own
phenomenal experience, James described its sense of continuity, change and
flow, and its contrasts in quality and pace. He distinguished the central focus
of conscious experience from its surrounding "fringe", and between what he
regarded as "subworlds" of experience such as the world of the senses,
philosophical and abstract beliefs and science. He went on to conceptualize
consciousness as a "theatre of simultaneous possibilities" selected through

active and passive attention. He also reflected on the personal and private character of conscious experience, and our sense of its close relationship with choice and purposive activity.

James certainly provides an articulate account of phenomenal consciousness but it is in complete contrast to the systematic approach of Wundt.[2] There is no attempt to utilise explicit procedures or trained observers. In fact, the method is not made explicit at all; the richly detailed account is simply asserted as being the case. We implicitly assume that it represents the product of James' reflection on his own experience and evaluate the account in terms of its concordance with our own phenomenal awareness where it tends to strike an easy chord. I recall that, when reading it in the past, this seemed the best account I had read of the broad nature of conscious experience. Only later, after a series of systematic phenomenological reflections on my own phenomenological consciousness (see below), did I begin to have doubts. One problem here is that, because of its lack of systematic elicitation, the account may well be subject to being constructed in terms of cultural and personal assumptions about it — what we expect conscious experience to be rather than as we actually experience it.[3] Unlike Wundt, James' account of conscious experience is not restricted to sensory awareness. It makes no separation between what is actually experienced and the complex of meanings which may be attributed to this.[4]

Phenomenological approaches in twentieth century psychology, psychotherapy and social science

If phenomenal experience was the obvious and core subject-matter for the early psychologists, that situation was soon to change. A few years into the twentieth century saw what in hindsight was a quite extraordinary shift of methodological stance in academic psychology. The change of attitude had been partly at least initiated by the problematic disputes about the findings from different psychology research laboratories. Was it possible to have thought without images, for example? The findings of Külpe and Titchener suggested contradictory answers. In retrospect, it has been suggested that their contrasting results are ascribable to differences in their methodology (Hunt 1995) but at the time they seemed to have more profound implications. It was with some relief that psychologists, in the USA at least, took up the banner of behaviourism and its promise of tangible progress akin to that of any other natural science. From being the preferred method of psychology, all forms of introspection became not merely neglected but actively proscribed.

But while phenomenological approaches largely disappeared from the diet of academic psychology for a large part of the twentieth century, they were kept alive in different ways through a variety of intellectual traditions and applications. As Solms notes in the previous chapter, psychoanalysis, for all its emphasis on unconscious motivation, essentially tries to work from and through the experiential standpoint of the patient. Psychoanalysts are not concerned with observable behaviour and situations as much as how the patient experiences these. The development of phenomenological and existential ideas in philosophy in the 1930s directly influenced not only some schools of psychotherapy (e.g. Binswanger 1958) but also the later anti-psychiatry movement (e.g. Cooper 1967). Laing in particular, set great store in working from the lived experience of the patient rather than external indicators such as behavioural or medical observations (see, for example, Laing 1959).

A very different and quite independent line of phenomenological-oriented enquiry is represented by work that is, loosely, within the sociological tradition, through Alfred Schutz (1962) to the work of Berger *et al.* (1966), Erving Goffman (1975) and even ethnomethodologists such as Garfinkel (1967). In spite of the dominance of behaviourism the phenomenological tradition even managed to manifest itself in US psychology in the form of the European import of Gestalt Psychology. This, in combination with European phenomenological and existential traditions in philosophy, subsequently provided important foundations for the most influential expression of a phenomenological emphasis in US psychology in the twentieth century — humanistic psychology. For Rogers (1951), for example, the phenomenal field of the person became the core focus of his work.

More recent and contrasting examples of a phenomenological approach

The preceding section shows how phenomenological approaches and the study of subjective experience were sustained in various forms and traditions throughout the twentieth century in spite of being essentially excluded from the orthodox empires of academic psychology. More recent years have seen a degree of liberalization and pluralization of psychological methodologies and perspectives and also an increasing focus on consciousness itself as a field of multi-disciplinary study. With these has come growing evidence within psychology itself (albeit at its periphery) of the acceptance that a phenomenological orientation is a legitimate stance to take. But rather than forming a coherent movement, theorists and researchers who have taken an explicitly phenomenological approach have mostly remained scattered and diverse.

The following four examples indicate some of the very different ways in which a phenomenological orientation has been expressed in more recent psychological theorising. Julian Jaynes (1979) in a controversial book which proposes that the origins of consciousness lie in what he calls 'the breakdown of the bicameral mind' draws, like James, on an eclectic range of resources to support his thesis: in this case they range from neurophysiological data to a scrutiny of the changing styles of literature and architecture in ancient times. Also like James, Jaynes is concerned to present a description of what phenomenological consciousness feels like, in this case, making vivid use of metaphor to try to convey its salient characteristics — e.g. 'a hidden hermitage where we may study out the troubled book of what we have done and yet may do. An introcosm that is more myself than anything I can find in the mirror. This consciousness that is myself of selves, that is everything and yet nothing at all....' (1979: 1).

Jaynes points out how we often talk about conscious experience as three-dimensional visual space (e.g. something is bright or fuzzy, at the forefront or put out of mind). For him though, the best metaphor to conceptualise consciousness is that of metaphor itself. He see consciousness acting, as metaphor does, as both an analogue and an operator: in other words, it both represents and transforms.[5] Jaynes' broad-ranging analysis is clearly in part derived from reflection on his own phenomenal consciousness but this is implied rather than made explicit and is done far less systematically even than in the case of James. There is no evidence of the employment of a specific phenomenological methodology here.

Robert Romanyshyn (1982) writes in the explicitly phenomenological tradition established by the Dutch psychologist van der Berg and the school of Amedeo Giorgi at Duquesne University in the USA. Like Merleau-Ponty (1962) before him, Romanyshyn's primary concern is to resist what he sees as the interiorizing and literalizing of the mind (what others such as Still [1998] have called 'cognitivism'). He stresses how subjective realities are not simply 'in our head' but are constituted by the conjunction of our thoughts and feelings with the objects and people that make up our world. Subjective experience consists then neither of concepts nor of things but the interplay between them. Psychological reality is a deepening of thoughts and feelings through the world of people, events and things in which we are immersed. Independently of Jaynes he agrees that what he calls 'psychological life' is well conceptualised as a metaphor, in that it involves experiencing one event through the medium of another, an experiential 'reality of reflection'. Romanyshyn is less eclectic in his use of supporting evidence than Jaynes but his assertions about the nature of experienced consciousness are based on several sources — not only accounts taken from the experiences of others and the history of ideas,[6] but also derived from his own experiences. As with Jaynes though, his phenomenological reflections are loose and unsystematic. There is no attempt at any kind of formal method for representing and / or analyzing the content of experienced consciousness.

Margaret Donaldson (1992) in her book *Human Minds* puts forward a developmental account of what she calls 'modes of mind' (stimulated in part by a growing interest in Buddhism). She discusses, for example, how a young child's experience develops from early 'point' or here-and-now awareness to subsequently encompass what she calls 'line' mode in which a child can incorporate past and future perspectives. She analyzes some of the different modes in which we as adults experience the world (e.g. 'intellectual' modes of apprehending the world in contrast to what she calls 'value-sensing' modes). She also distinguishes between construct modes (i.e. specific conceptualizations) and 'transcendent' forms (e.g. mathematics and mystical experience). To support her ideas, Donaldson analyses an interesting mix of source material from children's responses to questioning, to a poem of Wordsworth's. Although no direct reference is made to phenomenal consciousness, it is clear that her modes of mind clearly relate to different ways in which we experience the world. Again, however, we find no specific methodology developed to explore this area.

A different contribution yet again is made by the research of the Hungarian American psychologist Mihaly Csikszentmihalyi (1988, 1992). Rather than attempting a broad conceptualisation of phenomenal consciousness, his focus is on a specific aspect — what he calls 'flow' experience. He and his co-workers were led to this by their interest in the quality of life, and in which kinds of experience people find the most deeply enjoyable. By 'flow' he refers to a state of total absorption, where there is a 'merging of activity and awareness' and a rush of focused 'psychic energy' which is experienced as an end in itself. He details diverse examples of the experience of flow such as mountain climbing and dancing, and claims that (in spite of the achievement-oriented feel of many of the examples he gives) it is an experience that is found and valued universally. His analysis emphasizes the directive, generative and volitional functions of consciousness.

Unlike the other work mentioned so far in this section, Csikszentmihalyi's ideas are related to a specific series of research studies which utilised particular investigative techniques. These included interviews, questionnaires, diaries and 'experience sampling' where participants were randomly signalled by an electronic bleep and ask to record the nature and quality of their experience at the time. All these techniques essentially depend on some kind of retrospective verbal self-report. As such, they are of interest but do not reveal any novel method specifically designed to access and represent immediate phenomenal experience. Issues might also be raised about the validity of such self-reports of experiences. To what extent do they convey the particular qualities of phenomenal consciousness in such a way that others will understand clearly the nature of the experience concerned? How could we distinguish between say flow experience and the 'peak experience' made much of by Maslow (1973)? And how far do interpretations of elicited self-reports create what they look for: to what extent is the idea of 'flow', for example, a construction rather than an experience?

This brief review of a diverse sample of phenomenological approaches shows how they offer:
1. General descriptions of the characteristics of phenomenal experience (e.g. James) including the different forms this may take (e.g. Donaldson)
2. Ways of conceptualising phenomenal experience (e.g. the use of metaphor by Jaynes and Romanyshyn)
3. Differentiation of particular aspects of phenomenal experience (e.g. Csikszentmihalyi's flow experience).

What none of them do, however, is to develop and apply a specific methodology for accessing and representing phenomena — the immediacy, quality and feel of particular experiences such as the smell of coffee or the pain of a dentist's drill. These studies reflect the typical tendency of phenomenologically-oriented analyses to rest on general and unsystematic reflection on the part of the theorist or at most the use of verbal self-report from others. Since the early introspectionists, there has been little attempt to develop an effective method for accessing and representing immediate phenomenological experience. Phenomenological methodology is notable only by its absence.

Psychological research studies derived from phenomenological philosophy

So far, by phenomenological approach, I have referred broadly to psychological studies which focus on the first person perspective of subjective experience. There is a more specific and restricted use of the term phenomenology that is most identified with and given explicit (albeit opaque) expression in the writings of Edmund Husserl (1907, 1920).

While the focus of Husserl's work is on phenomenal experience, there is an extensive set of assumptions and theory that guides his way of conceptualizing and investigating this subject matter. For example, he claims, in contradistinction to philosophical realism, that no legitimate distinction can be made between subjective and external worlds. The notion of intentionality (derived from Brentano) refers to the idea that all experience is inevitably *of* something and therefore any separation between what is being experienced and experience itself is ultimately untenable. Husserl's emphasis is on the lived world of experience rather than the world as construed by science. This includes both sensory perceptions and our beliefs and thoughts (the inclusion of cognitions as part of phenomenal experience is something that I shall question later in this paper). In order to explore lived experience, it is necessary to suspend preconceptions, particularly assumptions about the nature of an external world. This 'bracketing' or suspension of preconceptions Husserl refers to as the *épochè*. Husserl's ultimate aim is *eidetic description* which involves going beyond the surface forms of experience to discover the invariants that he claims underlie these. Husserl propounds these and other ideas in considerable (and dense) detail. As part of this process, he illustrates the kind of description of experience he has in mind. He discusses the experience of a die, for example. While this can take many forms, depending on context, perspective etc., he argues that these are unified into a 'synthesis of identification'. This process of synthesis, he asserts, fundamentally underlies our lived experience.

Such examples of the application of his method which Husserl gives in his writings are relatively few and are given more to illustrate the points he is making than as exemplars of phenomenological research. In more recent years, phenomenological psychologists have attempted to use Husserl's and other notions derived from phenomenological philosophy as a basis for developing techniques for the phenomenological investigation of lived experience. These have resulted in a number of specific research studies, many of them conducted by colleagues of Amedeo Giorgi at Duquesne University. These have explored a variety of aspects of subjective experience including anger (Stevick, 1971), being at home (Buckley, 1971), being burgled (Fischer and Wertz, 1979), close friendship (Becker, 1987), being left out (Aanstoos, 1987), feeling guilty (Yoder, 1990), authenticity (Rahilly, 1993), longing (Palaian, 1993), insomnia (Copen, 1993), and the experience of coronary artery bypass surgery (Trumbull, 1993). Together with the work of Varela and his colleagues (see Chapter 6, this volume), these represent perhaps the most explicit examples of an attempt to develop a phenomenological methodology in psychology.

The methods used in these studies vary and some are more formal than others, but all centre on *eidetic reduction*: in other words their aim is to distil the 'invariant constituents' or the essential features of the phenomenal experience of their subjects, 'co-researchers' or the researchers themselves. This involves analysing interviews and written accounts (including literary sources) retrospectively focused on specific experiences of the phenomenon being studied. 'Eidetic reduction' is usually carried out by a team and involves:

1. *The epoché process*: the attempted 'bracketing' or putting aside presuppositions about the experience in question (not easy to do as the researchers admit).
2. Producing a *narrative digest*: often a summary obtained by deletion of detail.
3. *Thematic reduction*: this involves looking for the constituents of *specific* experiences. Significant statements are often selected to illustrate these.
4. Establishing the *thematic structure or fundamental constituents* of this kind of experience in general.

Thus, van Kaam (1969) in a variation of this process identifies the 'constituents' (i. e. the expressions in each protocol), reduces and transforms these into more precise terminology, and discards expressions which are specifically 'situated' or inessential. He then attempts a first 'hypothetical identification' or composite description. This is checked against protocols selected at random from the sample, and the description is revised accordingly. Polkinghorne (1989) also suggests that co-researchers should be asked for feedback as to how far this reflects their experience.

Two illustrations show the kind of results obtained by such methods. Register and Henley (1992) found the essential constituents of the experience of *intimacy* to be that it is strongly non-verbal and involves a sense of presence. Time is experienced as suspended, boundaries seem to dissolve and there is a paradoxical sense of both destiny (this was meant to happen) and suspense (not knowing where it might go next). Gifford-May and Thompson (1994) analysed accounts of *'Deep States'* of meditation. Essential constituents here included a sense of transcendence beyond the normal physical and mental boundaries of the self, a different sense of reality (boundless, oceanic) and the experience of positive emotions such as serenity and joy.

Such descriptions in themselves suggest some of the problems with this kind of analysis. Interesting they may be, but in what sense can they be considered to represent the 'essence' of the experiences concerned? These studies are based on the ideas and assumptions of Husserl's theory, which in themselves are open to dispute. How far, for example, is it really possible to adopt the suppositionless attitude of mind presumed by the notion of epoché? One might argue that studies in the psychology of perception indicate that perception is invariably constructive, involving the attribution of meaning of some kind, and that the notion of 'pure', concept-free perception is a chimera (see, for example, Dember 1965). A phenomenon is always constituted by the meanings we ascribe to it and our presuppositions are an intrinsic and insepa-rable part of this process. Even though experientially there may seem to be a shift in perspective in the epoché, this is hardly more than a matter of the partial shift from one set of assumptions to another. Furthermore, questions arise about the nature of eidetic reduction (i.e. that these studies are trying to distil the 'invariant constituents' or the essential features of a phenomenal experience). How far are the results obtained socially constructed and depen-dent on the reconstruction (and thus on the situation and personality) of the particular individuals concerned rather than representing some kind of invari-ant essence?

The most critical issue, however, turns on basic assumptions about the nature of experience. These studies follow Husserl in working from the idea that there are essences or structures underlying our experience of the world — highly questionable assumptions akin to notions of romantic or platonic ideals. How meaningful *experientially* is the notion of essential constituents? In effect, the results of these studies turn out to be abstractions based on interpretations of verbal accounts. They are concerned with general structural or thematic characteristics rather than specific content. They may capture some of the generalized meanings mediating or underpinning experience but such methods in no way offer a way of accessing the immediacy of direct experience. It would be difficult to see, for example, how they might be used to map the inter-relationships between direct conscious experience and its neurophysiological substrate. Again, what might have appeared to provide at least the basis for an effective methodology for accessing phenomenal consciousness in the sense specified in the introduction, leaves us as far as ever from the goal we seek.

Eliciting personal constructs and attempts to quantify consciousness

Before moving on in the next section to discuss some of the possible reasons for this dearth of an effective methodology for accessing phenomenal experience, I would like to comment briefly on two final candidates for consideration. Personal Construct Theory (Kelly 1955) is not only firmly focused on ways of making sense of people's experience, but offers specific methodologies for investigating this, especially in the form of repertory grid technique. Kelly in no way subscribes to the assumptions made by the studies discussed above and his work emerged from the very different tradition of American academic psychology and psychotherapy. Nevertheless, as a methodology for accessing phenomenal consciousness, PCT techniques might be considered to suffer at least one similar drawback. To elicit personal constructs is, at best, to access the cognitive infrastructures — the conceptual distinctions and meanings underlying our ways of making sense of the world (though in this case they are at least personal not general) rather than the actuality of immediate phenomenal experience itself.

Interesting work has been done by Ronald Pekala (1991) in developing measures for quantifying aspects of phenomenal consciousness. He and his co-workers have constructed a series of scales comprised of Likert-style items that attempt to measure intensity across several dimensions of conscious experience. These dimensions were selected initially from the scrutiny of studies of altered states and other studies of consciousness (e.g. Tart 1975; Silverman 1968) and subsequently refined through factor analytic techniques. The *Phenomenology of Consciousness Inventory* includes the dimensions of positive and negative affects, time awareness, intensities of imagery and self-awareness, concentration, volitional control and degree of lucidity. The scales are applied retrospectively (by the participants concerned) to memories of specific experiences which they have engaged in. The results can be plotted as profiles of intensity on each dimension (*pips* or *phenomenological intensity profiles*) or *psygrams* which graphically represent pattern relationships between PCI dimensions for specific states of consciousness.

Such scales attempt to quantify the broad dimensions of phenomenal experience and this has been found to be useful in enabling more specific characterizations and comparisons to be made of particular states of awareness such as hypnotic trance and out-of-body experiences. However, they depend on the application of pre-structured dimensions and make no reference to content, plotting only intensity along broad dimensions rather than the specifics of a phenomenal experience. One might well question how far the complex qualities of phenomenal consciousness can be effectively captured through quantified measures of this kind. While they represent a useful research tool, such inventories do not offer sufficient precision and detail to provide the kind of access to immediate experience that we might wish a sophisticated phenomenological methodology to provide.

Discussion: Why the failure to develop an effective phenomenological methodology?

Why this absence of an effective phenomenological methodology that this review indicates? One possibility is that the very idea of mapping experience makes invalid realist assumptions about the nature of subjective experience. Both the early introspectionists and, in a different way, the phenomenological psychologists of the Husserlian school assumed that phenomenal experience exists as a given to be introspected upon. However, the metaphor analogy of Jaynes and Romanyshyn draws attention to the fact that consciousness is not 'just there': it constructs as well as represents. George Kelly makes the same point with his concept of 'constructive alternativism'. As he puts it, events 'are subject to as great a variety of constructions as our wits will enable us to contrive...all our present perceptions are open to question and reconsideration...' (1970). This suggests that not only are there alternative ways of construing open to us but that people have considerable autonomy in the ways in which they use them. This idea of subjective experience as constructing as well as being constructed casts doubt on the realist notion that there is experience there to be introspected upon. For we are creating our consciousness in the very act of experiencing it. However, I would argue that this holds only for the meanings or interpretations that we give to our experiences rather than to the basic conscious events themselves. While there may be variety in the ways that we construe our bodies or the experience of deep pain, we cannot construct them away, any more than a non-hallucinating prisoner can deny the existence of the walls that incarcerate him.

The critical issue here is — what constitutes conscious awareness? A crucial distinction to make in considering this question is between the world as experienced and the meanings and significances we ascribe to this. I elaborate this point below.

I have reported elsewhere (Stevens 1997) on a systematic series of reflections on my own phenomenal experience. Based on these, my conclusion about the nature of phenomenal consciousness was that this is essentially perceptual. It consists of multimodal perceptual images. These include feelings and symbolic representations (such as spoken or imaged words and sentences) and the images which constitute phenomenal awareness are both stimulated by outside events and are internally generated in the more elusive and less defined form of remembered or imagined percepts.

Words and other symbols, of course, are not just sounds or images. They convey meaning. But what is this associated meaning? The important thing I discovered in my phenomenal reflections is that this meaning itself is not present in immediate awareness. When I hear or read a word or phrase (percept) or think about something (the image form) it is present in consciousness only as a sound or image. The meaning it implies, though, gives it a particular 'feel'. This 'feel' can often be articulated or unpacked through the generation of other verbal sequences denoting the associated meanings. Each of these verbal sequences will have their 'meaning feels'. The important point here, though, is that the thought or idea is not itself present in conscious awareness. I am only conscious of a thought in terms of the percept-images of the words that represent it.[7]

As far as conscious awareness is concerned, I am suggesting then that verbal sequences act as perceptual tags or anchors and provide a medium for accessing these meanings in awareness. They provide the means through which we both locate meanings and generate them. Thoughts and meanings only manifest themselves in conscious awareness through the medium of either words or images.

The same points regarding meaning apply to perception and imaging. Percepts and remembered images of course are not merely sensory. They carry meanings. But the meaning of the perception is implicit not explicit in our awareness. Percepts and images are 'informed by' meanings: the implicit meaning is present in awareness only as a particular kind of feel. For example, take the experience of being in a familiar room. The significances and the meanings that your experience of this room holds have no doubt changed over time. The implicit meanings or 'feel' of the room are now very different than the very first time you entered it. And yet in terms of immediate conscious awareness you see the same features as you did then.

To summarize the conclusions about phenomenal consciousness stimulated by my phenomenal reflections:

- Conscious awareness is essentially perceptual.
- The percepts and images (including words) which constitute it are linked to meaning systems.[8]
- Meanings are not themselves directly available in conscious awareness.
- Meanings can only enter consciousness if they are anchored in sensory forms of some kind (They manifest themselves only as particular 'feels' associated with particular percepts/images or words. These may be articulated through generating, in linear fashion, associated phrases and/or percepts.)

If one accepts a conception of consciousness such as this, it is not surprising that phenomenological methodology has proved as problematic as we have noted. It helps to explain why it has taken the very different forms included in this review. It also requires us in fact to make some important distinctions between different forms of phenomenological method.

If an investigator focuses (as Wundt tried to get his observers to) on basic phenomenological experiences rather than the implicit meanings (or 'feels') associated with them, then it should be possible to get reliable and communicable accounts. To take two examples: if several people were all to look at the same view (say a landscape) and try to see the scene as patterns of colour and shapes etc. and carefully report on what they see, there would be considerable consensus in their accounts. As Pekala (1991) has found also, a person is able to give reasonably reliable ratings of the intensity of his or her own immediate feelings such as anxiety or fear. However to ensure such achievements and to ensure consistency over labelling, we will probably have, as Wundt did, to train our observers. They would need to learn to introspect their inner worlds rather as a representational artist looks at the outer world, temporarily stripping the percept of its meaning, restricting themselves to noting lines and angles and patterns of light and shade. We can also supplement verbal accounts with quantitative information, for example from intensity ratings, and by establishing threshold levels and just noticeable differences. Using such procedures a great deal has already been discovered about the phenomenology of perception — about colours and taste dimensions, for example. Here, there is every reason to expect progress in relating phenomenological experience to both peripheral and central physiological processes.

However, if we turn our attention to the ways in which we *make sense* of our worlds then we are on much trickier ground. These, as we have seen, are likely to depend on *verbal accounts.* Words are, of course, our most powerful source of representing and articulating implicit meanings. By using them to trigger other people's implicit meanings, words are also the means we use to communicate our experiences to each other. If I wish to communicate to you an experience I have had, I can only do it through some system of symbolic forms, probably words. But, there are serious difficulties here for a listener who wants to understand what I am expressing. It is not a simple question of getting a record of the actual words I use or have in mind. It is about knowing what meanings they signify (i.e. about the meaning systems they relate to). One problem here is that communication depends on experiencers' abilities to express themselves: how articulate, how skilled and expressive they are in the use of language. Another is that the words used relate to a diffuse network of semantic assemblies both for speaker and listener: even if we attempt to articulate a particular cluster, where do we begin and stop? Thirdly, we depend on the researcher's or listener's ability to reconstruct or interpret what is heard. We share understanding with the speaker only in so far as we have equivalent semantic systems (and ones related to similar linguistic tags) which can be stimulated in us. These are very real difficulties confronting phenomenological research of this kind (as they were for the phenomenological research studies reviewed above). Such accounts can only be reconstructions, subject to the interpretative style of the subject and/or researcher and always open to change and negotiation.

The distinction I am making here is related to epistemology. The first form of investigation I have distinguished above remains (if not always comfortably) within the approach of the natural sciences. Like neurophysiology, it deals with the potentially observable and measurable. The aim is to describe what is there and what is going on in order to gain a general and nomothetic understanding. However, the second approach that is concerned with unpacking meanings demands a hermeneutic or interpretative epistemology. The epistemological distinction between the two forms of research is important for it means that with this second category of phenomenological method we cannot expect to find the same form of understanding. We cannot measure, observe and precisely define the symbolic content of which such meanings are constituted. For, firstly, research here involves articulating content which is implicit rather than a part of conscious awareness. Secondly, such material can only be articulated through interpretation and reconstruction.

Interestingly, this distinction which I make here on the basis of my perceptual-lingual[9] model of consciousness was broadly also Wundt's position. He was very clear that only the most basic experiences could be investigated experimentally. It was because Külpe and Titchener went beyond this to try to access more complex states that they were forced to rely more on retrospections and reconstructions: which is how the early introspectionists ran into the disputes and difficulties which led, it has been argued, to their premature demise. Wundt also believed that there is no way of directly accessing the complex integrations underlying his process of 'apperception', and by implication therefore linguistic and cultural meaning. Although he did hope for an eventual grand integration, he was careful to separate out his sensory psychology from his *Völkerpsychologie*.

I do not in any way mean to imply here that hermeneutic approaches have no relevance to the study of consciousness. But it is important to recognise that we are engaging in a different kind of phenomenological exploration. We are exploring the *meanings* through which people make sense of their world and their lives. In terms of my perceptual-lingual model, these are not explicitly part of conscious awareness. It is precisely because they can only be inferred and interpreted and are always open to re-interpretation and reconstruction that makes understanding our own experience and communicating with others such an endlessly fascinating business. But it does mean that, unlike our first approach, such explorations are not much use when it comes to understanding how conscious awareness relates to neurophysiological process.

The hermeneutic study of meaning is complicated in further ways. So far I have dealt with meanings from what we might call an 'individualist/cognitivist' perspective (Still 1998) as if they are 'in the mind'. But a lot of meanings, it might be argued, (though I would say *not* all) emerge from social interactions: in other words they are mutually or jointly constructed and depend for their existence on the relational framework of human society. We have to bear in mind then that much of the complex of our meaning systems is built on a social base and only expresses itself through joint action. This makes such meanings all the more difficult to conceptualise and access. It also suggests that discourse analysis (e.g. Potter and Wetherell 1987) may have some value as a supplement or contextualisation for phenomenological analysis.

I have suggested then that two distinctive epistemologies are involved in different forms of phenomenological research and that we need to be clear as to what each can and cannot do. I want to conclude by complicating the matter still further and proposing that a third epistemology (one that has attracted far less attention) may also be required in phenomenological research if it is to do justice to the nature of conscious awareness. This assertion derives from the curiously constructive nature of consciousness. To bring an idea or way of looking at something into mind is to give it a 'reality'. This is brought home to us by the notion of metaphor. A new metaphor encourages us to look at something differently, to attach a different feel or meaning to it. Through its means a new experiential reality is created. In conscious awareness, as with metaphors, we are not dealing with a reality waiting to be observed but experiences ever in the making. I have proposed elsewhere that we need a further epistemology to accommodate this extraordinary capacity of the human mind. I have called this 'transformational'. Its aim (in contrast to the *explanation* of nomothetic epistemology and the *interpretation* of hermeneutic approaches) is to *facilitate possibility* (Stevens 1998). For, as people and as psychologists, we have to live our consciousnesses (and perhaps help others to do so) as well as understand them. Because of the curious, potentially self-fulfilling effects when new ways of construing are offered to our consciousness, we in our analyses of consciousness, may (if unwittingly) play a part in this process. Labelling and describing states such as 'flow' or 'peak experiences' may help others to differentiate and become aware of facets of their experience or even to develop new forms of experiencing. This identifies a third function of phenomenological accounts. Perhaps as psychologists and phenomenologists (or philosophers and scientists interested in consciousness), we should acknowledge that our role may be, through the provision of accounts of varied forms of experience, to inspire as well to understand.

Notes

1. He assumed these processes to have physiological correlates, hence the title of his best-known work *Principles of Physiological Psychology*, 1874.

2. Interestingly Wundt was one of the few psychologists of the time not to applaud James' book.

3. Of course, this is also a problem, albeit to a lesser degree, even for systematic approaches such as Wundt's.

4. We will need to return to this elusive and difficult distinction between immediate sensory experience and the implicit meanings that feed into this in the later discussion.

5. To illustrate this double process, he gives an example of a metaphor: the phrase a 'blanket of snow' both *represents* a snowy scene and *transmutes* it by connotations of warmth and snugness.

6. For example, he mades use of Harvey's metaphor of the heart as a pump, to demonstrate how metaphor can work as a way of developing understanding.

7. In writing here about this notion of 'feels', I am struck by the similarity with Wundt's notion of *Gesamtvorstellung* or 'general impression', the implicit thought or concept which underlies but is not identical with its expression in words.

8. Attention or working memory (e.g. Baddeley and Hitch, 1974) and/or 'focal attentive processing' is probably the moment of integration between a percept and its underlying meaning systems.

9. The model is called perceptual-lingual because it asserts that phenomenal consciousness is essentially sensory and that the sensory content includes the images or sounds of words. Both sensory cues and linguistic tags (or words) serve as anchors for underlying implicit meaning systems.

References

Aanstoos, C. M. 1987. "A descriptive phenomenology of the experience of being left out." In F. J. van Zuuren, F. J. Wertz, and B. Mook (eds), *Advances in Qualitative Psychology: Themes and Variations*. Berwyn, PA: Swets.

Baddeley, A. D. and Hitch, G. 1974. "Working memory." In G. H. Bower (ed.) *The Psychology of Learning and Motivation*, Vol 8. London, Academic Press, 47–90.

Becker, C. S. 1987. "Friendship between women: a phenomenological study of best friends." *Journal of Phenomenological Psychology* 18 (1): 59–72.

Berger, P. L.and Luckmann, R. T. 1966. *The Social Construction of Reality*. Garden City, NY: Doubleday.

Binswanger, L. 1958. "The Case of Ellen West." In R. May, E. Angel and H. F. Ellenberg (eds), *Existence: A New Dimension in Psychiatry and Psychology*. New York: Basic Books.

Blumenthal, A. L.1975. "A Reappraisal of Wilhelm Wundt." *American Psychologist,* 30: 1081 -1088.

Boring, E. 1950. *A History of Experimental Psychology.* New York: Appleton-Century-Crofts.

Buckley, F. M. 1971 "An approach to a phenomenology of at-homeness." In A. Giorgi, W. F., Fischer, and R. Von Eckartsberg, (eds) *Duquesne Studies in Phenomenological Psychology.* Pittsburgh: Duquesne University Press.

Cooper, D. 1967. *Psychiatry and Anti-Psychiatry.* London: Paladin and Tavistock Publications.

Copen, R. 1993. "Insomnia: A Phenomenological Investigation", *Dissertation Abstracts International,* 53, 6542B.

Csikszentmihalyi, M. and Csikszentmihalyi, I. S. (eds). 1988. *Optimal Experience: Psychological Studies of Flow in Consciousness.* New York: Cambridge University Press.

Csikszentmihalyi, M. 1992. *Flow: The Psychology of Happiness.* London: Rider Press.

Danziger, K. 1990. *Constructing the Subject: Historical Origins of Psychological Research.* Cambridge: Cambridge University Press.

Dember, W. N. 1965. *The Psychology of Perception,* New York, Holt, Rinehart and Winston.

Donaldson, M. 1992. *Human Minds: An Exploration.* Harmondsworth: Allen Lane.

Fechner, G. T. 1860. *Elemente der Psychophysik.* Leipzig: Breitkopf and Härtel.

Fischer, C. T. and Wertz, F. 1979. "Empirical phenomenological analyses of being criminally victimized." In A. Giorgi, R. Knowles, and D. L. Smith (eds), *Duquesne Studies in Phenomenological Psychology,* Vol 3. Pittsburgh: Duquesne University Press.

Garfinkel, H. 1967. *Studies in Ethnomethodology.* Englewood Cliffs, New Jersey: Prentice-Hall.

Goffman, E. 1975. *Frame Analysis.* Harmondsworth: Penguin Books.

Gifford-May, D. and Thompson, N. L. 1994. "'Deep states" of meditation: phenomenological reports of experience." *Journal of Transpersonal Psychology* 26(2): 117–138.

Hunt, H. T. 1995. *On the Nature of Consciousness.* London: Yale University Press.

Husserl, E. 1907. *The Idea of Phenomenology.* The Hague: Martinus Nijhoff.

Husserl, E. 1920. *Cartesian Meditations.* Transl. D. Cairn, 1977. The Hague: Martinus Nijhoff.

James, H. 1920. *The Letters of William James.* Boston: Atlantic Monthly Press.

James, W. 1890. *The Principles of Psychology.* New York: Dover. (Published in 1950).

Jaynes, J. 1979. *The Origin of Consciousness in the Breakdown of the Bicameral Mind.* London: Allen Lane.

Kelly, G. A. 1955. *The Psychology of Personal Constructs.* New York: Norton.

Kelly, G. 1970. "A brief introduction to pesonal construct theory." In D. Bannister, (ed), *Perspectives in Personal Construct Theory.* London: Academic Press.

Laing, R. D. 1959. *The Divided Self.* Harmondsworth: Penguin Books.

Merleau-Ponty, M. 1962. *Phenomenology of Perception.* Trans. C. Smith. London, Routledge and Kegan Paul.

Osgood, C., Suci, G. J. and Tannenbaum, P. H. 1957. *The Measurement of Meaning.* Urbana Ill.: University of Illinois Press.

Palaian, S. 1993. "The experience of longing: a phenomenological investigation." *Disserta-*

tion Abstracts International, 54, 1678B.

Pekala, R. J. 1991. *Quantifying Consciousness: An Empirical Approach.* New York: Plenum.

Polkinghorne, D. E. 1989. "Phenomenological research methods," in R. Valle and S. Halling, (eds), *Existential-phenomenological Perspective in Psychology.* New York: Plenum.

Potter, J. and Wetherell, M. (1987) *Discourse and Social Psychology: Beyond Attitudes and Behaviour.* London: Sage.

Rahilly, D. A. 1993. "A phenomenological analysis of authentic experience." *Journal of Humanistic Psychology,* 33 (2): 49–71.

Register, L. M. and Henley, T. B. 1992. "The phenomenology of intimacy." *Journal of Social and Personal Relationships,* 9 (4): 467–81.

Rogers C. 1951. *Client-centered Therapy.* New York: Houghton.

Romanyshyn, R. D. 1982. *Psychological Life: From Science to Metaphor.* Milton Keynes: Open University Press.

Schutz, A. 1962. *Collected Papers.* The Hague: Martinus Nijhoff.

Silverman, J. L. 1968. "A paradigm for the study of altered states of consciousness." *British Journal of Psychology* 114: 1201–1218.

Stevens, R. 1997. "Western phenomenological approaches to the study of conscious experience and their implications." In J. Richardson and M. Velmans (eds) *Methodologies for the Study of Consciousness: A New Synthesis.* Kalamazoo: Fetzer Institute.

Stevens, R. 1998. "Trimodal theory as a model for interrelating perspectives in psychology." In R. Sapsford and A. Still (eds), *Theory and Social Psychology.* London: Sage.

Stevick, E. L. 1971. "An empirical investigation of the experience of anger." In A. Giorgi, W. F. Fischer and R. von Eckartsberg (eds), *Duquesne Studies in Phenomenological Psychology,* Vol 1. Pittsburgh: Duquesne University Press.

Still, A. 1998. "Theories of meaning." In R. Sapsford and A. Still (eds), *Theory and Social Psychology.* London: Sage.

Tart, C. T. 1975. *States of Consciousness.* New York: Dutton.

Trumbull, M. 1993. "The experience of undergoing coronary artery bypass surgery: A phenomenological investigation." *Dissertation Abstracts International,* 54, 1115B.

van Kaam, A. 1969. *Existential Foundations of Psychology,* New York, Image.

Wundt, W. 1874. *Grundzüge der Physiologishchen Psychologie.* Leipzig: Engelmann.

Yoder, P. 1990. "Guilt, the feeling and the force: A phenomenological study of the experience of feeling guilty." *Dissertation Abstracts International,* 50, 5341B.

CHAPTER 6

The Gesture of Awareness

An account of its structural dynamics[1]

Natalie Depraz
College Internationale de Philosophie

Francisco J. Varela and Pierre Vermersch
CNRS

This article proposes a description of the structural dynamics of the act of becoming aware based on the phenomenological method of *épochè* (or reduction), but also incorporating observations from psychological and contemplative sources. We propose as the core of this specific act an initial phase of *suspension* of habitual thought and judgement, followed by a phase of *conversion* of attention from "the exterior" to "the interior", ending with a phase of *letting-go* or of receptivity towards the experience.

Introduction

A new phenomenological approach

We wish to present here a structural description of the basic gesture of becoming aware. Such a description does not come from nowhere: our work is rooted in a renewed, contemporary phenomenology. The phenomenology we advance is characterized by the way it works: its operational, procedural or performative dimension. In a word, its *praxis,* its center is the practice of the so-called phenomenological reduction or *épochè.* It is characterized far more by its enaction than by its internal theoretical structure or an a priori justification of knowledge. Which amounts to saying that what is important to us is to actually *engage* directly in the description of phenomena. Only this allows moving forward in refining past work, and to confirm or invalidate past descriptions. That, rather than the discussion of the descriptions of other phenomenologists, past or contemporary, is our project. Nor are we interested in calling into question those of their doctrinal arguments that remain speculative, thus perpetuating the endless logic of commentaries upon commentaries. Our immediate purpose, we repeat, is to renew the very heart of the phenomenological approach as a method of categorical description and exploration of conscious life.

This stance towards phenomenology immediately implies a shift of philosophical paradigm, which leads takes us from hermeneutics to the pragmatic.[2] So it is from the philosophical horizon of pragmatism that the aptness and innovative nature of the following approach is best appreciated.

Épochè: The heart of the structural dynamics of bringing into consciousness

The description of the practice of *épochè* presented here is embedded within a larger project (cf. footnote 1) which aims to recapture the different steps in a process whereby something comes into my clear consciousness, something which inhabited me in a way which was confused, opaque, affective, immanent; something that is pre-reflective, and eventually becomes part of shared, intersubjective knowledge. According to the demands of the disciplines called upon, essentially: philosophy, psychology, cognitive sciences, and spiritual traditions (mostly Buddhism), we have variously called this gesture "phenomenological reduction", "a reflective act", "becoming aware", or "mindfulness".

The scope of the broad project just evoked cannot be discussed here in its entirety. It needs to be broken down into several component dimensions that can be roughly sketched as follows:

1. A *basic cycle* of dynamic components: the *épochè* itself and intuitive evidence as truth criteria;
2. Two optional steps, *expression* and *validation,* which allow for communication and shared knowledge of the act;
3. The multilayered *temporality* of the act of becoming aware, that lends its

necessary dynamic to the description.

Thus although *épochè* constitutes the real heart of the gesture that concerns us here, it is but an initial step, it primes the dynamic of the ensemble and gives the starting impulse. It is also a movement carrying across the other steps of becoming aware in the sense that it maintains the required quality of presence for such an exploration of experience.

Practicing épochè: between exercise and training

The three components of épochè

The present attempt at description follows a logic of *priming*, meaning that it is not presented as a finalized result. Rather, it is a first attempt at a thematic characterization of an individual experience, activated or reactivated individually and subjected to a progressive and intersubjective control. *Épochè* as a gesture is always complemented by a resulting intuitive evidence and its corresponding understanding in a minimal self-sufficient cycle. In other words, *épochè* and intuitive evidence call to each other, so to speak. *Épochè* finds its natural accomplishment in the intuitive evidence of a strong internal obviousness, antecedent to and qualified by a gradual process of filling-in which is a characteristic property of suspension, at the heart of *épochè*.

Let us now elaborate three principal phases we are proposing to describe the unfolding of *épochè* (Figure 1):

A. A phase of *suspension* of habitual thought and judgement. This is a basic precondition for any possibility of change in the attention which the subject gives to his own experience and which represents a break with a "natural" or non-examined attitude.

B. A phase of *conversion* or *redirection* of attention from "the exterior" to "the interior".

C. A phase of *letting-go* or of receptivity towards the experience

We call *épochè* the *ensemble* of these three organically linked phases, for the simple reason that phases B and C are always reactivated by and reactivate phase A. Note in passing that in this recursive movement, the suspending movement which begins the process, has a quality which is different each time around, at each step of the structuring of the reflective act.

epochè

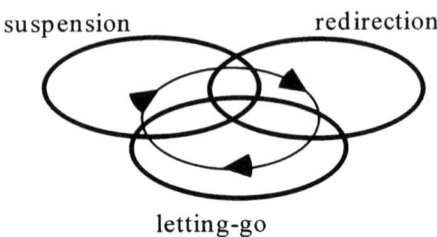

Figure 1. *Épochè*

Suspension and its immediate sequels

The initial suspension phase can be rooted or be started in at least three distinct ways:
- an external or existential event may trigger the suspending attitude. For example, confronting the death of others, or aesthetic surprise.
- the mediation of others can also be a decisive, for example a direct injunction to accomplish the act, or a rather less directive attitude, as is the case when someone plays the role of a model.
- exercises initiated by the individual, presupposing a self-imposed discipline including long phases of training and learning until the newly acquired habits are stabilized.

These three possibilities of priming are not exclusive, but come into play together, the one in relation to another. They amount to motivations that may develop from living in the world, and from intersubjective and individual life. All three motivations are not of equal importance, depending on the unique characteristics of the individual and his/her stage of development. But all converge in making possible and then maintaining phases B and C.

To speak of the "initial" phase, as if there was a supposed "starting point" regarding suspension, requires an immediate qualification. In some sense there cannot be of "starting point", since suspension has already taken place in one's life. Yet at the same time, it seems to unfold anew each time it is mobilized. What is needed for the reflective act to be set in motion? — a suspending move. So we seem to land into a paradox where we must already have in action that we are trying to trigger. Thus the very fact of posing this question in this manner shows that there is a problem. Considered in terms of the products of its activity, the precise moment of the initiation of the reflective act, its priming, is perhaps not relevant. But at the same time it is not possible to describe the reflective act other than in having put it into action, that is, unless we already know how to trigger its initiation. Thus we find ourselves in the provisional circle of having to describe an act in its very putting it into play, as in a bootstrap. The central nature of the starting up process is obscured by the fact that this beginning has already taken place for someone who uses it to describe this very same transition, as we are doing here.

This pragmatic Gordian knot cannot be resolved theoretically. Its circular character must be addressed by means of different *techniques* (methods, know-how, training) which permit a person to internalize or become masterful of such ongoing re-instantiation at every moment. Only an actual engagement with such techniques will also enable the evaluation of the difficulties which must be overcome in order that suspension be a stable capacity, accentuating the unusual character of becoming aware.

The two subsequent phases B-C are complementary and presuppose, as we have said, the initial phase as well as its sustained recycling. They correspond to two fundamental changes in the orientation of cognitive activity. B emerges as a change of *direction* of attention, which, distancing itself from a worldly show, takes an inward turn. In other words, instead of perception, what is invoked is largely what in philosophy is termed an *apperceptive act*: turning from the content of the world to the mental act which carries that perceiving. There is a massive obstacle to this change: the necessity of turning away from the habitual form of cognitive activity, usually oriented towards the exterior world. Change C consists in passing from the voluntary inward direction of attention to simple receptivity or an attitude of listening. That is, from B to C we pass from a "looking for" to a "letting come", a letting "reveal itself". The principal obstacle to this third phase resides in the traverse of an *empty time*, a time of silence, of the lack of take-up of the immediate givens which are available and already assimilated to consciousness.

Here, then, we are dealing with two reversals of the most habitual cognitive functioning, of which the first is the condition for the second; the second cannot happen if the first has not already taken place.

– A turning of the *direction* of attention from the exterior to the interior (B).

– A change in the *quality* of attention, which passes from the looking-for to the letting-come (C).

Whereas the first reversal remains governed by the traditional distinction between interior and exterior, that is to say, driven by a sort of an enhanced duality, and involves a portion of undeniably voluntary activity, the second is characterized by a passive, receptive waiting, which moves exactly in the opposite direction of the previous duality, a transient erasing of the inside/ outside distinction.

From the point of view of phenomenological philosophy, these two reversals match quite well the Husserlian version of reduction as reflexive conversion and the Heideggerian notion of pre-comprehension which lets the event happen.[3] In a similar way, in the Buddhist tradition of mindfulness, a principled distinction is made between the base-level *shamatha* as a voluntary movement where the attention is settled and its natural expansion via the coupling with a more panoramic consciousness (awareness-*vispasnya*), which is characterized by the letting go of voluntary searching, and the embracing of a mode of receptivity that is typically lived as openness (cf. Trungpa 1974; Varela, Thompson and Rosch 1991).

The non-habitual, unnatural character of these two reversals is manifest as the noticing of resistance, of difficulties in operating them, and typically require indirect strategies which allow them to be brought into effect (while avoiding the paradox of "be spontaneous!").

The difficulties in the conversion of gaze

Habitually engaged in the perception of others, in the grasping of worldly content, in the pursuit of goals or of interests linked in an immanent way with our everyday activities, attention is naturally interested in the world. It hardly ever turns away from the world spontaneously. Fink (1997) speaks here of a *Weltbefangenheit* (which can be translated as "imprisonment in the world"), and the Buddhist tradition of the snare of *samsara*. The inward direction of attention, turned away from the world, dis-interested, turned towards representations, towards thoughts, mental acts, and emotional tonality, is for many nonhabitual, to the extent that there is relatively little occasion to exercise it spontaneously or in response to a training demand.

Husserl approaches this reversal from the angle of a change of attitude in the relationship I maintain with the world. Under the heading of "change of attitude" (*Umkehrung der Einstellung*), it is clear that he doesn't mean just a modification of my existential state relative to the world, but indeed the conversion of the natural interest from an object, whatever it is, to the direction of the *act* which allows me access to it. Strictly speaking, it is the very core of reduction as the shift from the object to the act, or again, as passage from the *quod* to the *quomodo*, which is at play here. But it is true that the founder of phenomenology describes this "passing to the act" as a result of analysis, rather than something that is explicitly brought about by an explicit account of examples. Whence the paucity of references made to the difficulty of such a turn; the Husserlian description is hardly procedural or operational. The only indication of difficulty lies in the several places where Husserl discusses the ambivalence of this phenomenological conversion, given the bootstrap nature of the motivation to initiate suspension, as we have already discussed (Depraz 1999).

From a psychological perspective, Piaget's (1968) account of becoming aware allows for a precise evaluation of the difficulties of diverting the attention from the external world, from aiming at a goal, or from the perception of the effects of action; these attention attractors are more spontaneously pregnant than are mental acts or representation.

His principle of "making-conscious", which mobilizes attention from the perimeter towards the center, underlines the dynamics of that which mobilizes the attention in the natural attitude, that is, from the perception of a content (center), towards the means by which such an action is performed, i.e. the mental act which organizes and regulates the perceiving. This dynamic also shows at what point the taking of interest in that which is *not* the most directly pregnant is something secondary in the spontaneous motivation of the subject. Piaget has also shown the primacy of what may be called "positive" information which exists in a directly perceptible way over "negative" information which is only manifest because it is not present directly. In this light then, it is to be expected that to turn one's attention towards the mental acts which organize acting on the world, can only come as an acquired learning.

Pragmatic difficulties

But there are other equally pressing obstacles to this redirection of attention, which most practices acknowledge. Turning attention towards the interior is for some synonymous with turning it towards their intimacy, at the risk of becoming conscious of things which are in the domain of the peripheral, or even the repressed. So rejection is based on the refusal of full contact with one's own intimacy.

In a situation where I am in the presence of other people (interviewer, small groups), this reversal of attention presupposes the acceptance of relaxing the social control which I exercise over others by my gaze or talk. So it presupposes a confidence which enables me to authorize myself to turn my attention more towards my interior world than the social one. Assuredly, a change in the direction of attention towards the interior world is not necessarily an act of becoming aware. This reversal of attention is common to many practices, such as those involving making explicit cognitive knowledge, mindfulness meditation, or psychoanalysis. Psychotherapeutic practice in particular has emphasized how this condition could meet solid refusal.

The fact remains that it is difficult, in the framework of a description of this change of direction of attention, to grasp what it is that makes for so much difficulty in its enactment. Only knowledge of the techniques developed with the intention of aiding people to *produce* this change of attention (the outstanding example being the Buddhist tradition of mindfulness) give the measure of the wrenching which can constitute this reversal for some. The most obvious symptom of the magnitude of this difficulty seems to lie in the fact that these techniques *aim only to produce* this change of direction of attention, a little as if, once this change is induced, the rest (its exploratory reflective use) would go ahead automatically. These techniques commonly make use of the fact that this direction of attention towards apperception partly coincides with attention directed at kinesthetic and propioceptive sensations, its organic support. In bringing attention to breathing, or to what is tense and what is not, we are brought to center ourselves to the *lived body* as focal center, which can then be described as psychic or spiritual, and to leave the world as an extension beyond the bounds of the body.

So this turning back of the direction of attention presupposes becoming familiar with skilful *practices*. We can distinguish several types of prerequisites for progress in such practices: methodological, theoretical, and pragmatic.

The methodological pre-requisite concerns the suspension mentioned earlier, now with that singular quality that it is imbued with a real investment. In effect, the conversion of gaze is for the beginner incompatible with the simultaneous engagement in ordinary action. It implies a form of non-action which is at the outset, *per force*, completely literal: to remain in a sitting position, or in an attitude of attentive listening, or reclined on a couch. Engagement without action is generally very pregnant and creates a motivation and a centering of attention stronger and more immediate than an apperceptive turning back (from content to mental act) and the inhibition of action which it presupposes. However, to the extent that the practice passes from the level of a beginner to a greater mastery, suspension can co-exist in a completely natural way with action in a fully worldly situation. In fact, a fluid coexistence of this sort is precisely the measure of a form of *mastery*. Throughout the intermediate stages, most practices explicitly include transitional steps. A simple example is the alternation between sitting and walking meditation in *shamatha* training.

So the change in direction of attention corresponds to a *doing* from the point of view of cognition: it involves (or is caused by) a change of attitude in my relation to the world. Analyzed from the point of view of enabling techniques for enactment, it is essentially perceived as a lifting of control, in the sense where we could almost accuse the "natural" attitude (can we accuse an attitude!) of having a hypnotic influence which is very difficult to interrupt. This primacy conferred on the very idea of lifting control leads to the use of a language which is that of release, abandonment, letting-go.

Letting-go and the quality of attention

With the third phase, it is the *quality* of attention which changes tone: we pass from a conquering activity ruled by intentionality, which makes us *search out for* the interior to the detriment of the exterior, to a passive disposition of reception, to a *letting-come*, about which there is nothing passive other than the name. In fact, it eminently involves action.

Epochè also, in this phase of its accomplishment, aims at letting the reflection of the lived operate. In other words, it is an active movement of attention, which can be deliberative but, at the same time, presupposes *waiting* because what there is to reflect upon belongs by definition to the domain of the tacit, of the pre-reflective and/or the pre-conscious. So it involves maintaining a tension between a supported act of attention and an immediate non-filling. The immobile hunter knows at least what he awaits with vigilance and patience, even though here there is waiting without knowledge of the content of what is going to reveal itself. In varying degrees, the reflectable is not immediately available. It doesn't exist other than as a potential and will not come as revelation other than through a cognitive act borne by a particular intention. And so the gesture of letting-go presupposes a waiting, but is focused and open and so eventually void of content for a time, without any immediate discrimination other than "there is nothing", "it's foggy", "it's blurred", "it's confused", "nothing's happening".

This time of relative emptiness can be very brief or last several minutes, if not more. It is the time in which something first takes form, but can also be the time which the subject devotes to that which can create the object of this reflection. To the extent that he cannot "grasp" the object in a voluntary sense, this adjustment cannot take place other than structurally, without being able to immediately adjust itself to the detail of a content which is still not revealed.

It is a duration which is easily noticeable in the perception of stereoscopic images. Even when we have an expert ability at accessing this perception, there is a period when nothing is yet distinct, although we are already aware that we are no longer seeing in the normal way (the "natural attitude"). During that period, we sense the emerging of the form emerging up until the moment of brutally clear perception. We also see this type of phenomenon in psychotherapy, when the patient knows that something is in the process of coming back from his past, that he has the impression that "it is on the way to coming into consciousness". Sometimes he can even make out that that something comes from afar, from very far, without at all knowing the content of the scene from the past, or the words which are going to come back to him.

But even when it is objectively very brief, this empty period has the subjective duration of a radio blackout, where a silence of a few seconds appears eternal. In fact, it is subjectively very long, in contrast with the subjective rapidity of our more habitual conscious cognitive functioning. In the practice of letting-go, this slowing of the rhythm of expression and the period of arrested reflectivity is often a reliable criterion for the emergence of *épochè*.

To recapitulate: the difficulty of putting into action the gesture of becoming aware seems to have two inseparable aspects: (1) abandoning the habitual or "natural attitude", and (2) being able to become receptive, (which includes learning to know how do deal with the paradox of aiming at something which is involuntary!).

The pre-reflective dimension

This period which is at the same time empty and subjectively long seems to us to be the major obstacle to discovery and to the spontaneous putting into action of the act of becoming aware. It is difficult not to immediately succumb to the fear or worry that can be induced by that stance of receptive attention. This period is troubling for anyone with the naive belief in an instantaneous, permanent and mechanical mastery of cognition over its functioning. In fact this dimension of pre-reflective access implies that I can become conscious that I do things which are efficient and effective, without knowing (in a reflective sense) how I have arrived at that consciousness. What can also be troubling is to discover a new form of cognition which opens me to the revelation of novel properties and extraordinary aspects of the real to which I find I have been insensitive.

It is clear that in the initial gesture of redirection which modifies the direction of attention, it was necessary to inhibit or abandon immediate action in order to make way for the shift between content and the mental act underlying that content. In the second receptive stage that which needs to be abandoned is an immediate filling-in by projection of categories, expectations, and identifications. Here again, the quality of suspension re-appears in a new form; it fact it permeates every step of the act of becoming conscious.

With this idea of a suspension of judgement, we are very close to the Husserlian intuition of *épochès* interpeted in the widest sense as the principle of the absence of presupposition formulated as early as 1901 in the *Logical Investigations* (§7). But it remains the case that the Husserlian presentation is foundational and does not deal with these differentiated qualities of suspension which we repeatedly come up against in practice.

In more practical terms, we are also close to the attitude which guides psychotherapeutic practice: the professional opens his presence to the other and gives him his attention whist being vigilant not to interfere with the open reception of that which the other brings to light, by the therapist's own personal commentaries and his counter-transference to the patient. The practitioner takes simultaneously note of the verbal, the non-verbal (changes of posture, of gesture, of breathing — in rhythm, amplitude and localization — mimicry, micro-movements), the epi-verbal (what is said by means of the linguistic structures used and the categories of description of the world immanent in the patient's semantic choices), and the para-verbal (the variations of intonation). In psychoanalysis all this is not possible other than by a listening and an observation based on an open or "floating" attention, without grasping for something.

Perhaps we could apply the same analysis to the work of the painter:

> It is interesting to notice here that the phenomenological reduction [...] has a double action. It must make us forget at the same time that it makes appear. The reduction is at bottom in philosophy the equivalent of a technique of seeing in painting. We must forget what appear to be things when we look at them superficially and make appear in the thing itself that which it is in reality. And so the practice of phenomenological reduction is less a matter of seeing than of learning to see (Piguet 1975).[4]

In the tradition of mindfulness, the movement of letting-go is the very heart of what is described as the most "advanced" methods, the Mahamudra-Dzogchen schools of Tibetan Buddhism. The repeated practice of letting-go becomes non-paradoxical as soon as a pre-discursive component is introduced. In Rinzai Zen, the repetitive work with koans provides a classical framework; in the Tibetan schools, the emotional association with the manifest qualities of a living master ("devotion") is considered essential, so much so that the student is coached into a pre-discursive attitude (Namgyal 1987).

We may say, then, that "phenomenological reduction", "reflective act", "becoming aware", or "mindfulness" all stem from what is not available in normal reflection, they are rooted in the non-verbal, the pre-reflective, the ante-predicative. But this amounts to proposing that becoming aware stems from "nothing", in the sense that the lived experience which could be reflected upon is not immediately available. For, if it were, it would already have been brought under the spotlight of the reflexive attention; what we reflected upon can only modulate becoming awareness, but the fact remains that it is set into action, not the choice of content. So the reflective act stems from a "silent" or "empty" relation with experience. It is more at the contemplative level of reception, of listening or of impregnation than of the looking-for in a pre-determined way. It seems to arise from a modality which is more passive than cognition, even if we are well aware that that relative passivity is woven into the background by our categorical filters, whose permanent activity is hard to suspend. In this sense, our description of the reflective act is not about forcing a passive, mechanical reflection. The mirror which represents the person who operates the reflectivity is anything other than neutral. What is in play is to give oneself the possibility of not immediately in-forming reality by a form of thought through a language which is already available, thereby establishing a relative and provisional zone of silence from which to set off with a new relation to the reality of the lived. There is a fertile dimension of emptiness which escapes the parameters of a "natural" world or a language, from the point of view of experience. It enables penetration at an ontological level which is openness to more basic form, a penetration which cannot appear other than as *chiaro-oscuro* (subtle contrasts) supplied by the suspension in letting-go.

This cessation of the spontaneous movement that searches for "information" can only be relative. It involves a braking, an inhibition of habitual cognitive processes whose activity can completely eclipse the receptive dimension and make the reflective act impossible. It is the paradox whereby I can deliberately turn my attention towards the interior, not to look for something there, but to receive that which manifests itself there, or rather that which I am capable of letting manifest itself there.

Faced with this description of a reversal of the movement of attention and the difficulties it can meet in its realization, it might be that we are painting a dark picture. It could be thought that this gesture involves a reversal which continues *always* to be a great difficulty, if not a great mystery. But the period of reversal can be quick enough to pass unnoticed in the mind of someone who does not give it deliberate attention; the reflected content is sometimes easily accessible. The difficulty comes not just from the practice of the reductive act: it is perhaps also linked to the nature of that which is aimed at, or even with the relation which I maintain with that which is aimed at which can make the availability to reflection more difficult.

Conclusion

Let us now consider again the diagram (Figure 1) which shows the components of the basic cycle:

épochè

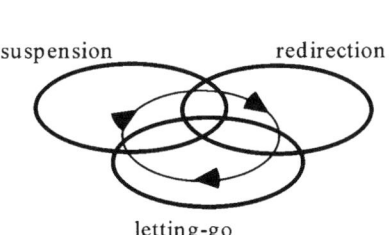

We can make out, at the heart of the process of becoming-aware which is the reflective act or the phenomenological reduction in action, the two sides of *épochè* which are the reflexive/redirection and the reception/letting-go, a correlated double movement. We can also describe its components as moments of emergence, as the unfolding of the process. The first unfolding, which leads to reflection (and on to expression) is characterized by a turning in on oneself; the second unfolding, which leads to a letting-go (and ends in a tacit intuition) is characterized by an openness to oneself.

In the first case, the described movement corresponds to a loop which leads back to itself without, however, closing in on itself, since from this loop the second movement sets out, that of receptivity towards oneself and the world. These two movements can be expressed by the metaphor of the braided axis, like diastole and systole, of contraction and dilation. The first axis is rooted in pre-reflective consciousness (pre-discursive, pre-noetic, ante-predicative, tacit, pre-verbal, pre-logical or non-conceptual; take your pick),[5] whose reflective capacity partially deploys the structure of pre-reflectedness, an intentional content. This is the *cognitive* axis of becoming-aware. The second axis is equally rooted in pre-reflective consciousness, but whose manifestations are not due to its reflective capacity, but to the parallel and indissociable gesture of letting go, intrinsically related to the affective and involuntary dimension of experience.[6] When the gesture of letting go intervenes, it becomes a moment of revelation, a receptive availability. Such is the *affective* axis of becoming aware.

These two axis are braided in single thread, as the unity of cognitive reflection and its inseparable affect, overlapping each other in a dynamic way in bringing each other about. This dynamic structure of metonymy between the core of what we have called *épochè* and the act of becoming aware in its totality is, indeed, remarkable.

Notes

1.   This text is adapted from a forthcoming book: *On Becoming Aware: The pragmatics of experiencing* by N.Depraz, F.Varela and P.Vermersch. As in the present paper, the order of the authors is strictly alphabetical and authorship a shared collective. A German version will appear in: R.Kühn und Michael Staudigl (Hg.), *Epoché und Reduktion*, Karl Alber Verlag (in press). For more on our views on the question of methodology the reader should consult Varela and Shear (1999).

2. In Anglo-Saxon literature, the closest antecedents to our attempt at a pragmatic phenomenology are the early efforts of Spiegelberg (1970), and more recently the pioneer work of Eugene Gendlin (1962). In the phenomenological tradition, Paul Ricouer (1950) is the only writer — so far as we know — to have tackled this question in his description of multiple "practical acts of consciousness" (attention, emotion, effort, habit), before having decided to abandon this project and turn to hermeneutics. In the German domain, Waldenfels (1993) has clearly formulated this need. Finally, the recent book by Marion (1998) should be noted in this context.

3. Cf. Bernet (1994), Introduction, as well as Courtine (1990), Marion (1989), and Henry (1991).

4. J.-Cl. Piguet (1963), op.cit. p.154. See also the much earlier letter from Husserl to Hofmannsthal of 1907 where Husserl makes use of a strict equivalence between the reductive and aesthetic attitudes (Cf. *Art et phénoménologie*, n°7, Bruxelles, 1991, p. 13–19).

5. For more details about this key distinction between pre-reflective/pre-reflexive and reflexive consciousness see the recent discussions in Gallagher (1998), Zahavi (1999), and Bermudes (1998).

6. Regarding these notions see *Analysen zur passiven Synthesis, Hua XI*, Den Haag, M. Nijhoff, 1966 ; Ricœur (1950), Montavont (1994), Mazis (1993), and more recently, Yamaguchi (1997).

References

Bermudes, J. L. 1998. *The Paradox of Self-Awareness*, Cambridge, MIT.

Bernet, R. 1994. *La vie du sujet*, Paris: PUF.

Courtine, J. F. 1990. "Réduction phénoménologique-transcendantale et différence ontico-ontologique." In *Heidegger et la phénoménologie*, Paris: Vrin, pp 207–247.

Depraz, N. 1999. "The Phenomenological Reduction as Praxis", in F. Varela and J. Shear (Eds) *The View from Within: First Person Methodologies in the Study of Consciousness*, Thorverton: Imprint Academic.

Fink, E. 1988. *VI. Cartesianische Meditation* (hrsg. G. Van Kerckhoven). Dordrecht: Kluwer. English translation by R.Bruzina, Indiana University Press: Indiana, 1997.

Gallagher, S. 1998. *The Inordinance of Time*. Evanston: Northwestern Univ. Press.

Gendlin, E. 1962. *Experiencing and the Creation of Meaning: A philosophical and psychological approach to the subjective*. Glencoe: Free Press; reprinted by Evanston: Northwestern University Press, 1997.

Henry, M. 1991. "Quatre principes de la phénoménologie", *Revue de Métaphysique et de Morale*, 1, 3–26.

Husserl, E., 1966. *Analysen zur passiven Synthesis, Hua XI*, Den Haag, M. Nijhoff.

Marion, J.L. 1998. *Etant Donné*, Paris: PUF.

Marion, J.L. 1989. *Réduction et donation*, Paris: PUF.

Mazis, G. 1993. *Emotion and Embodiment : A fragile ontology*, Evanston: Northwestern Univ. Press.

Montavont, A. 1994." Le phénomène de l'affection dans les *Analyses sur la synthèse passive* ", *Alter: Revue de Phénomeénologie No. 2*, Paris, Ed. Alter.

Namgyal, T. 1987. *Mahamudra: The Quintessence of Mind and Meditation*, Boston: Shambala,

Piaget, J. 1968. *Sagesse et illusion de la philosophie*. Paris: PUF.

Piguet, J. -C. 1975. *La connaissance de l'individuel et la logique du réalisme*, Neuchâtel: La Baconnière.

Ricœur, P. 1950. *Philosophie de la volonté I. Le volontaire et l'involontaire*, Paris: Aubier, 1950, reprinted 1988.

Spiegelberg, H. 1970. *Doing Phenomenology*. Den Haag: M. Nijhoff.

Trungpa, Ch. 1974. *Cutting Through Spiritual Materialism*, Boston: Shambala.

Varela, F and Shear, J. eds. 1999. *The View from Within: First-person methods in the study of Consciousness*. Thorverton: Imprint Academic,

Varela, F. Thompson E., and Rosch, E. 1991. *The Embodied Mind: Cognitive Science and human experience*, Cambridge, Mass.: MIT Press.

Waldenfels, B. 1993. *Edmund Husserl, Arbeit an den Phänomenen*, Frankfurt: Fischer.

Yamaguchi, Y. 1997. *Ki als leibhaftige Vernunft. Beitrag zur interkulturellen Phänomenologie der Leiblichkeit*. München: W. Fink Verlag,.

Zahavi, D. 1999. *Self-Awareness and Alterity*. Evanston: Northwestern Univ. Press.

PART 1C

Changing Conscious Experience

CHAPTER 7

Transforming Conscious Experience

Jane Henry
Open University

This chapter reviews the methods used to transform conscious experience in psychotherapeutic and personal development contexts, an area in which first person reports have always been accepted as legitimate data. The chapter compares the main approaches, looks at the diverse methodologies they use, indicates trends and outlines certain key findings from outcome studies. It also discusses the assumptions that underlie current practice, notably the stress on insight and catharsis, and places the privileged frames of deficiency and growth in historical perspective. It concludes by drawing attention to neglected practices that place greater emphasis on the socially embedded nature of consciousness, notably social support and active involvement in the world.

Introduction

By transforming conscious experience I mean a long term change in the way the self and the world are consciously experienced.

Many years ago the idea of transforming consciousness would have been restricted to devotees engaged in esoteric spiritual practices. Nowadays there is considerable interest in the idea of changing conscious experience among both professionals and the lay public. Professionals such as clinical psychologists, psychotherapists, counsellors and psychiatrists all aim to change the way individuals see themselves, their world or their place in it. Many people in the applied caring professions including nurses, social workers, carers and

Table 1. Some Psychotherapeutic, Personal, Professional and Spiritual Approaches to Transforming Consciousness

Behavioural			*Personal development*		
Positive reinforcement	-	Skinner	Positive thinking	-	Hay
Behavioural psychotherapy			Visualisation	-	Gawain
	-	Wolpe	Focusing	-	Gendelin
Behavioural modification	-	Bootzin	Hypnotherapy	-	Erickson
			Co-counselling	-	Jackins
			Neuro Linguistic Programming		
Cognitive				-	Bandler
Cognitive behaviour	-	Bandura	Alcoholics anonymous		
Cognitive therapy	-	Beck	Co-dependency	-	Brown
Rational emotive therapy	-	Ellis	EST	-	Erhardt
Psychodynamic			*Professional development*		
Psychoanalysis	-	Freud	Competence development		
Object relations	-	Klein	Focus groups		
Psychostructural	-	Kernberg	Mentoring		
			Team building		
Humanistic psychotherapies			Action learning		
Gestalt	-	Perls	Adventure training		
Person centred	-	Rogers	Creative problem solving		
Existential	-	Laing			
Psychosynthesis	-	Assagioli	*Spiritual development*		
Psychodrama	-	Moreno	Buddhism		
Primal therapy	-	Janov	Hinduism		
Family therapy	-	Haley	Sufism		
			Jewish Kaballa		
Systemic			Christian mysticism		
Family therapy					
Group therapy			*Attentional approach*		
Encounter group			Mindfulness		
Cognitive analytic therapy			Transcendental meditation		
			Zen		
Psycho-physical					
Bioenergetics	-	Lowen	*Energetic approach*		
Massage	-	Rolf	Tai chi		
Subtle energy	-	Acupuncture	Shiatsu		
Movement	-	Alexander Technique	Kinesiology		
Relaxation	-	Biofeedback	Polarity therapy		

(Source: Henry, J. 1999, p. 580. Adapted and extended)

clergy are also very much concerned with developing and improving conscious experience. Among the lay public there is considerable interest in personal and spiritual development as routes to consciousness transformation.

One of the problems is that people are faced with numerous different approaches to transforming consciousness. For example Karasu (1986) cites 450 therapeutic approaches alone. Table 1 indicates the range of approaches facing individuals interested in transforming consciousness through psychotherapeutic, personal, professional or spiritual development.

Schools

Although practices in this area are underpinned by very different theories, approaches to transforming consciousness in the clinical domain can be grouped under six major schools: psychobiological, behavioural, cognitive, humanistic, psychodynamic and systemic. In addition to employing strategies that derive from a humanistic orientation, personal development offers approaches that aim to transform the mind through work on the body. Spiritual practice offers further approaches including the attentional, and energetic. Table 2 contrasts the focus, model of the person, goal and approach used in each of these schools.

By and large psychiatrists incline towards the psychobiological, many clinical psychologists favour cognitive-behavioural approaches, psychoanalysts follow psychodynamics, and many psychotherapists employ humanistic approaches. An indication of the main focus, goal and type of methodology associated with each approach follows.

The *psychobiological* approaches consciousness by seeking to correct physiological imbalances through the use of drugs, or treat them through other biological interventions such as ECT and, in extreme cases, surgery. A depressive facing a psychobiological practitioner is likely to be given anti-depressants such as Prozac.

Behaviourists assume that the mind develops unhelpful habits through conditioning and seeks to transform these by counter-conditioning and selective reinforcement of helpful habits. Alternatively they see the problem as one of skill deficiency and seek to input absent social skills to improve relationships (and therefore the subjects' sense of well-being). Nowadays many practitioners identify themselves as cognitive-behavioural, an approach which

Table 2. Transforming Conciousness: Key Schools Focus and Concerns

	Psychobiology	Behavioural	Cognitive	Psychodynamic
Focus	Internal	Environment physiology and genes	Present and learning	Past thoughts
Model of person	Medical	Programmable	Habitual	Repressed
Emotion	Largely chemic -ally controlled	Conditioned response	Determined by thoughts	Excess psychic energy
Problem	Biological defect	Faulty conditioning Skill deficiency	Incorrect thinking	Unconscious disowned affect Denied
Cause	Genes/disease	Bad habits	Socialisation	Early socialisation
Goal	Control physiological imbalance	Control behaviour	Insight into relationship between thought & feeling	Insight into relationship between early experience & current state
Treatment	Correct biological imbalance	Counter conditioning to eliminate or control maladaptive behaviour	Replace faulty thinking via disputation/ rehearsal etc	Insight plus release through transference
Examples	Anti-depressant medication	Desensitization	Rational emotive therapy	Transference
Data	Physiological, performance	Behaviour	Self report, dialogue, written work	Clinical interview
Theorists	Sargeant	Wolpe, Skinner Pavlov	Beck, Ellis Meichenbaum	Freud, Erikson Klein, Lacan

(Source: Henry, J. 1998a)

Table 2 (continued)

Humanistic	Systemic	Attentional	Body	Energetic
Present feelings socialisation	Present relationships	Mind's focus of attention	Body	Subtle energy
Self actualising	Socially embedded	Illusory	Embodied	Multilayered energetic
Valuable guide to action	Influenced by others	Influenced by misleading thoughts	Reflected in physical rigidities	Repressed emotion blocks energy flow
Lapsed growth Denied 'unfinished' business	Inappropriate relating	Attachment	Physical and mental blocks	Energy blocks
Denied affect	Poor socialisation	Excessive thinking	Trauma, bad habit	Trauma
Insight into self plus discharge feelings	Insight into family/ group dynamics, new behaviours with key others	Calm mind, diminish intrusive thoughts	Release body and mind	Balance and/or boost energy
Develop trust, self awareness, express feelings, explore possibilities	Observe group interacting, dialogue, point out patterns, make interventions	Meditation, contemplation relaxation	Massage, movement hold positions	Healing, exercises
Catharsis	Family therapy	Mindfulness meditation	Rolfing, Alexander Technique	Reicki, Therapeutic Touch
Counselling interview	Observe group, interaction, discussion	Observation of own cognitive patterns	Felt sense	Subtle sense
Rogers, Perls Moreno, Laing Kelly	Haley, Minuchin	Teasdale, Kabat-Zinn	Lowen, Reich	

combines elements of the behavioural and cognitive approaches. Depressives undergoing behavioural treatment might find themselves on a programme that rewards constructive behaviour with time spent doing things the depressive appears to like and that aims to teach them any social skills in which they appear deficient, for example social rewardingness.

The *cognitive* approach assumes that a dissatisfied consciousness has developed unconstructive patterns of thought such as negative thinking and unwarranted generalization. Practitioners seek to transform consciousness through a rational analysis of the patient's situation and challenges to the mind's prevalent mental conceptions, for example through disputation. The depressive might find a cognitive therapist challenging their negative thoughts in an attempt to get them to reframe their negative understandings into something more realistic and useful. They are also likely to find themselves with homework, for example keeping a log so they have a better understanding of the activities that appear to set off depressive feelings and those that give them a sense of mastery.

The *psychodynamic* approach pays considerable attention to early socialisation. It assumes that denied affect from early life accounts for certain irrational thoughts and behaviour and seeks to offer insight into the underlying causes. It focuses on the unconscious, transference and object relations as routes to unearthing defensive distortions. The psychodynamic practitioner would probe the depressive's early life and seek to show how they appear to be repeating patterns generated there.

The *humanistic* school focuses on present feelings and stresses the importance of expressing feelings. Most humanists value catharsis, on the understanding that the unfinished business of pent up emotion needs discharging. The goal is to facilitate agency. The depressive would be encouraged to relive and express their negative feelings fully, as well as to focus on what they wish for in life.

All the approaches mentioned so far tend to treat individuals in isolation. In contrast, *systemic* and *group* therapies focus on relationships with significant others, such as members of family groups or the other members in the client's therapy group. Family therapy and co-dependence focus on inappropriate patterns of interaction. Family therapists observe families relating so that they can identify recurring patterns, family scapegoats and reveal how members collude in maintaining this behaviour. In examining a depressive they might seek to locate patterns that seemed to bring forth a depressive position, and to note collusion and power relations.

Though the discussion above has emphasised the diverse premises under-pinning the schools described above, in the last twenty years there has been increasing interest in eclectic approaches and a significant proportion of therapists would now choose this attribution for themselves.[1]

Certain spiritual practices for transforming consciousness parallel those undertaken by therapists and vice versa. For example both Buddhism and cognitive psychotherapy employ a practice of thought stopping, and the process of desensitization can be seen as having parallels with Buddhist procedures that encourage the development of loving kindness, in that adepts are encouraged to deal with less troublesome material before tackling more challenging material.

However there are also fundamental differences. Notably, while Western therapies focus on the contents of consciousness, many spiritual practices concentrate more on the processes that give rise to them. Spiritual practice tends to focus less on the use of rational analysis as a means of achieving conscious insight. Instead it emphasises contemplation, with a view to quiet-ing the mind (not clarifying relationships amongst the stories it tells). In attending to the processes that give rise to the mind's chatter, and disassociat-ing from it, rather than engaging with the content, meditators seek to transform consciousness though a shift of attention. Recently psychologists have been making use of such approaches in clinical settings (Teasdale et al. 1995; Kabat-Zinn et al. 1992). Typically people are taught how to meditate and are encouraged to do so regularly. The focus of the mind's *attention* appears to shift as people realise the transitory and arbitrary nature of the day to day chatter in their minds. Assuming that they were judged stable enough, a depressive might be taught meditation and encouraged to meditate every day, the practice itself being expected to improve the patients condition by redirect-ing attention.

In professional settings, attempts to transform consciousness draw on two main approaches — competencies and reflection. Trainees are encouraged to spend time reflecting on what their key goals are and what they need to do to achieve them; where appropriate they are also encouraged to develop the competences needed to achieve these.

In self help settings we find several other approaches to consciousness transformation, many of which parallel those employed by humanistic thera-pists. One practice emphasised is *positive thinking* and the power of affirmations (e.g. Peale 1953). Here the depressive might be encouraged to write out several positive statements about themselves and what they wanted and be encouraged to repeat these x times every day. The idea of focusing on positive outcomes is shared with certain spiritual practitioners, (e.g. certain forms of Raj Yoga).

Nowadays the human potential movement also embraces approaches that seek to transform the mind through the *body*. These include the use of manipulation and movement (e.g. biodynamics, aromatherapy, Rolfing). Here the practitioner would seek to release the bodily tension held by the depressive assuming their mood would lighten as these long standing armours were released. Others purport to work on subtle *energy* channels (long recognised in the East as *chi* or *prana*) though Tai Chi, Shiatsu or various forms of healing. Here the depressive is assumed to be suffering from 'blocked energy' and the practitioner would seek to unblock certain paths, and strengthen others with a view to rebalancing the system of subtle energy assumed to run in the body.

Methods

Each school has their own favoured routes to transforming consciousness. We have seen in Table 2 how their rationales differ. Table 3 indicates the wide range of methodologies encompassed by the different traditions.

However there may be more parallels than are at first apparent. With the exception of the psychobiological approaches, many practitioners rely very largely on verbal discussion. Table 4 indicates some of the different forms of verbal discussion used.

The majority of the orthodox approaches to transforming consciousness in the clinical area are heavily dependent on introspection. Typically the client describes their feelings in conversation with an expert. This normally occurs face to face in dyads or small groups, the goal being to bring troubling feelings to the surface and offer insight into their cause. Perhaps the majority of those seeking to transform consciousness (including counsellors, therapists, psycho-analysts and trainers) rely solely or very largely on verbal discussion, basically comprising reflection on goals and discussion of problematic feelings.

Cognitive therapists and psychosynthesis advocates also employ written homework, such as an activity log or autobiography. Humanistic therapists employ a range of other media including creative expression of feelings

Table 3. Transforming consciousness: Methods

Psychobiological
  Drugs
  Biofeedback
  Electro convulsive therapy
  Surgery

Behavioural
  Counter conditioning
  Desensitisation
  Aversion therapy
  Positive reinforcement
  Skill development

Cognitive
  Thought catching
  Reality testing
  Activity scheduling
  Cognitive rehearsal
  Disputation

Psychodynamic
  Clinical interview
  Life story
  Free association
  Active imaging
  Transference

Humanistic
  Genuineness, warmth,
    positive regard
  Affective self disclosure
  Expressive (drama, art)
  Cathartic (breathing)

Systemic
  Group discussion
  Interpersonal dialogue
  Observation
  Interpretation and comment
  Paradoxical intervention

Psycho-physical
  Massage
  Movement
  Holding
  Touch

Personal development
  Reflection
  Visualization
  Positive thinking
  Body work

Professional development
  Reflection
  Assertiveness
  Negotiation
  Group support
  Role play
  Co-operative enquiry
  Adventure training

Spiritual development
  Service
  Devotion
  Ritual
  Yoga
  Asceticism
  Surrender

Attentional
  Relaxation
  Contemplation
  Mindfulness
  Meditation

Energetic
  Exercises
  Energy balancing
  Energy building
  Healing

(Source: Adapted and extended from Henry, J. 1998a)

Table 4. Media for transforming consciousness

Verbal	Reflection	Share, Relive, Challenge, Reconstrue
discussion	Pair work	Psychotherapy, Counselling, Co-counselling
	Small group	Group therapy, Family therapy, Co-dependency
	Large group	EST, Insight, Life Training
Reflective	Narrative	Autobiography, Journal, Story telling, Myth
writing	Reporting	Activity log, Mood rating, Mapping
	Imaginative	Metaphor, Unsent letter, Epitaph
Expressing	Drama	Psychodrama, Role play
emotion	Art	Art therapy
	Music	Music therapy
Imaging	Rehearsal	Mental rehearsal, Good resource
issues	Visualising	Guided fantasy, Active imagination
	Contemplative	Meditation, Contemplation
Body based	Massage	Bioenergetics, Biodynamics
	Movement	Tai Chi, Dance
	Invasive	Drugs, ECT
	Relaxation	Biofeedback, Breathing

(Source: Henry 1999, p. 593)

(through drama, art or music), use of the imagination through imaging (or visualisation) and bodywork.

The dominance of verbal discussion in the clinical area means that *self-report* has remained central. Contrary to the distrust of introspection seen in most other areas of consciousness studies, clinical work has necessarily continued to depend heavily on self report, indeed self report forms the basic subject matter in most traditions. These reports have been accepted at face value and, until recently, their validity has barely been questioned. Yet the validity of accounts about people's lives is problematic. As far back as the late 1970s, Nisbett and Wilson (1977) cast doubt on people's ability to recognise their own motivation by showing that people were unable to provide accurate reasons for certain decisions. Ericsson and Simon (1980) have pointed out that retrospective accounts and interpretations of personal experience of the kind used in clinical work are much more likely to be invalid than a contemporaneous account.

There are a number of other reasons for questioning the validity of personal accounts. We know that memories are reconstructed anew rather than pulled out of the mind's film library ready-made. Historians find that people's accounts of war are remembered and recounted differently as people age from 30, and 40 to 50. Work on the false memory syndrome has revealed many instances where people have constructed false histories and believed them to be true (Loftus 1994.) We also know the mind is subject to numerous cognitive biases, witness studies show what unreliable witnesses we are, and hypnosis and split brain experiments illustrate our need to rationalise away our actions (Tversky and Kahneman 1974). Some clinical practitioners argue that the literal validity or otherwise of personal accounts is immaterial; for clinical purposes all stories can be treated as narratives which reveal some aspect of the person whether or not they are literally true. Nevertheless, in some cases, a more circumspect attitude to clinical material seems in order.

Outcomes

Naturally, with a range of approaches underpinned by such different theories and methodologies people have been keen to establish their relative effectiveness. The various psychotherapies have been extensively researched (Bergin and Lambert 1994). Meta-analyses show that psychotherapeutic approaches are considerably more effective than placebo or spontaneous recovery over a wide range of conditions (so Eysenck's [1952] charge that psychotherapeutic approaches to change are ineffective is no longer tenable).

However, fascinatingly, it has been hard to prove the superiority of one approach over another — all approaches seem to work with some of the people some of the time (Luborsky et al. 1975; Bergin and Lambert 1994.) This has led many commentators to look for common factors among the diverse traditions that could account for this finding. The common factors seem to have more to do with client expectations, therapist characteristics and the relationship between them than the merits of any particular technique. Lambert et al's (1986) review attributed 30% of the variance in outcome to common factors, 15% to client factors and 15% to technique; spontaneous remission accounted for the other 40%. Fiedler (1950) found expert therapists had more in common with expert therapists from other schools than novices in the same school.

A number of studies show that a good relationship between the therapist and client is more important than the approach used (Lambert 1989; Stiles et al. 1986). Key therapist characteristics are warmth, understanding and empathy, the ability to present a new perspective and help the client to see things in a positive light. Client characteristics are also important; people with positive expectations, strong egos and adequate defences are likely to fare better than those with low-self esteem and little faith in the process.

There are also differences in what clients and therapists perceive to be the important factors. While therapists stress the importance of insight, clients tend to stress the importance of reassurance and being understood (Murphy 1984; Llewelyn 1988).

For a small percentage of people the process of psychotherapy is harmful (Elkin et al. 1989; Lambert and Bergin 1992). A confrontative style on the part of the therapist appears to increase the risk of a negative outcome (e.g. Lieberman et al. 1973). Interestingly, confrontational approaches are now much less popular than they used to be. In large group work EST has largely given way to the less confrontational Insight and Loving Relations Training, and in small group work, in place of the forceful challenge typical of marathon encounter groups, we now find groups laying greater stress on support.

Process

It is clear that a good therapeutic alliance between the client and therapist or counsellor is critical. One interpretation of this finding is that helping relationships are social influence processes. For example Frank (1961,1982) postulates that depressed people suffer low self-esteem, and are unable to help themselves. He suggests that the therapist's task is to restore hope and morale in the client. They then feel able to get out more and begin to socialise in a normal way and so start to feel better about themselves and their life. It has been suggested that this kind of influencing process has parallels with the use of placebo and faith healing (Frank 1961).

An alternative interpretation focuses more on the cognitive changes that seem to accompany consciousness transformation — changing the client's constructs and schemas (Stein 1992) and transforming their sense of meaning (Power and Brewin 1997).

It practice, it seems that psychotherapeutic and personal development approaches to transforming the conscious mind almost invariably involve at least three elements: social support, learning and changing perspectives, and new behaviour. Two factors usually assumed to be central to this process are insight and catharsis.

Insight

Most Western approaches to transforming consciousness, including the cognitive, psychodynamic, and humanistic, assume that the key to transformation is *insight,* an explicit understanding of the nature of the problem. Typically therapists ask clients to report and reflect on their feelings and seek to give them insight into the causes underlying it — self awareness though a rational analysis of the problem. The assumption is that self awareness is inherently transformative, and that understanding the nature of the problem will of itself instigate new behaviour that gets around it. This essentially rational, cognitive strategy is entirely in keeping with the Western rationalist ethos.

However this reliance on conscious insight is problematic on several counts as explained below.

The idea of improving insight generally presupposes that there is a central controlling self, able to act on new understanding. This idea of a unitary *self* is normally taken for granted, however the existence of a central self is under challenge from sources as diverse as cognitive psychology's emphasis on the role of parallel processing by sub-sections of the brain, and the Buddhist idea of no self. Though they use different terminology many clinical traditions have long recognised the presence of competing subpersonalities (ego states, complexes, sub-selves, identity states, self-schemas, archetypes). Clinically the goal has been to get the different parts to recognise each other and reach agreement. It is probably too simplistic to expect a correspondence between physical and mental levels, as revealed by brain scanning, such as MRI, and the different concerns of subpersonalities, but it would be fascinating if there were parallels.

Even if the idea of a mediating self is accepted one can question whether insight is sufficient to transform consciousness. At face value it seems that people who understand their problems would be better placed to deal with them, but often people find they understand their problem only too well and be no nearer changing. They may still be caught in habits that are hard to break, or lack appropriate skills or resources. Often some *mediating variable,* such as confidence, support or attention from a valued other or new behaviour, can be just as effective at transforming mood and the way things seem, as insight into their cause.

More fundamentally one can challenge the merits of prescribing accurate self awareness as a route to well being. In the late 1980s Taylor and Brown

(1988) undertook a series of studies showing that happy people tended to hold unrealistically positive self images and expectations about their likely success in the world, whereas depressives and those with low self-esteem tended to hold more accurate conceptions of themselves and their prospects in life. This work on the adaptive potential of an inflated self image and overly optimistic view of the world calls the self awareness strategy into question (Colvin and Block 1994 and Taylor and Brown 1994 present a discussion of this issue). Hillman and Ventura (1991) add that given the state of the world it might be entirely rational to be depressed about it.

Prochaska has provided a helpful model that suggests that insight may be useful early on in the change process, where people are not very aware and value clarification of problematic experiences, but that it may be less useful

Table 5. Prochaska's theory of Change

Stages

Precontemplation
Contemplation
Preparation
Action
Maintenance
(Relapse)

Ten Processes

Consciousness raising
Counterconditioning
Dramatic relief
Environmental reevaluation
Helping relationships
Reinforcement management
Self liberation
Self reevaluation
Social liberation
Stimulus control

Problem Level

Problematic behaviour
Maladaptive cognitions
Intrapersonal conflict
Interpersonal conflict

further along the change process. For better assimilated issues the more action-oriented cognitive behavioural approaches might be more useful to help restructure schemas and instigate behaviour change (Prochaska and DiClemente 1982.) Table 5 also shows Prochaska's attempt to summarise the different problem types and therapeutic processes that are used to change consciousness.

Wilber takes this one stage further arguing that therapeutic approaches are useful for the early stages of personal development and spiritual development approaches for more advanced stages (Wilber et al. 1986). Clarkson presents a similar model (Clarkson and Lapworth 1992). Both models also relate particular therapeutic approaches to particular pathologies, see Table 6.

Table 6. Stages of psychotherapeutic and spiritual development, corresponding psychopathology and treatment

Stage	Pathology	Treatment
Sensoryphysical	Psychoses	Physiological (pharmacology)
Phantasmal emotional	Narcissistic/Borderline	Structure building (psychostructural)
Representational mind	Psychoneuroses	Uncovering (psychoanalysis, psychotherapy)
Rule/Role	Script pathology	Script analysis (cognitive, family therapy)
Formal reflective	Identity neuroses	Introspection (reflection)
Existential	Existential pathology	Existential therapy (humanistic therapies)
Psychic	Psychic disorder	Yogic path (yoga)
Spiritual*	Subtle pathology	Spiritual path (contemplation)

(Source: After Wilber, in Wilber et al 1986, Chapters 3-5)

---

* Wilber differentiates between the subtle and causal stages of spiritual development.

Catharsis

Many humanistic practitioners assume the body is intimately linked to the mind and that consciousness may be transformed if individuals experience catharsis to release pent up emotion. Hence humanistic therapists encourage clients to express their feelings, as holding these in is assumed to be detrimental. This route to transformation entails reliving experiences, expressing previously denied feelings and discharging these through catharsis. This assumes emotions are fixed entities that are stored until release.

Practitioners favouring catharsis tend to assume emotions are primary. However it is quite easy to show that emotions usually follow thoughts rather than predate them. For example we might get angry with someone who falsely accused us but not if we thought the judgement fair.

In certain cases concentrating on negative feelings is counterproductive. For example with individuals already engulfed with feelings, where restimulation is likely (when a feeling or situation brings up a well rehearsed set of negative thoughts (Jackins 1989)) or with borderline personalities who need ego strengthening (Kernberg 1984). Unfortunately many practitioners still assume catharsis is universally beneficial and give scant attention to these contraindications.

The idea that expressing anger, for example, is a good thing is in any case a very Western notion. Many other cultures view the expression of anger as childish and something to be avoided. Eskimos for example barely recognise the term. Tibetans, whilst recognising frustration, discourage identification with anger. They are more likely to encourage avoiding the circumstances that could engender anger on the grounds that this could fuel the stove, making it more prone to discharge (Jinpa 1998) — a very different idea about the best way forward than the humanistic stress on the merits of uncorking the bottle.

History

Western attempts to transform consciousness reflect their time and culture. Both the attention now given to personal development and the adoption of psychological ways of transforming experience is largely a recent phenomena.

Growth v. acceptance

Interest in psychological ways of transforming conscious experience developed in the 19th century. This was a time of economic growth and geographic expansion. Our ideas of personal growth seem to have borrowed from the conceptions of economic growth current at that time, and this influence lives on. We still speak of personal growth rather than acceptance and we seek to fix ourselves much as we seek a technological solution to fix the planet's problems.

Yet there appears to be a limit to this goal. Evidence is building that temperament (e.g. extraversion, neuroticism, agreeableness) has a genetic component (Goldberg 1993). If this is the case the extent to which we can transform say, a neurotic consciousness is probably limited, though we can of course improve our coping skills. In this view the enlightened master may still retain a few idiosyncratic neurotic quirks.

The rosy discourse of personal growth leads one to expect that it is possible to resolve personal difficulties caused by problematic feelings or a sense of inadequacy, but empirical evidence calls this into question. Empirical studies suggest that major life trauma such as loss of, or absence of, a child stays with people throughout life.

The way the Western discourse of growth is framed tends to reflect the Western tendency to think linearly. Many developmental theorists have presented their theories as a series of vertical stages (whether this is Piaget and Perry's ideas of child and adult cognitive development, Kohlberg's notions of moral development or Erickson's stages of man). Staged conceptions of development are also allied to Western notions of economic growth, evolutionary thinking and technological fix. Table 7 lists some of the vertical conceptions of staged growth.

In contrast, Eastern conceptions of personal development have drawn on rather different metaphors that also have their origins deep in culture and history. For example the idea of development as a *cycle* features prominently in the East. This accords with the Hindu conception of a cyclical version of world history. In the East we also find a greater stress on self acceptance and forbearance (rather than the idea of personal growth and fixing and transforming oneself). The idea of self acceptance perhaps follows from the cyclical conception of development.

In China the idea of balance and harmony features strongly. This again suggests a different sort of development, less a question of transformation than

Table 7. Vertical stage models of the development of consciousness

Piaget	Kohlberg	Loevinger	Erikson	Maslow	Wilber
1 Sensorimotor	Hedonism	Impulsive	Trust v mistrust >hope	Physiological	Senses
2 Preoperational			Autonomy v shame >will	Safety	Emotional
3 Concrete operations	Obedience to avoid punishment	Self protective	Initiative v guilt >purpose	Love	Representational
4	Bargain for reward	Conformist	Industry v inferiority >competence		Rule/Role
5 Formal operations	Approval conform	Self aware	Identity v confusion >fidelity	Esteem	Reflective
6	Duty to social order	Conscientious / Individualistic	Intimacy v isolation >love		Existential
7 Post formal	Contract and commitment	Autonomous	Generativity v stagnation >care	Self-actualisation	Intuitive
8	Conscience or principle	Integrated	Integrity v despair >wisdom		Spiritual

Key: > resolves to
(Source: Henry, J. 1996a)

the need to balance different parts and aspects, and adopt a middle way. Chinese medicine and spiritual exercises (Tai Chi and Shiatsu) aim for a balance of energies.

The idea of a sudden metamorphosis or instantaneous transformation of consciousness is rare, but is found in spiritual practice, through the idea of instant enlightenment as in Zen or Kundalini experiences, both of which are reputed to have the power to transform consciousness fundamentally in an instance.

Heritage of deficiency

In addition to the historically rooted idea of personal growth, we tend to frame notions of consciousness transformation within a rhetoric of deficiency. Foucault (1975) has documented how our conceptions of the psychologically disturbed have changed from viewing them as bad and in need of discipline to mad and in need of locking away. The modern conception borrows from the medical model, to view neuroses as abnormal, deficient and in need of treatment to cure the problem. Even nowadays most Western methodologies for transforming consciousness derive from attempts to cure people with abnormal personalities. So our repertoire of approaches derive largely from work on pathology, deficiency and failure not success and well-being.

One consequence is that history has inclined us to perceive people with personal problems as deficient and in need of treatment rather than going through a natural grieving process after one of life's blows. We have also tended to frame attempts to transform consciousness by starting with the empty side of the glass — the presenting problem rather than the full side — the desired outcome. Most clinical workers seeking to engender change start from an analysis of what is wrong, seeking to understand this and fix it. Some change specialists argue that focusing on the problem is counterproductive as it can lead to a vicious circle of increasingly negative thoughts. They advocate change strategies based around dissociating from the negative, visioning, starting with an image of what they want rather than what's wrong, and identifying with the positive (Bandler 1985). They argue that starting with the vision of where you want to be rather than analysing current problems leads to a more satisfactory and different outcome (Fritz 1989).

Though our heritage inclines us to analyse problems and seek strategies to fix them, a few practitioners have begun to take the alternative route of modelling success instead of examining deficiency (Maslow 1968; Csikszentmihalyi and Csikszentmihalyi 1988; Covey 1989, Seligman and Csikszentmihalyi 2000).

Such work as there is on the psychology of well-being suggests very different strategies for transforming conscious experience. For example Csikszentmihalyi (1988) has undertaken a series of studies on what people are doing when they feel a sense of well-being. He noted common characteristics across these activities and called the resulting state of mind 'flow'. In this state people had a clear goal that they had a chance of achieving, they were in control of their actions and received feedback on their progress, they were absorbed in the activity, their sense of time altered and they lost their sense of self. A distinguishing feature of the activities that featured (which ranged from gardening, through sport to parenting) is that people were actively engaged in tasks, not passive bystanders. The implication of this work is that we are better off engaging in a physical activity we enjoy than passively watching TV; also that well-being is associated with absorption and a focus outside the person rather than navel gazing introspection.

In a review of work on the psychology of happiness Argyle (1987) notes that well-being is found more often in those who are part of and are supported by a social network. The implication here is that we might be better keeping up friendships than spending time analysing feelings about apparent problems. The pre-eminence of the talking cure has led to the neglect of other potentially efficacious strategies, for example the benefits of exercise on depressive neurochemistry (McCann and Holmes 1984) or simply spending time in nature.

Neglected frames

Intuitive and embodied

It can be seen from this rapid survey of the methods used that the predominant approach used to transform consciousness in the West employs professionals who rely largely on rational strategies. Therapists aim to analyse the problem and develop self-awareness. Similarly professional development practitioners encourage people to reflect on learning points. Even those advocating visions prefer these to be explicit goals that people can plan towards. This is entirely in keeping with the rationalistic ethos that has held sway in the West since Descartes.

Thus professional strategies for change (like education itself) privilege a rational analysis of problems and neglect intuitive, embodied and more socially embedded approaches.

Recent work on consciousness has revealed that much more information processing, perception, learning and decision making goes on at an unconscious level than had been suspected. It further reveals that explicit understanding can lag behind unconscious know-how, that the unconscious can grasp complex patterns that the conscious mind fails to understand and that in certain circumstances the conscious mind believes itself to be adopting a strategy at odds with that actually being practised by the unconscious mind (Berry and Dienes 1992; Lewicki et al. 1992). The effect of this work is to show that the conscious mind is much less important than had been believed hitherto. Feeling this to be the case, certain clinical practitioners have directed their change efforts at implicit learning and the unconscious. For example Erikson (1980) reasoned that by the time people came to him for treatment their conscious resources had failed to solve their problems. He used indirect hypnotic inductions (of which the person was unaware) and suggestive narratives, in an effort to bypass the rational conscious mind and speak directly to the unconscious. Whilst many attempts to change consciousness try to do so by making the implicit explicit, this strategy aims to bypass explicit reasoning.

In the human potential movement there has been a marked shift of interest away from rational talking therapies towards previously neglected strategies. For example there has been increasing interest in *intuitive* approaches employing imaging and visualisation. There is also a lot more interest in *embodied* approaches that start by engaging with the body in an attempt to transform the mind, for example through massage as in Rolfing or aromatherapy or through movement as in Tai Chi or Shiatsu.

The author has conducted a number of workshops with different client groups including managers, psychologists, therapists and the general public.[2] Asked to describe what strategies have helped them transform their consciousness long-term, the most common responses are attending to and giving time to intuitive promptings, support from friends, the use of physical exercise, or simply being in nature. Other approaches cited include 'following your bliss' and risking commitment or surrender. Talking about problems features but is cited much less frequently (Henry 1998a). Methods cited as failing to effect any change included exhortation, reading about problems, talking about problems, and making plans, (which is not to say that these methods do not work for some people). What is interesting is the lack of attention given to analysis

of the problem, insight into their cause, or consciously acquired self awareness, yet it is precisely these sorts of approaches than most personal change
professionals seem to favour.

If consciousness change strategies were based on methods highlighted in
experiential accounts and those suggested by studies of well-being we might
find a different menu of approaches on offer, in particular strategies that allow
time for intuitive processes that involve quietening rather than analysing the
mind, entail social support, and embody practices such as walking in nature.

Social and political

Up to this point our discussion has taken it for granted that we are concerned
with transforming consciousness within a single individual and, in most cases,
that the problem resides within that individual's consciousness. Such an
approach is in keeping with the individualistic sense of self found in the West.
However it can be criticised as being overly concerned with the individual and
failing to appreciate the extent to which people's states of consciousness arise
out of their social situation. The implication is that many problems of consciousness reside as much in the social and environmental situation in which
people find themselves rather than solely within some aspect of their individual psyche.

Given these concerns, it is ironic that there has been a vast expansion in the
areas of life deemed suitable for psychological scrutiny: victims of crime,
criminals, the soon to be redundant and the infertile all regularly face a
counsellor to attend to the needs of their conscious minds. Indeed few people
escape the attention of the consciousness transformation experts in their modern
day guises as counsellor, therapist, trainer, cleric or day-time TV pundit.

Rose (1990) decries the psychologization of experience that he sees in
this psychotherapeutic approach to consciousness raising. He argues that this
therapeutic approach has been overextended into inappropriate fields, colonis-
ing areas such as personnel and training and the caring professions; that it
has been inappropriately applied in mundane matters such as debt, and inappropriately used to pathologise tragedies such as bereavement which are an
inevitable part of life. Rose argues that this psychological orientation overem-
phasises the importance of personal relationships and disempowers the individual.

Countries with a more communal sense of self, such as the Native

Americans and many African societies, have long tended to treat the psyche in a social context rather than isolated from it, as in the individualistic West.

There are however some approaches to consciousness transformation that take greater account of the social situation that people find themselves in. Therapeutic approaches like family therapy and co-dependence recognise the ever present influence of significant social peers, and attribute aspects of behaviour to the situation as much as to the individual psyche. Though there is increasing interest in these systemic and embedded approaches, at present this orientation is a minority one.

The politically concerned also often find the personal approach to transforming consciousness wanting. For example Hillman and Ventura (1991) point out that the focus on developing the person in many human potential and psychotherapeutic movements draws attention away from the possibility of acting in the world in a way that might bring about political change and social improvement. The same critique of egocentricity is often made against spiritual practitioners.

Many political activists frame the transformation of consciousness as a social process of consciousness raising, that arises through dialogue among people with conflicting viewpoints acting in the world, rather than a solitary analysis of an individual psyche (Freire 1975). There are now some approaches to consciousness transformation that are embedded within social action, for example co-operative inquiry, action learning and participatory action research. Freire (1978) would take this one stage further and argue that the transformation of individual and social consciousness are interdependent, and that dialogue and engagement in society are needed for people to be able to recognise and transform their false consciousness.

Table 8 summarises the privileged practices in consciousness transformation and those neglected by the mainstream.

Table 8. Privileged practice in consciousness transformation

	Privileged	*Neglected*
Psychological	Conscious insight	Contemplation
Physical	Disembodied	Embodied
Social	Individual	Social
Political	Isolated	Engaged
Historical	Pathological	Well-being
Cultural	Growth	Acceptance
Professional	Expert	Self-managed

(Source: Adapted from Henry, J. 1998b)

Conclusion

Psychological approaches to consciousness transformation are characterized by a diverse theoretical base. However in practice many traditions rely heavily on verbal discussion of people's life experiences and their reactions to these. In contrast to other areas of psychology, in the clinical area introspective self reports have always been accepted as legitimate data.

Research on outcomes suggests that therapeutic effectiveness has more to do with the therapeutic alliance between the client and therapist than the particular method adhered to. In the informal sector there has been a shift away from individually oriented talk-based approaches to greater use of intuitive, contemplative, and physically embodied approaches. This area has generally conceptualised the problem of consciousness transformation as a matter for the individual. However there are now a number of approaches that are more socially embedded.

Psychotherapy, personal and professional development are still dominated by a discourse of growth, deficiency, insight, and catharsis. These privileged practices led to a neglect of other practices that emphasise social support and active involvement in the world. Studies of well-being suggest the latter are important strategies for achieving well-being.

Notes

1. For example a study of all the clinical psychologists in the NHS found 39% claimed to be eclectic practitioners and 41% cognitive-behaviourist (Rowan 1998).
2. The workshops on effective and ineffective strategies for personal change include two run for the Open University Experiential Research Group in 1995 and 1997, one at the First Annual Consciousness and Experiential Psychology Conference 1997, another at the 6th International Conference on Experiential Learning in Finland in 1998, and a fifth at the OUBS MBA Creative Management residential school in 1999; in addition to one at a London Salon on Personal Change in 1995.
    Some of the material on which this article is based was previously published in the British Journal of Psychology, 1999 no 4.

References

Argyle, M. 1987. *The Psychology of Happiness.* London: Methuen.

Bandler, R. 1985. *Using your Brain for a Change*. Mob, Utah: Real People Press.

Bergin, A.E. and Garfield, S. L. 1994. *Handbook of Psychotherapy and Behaviour Change*, 4th Edition. New York: Wiley.

Bergin, A.E and Lambert, M.J. 1994. "The effectiveness of psychotherapy." In A.E. Bergin and S.L. Garfield (eds), *Handbook of Psychotherapy and Behaviour Change*, 4th Edition, New York: Wiley.

Berry, D. and Dienes, Z. 1992. *Implicit Learning*. London: Lawrence Erlbaum.

Clarkson, P. and Lapworth, P. "Systemic integrative psychotherapy." In *Integrative and Eclectic Psychotherapy*, W. Dryden (ed.). Buckingham: Open University Press

Colvin, C. and Block, J. 1994. "Do positive illusions foster mental health? An examination of the Taylor and Brown formulation," *Psychological Bulletin*, 116(1): 3–20.

Covey, S. 1990. *The Seven Habits of Highly Effective People*. New York: Fireside

Csikszentmihalyi, M. & Csikszentmihalyi, I.S. (eds) 1988. *Optimal Experience: Studies in the flow of consciousness*. New York: Cambridge University Press.

Dilts, R. *Changing Belief Systems with NLP*. Cupertino, CA: Meta Publications.

Elkin, I., Shea, M.T. Watkins, Imber, S.D., Stotsky, S.M., Collins, J.F., Glass, J.D., Pilkonis, P.A., Leber, W.R., Docherty, J.P., Feister, S.J. and Parloff, M.B. 1989. National Institutes of Mental Health treatment of depression collaborative research programme: General effectiveness of treatments, *Archives of General Psychiatry*, 46: 971–982.

Ericsson, K.A and Simon, H.A. 1980. "Verbal reports as data," *Psychological Review*, 87: 215–251.

Erikson, M.H. and Rossi, E.L. and Rossi, S. 1976. *Hypnotic Realities: The Induction of Clinical Hypnosis and Forms of Indirect Suggestion*. New York: Irvington Press

Eysenck, H.J. 1952. "The effects of psychotherapy: an evaluation," *Journal of Consulting Psychology*, 16: 319–24.

Fielder, F.E. 1950. "Comparisons of therapeutic relationships in psychoanalytic, non-directive and Adlerian therapy," *Journal of Consulting Psychology*, 14: 436–45.

Foucault, M. 1975. *The Birth of the Clinic*. New York: Vantage Books

Frank, J.D. 1982. "Therapeutic components shared by all therapies." In J.H Harvey and M.M Parks, The Master Lecture Series, Vol. 1, Psychotherapy Research and Behaviour Change, Washington DC: American Psychological Association, 73–122.

Frank, J.D. 1961. *Persuasion and Healing*. Baltimore: John Hopkins Press.

Freire, P. 1978. *Pedagogy in Progress*. London: Writers and Readers Publishing Co-operative.

Fritz, R. 1989. *The Path of Least Resistance*. NY: Ballantine.

Goldberg, L.R. 1993. "The structure of phenotypic personality traits." *American Psychologist*, 48: 245–47.

Haworth, J. T. 1997. *Work, Leisure and Well-being*. London: Routledge.

Henry, J. 1999. "Changing conscious experience: comparing clinical approaches, practice and outcome." *British Journal of Psychology*, 90, 4, 587–607.

Henry, J. 1998a. "Methods for personal change." Paper and workshop presented to 6th International Conference on Experiential Learning, University of Tampere, Finland.

Henry, J. 1998b. "Privileged practice in personal development." *Lifelong Education in Europe*, 3: 161–164.

Henry, J. 1996a. "Transforming Experience." Paper presented to BPS Annual Conference, Brighton.

Henry, J. 1996b. "Developing and changing experience." Paper presented to 5th International Experiential Learning Conference, Cape Town, S Africa.

Hillman, J. and Ventura, M. 1991. *One Hundred Years of Psychotherapy and the Worlds Not Getting Any Better.* San Francisco: Harper.

Jackins, H. 1989. *Fundamentals of Co-counselling Manual.* Riverside Press.

Jinpa, Geshe Thubten. "Tibetan attitude to emotion," Presentation to 2nd Psychology of Awakening Conference, Dartington, Devon.

Kabat-Zinn, J. et al. 1992. "Effectiveness of a meditation-based stress-reduction programme in the treatment of anxiety disorders." *American Journal of Psychiatry,* 149: 936–943.

Karasu, T.B. 1986. "Specificity versus non-specifity," *American Journal of Psychiatry,* 143: 687–695.

Kernberg, O.F. 1984. *Severe Personality Disorders: Psychotherapeutic Strategies.* New Haven Conn: Yale University Press.

Lambert, M. J. and Bergin, A.E. 1994. "The effectiveness of psychotherapy." In Bergin and Garfield op.cit.

Lambert, M.J. and Bergin, A.E. 1992. "Achievements and limitations of psychotherapy research." In D.K. Freedheim (ed.) *History of Psychotherapy: A century of change,* Washington DC American Psychological Association, 360–390.

Lambert, M. 1989. "The individual therapists contribution to psychotherapy process and outcome." *Clinical Psychology Review,* 9: 469–85.

Lambert, M.J. 1986. "Implications of psychotherapy outcome research for eclectic psychotherapy." In J. C. Norcross (ed.) *Handbook of Eclectic Psychotherapy,* NY: Brunner/ Mazel, 436–62.

Lewicki, P., Hill, T. and Cryzewska, M. 1992. "Non-conscious acquisition of information." *American Psychologist,* 47: 796–801

Lieberman, M.A., Yalom, I.D. and Miles, M.B. 1973. *Encounter groups: First facts,* New York: Basic Books.

Llewelyn, S.P. 1988. "Psychological therapy as viewed by clients and therapists," *British Journal of Clinical Psychology,* 27: 223–37.

Loftus, E.F. 1994. "The repressed memory controversy," *American Psychologist* 49: 5, 443–45.

Luborsky, L., Singer, B. and Luborsky, L. 1975. "Comparative studies of psychotherapy: is it true that 'every body has won and all must have prizes'?" *Archives of General Psychiatry ,* 32: 995–1008.

Maslow, A. H. 1968. *Towards a Psychology of Being,* New York: Van Nostrand

McCann, I.L. and Holmes, D.S. 1984. "Influence of aerobic exercise on depression." *Journal of Personality and Social Psychology,* 46: 1142–7.

Murphy, P.H., Cramer, D. and Lillie, F.J. 1984. "The relationship between curative factors perceived by patients in their psychotherapy and treatment outcome: an exploratory study," *British Journal of Medical Psychology,* 57: 187–92.

Nisbett, R.E., & Wilson, T.D. 1977. "Telling more than we can know: Verbal reports on mental processes," *Psychological Review,* 75: 522–536.

Peale, N. 1953. *The Power of Positive Thinking*, Kingswood, Surrey: Cedar

Power, M and Brewin, C. R. 1997. *The Transformation of Meaning in Psychological Therapies: Integrating theory and practice,* London: Wiley.

Prochaska, O. and DiClemente, C.C. 1982. "Transtheoretical therapy towards a more integrative model of change," *Psychotherapy: Theory, Research and Practice*, 19: 276–88.

Rose, N. 1990. *Governing the Soul*. London: Routledge.

Rowan, J .1998. "Change processes in humanistic and transpersonal therapies," Presentation to Comparing Change Processes Round Table, BPS Annual Conference, Brighton.

Seligman, M. E. and Csikszentmihalyi, M. 2000. Positive Psychology, Special Issue of *American Psychologist*, 55, 1, 1–196.

Stein, D. J. 1992. "Schemas in cognitive and clinical sciences an integrative construct." *Journal of Psychotherapy Integration, 2*, (1), pp. 45–63.

Stiles, W.B., Shapiro D.A., and Elliot, R. 1986. "Are all psychotherapies equivalent?" *American Psychologist*, 41(2) 165–80.

Taylor, S.E. & Brown, J.D. 1988. "Illusion and well-being: A social psychological perspective on mental health." *Psychological Bulletin*, 103: 193–210.

Taylor, S.E. & Brown, J.D. 1994. "Positive illusion and mental well-being revisited: Separating fact from fiction," *Psychological Bulletin,* 116(1): 21–27.

Teasdale, J., Segal, Z. and Williams, M. 1995. "How does cognitive therapy prevent depressive relapse and why should attentional control (mindfulness) training help?" *Behavior Research and Therapy*, 33(1): 25–39.

Tversky, A. and Kahneman, D. 1974. "Judgement under uncertainty," *Science,* 183: 1124–31.

Wilber, K., Engler, J. and Brown, D.P. 1986. *Transformations of Consciousness*. Shambala: Boston.

CHAPTER 8

Clinical Implications
of an Intersubjective Science

Janet Richardson

King's College, London

This chapter explores the positive therapeutic effects that could, in part, arise from the intersubjective experience shared by the patient and practitioner. The chapter draws on a theoretical analysis of intersubjectivity from both psychological and clinical perspectives, supported by research evidence. Case studies from clinical practice illustrate the potential contribution of 'shared consciousness' or intersubjective experience to a therapeutic outcome. The concept of empathy as shared experience, and the extent to which this approach (or skill) can be taught will be examined. The ideas in this chapter have developed from my own background in psychology, and my experience of nursing theory and clinical practice.

The potential for an intersubjective science

Much of medical care is aimed at the exploration of physical/biological processes in order to understand and treat diseased bodies (and to some extent diseased minds). Efforts are made to examine 'objective' measures of disease and seek 'objective' outcome measures in order to monitor the success or otherwise of treatment. This is exemplified in the randomised control trial where strenuous efforts are made to control for extraneous variables in order to observe and measure the effect of the intervention. Subjective experiences of disease and illness are beginning to receive attention in medical research (Britten 1995; Pope and Mays 1995). However it is the 'objectivist' paradigm that currently dominates both medicine and science. For example it is a commonly held view in psychology that perceptions are private and 'subjective' and that physical objects are public and 'objective' (Velmans 2000). This view influences the way private experiences and physical objects are thought of and interpreted. Greater importance is assigned to physical events as they can be observed 'objectively'. In contrast, subjective experiences are elusive and difficult to measure as feelings and experiences can only be reported by the experiencer. Consider, however, the importance given to research into pain (a subjective experience) and its management, with over 148,000 publications listed on the Medline database from 1996–1998 (Velmans 2000). This makes it clear that subjective experiences have been investigated by science. In the light of this (and other considerations) Velmans presents a persuasive reanalysis of private versus public phenomena:

> "Each (private) observation or experience is necessarily *subjective*, in that it is always the observation or experience of a *given* observer, viewed and described from his or her individual perspective. However, once that experience is shared with another observer it can become *intersubjective*...... To the extent that an experience or observation can be *generally* shared (by a community of observers), it can form part of the data-base of a communal science".

This approach suggests the possibility of an intersubjective science in which our phenomenal worlds can be rigorously explored and interpreted.

The potential application of an intersubjective science to a clinical setting is interesting. Indeed there is a strong tradition within nursing of studying the 'lived experience' of illness through the methodology of interpretive phenomenology (Benner 1994a). In this method "The interpretive researcher creates a dialogue between practical concerns and lived experience through engaged reasoning and imaginative dwelling in the immediacy of the participants' worlds" (Benner 1994b: 99). Benner suggests that nurses are well suited to phenomenology as they are accustomed to getting the person's story. The interpretive phenomenologist applies a range of skills in the research methodology that are completely conducive to a therapeutic encounter: open listening, active listening, and allowing the interviewee to shape the telling of the story. In order to interpret the data the researcher is required to move into the phenomenal world of the participant.

This intersubjective science, based on observation, reporting, interpreting and understanding a person's experience is not in conflict with an 'objective', third-person approach. Indeed such an approach is complementary to a third-person approach. In particular, the combination of first and third-person approaches to the evaluation of clinical interventions can provide a more detailed picture of what is inevitably a complex process. For example, through a third-person approach it might be possible to report the blood gasses and other clinical features of patients who have chronic obstructive pulmonary disease. But it is the phenomenological approach that would reveal how patients who have this condition make sense of it in terms of fighting a battle and 'going to war'. This methodological approach will be explored more fully later in the chapter.

The process of patient assessment

For a practitioner, the first point of contact with a patient involves taking a history. Though essentially a fact-finding enterprise, the history-taking is (potentially) the beginning of the therapeutic relationship. During this initial period of questioning, the practitioner's response (or lack of response) to the patient's answers and subtle cues, such as facial expression and body language, will demonstrate her skills in 'active listening'. When the patient consciously (or unconsciously) processes the practitioner's response, he will adjust his participation in this process, appropriately elaborating or restricting his answers to the questions. Taking a history is rather like encouraging someone to tell a story — the patient's personal story. However in healthcare the patient is often expected to tell their story in a way which is tightly ordered and structured. This serves the obvious purpose of ensuring that nothing important has been missed, such as a family history of high blood pressure.

What this approach can fail to uncover is the extent to which the clinical problem affects the patient's life. There is also an expectation that the patient's story will be told in a language that is familiar to professionals, a 'clinical language'. The facts can then be ordered so that a pattern can be recognised, and appropriate treatment prescribed. This process is particularly important for junior and inexperienced staff who may not have fully assimilated all the relevant questions into their natural repertoire.

However this approach to taking a patient's history can easily interrupt the flow of the narrative. For example Beckman & Frankel (1984) found that patients were interrupted by their doctors approximately eighteen seconds after they began to speak. In contrast, excellent physicians are those who spend time with the patient and are able to gain an understanding of both the clinical problem and the patient's life situation (Landau 1993). The form of questioning used in taking a medical history attempts to identify symptom patterns in order to detect the presence or absence of 'disease'. 'Illness' however refers to how the sick person and wider social network *respond* to symptoms and disability (Kleinman 1988). This illness *experience* may be overlooked in attempts to record and categorise symptoms, particularly as it requires an explanation and understanding in 'common-sense' that is accessible to lay-persons within the patient's social group and culture. It also requires an understanding of the extent to which the problems impact on the patients' everyday lives.

Disease is what medical practitioners are trained to see, so they reconfigure the patient's problems as narrow, technical problems, and may be unconcerned with patients' narratives and causal beliefs (Kleinman 1988). For the patient *illness* has meaning. Yet (biomedical) healthcare is organised in order to pursue the biological mechanisms of disease, and to avoid the exploration of its meaning.

The meaning associated with an illness will depend on social and cultural factors, but also the limitations and trajectory of the illness. For example an elderly patient experiencing post-operative pain following a total hip replacement might interpret the pain as necessary for healing. She might expect that it will be of short duration, followed by increased mobility and the absence of the chronic pain she has suffered for the past two years or more. In contrast, a patient experiencing pain following a mastectomy for the removal of a malignant tumour might wonder if this is the kind of pain she can expect to experience for the rest of her life. She will be concerned about the results of the histology, the cancer may have spread more widely than was originally thought; it might recur; how will she cope with her family and young children? The pain takes on a sinister meaning associated with uncertainty, possible future suffering and, ultimately, her possible death.

Through detailed inquiry and active listening the practitioner can enter the patient's phenomenal world of illness. Kleinman (1988) proposes a clinical method for the care of the chronically sick. This involves the 'empathic witnessing' of the experience of suffering through sensitively facilitating the patient to tell their story of the illness.

Stories

Stories play a major part in our lives as human beings, and we need to be able to tell them (Gersie 1997). In predominantly oral traditions they are the main mode of transmission for important information such as traditional practices, rituals, the use of medicinal substances, and cultural history. We construct who we are through stories, stories about childhood, what we did on holiday, how we came to be in the job we are in, how we met our partner and fell in love. All our stories are expressions of ourselves and are necessary to weave the web of meaning within which we can live our lives. They provide the context of normality within which we live (Mair 1989). Storytelling is a way of placing life changes and rites of passage in a mythical and wider cultural context.

Stories not only provide context and meaning to our lives, they can be a tangible way of sharing thoughts and feelings which, in normal conversation, we feel unable to express. By placing our experiences in a mythical and imaginative context, particularly in times of pain and distress, it is possible to express and explore that distress in a profound and deeply meaningful way (see for example Mellon 1992). Storymaking can be an important therapeutic activity, for example in dealing with life changes, loss and bereavement (Gersie & King 1990; Gersie 1991, 1997).

Storytelling also serves the healing professions very well. Case studies are written for professional journals in order to communicate new findings in treatments and healthcare practices; 'cases' are presented to colleagues that tell a story about a normal or unusual 'picture' of a 'disease'. But stories are also told about patients communicating their courage and understanding in the context of their illness (see for example Lynn 1993; Remen 1996). Such stories, communicated beautifully, capture the qualities and depths of the human condition, which are inevitably encountered during the course of the lives of health professionals and lay-people alike.

Stories inevitably play a central role in counselling and psychotherapy. Studies of different psychotherapy models suggest that there is little difference in outcome between contrasting therapeutic orientations (Barkham 1992). However therapist variables appear to exert a strong influence on therapeutic outcome irrespective of theoretical orientation (Barkham 1992; Norcross & Arkowitz 1992). The quality of the therapeutic relationship can provide a space in which the patient is able to tell their story, and foster the feeling that their story is important (Schreiber 1996). This story telling and listening enables an exploration of meaning, the defining or re-defining of meaning, and this in itself may lead to a therapeutic outcome (Charlton 1991; Mair 1997).

The simple process of telling one's story can have therapeutic value, and good communication between patients and their practitioners is recognised as an important aspect of treatment. For example, evidence suggests that patients value the opportunity to talk to their doctors about their difficult life situations, and they stress the importance of feeling that the doctor understood their problems (Abyholm and Hjortdahl 1999). Clinician-patient communication styles that emphasise the psychosocial aspects of care have positive effects on both adherence to preventative health measures and health outcomes (Bertakis et al. 1998; Stewart et al. 1999; White and Malik 1999).

Case study 1

Consider the following case study, taken from clinical practice. The patient was referred to the Complementary Therapy Centre at Lewisham Hospital, South East London (Richardson 1995a,b, 1996, 1999) and was presented by the acupuncturist in a case presentation session:

A woman presents to the clinic for acupuncture treatment. She has been referred by her general practitioner with a clinical problem of 'chronic low back pain'. She is 54 years of age, she has had her back problem for 8 years and has been treated with a range of methods: bed rest, traction, physio-therapy, and non-steroidal anti-inflammatory drugs. She is also under the care of the orthopaedic team. The patient has no experience of acupuncture and is somewhat nervous and apprehensive about the consultation.

The acupuncturist begins to take a detailed history, asking questions that are unfamiliar to the patient. It becomes apparent during the history taking that the patient is also suffering from a frozen shoulder. The patient noticeably begins to relax. This is clearly a consultation where she is being taken seriously and the acupuncturist is taking time in listening to her history. The acupuncturist then asks a further question "How did you come to have this pain?". The patient draws a deep breath and says "You are the first person to ask me that". She then begins to weep. This is clearly an important moment in the consultation and the acupuncturist holds that moment and gently begins to explore it with the patient. "Perhaps you would like to tell me about it?" At this point the patient unpacks her story. When her son was 7 years old he started to have fits. The GP suggested that these were not serious and that the boy would grow out of them. But the fits got worse, no investigations were performed until he suffered some limb paralysis at the age of 19. Finally a brain scan revealed an inoperable tumour. Distraught and angry, our patient decided to care for her son at home. This she did until he died. However she was unaware of the range of possible services which could have supported her in this home care, and they were never offered. Consequently she struggled with the physical care which involved lifting and moving her son, who was by then aged 21. This resulted in physical damage to her back. The emotional care, the love and concern for her son, and her own distress, were intertwined with her anger with medical staff for failing to take his condition seriously and to investigate appropriately. Her physical and emotional state appeared to be unresolved after 8 years of 'treatment'.[1]

The outcome for this patient was a positive one. She was treated with a course of acupuncture, but only after she had been given the time and space during which she could tell her story to someone who was completely present for her. After three treatments her frozen shoulder was greatly improved. She was discharged following her sixth treatment, her physical problems resolved, and her emotional world had moved on to a place from which she could begin the lengthy process of healing.

A discussion with the practitioner following that first consultation re-vealed an interesting phenomena. The practitioner reported how she experi-enced the emotional distress and anger experienced by the patient, and felt the physical tension of the patient's back problem in her own back. The practitioner was also consciously aware that in allowing the patient to tell her story and share her distress, and in honouring the story, the healing space[2] the patient had been denied in previous treatments could be created. It was the practitioner's opinion that if the patient had not been able to unpack her story in that first consultation, she would still have a chronic back problem.

Empathy and intersubjectivity in clinical practice

The process described above might be interpreted as a form of empathy. The concept of empathy is fundamental to the healing relationship and could be defined as 'respect for and openness to the concerns of the patient and her family' (Levasseur & Vance 1993). Though empathy can clearly be used as a specific and conscious intervention, it is also possible that some of the positive outcomes of therapeutic interventions which are due to so called non-specific (placebo) effects, may result from the practitioner's mobilisation of empathy, either on a conscious or unconscious level. Empathy is a fundamental underpinning of the therapeutic relationship in counselling and psychotherapy. Empathy requires that the practitioner enter the private perceptual world of the other and becomes thoroughly at home in it (Rogers 1975).

Halpern (1993) suggests that clinical empathy is an 'emotional resonance' where the goal is to understand in a detailed and experiential way what the patient is feeling. Halpern suggests that this is a process that requires emotional engagement. The ability of a therapist to empathise and 'be with' a patient may, however, be constrained by that practitioner's own fears and anxieties. For example Jacobs (1989) reports:

> 'I may not like what a patient is doing. I may be angry. But I try to keep these feelings against a background of the overall dialogic attitude that I am maintaining. This dialogic attitude is often not communicated in words, really; it develops over time, and is more often sustained by non-verbal behaviour or by tone of voice than by any words spoken. In a few instances recently, when I confronted patients in my anger, I could really feel my ability to be with the patients in my anger and still be open and receptive to them. The vibrancy of the meetings was remarkable. This was very different from times when I have set limits out of my own frustration, been psychologically cut off from the patient's experiences, and wanted them to do something to make me feel better'.

Thus the practitioner's own feelings, perceptions and processes will affect his or her ability to enter into the patient's perceptual world and may determine the possibility of an intersubjective sharing between practitioner and patient.

It is possible to develop empathy through the exploration of the patient's narrative. Through narrative knowledge humans come to recognise themselves and each other, telling their stories in order to know who they are (Charon 1993). Much of the work of the clinician involves listening to patients' stories and making sense of their accounts of illness and how individual and family lives are affected. Charon suggests that it is only with narrative competence that a clinician can deliver empathic care. Through the process of listening to and telling stories it is possible for individuals to move into a shared space, where time seems to stand still and the boundaries between self and other appear to merge.[3] Where the distinctions between the storyteller and the listener dissolve, there is only the presence of the story.

Consider Figure 1 below. This figure is re-produced from a chapter by Velmans (1998) in a book on virtual realities. It is pictorial representation of a dream (my dream), in which people are enclosed in bubbles which are virtual worlds. While people are enclosed in their virtual worlds they engage in relationships, but there is no genuine contact between them. In intersubjectivity however, the boundaries of the bubbles become semi-permeable, and there is genuine engagement and openness to each other. This is the space in which empathy can exist.

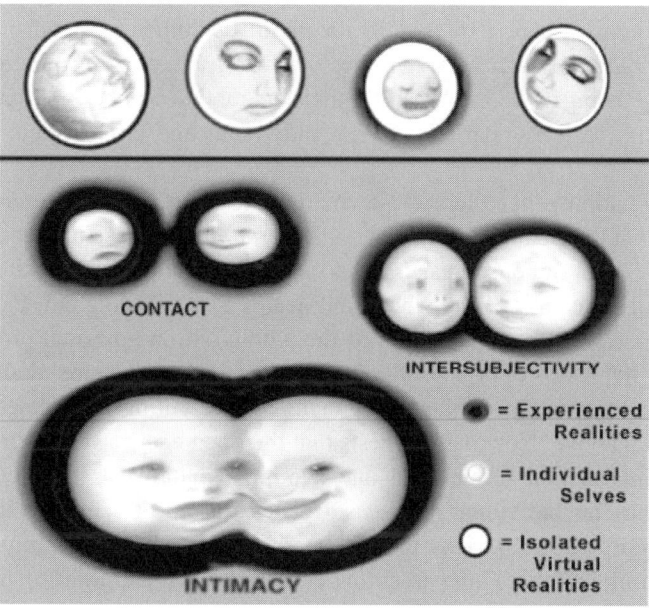

Figure 1. Experienced realities: Intersubjectivity in relationships

Health professionals reading this chapter may have observed a consultation where the patient and practitioner appear to be communicating, but real engagement is not taking place. The practitioner is 'in his head', taking in facts, working through patterns (under time pressure), and making notes, but he is not really engaged in the process. Consequently in his lack of engagement he misses vital cues which are not followed through. Or perhaps he decides that because of time pressure or his own fears and anxieties he is unable to explore some of the concerns the patient is expressing. He communicates to the patient that he is only seeking answers to his questions and does not require full elaboration (the patient's story). In contrast there are consultations that look something very like the intersubjectivity picture, where both patient and practitioner are fully present in the consultation, sharing the experience from their relative perspectives. However this 'intersubjective' form of engagement requires a degree of openness from the patient who has to be willing, under the appropriate circumstances, to share their experience with the practitioner. It also requires that the practitioner is comfortable in facilitating the process and sharing the patient's story. These themes of 'openness' and 'engagement' are explored in detail in a number of nursing theories (Rogers 1992; Newman 1994). In these theories human beings are described as 'unitary' beings who are 'open' in their interaction with their environment; there are no real boundaries between individual and environment (George 1995a).

In developing her theory, Newman drew on physicist David Bohm's discussion of implicate and explicate order, and Moss's presentation of love as the highest level of consciousness (George 1995b). For Newman, disease is a meaningful reflection of the whole and health is 'expanding consciousness'. Newman sees health as a 'pattern of the whole within a normal progression toward higher levels of organisation'. The 'open energy systems' described by Newman appear to be similar to the picture representing intersubjectivity in the diagram above. Newman suggests that the open energy systems remain in constant interaction, influencing one another's patterns as they evolve together. Thus an individual's dis-ease relates to and affects the patterns of others (George 1995b). This particular approach appears to imply that the separation of *Self* and *Other* is not as clearly defined as might be imagined. This approach also suggests that the ability to manifest 'openness' and 'engagement' may be a product of how aware individuals are of self, and the relationship of self to other.

Presencing and the healing effect

By following Newman's theory of interacting open energy systems and 'patterns' of expanding consciousness, it is possible to see similarities between her theory and the role of empathy and 'presence' in the therapeutic relationship. Indeed Newman (1994) states that the intention of nursing is to:

"enter into the process with the client to be present with it and live it, even if it appears in the form of disharmony, catastrophe, or disease".

Rowan (1998) suggests a therapeutic relationship that 'goes beyond empathy' which is similar to that outlined by Newman. He calls this 'linking' and describes a process by which one person's world overlaps with another's, where the practitioner can be with the patient from the inside and share their subjective experience. Robbins (1998) also describes a process which he suggests is a form of 'therapeutic presence' which requires openness and awareness of the intersubjective space between therapist and patient:

"In order to understand an experience, I must first feel its contours, touch the very texture of its existence, and take the substance of the interaction into my body".

The importance of understanding the experience of the patient is not new to nurses who, over thirty years ago were advised to get inside the skin of their patients in order to know what they need (Henderson 1960). The following case study is a lovely example of a brief moment of this demonstrated in clinical practice:

Case study 2

During my clinical and teaching work with an acute pain team in a general hospital, I was fortunate to observe and share this experience of clinical practice with a colleague. My colleague, a Clinical Nurse Specialist in Acute Pain is called to assess a patient. The patient is recovering from major surgery that she had two days earlier. She also has an unrelated chronic pain problem that was not fully assessed and treated prior to surgery. The nurse assesses the patient who is clearly in severe pain at rest. A further pain-killing drug exhausts what is available on the drug chart. The anaesthetist is called to revise the medication. While awaiting the anaesthetist the nurse shares the patient's feelings of helplessness. The nurse remembers what she knows about therapeutic touch and suggests to the patient that providing gentle support for her head might be useful. Removing the back of the bed and the pillows, the nurse gently cradles the patient's head, focusing her intention on supporting and being with the patient. When asked why she did this she later reported "I felt as if I was experiencing the patient's pain and distress and there was nothing I could do but be with that patient". She explained that she was aware of how therapeutic touch could be used as a way of communicating with patients, particularly when "There was nothing I could *say* that would help".

Nurses frequently use touch as a means of communication and to provide comfort to patients who are in pain or distress (Sayer-Adams and Wright 1995). Physical contact between nurse and patient may take place in different contexts and for different reasons. The physical contact in itself may contribute to a therapeutic outcome, though this is likely to be determined by the nature and purpose of the contact, and the intent of the nurse. For example instrumental touch is the deliberate physical contact made as part of a procedure, such as the dressing of a wound, whereas expressive touch, such as a hug to comfort a patient or relative, is a demonstration of concern and support. In contrast, therapeutic touch involves mobilising the *intent* of the nurse and the transferring of 'energy' in order to produce a positive therapeutic effect (Tutton 1991). A practitioner's awareness of self and his or her own personal stories will no doubt influence and empower that professional's *intent*, that is the ability to utilise *intention* therapeutically in the context of a healthcare relationship. Whether consciously using touch as a therapeutic intervention or providing some form of psychotherapeutic action in the context of nursing, it appears that there is something about the quality of the relationship and the quality of 'presence' that is important in the therapeutic interaction (Ersser 1991).

Benner (1984) demonstrates through phenomenological research, how a healing relationship between a patient and a nurse can positively affect the therapeutic outcome or the ability of the patient to deal with life-threatening illness. Benner provides examples of how a healing relationship, using therapeutic goals and intentions can help patients to change their behaviour, by helping them to interact in a more satisfying way with other people. In contrast to the dominance of cure in medicine, Benner's work emphasises the caring and empowering work of nursing and shows how this can have profound effects on patients' physical, social and emotional wellbeing. Benner's research of 'novice' and 'expert' nurses shows that several stages occur in the development of the healing relationship. The first, mobilising hope for the nurse and the patient, requires the nurse to recognise that the patient has the capacity to make positive life changes and then makes a conscious decision to help this. In this way, the patient's sense of hope is mobilised. In the second stage the nurse helps the patient to find an acceptable interpretation or understanding of the illness, pain, fear, anxiety or other stressful emotion. In the third stage the nurse assists the patient to use appropriate social, emotional or spiritual support, provided by the nurse and others, for example family. Once the healing relationship is established, subtle interventions and ways of 'being with' a patient appear to make a positive difference in recovery. Such skills are predominantly found in expert rather than novice nurses (Benner 1984). Benner suggests that this expert behaviour emerges out of a (personal) way of being, and of being in relation to others. However it is also possible that training, experience and confidence enable practitioners to work with patients in this particular way. Much of Western health care is focussed on procedures for gathering information and making a diagnosis (blood tests, x-rays and so on), and interventions to help patients to recover, such as surgery or drugs. The concept of *doing to* a patient is prevalent in Western medicine, whilst the notion of *being with* is not usually part of the health care curriculum, and is infrequently practised let alone understood. What Benner describes as 'presencing', is, on the surface, simply staying with the patient during a time of pain, discomfort or loss. It is however a form of communication which requires little verbal activity and is, to a large extent, dependent on the practitioner's own emotional/spiritual development and their sense of humanness.

This healing and caring approach taken by nurses might be defined as empathy, presencing, or intersubjectivity. It has been eloquently described by Henderson (1960: 4):

> 'The nurse is temporarily the consciousness of the unconscious, the love of the life of the suicidal, the legs of the amputee, the eyes of the newly blind, the means of locomotion for the infant, knowledge and confidence for the young mother, the voice for those too weak or withdrawn to speak'.

The therapeutic relationship and placebo effects

Attempts to understand the role of non-specific (placebo) effects in clinical practice are well documented (see for example White et al. 1985; Peters 2001). The terms 'placebo' and 'placebo effect' are often used interchangeably. However it is important to make a clear distinction between the two terms. A *placebo* is an inert substance used to persuade an individual that s/he has received an active, usually therapeutic, intervention. The *placebo effect* is an effect rather than a substance. It is mediated by undefined mechanisms which facilitate a therapeutic change, but which are usually viewed as less valid than pharmacological or other 'active' interventions (Watkins 1994). There is no evidence that the placebo effect differentiates between organic and mental illness, or that specific groups of the population are 'placebo responders' with a particular type of mentality (Wall 1996). In studies of pain (a multidimensional experience) all dimensions appear to be equally involved in the placebo response, either separately or together. The non-specific effects that bring about a placebo response can be extremely powerful, are complex in nature, and are thought to be an essential component of all forms of medicine and healing (Helman 1984; White et al. 1985; Lewith 1993).

The *power* of the placebo effect has been demonstrated in a number of studies (for example Cobb et al. 1959; Dimond et al. 1958; Moscucci et al. 1987). The *nature* and *cause* of such effects however are poorly understood, and have been attributed to an interaction of the self healing properties of the body, changes induced by therapist and environment, the cultural context, the power of expectancy and belief and physical/pharmacological interventions (Helman 1984).

Hodges & Scofield (1995) propose a 'healing model' as a primary mechanism underlying much of conventional and complementary medicine. This model incorporates many of the factors thought to bring about a placebo response, in particular the role of the therapeutic relationship. Within this model it is possible to conceptualise a 'healing effect' that potentially underlies and contributes to all forms of therapeutic intervention. Given the power of this effect, it might be more useful to view it positively rather than to be dismissive, and to attempt to mobilise it for the benefit of the patient.

Frank (1961) examined similarities between psychotherapy and placebo effects in medicine and suggested that some of the basic ingredients in all therapies include: arousing hope, emotional arousal, encouraging changed activity and encouraging new ways of understanding oneself and one's problems. Benner (1984) found that arousing hope was the first step in the development of the healing relationship in nursing. Frank (1984) suggested that different psychotherapeutic models shared the following therapeutic components: confiding relationship with a helping person, a healing setting, a conceptual scheme or myth to explain symptoms, and a ritual to help resolve symptoms. These components are clearly common to all therapeutic relation-ships from Western medical interventions to shamanic interventions (Helman 1990; Kakar 1982).

If 'relationship' is an important component of a therapeutic encounter then it is essential that this relationship can be evaluated and that practitioners can be taught how to maximise its effects. The following two sections of this chapter will explore the application of qualitative research methods in the context of an intersubjective science, and the use of education to foster an empathic therapeutic approach in clinical practice.

The use of qualitative research in intersubjective science

Polkinghorne (1991) suggests that quantitative and qualitative research meth-ods "are not oppositional: merely different". Quantitative research is grounded in deductive reasoning. Hypotheses are generated on the basis of prior knowl-edge in order to test a theory or set of propositions. Quantitative research is, therefore, most frequently applied to areas of research where much is already known. In contrast, where very little is known about the phenomena in question, inductive theory can be applied in order to bring new knowledge into view. This can be achieved through the use of qualitative research methods. Rather than test hypotheses, these are based on 'research questions', which are designed to gain a deeper understanding of phenomena and could lead to the generation of hypotheses at a future time.

Qualitative research is appropriate for asking questions about experience. Consider for example a patient with cancer. Observing the clinical signs such as blood cell count, tumour markers, and using diagnostic imaging will reveal the extent to which their cancer is responding to treatment. A quality of life survey will give an indication of the effects of the cancer and the treatment on the patient's life. However an in-depth qualitative interview will provide a deeper understanding of the patient's experience; it will reveal 'what it is like' to be that person.

Qualitative research is "multi-method in focus, involving an interpretive, naturalistic approach to its subject matter" (Denzin and Lincoln 1994: 2). A number of qualitative research methods exist, some of which are grounded in a particular philosophical perspective. It is impossible to summarise in this chapter the range of qualitative approaches available. Readers requiring greater details of methods and their respective philosophical positions should refer to Denzin and Lincoln (1994). However, a number of approaches will be mentioned here in order to illustrate their potential usefulness in an intersubjective science.

Ethnography

Ethnography relies substantially, or in part, on participant observation (Atkinson and Hammersley 1994). This approach seeks an understanding of a particular 'culture' where the culture is viewed as a system of knowledge used by those within it to interpret experience and generate behaviour (Aamodt 1991). There is a strong emphasis on exploring particular social phenomena. The ethnographer gathers data by observing the culture and making 'field notes'. They may also ask questions regarding the meaning of practices, behaviour and experiences. The 'culture' that is the focus of the research could, for example, be a breast clinic where women attend for chemotherapy. Through observations of the interaction between patients and nurses, the researcher might note that patients seem anxious about their treatment, but the anxious behaviour is reduced following an interaction with the nurse. Repeated observation of this expression of anxiety and its resolution might lead the researcher to interview the patients and ask them to:

"Tell me what it is like coming to the clinic"

In attempting to understand the culture of the clinic and how anxiety might be perceived and dealt with by the nursing staff the researcher might also interview the nurses and ask:

"How do you think patients feel when coming to the clinic for their treatment?"
"Is there anything you do to make them feel at ease?"

So in the ethnography, the researcher will observe and ask questions of others involved in the culture, such as the health professionals. The interview data will be interpreted in the context of the observations (field notes) in order to present a complete picture of the culture. In ethnographic research it is possible for the researcher to become so completely absorbed in the participant's experience that they are unable to separate this from their own reality. This is often defined as 'going native'.

Grounded theory and phenomenology

Narrative can provide a framework for understanding subjective (first-person) accounts in qualitative research (Sandelowski 1991). Language is the central medium for narrative research and the researcher encourages the participant to reveal their story. The purpose of the story in qualitative research is to enable the researcher to understand, interpret, and ultimately communicate to others, the lived experience of the participant. Depending on the theoretical tradition of the qualitative researcher, individuals' narratives may also be analysed for common themes that can lead to the generation of theories.

Phenomenology is concerned with the study and interpretation of subjective experience. According to Husserl, human consciousness actively constitutes the objects of experience (Holstein and Gubrium 1994: 263). As individuals we assume that the world we experience is similar to that experienced by others. "We take our subjectivity for granted, overlooking its constitutive character, presuming that we *intersubjectively* share the same reality" (Holstein and Gubrium 1994: 263). In interpretive phenomenology the researcher "seeks to understand the world of concerns, habits, and skills presented by participants' narratives " (Benner 1994: xiv).

Grounded theory is "a general method for developing theory that is grounded in data systematically gathered and analyzed" (Strauss and Corbin 1994: 273). It is a method that is applicable to quantitative and qualitative methodologies, but is particularly useful for the analysis of interview and focus group data. In contrast with phenomenology, interviews with patients and practitioners are explored and analysed in order to find common themes and to generate theories. In grounded theory the researcher moves towards producing theory based on the themes arising from the research, and the relationships between those themes (Strauss and Corbin 1994: 278). Grounded theory researchers are interested in patterns of action and interaction between and amongst participants, rather than creating theory based on the discourse of a particular individual. These patterns form an intersubjective reality for the participants and the resulting theory can be applied and further tested or developed within the wider community.

In qualitative research the researcher's own experience and knowledge will, to some extent influence their observations, questioning, and interpretation of data. Needless to say, important questions arise regarding the rigour of qualitative research. Such issues cannot be explored in full in this chapter.

They are however explained in some detail in a number of texts (for example Lincoln and Guba 1985; Morse 1991; Morse and Field 1996). Essentially, rigour in qualitative research is demonstrated through clarity in the data gathering, data analysis and interpretation process — for example by the use of an audit trail, and by attending to the key aspects of 'trustworthiness' set out by Guba and Lincoln (1985).

An intersubjective science of consciousness might explore relationship with self and others through the use of qualitative research methods. For example a researcher may be interested in the therapeutic process and the extent to which a shared understanding and experience of the process is taking place. Interviews would be focused on questions such as "what was your experience of the consultation?" "What was happening in the consultation?" The data would be analysed in order to identify shared themes suggestive of an overlap (or not) in the experience of the two people involved. Where conscious processes are to be the subject of investigation it is possible to use a qualitative approach to understand and interpret the effects of practices that are intended to alter conscious experience. By collecting qualitative data from a number of participants and identifying common themes/experiences, the data becomes 'intersubjective'. That is, the experience of one participant can be validated by similar experiences in others.

Developing the therapeutic relationship: The use of narrative and empathy in clinical practice

It may be possible to mobilise 'healing' factors by attending to patient expectations, the provision of good quality information, the use of deep relaxation (or hypnosis), and the use of distraction techniques. Perhaps fundamental to all these activities is the power of the relationship between patient and practitioner. Our ability as practitioners to work with narrative, to hear the story, and be open to the suffering is a good place to start. The healing process may begin in a particular point of focus and shared consciousness (or intersubjectivity), where the patient feels that their experience is deeply understood, and therefore their personhood is valued.

Charon (1993) suggests that practitioners can be taught to improve their narrative competence by:
– Writing from the patient's point of view. In particular, when a patient

consultation has resulted in the practitioner feeling angry or frustrated, it can be useful for them to think their way into the patient's circumstances, and feelings that may have contributed to the behaviour which resulted in the practitioner's own frustration.
- Reading serious fiction can exercise narrative skills and expose practitioners to other lives and realities.
- Recognising the way in which 'clinical' judgements may be influenced by the practitioner's own experiences. For example our own unheard stories and unfinished business.

Charon's approach to the development of narrative competence can also be used to enable practitioners to develop empathy. Arguably empathic care is fundamental to the assessment and management of pain. Whilst attempts to measure pain and the effectiveness of treatments are well documented (Turk and Melzack 1992), pain remains a private and personal experience. Factors such as age, gender and previous experience of pain influence pain perceptions (Carr 1997), but they also play a part in how practitioners assess pain. The patient who, following surgery, is seen laughing and joking with relatives may get a frosty reception from the nurse when he asks for pain relief as soon as his relatives have left the ward. The nurse may feel that the pain cannot be so bad, as a moment ago the patient was laughing. However this interpretation would reflect a serious misunderstanding about the role of attention in the perception of pain. One way of dealing with this is to facilitate an empathic understanding of the pain experience through the use of stories.

In a session where I was teaching hospital staff pain assessment and management, I asked participants to imagine, and write a story as if they were a patient in pain. They were encouraged to consider both their own experiences of pain, and their 'professional' experiences and observations of patients in pain. A hospital pharmacist wrote the story below. It demonstrates the practitioner's understanding of how chronic pain can affect a person's life. It also shows how it was possible for this young (healthy) professional to 'get under the skin' of an illness experience by allowing himself to consider the patient's perspective:

> "I wake up in the morning after what can be described as sleep. And the pain hits me. My knee's been in the wrong position all night and I know it's going to cause me grief all day. It takes me all my time to manoeuvre to the edge of the bed. And I feel sick as I endure the pain of bending the knee to stand up. I can feel the bones scraping together as my cartilage has been eroded away by

rheumatoid arthritis. My volterol takes the edge off it and my doctor tells me the methotrexate will slow down the progress of the disease, but isn't it too late for that? I'm already nearly crippled. Getting down the stairs is a nightmare. The pain is getting worse with every step. I need a new knee now! My hands are bent and twisted with the disease too, so eating breakfast takes a while. I get in the car and the pain returns as I bend the knee again. Every time I have to use the clutch the pain shoots through. Even the simplest thing like getting out of the car fills me with dread when every move is greeted with a stabbing pain from my eroded knee. Every night I go to bed and try to get as comfy as possible, knowing the pain will return after only 3–4 hours sleep. Knowing that the next day will start with pain again as soon as I wake".

Teaching in this way encourages professionals to consider the patient's story, and to develop their own narrative skills. It also helps them to begin to view the experience from the patients' perspective.

Conclusions

Narratives in research can reveal practices and concerns that are embedded in the social and moral culture of healthcare (Wros 1994). Through the development of an 'intersubjective science' and the use of qualitative and narrative research it is possible to begin to understand 'what it is like' for our patients. "That is, through the sharing of a similar experience, subjective views and descriptions of that experience potentially converge, enabling intersubjective agreement about what has been experienced" (Velmans 1999).

An intersubjective science could focus research on illness rather than disease. For example attempting to understand what it is like to live with chronic illness (Benner et al. 1994). This research approach, conducted within a rigorous methodological framework (see for example Benner 1994a), is not simply about developing an interesting form of inquiry. It could facilitate the healing professions in understanding the patients' experience. So that they are able to help patients to live with their illness, find meaning in the experience.

Perhaps our development as practitioners includes the process of empathy, the ability to 'be with' our patients, providing the 'presencing' to which Benner (1984) refers. If this quality of relationship can make important differences to therapeutic outcomes, these skills might need a more prominent place in the education of healthcare professionals. Katz (1963) suggests that with discipline, empathy or empathic understanding can become a fully reputable scientific technique, and that when empathy is used in a professional way, it becomes more consistently effective. Empathy requires openness, but it is important to acknowledge that being open also requires us to be vulnerable (George 1995b). By focusing on our own openness (in the context of our relationships with patients), and being aware of our personal stress and limitations, we might be more able to effect a therapeutic process. This way of 'being with' and working with patients requires us to consider how we might retain appropriate vulnerability, whilst ensuring that our own personhood remains intact.[4]

Although it is possible, through research, to tease out some of the variables that contribute to a therapeutic outcome (over and above the 'active' intervention), the interaction of social, cultural and personal factors remain complex. It may however be possible that some practitioners are, simply, more 'therapeutic' than others. Needleman (1985) talks of the indefinable, yet instantly recognisable qualities that manifest when a practitioner is also a 'healer'. These 'indefinable' qualities may be grounded in an intersubjective process. That is, an ability to move, through the use of narrative, empathy and openness, into a shared (healing) space with the patient. This is a space in which the world of the patient overlaps with the world of the practitioner, and where the 'doing' is less important than the 'being'.

Notes

1. This case (history) is presented to the reader as it was presented to the practitioner by the patient. It is not my intention to draw any conclusions or make any judgements about the professional management of the patient's son.

2. King (1990) provides an operational definition of 'space' where space exists in all directions, is the same everywhere, and is defined by the physical area known as "territory" and by the behaviours of those who occupy it. Space is characterised as universal, but may be personal, subjective, situational or dependent on relationships in the situation, or based on the individual's perception of the situation (George 1995c).
    In Newman's theory, 'space' is discussed in conjunction with time and movement on the basis of the following relationships (see George 1995b):

    (i)   time and space have a complementary relationship
    (ii) movement is a means by which space and time become reality
    (iii) movement is a reflection of consciousness
    (iv) time is a function of movement
    (v)   time is a measurement of consciousness

3. For example in my training in transpersonal counselling skills this 'space' was described as: the moment when the dialogue between counsellor and client becomes a dance, and

the room seems to disappear.

4.   One mechanism through which this vulnerability and openness can be contained is in relationship with another professional who acts as 'supervisor'. This is common practice for psychotherapists and counsellors, and is now a basic requirement in clinical nursing (clinical supervision).

Acknowledgements

I would like to thank Jessica Darling (Acupuncturist) and Karen Gardiner (Clinical Nurse Specialist in Acute Pain) for sharing their case studies with me. Also Julie O'Callaghan for sharing her research and Andrew Turton for allowing me to use his pain story.

References

Aamodt, A. M. 1991. "Ethnography and epistemology: Generating nursing knowledge." In: Morse J. M. (ed.). *Qualitative Nursing Research A Contemporary Dialogue*. California: Sage Publications.

Abyholm, A. S. and Hjortdahl, P. 1999. "Being believed is what counts. A qualitative study of experiences with the health service among patients with chronic back pain." *Tidsskrift for Den Norske Laegeforening*. 119 (11): 1630–2.

Atkinson, P. and Hammersley, M. 1994. "Ethnography and Participant Observation." In: Denzin, N.K. and Lincoln, Y.S. (eds) *Handbook of Qualitative Research*. California: SAGE Publications Inc.

Barkham, M. 1992. "Research on integrative and eclectic therapy." In: Dryden, W. (ed.) *Integrative and Eclectic Therapy: A handbook*. Buckingham, UK: Open University Press.

Beckman, H. and Frankel, R. 1984. "Evaluation of humanistic qualities in the internist." *Annals of Internal Medicine* 99: 720–24.

Benner, P. 1984. *From Novice to Expert: Excellence and Power in Clinical Nursing Practice*. California, USA: Addison-Wesley Publishing Company.

Benner, P. (ed.) 1994a. *Interpretive Phenomenology. Embodiment, Caring and Ethics in Health and Illness*. California: Sage.

Benner, P. 1994b. "The tradition and skill of interpretive phenomenology in studying health, illness and caring. In: Benner, P. (ed.) *Interpretive Phenomenology. Embodiment, Caring and Ethics in Health and Illness*. California: Sage.

Benner, P., Janson-Bjerklie, S., Ferketich, S., Becker, G. 1994. "Moral dimensions of living with a chronic illness." In: Benner, P. (ed,) *Interpretive Phenomenology. Embodiment, Caring and Ethics in Health and Illness*. California: Sage.

Bertakis, K.D., Callahan, E.J., Helms, L.J., Azari, R., Robbins, J.A., Miller, J. 1998. "Physicians practice styles and patient outcomes: differences between family practice and general internal medicine." *Medical Care* 36 (6): 879–91.

Britten, N. 1995. "Qualitative interviews in medical research." *British Medical Journal* 311: 251–3.

Carr, E. 1997. "Factors influencing the experience of pain." *Nursing Times* 93 (39): 53–54.

Charlton, B. G. 1991. "Stories of sickness." *British Journal of General Practice* June 222–223.

Charon, R. 1993. "The narrative road to empathy." In: Spiro, H., Curnen, M. G., Peschel, E., St James, D. (eds) *Empathy and The Practice of Medicine*. New Haven: Yale University Press.

Cobb, L.A., Thomas, G.I., Dillard, D.H, Merendino, K.A, Bruce, R.A. 1959. "An evaluation of internal mammary artery ligation by a double blind technique." *New England Journal of Medicine* 20: 1115–1118.

Denzin, N. K. and Lincoln, Y. S. (eds) 1994. *Handbook of Qualitative Research*. California: Sage Publications.

Dimond, E.G., Kittle, C.F., Crockett, J.E. 1958. "Evaluation of internal mammary ligation and sham procedure in angina pectoris." *Circulation* 18:7 12–713.

Ersser, S. 1991. "A search for the therapeutic dimensions of nurse-patient interaction." In: McMahon, R. and Pearson, A. (eds) *Nursing as Therapy*. London: Chapman & Hall.

Frank, J. D. 1961, 1984. *Persuasion and Healing: A Comparative Study of Psychotherapy*. 1st & 2nd edn John Hopkins University Press.

George, J.B. 1995a. *Nursing Theories: The Base for Professional Nursing Practice* (4th ed). New Jersey: Prentice Hall International Editions.

George, J.B. 1995b. "Margaret Newman." In: George, J. B. *Nursing Theories: The Base for Professional Nursing Practice* (4th ed). New Jersey: Prentice Hall International Editions.

George, J.B. 1995c. "Imogene M. King." In: George, J. B. *Nursing Theories: The Base for Professional Nursing Practice* (4th ed). New Jersey: Prentice Hall International Editions

Gersie, A. and King, N. 1990. *Storymaking in Education and Therapy*. London: Jessica Kingsley Publishers.

Gersie, A. 1991. *Storymaking in Bereavement: Dragons Flight in the Meadow*. London: Jessica Kingsley Publishers.

Gersie, A. 1997. *Reflections on Therapeutic Storymaking: The Use of Stories in Groups*. London: Jessica Kingsley Publishers.

Halpern, J. 1993. "Empathy: Using resonance emotions in the service of curiosity." In: Spiro, H., Curnen, M.G., Peschel, E., St James, D. (eds) *Empathy and The Practice of Medicine*. New Haven: Yale University Press.

Helman, C. G. 1990. *Culture Health and Illness*. 2nd Edition Oxford: Butterworth Heinmann.

Henderson, V. 1960 *The Basic Principles of Nursing Care*. London: International Council for Nurses.

Hodges, D. and Scofield, T. 1995. "The healing effect — Complementary medicine's unifying principle?" *Network* 58:3–8.

Holstein, J.A. and Gubrium, J.F. 1994. "Phenomenology, ethnomethodology, and interpretive practice." In: Denzin, N. K. and Lincoln, Y. S. (eds) *Handbook of Qualitative Research*. California: Sage Publications Inc.

Jacobs, L. 1989. "Dialogue in gestalt theory and therapy." *Gestalt Journal* 8(1): 25–37.

Kakar, S. 1982. *Shamans, Mystics and Doctors*. London: Mandala Books.

Katz, R. L. 1963. *Empathy: Its Nature and Uses*. New York Free Press.

King, I. 1990. *A Theory for Nursing: Systems, Concepts, Process*. Albany, NY: Delmar.

Kleinman, A. 1988. *The Illness Narratives: Suffering, Healing and The Human Condition*. USA Basic Books.

Landau, R. L. 1993. "….And the Least of these is empathy." In: Spiro, H., Curnen, M. G., Peschel, E., St James, D. (eds) *Empathy and The Practice of Medicine*. New Haven: Yale University Press.

Levasseur, J. and Vance, D. R. 1993. "Doctors nurses and empathy." In: Spiro, H., Curnen, M. G., Peschel, E., St James, D. (eds) *Empathy and The Practice of Medicine*. New Haven: Yale University Press.

Lewith, G.T. 1993. "Every doctor a walking placebo." In: Lewith, G. T and Aldridge, D. (eds) *Clinical Research Methodology for Complementary Therapies*. London: Hodder & Stoughton.

Lincoln, Y. S., and Guba, E. G. 1985. *Naturalistic Inquiry*. Beverly Hills, CA: Sage.

Lynn, J. 1993. "Travels in the Valley of the Shadow." In: Spiro, H., Curnen, M. G., Peschel, E., St James, D. (eds) *Empathy and The Practice of Medicine*. New Haven: Yale University Press.

Mair, M. 1989. *Between Psychology and Psychotherapy: A poetics of experience*. London: Routledge.

Mair, M. 1997. "Conversational Inquiry: Questioning our understanding." In: Richardson, J. and Velmans, M. (eds) *Methodologies for the Study of Consciousness: A New Synthesis*. Proceedings of An International Symposium.

Mellon, N. 1992. *Storytelling & The Art of Imagination*. Dorset: Element Books.

Morse, J. M. (ed) 1991. *Qualitative Nursing Research: A Contemporary Dialogue*. California: Sage Publications,

Morse, J. M., Field, P. A. 1996. *Nursing Research: The application of qualitative approaches*. Cheltenham, England: Stanley Thornes.

Moscucci, M., Byrne, L., Weintraub, M., Cox, C. 1987. "Blinding, unblinding, and the placebo effect: An analysis of patients' guesses of treatment assignment in a double-blind clinical trial." *Clinical Pharmacology & Therapeutics* 41 (3): 259–265.

Needleman, J. 1985. *The Way of the Physician*. London: Arkan.

Newman, M. A. 1994. *Health as Expanding Consciousness* (2nd ed). NY: National League for Nursing.

Norcross, J. C., Arkowitz, H. 1992. "The evolution and current status of psychotherapy integration." In: Dryden, W. (ed) *Integrative and Eclectic Therapy: A handbook*. Buckingham UK: Open University Press.

Peters, D. 2001. *The Placebo Response: Biology and Belief in Clinical Practice*. London: Churchill Livingstone.

Polkinghorne, D. E. 1991. "Two conflicting calls for methodological reform." *The Counselling Psychologist*. 19 (1):1 03–114.

Pope, C. and Mays, N. 1995. "Reaching the parts other methodologies cannot reach: An introduction to qualitative methods in health and health services research." *British Medical Journal* 311: 42–5.

Remen, R. N. 1996. *Kitchen Table Wisdom.* London: Pan Books.

Richardson, J. 1995a. "Complementary therapies on the NHS: The experience of a new service." *Complementary Therapies in Medicine* 3: 153–157.

Richardson, J. 1995b. "Complementary Therapy and Research Centre, Lewisham Hospital. *Health and Hygiene* 16: 111–115.

Richardson, J. 1996. "Non-conventional therapy in the NHS: Can it work?" *International Journal of Alternative and Complementary Medicine* July. 20–21.

Richardson, J. 1999 *Assessing the Impact of Complementary Therapy on Health Status: A Service Evaluation of the Benefits of Acupuncture, Homoeopathy and Osteopathy Using the SF-36 Health Survey and a Waiting List Control Group.* Unpublished PhD Thesis, King's College, London University.

Robbins, A. (ed) 1998. *Therapeutic Presence.* London: Jessica Kingsley Publishers.

Rogers, C. 1975. "Empathic: An unappreciated way of being." *Counselling Psychologist* 5(2): 2–10.

Rogers, M. E. 1992. "Nursing science and the space age." *Nursing Science Quarterly* (5):27–34.

Rowan, J. 1998. "Linking: Its place in therapy." *International Journal of Psychotherapy* 3 (3): 245–354.

Sandelowski, M. 1999. "Time and qualitative research." *Research in Nursing & Health.* 22 (1): 79–87.

Sayer-Adams, J. and Wright, S. 1995. *The Theory and Practice of Therapeutic Touch.* London: Churchill Livingstone.

Schreiber, R. 1996. "(Re)Defining my self: women's process of recovery from depression." *Qualitative Health Research* 6: 469–91.

Stewart, M., Brown, J. B., Boon, H., Meredith, L., Sangster, M. 1999. "Evidence on patient-doctor communication." *Cancer Prevention and Control* 3 (1): 25–30.

Strauss, A. Corbin J. 1994. "Grounded theory methodology." In: Denzin, N. K. and Lincoln, Y. S. (eds) *Handbook of Qualitative Research.* California: Sage Publications.

Turk, D. C., Melzack, R. 1992. *Handbook of Pain Assessment.* New York, USA: The Guilford Press.

Tutton, E. 1991. "An exploration of touch and its use in nursing." In: McMahon, R. and Pearson, A. (eds) *Nursing as Therapy.* London: Chapman & Hall.

Velmans, M. 1998. "Physical, psychological and virtual realities. In: Wood, J. *The Virtual Embodied: Presence, Practice, Technology.* London: Routledge.

Velmans, M. 1999. "Intersubjective science." *Journal of Consciousness Studies* 6 (2/3): 299–306.

Velmans, M. 2000. *Understanding Consciousness.* London: Routledge.

Wall, P. D. 1996. "The placebo effect." In: Velmans, M. (ed) *The Science of Consciousness Psychological, Neuropsychological and Clinical Reviews.* London: Routledge.

Watkins, A.D. 1994. "The role of alternative therapies in the treatment of allergic disease." *Clinical and Experimental Allergy.* 24: 813–825.

White, M. K. and Malik, T. 1999. "Teaching clinician-patient communication in the treatment of breast disease." *Journal of Womens Health* 8 (1): 39–44.

White, L., Tursky, B., Schwartz, G. (eds) *Placebo: Theory, Research and Mechanisms.* New York: The Guilford Press.

Wros, P. L. 1994. "The ethical context of nursing care of dying patients in critical care." In: Benner, P. (ed) *Interpretive Phenomenology. Embodiment, Caring and Ethics in Health and Illness*. California: Sage Publications.

CHAPTER 9

The Nature and Transformation of Consciousness in Eastern and Western Psycho-Spiritual Traditions

David Fontana
University of Cardiff

The enduring fascination of consciousness research

Leading neurosurgeon Sir John Eccles once posed the question 'Why do we have to be conscious at all? We can in principle explain all our input-output performances in terms of the activity of the neuronal circuits; and consequently consciousness seems to be absolutely unnecessary' (Eccles 1976). And yet consciousness is there, and has intrigued men and women from the beginnings of recorded history, as evidenced by the analyses of levels of consciousness first referred to nearly 3,000 years ago in the Upanishads, and greatly enlarged upon during subsequent centuries in the Brahma-Sutras, in the Bhagavad Gita, in the writings of Yogacara Buddhism and in those of Plato, Plotinus, and other notables in the various civilisations that flourished around the Mediterranean Basin in the centuries before and after the Common Era (for surveys of the Eastern and Western traditions respectively see e.g. Nielsen et al. 1988, and Godwin 1981).

We can admire not only the complexity of the models of consciousness arising from these analyses, but also the activities of mind which the sages associated with them practised and taught, and which perhaps have scarcely been bettered as exploratory and transformational tools. As we examine aspects of these models and activities we can identify common features among them and among the great traditions with which they are associated such as Vedanta, Buddhism, Jainism, and Taoism in the East, and gnostic and mystical Christianity, the Hebrew Kabbalah, and the various mystery traditions in the West.

It is impossible as yet to know what prompted the sages concerned and now prompts modern man to inquire into the nature of consciousness, but there is no doubt that it is our direct experience of conscious processes — together with our ability to reflect upon these processes — that allows us to pursue this inquiry. No matter how sophisticated our methodology and our instrumentation for exploring the outer world (including our own brains), it is our capacity for direct experience that is the ultimate tool in consciousness research. Yet in spite of its central role in our effort towards inquiry and understanding, science has never been particularly happy with the concept of a psychology of direct inner experience. The private nature of this experience, together with the absence of an agreed language for communicating much of what it reveals, leaves scientists unable to approach it with the degree of objectivity available to them in other fields of endeavour, and regarded as essential for the operation of disciplinary rigour.

Western science and the neglect of consciousness

The reluctance of Western science to engage fully with a psychology of inner experience is understandable, but has left us with a major gap in our knowledge of what it means to be human. Indeed, it would be accurate to say that in the Western world we have learned more about how individuals experience themselves and their relationship with the outer world from the arts than from the sciences. Poets, dramatists and novelists have presented us with much profounder insights into our experiential selves than have psychologists and social scientists — a state of affairs which helps explain the enduring popularity of the arts, and the reason why many find the sciences unattractive and lacking in real relevance to self-understanding. People recognise in the arts representations with which they can identify, and which mirror and to some extent resolve their multivarious human concerns.

Theology and philosophy have rivalled the arts in their readiness to explore inner experience, theology with its concern for that least material of all supposed human attributes — the soul and for the mystical states associated with it, and philosophy with its concern to address questions on the nature, meaning and purpose of mind. However, although developing largely from these philosophical concerns, the fledgling subject of psychology quickly abandoned them in favour of methodologies based upon those of the physical sciences, and which hold that only phenomena which can be observed and quantified, and whose qualities can be assessed and agreed upon by more than one observer, are appropriate for exploration. Incidentally, in turning its back upon human experience, psychology also turned away from one of its founding fathers, William James, who wrote "experience moulds us every hour, and makes of our minds a mirror of the time- and space-connections between the things in the world" (James 1890: 619).

The two major forces that dominated psychology prior to the development of humanistic and later transpersonal psychology, namely behaviourism and psychoanalysis, were concerned respectively with responses to stimuli from without and stimuli from within, rather than with a recognition that in actual experience the individual and the environment are inextricably intertwined, and in effect co-constitute each other. Neither behaviourism nor psychoanalysis, for all their undoubted value, operated on the premise that neither the individual nor the environment have psychological meaning when viewed independently of each other. A true psychology of experience requires not only a recognition of this inter-dependence, but also of the ability of the individual to operate as an active agent who can reflect upon experience, make choices between different options, manifest intentionality, and engage in what existential-phenomenological psychology refers to as *prereflection* (a form of knowing which appears to exist before it finds expression in cognitive manifestation, somewhat akin to the innate pattern-making quality recognised by gestalt psychology — see e.g.Valle and Mohs 1998).

The value of the great traditions

We therefore have a particular need to supplement knowledge derived from Western psychology with the results derived from direct experience by the traditions — and particularly by the Eastern traditions — to which I have just referred. Before discussing how this might best be done however, it is necessary to confront the issue of accuracy. How accurate are the models derived from the Eastern traditions likely to be? What warrant do we have for regarding them as having anything of value to tell us about consciousness? Might not these models be hopelessly inadequate for our needs? The way in which such models can be put to possible test will be discussed in due course below, but our initial excuse for extending a degree of provisional credibility to them is that they have stood the test of time. Rather like the hold that the arts have upon human attention, they would seem to have endured because people recognise in them aspects of themselves. Further, by working with the practical techniques associated with these models, individuals have made inner discoveries which again accord with what these models tell them.

Good psychology takes into consideration the accounts that people give of themselves — indeed regards these accounts as part of the essential raw material of the subject. Once heeded, these accounts can and should be subjected to careful scientific scrutiny, but in and of themselves, particularly if they manifest uniformity and consistency, they serve as an essential starting point for psychological investigation. This is perhaps especially so of accounts of inner experience, and in the present context of accounts of inner experience that show common features across the long-established Eastern and Western traditions under current discussion. Given their complexity and ubiquity, the task of explicating these models is well beyond the scope of one short chapter. So the most practical way of approaching them is to look for these common features — an approach which has the additional value of allowing us to identify the most powerfully affirmed aspects of the models concerned.

Common features among the great traditions

The most obvious of these common features is the belief that normal consciousness is only a very small part of our potential for inner experience. Another prominent feature is the conviction that the purpose of human life is to realise the fullness of this potential, and thus to achieve identification with the source from which it arises. A third common feature is that one passes through a number of interconnected levels on the way to realising this potential. Buddhism identifies 26 such levels, but rather than use these I am going to draw upon the largely compatible Advaita model in Vedantic Hinduism (articulated in particular by the 9th Century philosopher Shankara) which Wilber (1993) calls the most spectacular and consistent system of all, a judgement which my own experience leaves me happy to accept. The Advaita model recognises 19 levels, but without grave injustice these can usefully be condensed into five major ones, of which the remainder can be seen as subsections. Of these five, three can in turn be grouped under a single heading, as indicated at the appropriate point below.

The Advaita-Vedanta model of consciousness

The lowest level of consciousness recognised in the Advaita model is the *material level*, a level at which we identify consciousness exclusively with sense data, and the self is seen as synonymous with the physical body. Almaas (1988) puts it that through this identification with the physical body,

> Consciousness becomes increasingly anchored in physical reality... It becomes less aware of the dimension of Being and, in most instances, loses its contact with it. The unity of Being is lost, and the world appears more and more fundamentally physical. (Page 282)

The term 'Being', as used here by Almaas, can be taken to mean what the great traditions refer to as the source from which human life arises, and about which more will be said when we come to discuss the highest level of consciousness in the Advaita model in due course. Essentially the point being made is that by identifying consciousness with the material substance of the physical body we come to convince ourselves that materiality is the primary force behind being, and that the way to explore being is therefore through the material world. Attempts by Western scientists to equate consciousness with brain functioning would be seen by the great traditions as belonging to this material level of thinking, and the high intelligence of those scientists whose work engages only with this level would therefore not be regarded by the great traditions as evidence of advanced levels of consciousness.

The next three levels of consciousness in the Advaita model, in ascending order, are the *vital*, in which consciousness becomes aware of the mortal nature of the body, and experiences the will towards its preservation; the *discriminative* in which consciousness begins to categorise the objects and the events presented to it by experience, and in which it may recognise that there is an important categorical distinction between turning inwards towards the non-material world of thought, intuition, and perhaps spiritual awareness, and turning outwards towards physical sensation and the material world; and the *ratiocinative* in which consciousness is characterised by the capacity for analytical and rational thought, and evidences itself in the higher levels of abstract thinking, philosophical debate and advanced theory-building.

Above these is the fifth level, known as the *causal*, which consists of pure contentless awareness, sometimes referred to as consciousness in and of itself, the ground from which consciousness with content arises. Such a level is almost impossible to describe adequately to those who have not experienced it. At each of the previous levels we are conscious *of* something, whether it be sense data registering the presence of the outer world, or thoughts arising from our own minds. At the causal level, consciousness is said to be pure and clear, present in all its fullness, but not clouded by the arising and passing away of sensation or of mentation. In Buddhism, an appropriate metaphor for this state is the cloudless sky, spacious and unsullied, self-existent and timeless.

It is important to recognise that there is nothing necessarily spiritual or mystical about the first four levels of consciousness. Each of them can be used in different ways. As the child develops, he or she will usually acquire at least the first three of them. It is also important to recognise that the earlier levels are not left behind in the course of this development but carried with us (a useful analogy would be with Brunerian as opposed to Piagetian theories of cognitive development), and that we can be operating at more than one of these levels at the same time. Thus an advanced thinker may be operating at the ratiocinative level, but may also be so firmly located at the material level that his or her erudite theory building is entirely concerned to explain everything in material terms (as e.g. would a convinced Darwinian). On the other hand, he or she may see the material level as relating only to a limited range of experience, and may use ratiocination to explain things in non-physical terms (as e.g. would an avowed Platonist).

Varying experiences of consciousness

Crucially, the Advaita model recognises that as consciousness become more developed and advances through the various levels, it gains the potential to see reality in different ways, even though this potential may not be put to use. At the material level, consciousness does not allow us to see this reality in other than material terms. A gross level of consciousness only enables us to see a gross universe. However, our capacity to see behind this grossness increases as consciousness becomes more refined, so that by the time we reach the causal level we are able to recognise — through direct experience as did Shankara and other Hindu sages of many centuries ago — that reality consists of a unified energy field in which the world of form, the individual, and the unitary source of all phenomena (the Divine, the Absolute) are ultimately identical with each other.

The four levels of consciousness below the causal level are described in the Advaita model, as we move back downwards, as representing increasingly limited aspects of our consciousness. But the model recognises a further level, this time above the causal and off the scale so to speak, which is referred to as *Brahman*, that is the primal, undifferentiated, unitary source of all phenomena, i.e. the very Divine or Absolute from which all else arises. In the Hindu pantheon Brahman is the divine aspect above the manifest trilogy of *Brahma* (the creator), *Vishnu* (the preserver), and *Siva* (the agent of change). The direct parallel within Christianity is with what Eckart and other mystics referred to as the Godhead, the ground of our being, which lies beyond the Trinity of Father, Son and Holy Spirit. Brahman, like the Godhead (and *Nirvana* in Buddhism, and *Ishatpragbhara* in Jainism) is that Absolute being or state, call it what one will, about which nothing definitive can be said, because whatever terms we use impose limitations upon it, and therefore cannot be other than partial and thus incorrect. Brahman is that refined level of consciousness, above even the content-less awareness of the causal level, which can only be directly experienced in the deepest level of mystical experience (termed *nirvikalpa samadhi* in Sanskrit), and which cannot be put into words. The Buddhist Lankavatara Sutra puts it that "The highest Reality is unthinkable", and is thus empty (or void) of the limited consciousness operative at all levels right up to the point at which the causal level is realised.

If the highest Reality or Brahman level of consciousness is only experienced by enlightened beings such as the Buddha and Christ, we lesser mortals had better restrict our discussion to the five, more effable, levels that lie below it. In the Sanskrit terminology used by Advaita Vedanta, the causal level is referred to as the bliss body of consciousness (Sanskrit *karana-sarira*), the ratiocinative, discriminatory and vitality levels collectively as the subtle body (*suksma-sarira*), and the material level as the gross body (*annamayakola*). For convenience I shall use these three Sanskrit terms to refer to these broader groupings.

A fourth common feature among the great traditions is that the consciousness of the great sages in both Eastern and Western traditions is said to run continuously throughout waking life, dreaming sleep and dreamless sleep (this phenomenon is well known in the East, less so in the West, but see Regardie 1972 for a reference to its authenticity in the Western traditions). Consciousness of this kind is difficult for many of us even to imagine. However, in dreaming sleep it would seem to be comparable to (perhaps identical with) the phenomenon now known to Western science as lucid dreaming, a form of dreaming in which the dreamer is fully aware of the fact that he or she is dreaming, and is able in consequence to take control of the dream state (see e.g. LaBerge 1985). Consciousness in dreamless sleep can perhaps best be thought of as a state akin to the deep meditation of *karana-sarira* (causal) consciousness, in which the mind is fully aware, but serenely empty of all content.

Other common features among the great traditions

The descending hierarchy of consciousness represented by *karana-sarira, suksma-sarira* and *annamayakola* is sometimes referred to as an evolution away from Brahman, and a fifth common feature among the great traditions is that a broadly equivalent hierarchy of descent (though some of the details differ). This is found in Buddhism, where it is spoken of as a progressive movement away from the Dharmadhatu. It is also found in Christian mysticism and Gnosticism where it is described as a progressive exile from the Godhead, in Jainism where it is thought of as movement away from Kaivalya, in Hebrew Kabbalism where it becomes a descent from Ain Soph, and in Taoism where it is said to be a progressive loss of harmony with the Tao.

A sixth common feature is that all the above traditions agree that thinking, as an activity, can impede attempts to raise consciousness from *annamayakola* to *karana-sarira*. If consciousness is lost in undisciplined thinking — the kind of discursive stream-of-consciousness thinking in which we typically spend so much of our time — it is heedless to the subtle inner states which lead towards *karana-sarira*. A further hindrance to the development of consciousness — stressed more in the Eastern traditions than in the Western — is our tendency to think always in terms of opposites. This oppositional thinking leads to an essentially individualised, even fragmented view of reality, and thus one which is at odds with the concept of the underlying unity said to be experienced in *karana-sarira*. Nagarjuna, the second/third century founder of the Buddhist

Madhyamika philosophy and one of the greatest of Eastern thinkers, pointed out that each linguistic proposition excludes its opposite, and therefore all such propositions are purely relative, and no relative statement can adequately describe the true nature of reality (see e.g. Williams 1989).

An assault upon the meaning of self

The complexities and subtleties of the models proposed by Vedanta and the other great traditions represent in fact nothing less than an attempt to recognise the very source from which our consciousness arises. We may well consider it impossible for an apparently self-contained system such as consciousness to comprehend the totality of itself, but to the traditions concerned consciousness is seen not as self-contained but as a fluid, open dynamic which stretches into the infinity beyond *karana-sarira.*

Many Western scientists are paying increasingly attention to the hierarchical models of consciousness enshrined in the great traditions, with Buddhist versions attracting the greatest attention, probably because Buddhism is better-known in the West than is Advaita Hinduism (in spite of the attention focused upon the latter by influential writers such as Isherwood and Huxley — e.g. Isherwood 1963). One of the many reasons for this attention is that Eastern models link consciousness closely with concepts of the self, concepts that have proved particularly troublesome for Western philosophy and more recently Western psychology. The fundamental issue addressed in Eastern thought is whether we are conscious of a self (or more accurately, whether self is present in *karana-sarira*), or whether consciousness creates a self for us. In other words, is self something enduring beyond the ever-changing flux of conscious thinking, or is it simply a feature of this flux?

However, problems arise for Westerners not only over the precise meanings of the original Pali, Sanskrit, Tibetan or Chinese texts in which the self is discussed in Eastern psychology, but from a failure adequately to take account of the religio-cultural milieu from which this psychology arose, and within which it went through its various stages of development. Many Western commentators have little knowledge of this milieu, and show in addition the Western tendency mentioned earlier towards oppositional thinking. Eastern thinkers are often more at ease with a 'both and' rather than an 'either or' approach to fundamental questions. To the Westerner — and particularly to the Western scientist — a 'both and' approach introduces paradox. Thus to the Westerner the self is either an enduring reality, or a transient creation of the conscious mind. To the Eastern thinker, the self is both of these things, and needs to be understood differently at each of the five levels at which consciousness operates. At *annamayakola* the self is a creation of consciousness, linked essentially to the body and to the material world, and as transient as the body and material existence. It was this self that the Buddha denied as enduring (*anatta*). At the level of *karana-sarira* by contrast, the self (the *Atman,* often written in translation as the Self) is seen as identical with *Brahman*, the Absolute (see e.g. Krishnananda 1969). It is this self to which one of the classics of Buddhist literature (the *Dhammapadha*) refers when it tells us "The Self is lord of self".

This insistence that our real nature is not discoverable if consciousness is operating only at the *annamayakola* or *suksma-sarira* levels is a seventh unifying feature among the great traditions. Buddhism shows particular reticence in defining what lies behind the illusory *atta* or self-identity with which normal consciousness usually identifies itself. The Buddha is said to have maintained a 'noble silence' (i.e. the silence of one who knows but does not speak) when questioned about it, preferring to teach practices for its realisation, rather than to attempt the impossible by putting it into words. In his view such an attempt is as profitless as the attempts by some non-Vedantic Hindus to speculate about the nature of Brahman. As Wilber (1993) points out, thinking about our own essential nature only succeeds in creating a dualistic separation from it. Instead, "We are always already directly in touch with ... (it) ..., but we cannot see It, name It, or think of It, for in so doing we turn it into an illusory object! ... If my eye tries to see itself, what will it see? Totally, completely, absolutely, it will see nothing!" (1993: 320).

Wilber goes on to say "We postpone our awakening, we postpone seeing what is already the case because we insist on retaining the primary dualism, on seeing It as an object, as something we can grasp or perceive, while It actually is that in us right now which is trying to grasp and perceive!" (1993: 321). In other words, that which is looked for is that which is looking. We are each the answer to our own question — in fact, question and answer are one and the same. When we realise this (by direct experience, not by precept), we have reached the level *karana-sarira*.

The path of the great traditions

To know, as opposed to supposing or believing, that ultimate reality is not to be found in the world of form or in deconstructionist, reductionist paradigms, but within the mysteries of consciousness itself, requires a tremendous, transformative leap by that same consciousness. Such a leap involves the realisation that far from being secondary to matter and to sense data, consciousness is in fact primary. As the Vedantists emphasised over two thousand years ago, this primary consciousness is in fact one indivisible whole, with individual consciousness both a reflection of it, and the thing in itself (another — and prime — example of the paradox to which reference has just been made). Thus if we realise the indwelling Atman or the Buddha mind or the Christ within, we realise Brahman and thus the nature of all things.

This teaching is echoed in the belief at the heart of the Western Hermetic mystery tradition, rooted in ancient Egypt, that Macrocosm and Microcosm are one ('as above, so below'), the latter merely the visible manifestation of the former (Regardie ibid., 1972). From within the Christian mystic tradition, Eckart put it that "For in that essence of God which is above being and distinction, there I was myself.. ." (see e.g. Walshe 1981). And in one of the most overlooked passages of the New Testament, St. John tells us that ".... as many as received him, to them gave he power to become the sons of God" (John 1:12).

This 'consciousness only' (or 'mind only') philosophy, a form of subjective idealism, is in fact apparent at exalted levels in every one of the great traditions. In answer to Eccles' earlier question as to the purpose of consciousness it affirms that we are conscious because consciousness is the root of everything else. Such an understanding is now apparent in the thinking of some physicists. Goswami puts it that 'not matter but consciousness is the stuff of creation, being constitutive of all things, and the true foundation of knowledge, perception and understanding' (Goswami et al. 1995), with quantum nonlocal correlations an actual expression of the nonlocality of consciousness.

The transformation of consciousness

An eighth unifying feature among the great traditions is that the transformation of consciousness depends crucially upon discarding the notion of the small, deluded self — 'dying to self' as Western mysticism puts it, or rejecting a 'taking-on of self' as the Buddha had it. This is done either by surrendering to a greater power (to God in Christianity, to Amitabha Buddha in Pure Land Buddhism, to one of the many manifestations of Brahman in Hinduism), or by a minute self-analysis which reveals the empty nature of the self with which we normally identify (as in Advaita Vedanta or Zen Buddhism). Such transformation leads not to the loss of individual consciousness, but to its expansion into universal consciousness (Aurobindo 1957). The Hindu sages described this as the dewdrop slipping into the shining sea, but one can equally well say that the dewdrop realises it is the shining sea.

A ninth feature is the stillness of mind, as in meditation, in which much of the work upon consciousness must be done (some of the similarities between the meditation techniques used by the great traditions are covered in Fontana 1992). A tenth feature is the need for awareness, or mindfulness. We are constantly admonished to 'wake up' in order to experience the direct reality of being alive. Various techniques are given to help in this awakening (see e.g. Tart 1988), all of which emphasise the need for concentration, and for a contemplation of experience that is no longer overlaid by linguistic preconceptions and preconditions (stripped of preconceptions, even time emerges not as a dimension of reality but simply as a process of change). Direct contemplation allows us to develop what Buddhism calls 'right view', a perception of the world as it really is, without delusions.

An eleventh feature is the creative use of imagination, in particular of visual imagination. As consciousness is considered primary, the images and visions held within the mind at all levels below *karana-sarira* are believed to have a profound effect upon our experience of the outside world and of ourselves. In order to purify this inner theatre, the Buddhist builds up a highly detailed mental picture of the Buddha, replete with the symbols of all his various attributes, and then visualises the absorption of this image into his own being, thus internalising the qualities of the Buddha — or, if we prefer to put it a rather different way, awakening the inborn Buddha-like potentialities that are already there. The Christian mystic uses images of Christ (readers unfamiliar with the place of visualisations in Christian meditation may like to consult *The Spiritual Exercises* of Ignatius Loyola — see e.g. Corbishly 1963), the Hindus use images of Vishnu, Siva or Krishna, the Jains images of jinas such as Parshva or Mahavera, the Taoists images of Kuan Yin or of one or other of the eight immortals.

A twelfth unifying principle, and the last for which I have space (there are others), is the emphasis placed by each of the great traditions upon non-attachment to the world of form. This is a subtle concept often taken to mean indifference, but the real meaning is non-attachment to the greed or hostility within ourselves that covets and acquires on the one hand, and hates and destroys on the other (referred to for convenience in Buddhism as grasping and aversion). The non-attachment experienced by the transformed consciousness is said to feel love and compassion for all things, yet to desire nothing for itself. One of the most important — and the most difficult — steps in the development of this non-attachment is to cease identification with the body and therefore with its various desires. As we have seen, the *annamayakola* (material) level of consciousness is characterised by identification of consciousness with the physical body, an identification which leads us to see sense data and the material world as primary reality.

Efforts to bring about the cessation of one's identification with the body have been prominent in all the great traditions. They lie behind the practices of religious asceticism, of self-denial, chastity, fasting and even of physical self-mortification found in these traditions, and our revulsion at some of the excesses engaged in by certain practitioners should not blind us to the fact that the original purpose behind the practices was not denial or repudiation of the body and of the physical world, but a recognition of the need to raise one's levels of consciousness above *annamayakola*. Except in the Western Gnostic traditions, the material world was not seen as bad in itself. In fact, as already made clear, at the highest level of realisation it was recognised as one with the Absolute (primary consciousness), and one with our individual consciousness. But the identification of consciousness only with the body was regarded as leading to the deluded view that matter, as it presents itself to us through the gross consciousness of *annamayakola*, is the real stuff of existence.

To assist the process of disidentification, one of the oldest forms of meditation practised within the Hindu tradition employs a mantra consisting of the words 'I have a body, but I am not the body'. Sometimes the further words are added 'I have thoughts, but I am not my thoughts', which brings us to a second, equally important part of the transformation process, namely the acquisition of control over the processes of thinking. Again, there is no real suggestion that thinking is bad in itself. In fact, thought is recognised as one of the most powerful and valuable tools of consciousness. But the unbridled use of thinking, as indicated earlier in the chapter, is regarded by all the great traditions as a major hindrance in the development of consciousness. Just as consciousness can identify itself with the physical body and with sense data at the *annamayakola* levels, so at *suksma-sarira* it can identify itself with thinking. One of the first discoveries one makes in meditation is that when thought ceases — as it will do, even if only fleetingly in the early stages — consciousness is nevertheless still there. Except in the case of the very advanced meditator consciousness is unlikely to be operating at the *karana-sarira* level, and there will still in all probability be some awareness of sense data such as sounds and bodily sensations, but thoughts will no longer form the persistent content of consciousness, and the meditator will come to recognise the truth of the mantra that we have thoughts, but are indeed not our thoughts.

A third vital step in the development of consciousness common to all the great traditions — and again related to thinking — is what the Buddhists call 'mindfulness'. Instead of being lost in thought as one goes about daily life, consciousness is kept focused clearly and steadily upon whatever it is one is doing. In Zen Buddhism this is expressed in such teachings as 'when walking just walk, when sitting just sit, when eating just eat'. In monastic life, whether Eastern or Western, periods of silence during meals and at other times of the day (even, in some closed Western monastic orders, throughout waking life) are used as an aid to this mindfulness. The whirling 'dance' of the Dervish order within Sufism, in which the practitioner keeps his mind firmly fixed on the awareness that as he spins he is turning always towards God, is another example. Kinhin, the Buddhist walking meditation, in which the walker takes small very slow steps with the mind focused upon each minute sensation as he or she does so, is yet another. In all these practices, consciousness is seen as separate from thoughts or from the body; it observes and notes what the body is doing, but without involvement or identification. In Tibetan Buddhism the use of small hand-held prayer wheels which the practitioner keeps constantly spinning, and the Jesus prayer ('Lord Jesus Christ Son of God, have mercy upon me') repeated silently and unceasingly or whispered by Orthodox Christian monks are further examples. In all these practices, if extraneous thoughts arise, they are viewed with the same detachment as one views the movements of the body.

The relevance of higher states of consciousness

At the risk of straying too far into the field of values, the question as to why we should concern ourselves with whether or not such a state of consciousness as *karana-sarira* actually exists needs to be addressed. A further question might be whether or not, if such a state does exist, it is anything more than a curiosity. Some might argue in fact that it borders upon the pathological, and is actively counter-productive in terms of human effort and achievement.

These questions can be taken together. We have an impressive body of literature from the great traditions that the state is a reality, and that it appears to have a profound effect upon the subsequent behaviour of those who experience it. The founders, and indeed many of the major figures within these great traditions, appear to have experienced it, and their impact upon world history has been far-reaching. It might in fact be fair to say that they have been responsible for shaping much of the civilisation of both the Eastern and the Western worlds. This is not the place to argue whether or not the civilisation that has resulted is superior to what might have emerged in the absence of the great traditions. Judgement here must rest upon personal conviction rather than upon the weighing of often highly conflicting evidence. But there is no denying that at their best the traditions have added immeasurably to social cohesion, to education, and to man's concept of himself and life's purpose. Arnold Toynbee puts it that what he calls the 'essential truths' taught by the great traditions are valid without regard to time or space, and are indispensable for human life — without them in fact humanity would not be human (Toynbee 1956).

To this we can add the cultural impact of what appear to be *karana-sarira* experiences. Much of the world's greatest architecture, music, painting, sculpture, philosophy and literature has been produced in homage to those who have had such experiences — Christ, the Buddha, Mohammed, Padmasambhava, Mahavira, and semi-mythological figures such as Krishna. Many of these works may well have been created by artists who had themselves experienced *karana-sarira*. This may be true of the anonymous artists responsible for Greek sculpture, and who worked in the belief that the perfect form was already present within the stone, and required only to be revealed by the hand of someone inspired by the deity concerned. It is said to be true also for the builders of Europe's gothic cathedrals, and it is probably true for Bach, Verdi and many other creators of sacred music. The icons which are such a feature of the great art of the Greek and Russian Orthodox Churches are claimed always to be created while the artist is in a higher state of consciousness and at one with the divine or saintly beings he is portraying. The Gregorian chants which are such a feature of the Roman Catholic Church were not only created while the musician was in a higher state, but were intended to raise the consciousness of the listener to the same exalted level.

Leaving aside for the moment the more directly claimed spiritual benefits of karana-sarira consciousness, it would seem therefore to be a particular aid to creativity (from wherever one believes creative inspiration to arise), possibly in the sciences as well as in the arts (see e.g. Ghiselin 1952 for an anthology of first-hand accounts of the creative process). The reality and the relevance of *karana-sarira* would therefore appear to be well-attested by history. The extent to which succeeding generations have identified with the teachings of the great traditions and have appreciated the sacred art and architecture associated with them also seem to discount the notion that there is anything pathological per se about it.

It is possible, of course, to point to instances of so-called spiritual masters who appear to have experienced *karana-sarira* but who have nevertheless been responsible for leading followers sadly astray. Such men and women have rarely made much of a mark upon history, and it is possible that on returning to lower levels of consciousness their error lay in identifying the sense of oneness with the Divine apparently experienced in *karana-sarira* with their own limited egos. The ancient Greeks appeared to know all about this error, which they named hubris, and which they recognised as leading inevitably to disaster (nemesis) for those who committed it and for their followers.

It is also possible to point to saints such as the great Hindu sage Ramakrishna who, although their influence was uniformly good, would sometimes lie trance-like in *karana-sarira* for days on end, requiring to be cared for by their devoted followers. Such behaviour might be described by some as psychotic, but the effectiveness of such saints in influencing the levels of consciousness and achievement of others when they emerged from *karana-sarira* (there are Ramakrishna-Vedanta centres all over the world) would appear to contradict this description.

Conclusions as to the spiritual as opposed to the purely psychological benefits of *karana-sarira* consciousness must be left to individual judgement. Personal conviction rather than appeals to evidence would seem to play the major part in such a contentious area. All that can be said is that for those who accept the idea of a spiritual dimension to humankind, *karana-sarira* consciousness would seem to provide appropriate direct experience. I know of no accounts given by anyone reaching this level of consciousness which have failed to report the feelings of eternity, infinity and unity that bring conviction that man is more than a material phenomenon. It would seem in fact that it is direct awareness of these ineffable states that defines *karana-sarira* (for an excellent recent collection of papers on what might be called the psychology of spirituality see Tart 1997).

A rapprochement between Western science and the great traditions

The great traditions speak of four manifestations accessible to the various levels of consciousness, namely matter, life, mind and spirit (the so-called 'Great Chain of Being'). A comprehensive scientific exploration of consciousness clearly needs to take each of these into account. In doing so, it might succeed in bringing about a reconciliation of some kind between science and religion on terms acceptable to both camps. In one of the most perceptive explorations of the possible way towards such a reconciliation, Wilber (1998) points out that much of modern science has attempted to replace the Great Chain of Being with a 'flatland' concept that holds matter (or matter/energy) to be all there is. Such a concept suggests that part at least of science is fixated at the *annamayakola* level, however capable may be the powers of ratiocination of the scientists concerned. Our consciousness of matter, whether in the form of objects, bodies or brains, is certainly the stuff of orthodox scientific enquiry, but as we move up through *suksma-sarira* to *karana-sarira*, so we need other forms of inquiry. As Wilber puts it, our problem is that the current differentiation of cultural values between the spheres of art, spirituality, science and morals has allowed 'a powerful and aggressive science to begin to invade and dominate the other spheres, crowding... (them) ... out of any serious consideration in approaching 'reality''. If we are to integrate spirituality and science, we have therefore to find a way of reconciling the Great Chain of Being with the various disciplines operating within these areas of cultural differentiation.

In attempting such a reconciliation, Wilber starts with the recognition that each stage of the Great Chain of Being has an identifiable discipline associated with it. Thus matter is the province of physics, the body that of biology, the mind that of psychology, the soul that of theology, and the spirit that of mysticism. This being the case, the need is for a sensory-empirical science which can do for the spiritual level something of what is done by the other disciplines for the lower stages of the Chain. Such a sensory-empirical science would of course be unable to penetrate directly into any of the levels of consciousness in the way in which physics is able to penetrate into matter, and the life sciences are able to address life energies, but it would nonetheless be able to register their physical correlates. Wilber cites as an example the fact that the deeper levels of transcendental meditation are shown by research to correlate with real and sometimes dramatic changes in physiological states — to such an extent in fact that he considers we can postulate the existence of a fourth level of consciousness over and above those of waking, dreaming, and dreamless sleep, a level which may in fact access *karana-sarira*.

Wilber also points out that meditators typically check their inner experiences with advanced fellow practitioners 'much as mathematicians will check their interior proof with others who have completed the injunctions'. Thus if physiological measurements indicate that consciousness does appear to consist of various different levels, we may then be able to establish what these levels are like by identifying consensus among the accounts given by those people who experience them.

Modern science, as Wilber points out, has both narrow and broad aspects. Narrow or flatland science concentrates only on sensory experience and thus operates only at the *annamayakola* level, whereas broad science takes account of direct experience wherever it occurs, whether sensory, mental or spiritual, and therefore can take some note of higher levels. Narrow, flatland science is the science of objects and processes and systems, whereas broad science is the science of self, self-expression, aesthetics, morals, ethics, values and meaning. The scientific method, which proceeds by hypothesis-making and testing can be applied to broad as well as to narrow science, and thus has the potential to bring the higher levels of consciousness under something of the same scrutiny applied to the physical and life sciences. In doing so, consciousness need not be reduced to the material level because the unifying thread in our enquiry will remain that of direct experience.

To Wilber's proposal that we attempt to demonstrate the reality of higher levels of consciousness by their physiological correlates and by consensus among the accounts given by those who have been there, we can add a further appropriate research strategy, namely the exploration of the influence that an experience of these levels has upon observable behaviour. For example we can explore the influence which it appears to have upon personal and social relationships, upon self-concepts, upon moral and belief systems, upon affect, attitudes, and even upon eating and sleeping needs and physical and psycho-logical health. The most orthodox of behavioural psychologist could hardly deny either the science of such exploration, or the potential interest of the results it may yield.

The need for direct experience

One final point. As made clear at the outset of this chapter, it is *direct* experience of conscious processes — together with our ability to reflect upon these processes — that allows us to pursue our inquiry into the nature of consciousness. It would therefore seem appropriate that researchers should be concerned to explore not only the consciousness of others, but that of them-selves. Wilber's advice is indeed that if we wish to understand the highest level of consciousness we should 'Enter that state (ourselves) and find out. For the almost universal consensus of those who do is that this state begins to disclose the divine' (Wilber ibid. 1998: 198). Roll (1997) makes a similar point when he says 'The larger states of awareness can best be understood by explorers who are able to go there, or are willing to be guided by those who can. You cannot draw a reliable map without knowing the land' (Roll 1997: 67). No indeed.

References

Almaas, A. H. 1988. *The Pearl Beyond Price: Integration of Personality into Being: An Object Relations Approach*. Berkley: Diamond Books.
Aurobindo, Sri. 1957. *The Synthesis of Yoga*. Pondicherry: Sri Aurobindo Ashram.
Corbishley, T. (translator) 1963. *The Spiritual Exercises of St. Ignatius Loyola*. Wheathampstead, Herts.: Anthony Clarke.
Eccles, Sir John (ed.) 1976. *Brain and Conscious Experience*. New York; Springer-Verlag.
Fontana, D. 1992. *The Meditator's Handbook*. Shaftesbury UK and Rockport USA: Element Books.
Ghiselin, B. (ed.) 1952. *The Creative Process*. California: University of California Press.
Godwin, B. 1981. *Mystery Religions in the Ancient World*. London: Thames & Hudson.

Goswami, A., Reed, R. and Goswami, M. 1993. *The Self-Aware Universe.* New York: Tarcher-Putnam.

Isherwood, C. 1963. *Vedanta for the Western World.* London: Unwin Books.

James, W. 1890. *Psychology.* New York: Henry Holt.

Krishnananda, Swami 1969. *The Philosophy of Life.* Sivanandanagar: Divine Life

LaBerge, S. 1985. *Lucid Dreaming.* New York: Ballantine Books.

Nielsen, N. C., Hein, N., Reynolds, F. E., Miller, A. L Karff, S. E., Cowan, A. C., McLean, P., and Erdel, T.P. 1988. *Religions of the World.* New York: St. Martin's Press (2nd edn.).

Regardie, L. 1972. *The Tree of Life.* York Beach, Maine: Samuel Weiser.

Roll, W. 1997. My search for the soul. In C. Tart (ed.) *Body Mind Spirit: Exploring the Parapsychology of Spirituality.* Charlottesville: Hampton Roads.

Tart, C. 1988. *Waking Up.* Shaftesbury UK and Rockport USA: Element Books.

Tart, C. 1997. (ed.) *Body Mind Spirit: Exploring the Parapsychology of Religion.* Charlottesville: Hampton Roads.

Toynbee, A. 1956. *An American's Approach to Religion.* London: Oxford University Press.

Valle, R, and Mohs, M. 1998. Transpersonal awareness in phenomenological inquiry: philosophy, reflections, and recent research. In W. Braud and R. Anderson (eds.) *Transpersonal Research Methods for the Social Sciences: Honoring Human Experience.* Thousand Oaks Cal.: Sage.

Walshe, M. 1981. *Meister Eckart: German Treatises and Sermons, Vol. II.* London: Watkins.

Wilber, K. 1993. *The Spectrum of Consciousness.* New York: Quest (2nd edn.).

Wilber, K. 1998. *The Marriage of Sense and Soul: Integrating Science and Religion.* Dublin: Newleaf.

Williams, P. 1989. *Mahayana Buddhism: The Doctrinal Foundations.* London: Routledge.

PART 2

Maps of Consciousness Studies

CHAPTER 10

Modern Science and the Mind

Alwyn Scott
University of Arizona

As the present century draws to its close, the physical sciences take pride in several achievements that have led to striking advances in communications, computer engineering, transportation, and the manufacture of useful goods. The generation and propagation of electromagnetic waves over some twenty orders of magnitude (from geophysical waves to cosmic radiation) is now well understood, as is the theoretical relationship between atomic properties and the details of chemistry. Although corresponding advances in the technology of war cast a shadow over this esteem, none doubt that our knowledge of inanimate matter extends far beyond that of a hundred years ago. Thus it seems appropriate — as we move from the century of physics into the century of biology — to assess the contributions that science may be expected to make toward a better understanding of living organisms and the human mind.

As a basis for biology, recent advances in the area of *nonlinear science* are of particular interest, and, although poorly understood by the general public, these results and perspectives promise to be even more useful guides in forthcoming studies of the human brain. The aim of this chapter is to define the modern concept of nonlinearity and describe the role it is expected to play in future developments of biology and the social sciences.

An effort is made to avoid the overselling of science, a standard failing of physicists and mathematicians. Thus the chapter winds down with a discussion of how and why modern science may be insufficient to the task of understanding the nature of mind, suggesting that complementary insights from the humanities may yet be needed.

What is nonlinear science?

Or to put it another way: What is nonlinearity? As used in scientific circles of today, the term does not mean "curved" as opposed to "straight," nor does it imply the opposite of "linear thinking," through which one plods rationally from some rather obvious axioms to a dull conclusion. Instead, it is a precise statement about the *nature of causality*. Let's think about this.

Suppose that a series of experiments on a certain isolated system have shown that cause $C(1)$ gives rise to effect $E(1)$, and similarly $C(2)$ induces $E(2)$. This system is linear if

$$C(1) + C(2) \text{ causes } E(1) + E(2)$$

and it is *nonlinear* if the result of combining

$$C(1) + C(2) \text{ is } not \text{ equal to } E(1) + E(2).$$

Thus for a linear system any cause can be arbitrarily divided into convenient components $C(1)$, $C(2)$,...$C(n)$, whereupon the effect will be conveniently divided into $E(1)$, $E(2)$,...$E(n)$, allowing the effects of individual causes to be sorted out. Although useful for mathematical analysis and often approximately satisfied in studies of inanimate matter, this property is rare in the biological realm.

In other words, linear systems are easier to analyze and understand than nonlinear systems because a complex cause can be expressed as a convenient sum of simpler components, and the combined effect is the sum of the effects from each component of the total cause. For this reason linear models have been favored by physical scientists and philosophers, especially during the present century. In biology, however, the assumption of linearity is rarely justified. Examples? One bite stimulates the appetite while ten satisfy and twenty nauseate; a story told once can be amusing but told over again it becomes boring if not painful; one sperm will fertilize an egg, two can do no more.

Nonlinear systems are more difficult to analyze precisely because they are more interesting. More can happen — new *things*, new atomistic building blocks may *emerge* at each level of description — and that is why the phenomena of life and mind are so rich (Scott 1995). Some call these emergent entities "holons" (Wilber 1995).

A team of bicycle racers, a flock of geese, and a school of fish demonstrate this idea, where the emergent team, flock, and school are held together by nonlinear attractive forces that arise because the surrounding fluid (air or water) moves with them, but there are many variations on the theme. The atoms of hydrogen and carbon in a molecule of benzene are bound together by a combination of electrostatic and chemical valence forces; the membrane of a living cell organizes itself as a molecular bilayer in response to the shape and charge distribution of lipid molecules and the large dielectric constant of water; and the flame of a candle expresses a balance between the nonlinear localizing effect of combustion and the dispersive effect of thermal diffusion. At yet higher levels of description, one can consider the formation of a nerve impulse or the ignition of a burst of nervous activity, the development of a human being or the growth of a city, a memory or a poem. It is, in fact, difficult to think of a biological or social entity that does not take advantage of nonlinearity, as here defined, to establish its integrity, its oneness.

Nonlinear science comprises the study of all nonlinear systems, from the solitons carrying bits of information along optical fibers to the tsunamis that emerge from suboceanic earthquakes and suddenly ravage a coastal village, from Jupiter's Great Red Spot to a local mode of vibration in a molecule of benzene, from the dynamics of a nerve impulse to the musings of a brain. Clearly emergent phenomena are destined to play a role in biology and the social sciences (Scott 1999).

How many proteins are out there?

As the most simple of biological structures, consider a protein molecule. Some 200 amino acid molecules, each chosen from 20 candidates, are determined by a DNA code, constituting the *primary structure* of a protein. How many different proteins can there be? For a protein of only one amino acid, there are 20 possibilities. For two amino acids, there are 20 times 20 or 400 possibilities. For 200 amino acids, there is a number of proteins that is equal to 20 multiplied by itself 200 times, which is also said to be "20 raised to the 200th power." This is a finite number, but a rather large one.

With reference to the frequent appearance of such large finite numbers of possibilities in biology, Walter Elsasser (1966) has proposed the concept of an *immense number*, which is defined to be larger than 10 raised to the 110th power. (In ordinary arithmetic, this is written as a one followed by 110 zeros.) Why was this particular value chosen for the definition of immensity?

The mass of the universe measured in units of the hydrogen atom (in other words, the atomic mass of the universe) is about 10 raised to the 80th power, and the age of the universe measured in picoseconds (about the period of a molecular vibration) is about 10 raised to the 30th power. Multiplying these two factors gives 10 raised to the 110 power.

Thus an immense number is a finite number that is larger that the atomic mass of the universe times its age in picoseconds. Although finite, there is no way that an immense number of possibilities can be sequentially investigated. No such list could ever be constructed in any possible computer memory, and even if it were (say in the mind of God) there would never be enough time to examine it.

Since 20 raised to the 200th power is greater than 10 raised to the 110th power, the number of possible protein molecules is immense. The process of biological evolution — which is engaged in the business of trying out new proteins and saving the primary sequences of useful ones in genetic codes — will thus never run out of new proteins to try. This simple fact has interesting consequences for the course of evolutionary history.

Fossils of bacterial cells are found imbedded in rocks that are estimated to be 3500 million years old — the oldest in which such evidence could be expected — and this amazingly robust form of life dominated the Earth for at least two thousand million years (Margulis and Sagan 1995). Think of it. For more than two billion years (forty-five percent of her present life) our fair planet was covered from equator to poles by ever thickening layers of slimy bacteria of countless sorts, struggling to live, multiply, and improve their chances of survival. It was on the many anvils of this Archean workshop that much of the basic machinery of life was forged. An ever changing staff of bacterial blacksmiths labored day and night to find useful sizes and shapes for protein molecules. Why did it take them so long? Because the number of possible proteins they explored is immense, so their task will never end. There will always be interesting proteins out there, waiting to be discovered by the ongoing process of evolution.

The dynamic hierarchy of biology

But the proteins constitute just one level of biological description. Emerging from the molecules (amino acids) of chemistry, proteins provide a basis for biochemical cycles, changing energy from one form to another and altering biochemical structures. Biochemical cycles, in turn, supply the energy and molecular constituents needed for replication processes, involving DNA, messenger RNA, and protein synthesis. And so on, up through the structure of an organism, to its interaction with the environment, as is suggested by Diagram 1.

Biosphere

Organism

Organs

Individual cell

Homeostatic processes

Intercellular interactions

Replication

Biochemical cycles

Proteins

Chemistry

Diagram 1.

There is nothing original about constructing such a diagram for the hierarchical structure of a living organism; it has been noted and discussed by several authors over the past decades. Nonetheless certain points concerning its structure are to be made.

1. At each level of the diagram, first of all, there is a nonlinear dynamic system, following rules of behavior that the scientists of that level (be they chemists, biochemists, cytologists, physiologists, or ecologists) are working to discover.

2. Out of the nonlinear dynamics of each particular level emerge new entities that provide the basis for (or "atoms" or "holons" of) the nonlinear dynamics of the next higher level.

3. The possible number of new atomic entities that may emerge from each level is immense, just as for the proteins; thus construction of higher levels from a knowledge of the properties at lower levels is not feasible.

4. Closed loops of causal implication are particularly strong within each level, indeed this is why the new entities characterizing that level emerge, but there are significant interactions among adjacent levels. Longer range interactions are also possible: for example a poisonous substance ingested from the biosphere may modify the functioning of certain physiological processes, or the evolutionary discovery of a new protein may make possible a novel behavior of the organism. Thus — like the ouroborus of mythology, biting its own tail — myriad closed loops of causal implication are expected to thread their ways through the entire hierarchical structure, branching and contracting in countless ways.

Where in this slithering nest of involuted causality is the "physiological substrate of life"? What is life? Does it emerge — in some manner that is yet to be understood — from all levels of the nonlinear dynamic hierarchy?

The dynamic hierarchy of the brain

The neocortex of the human brain contains more than ten thousand million neurons, leading one to ask (as we did for the proteins): How many brains can there be? Using the simplest model of an individual neuron, a single switch, this number has been very conservatively estimated as about 10 raised to the 10 raised to the 17th power (Scott 1995). Although finite, this is such a *very* large number that one is tempted to call it *hyperimmense*. If it were written out in the normal manner as

$$1,000,000, \ldots ,000,000,$$

some two hundred billion books would be required. Given all of these possibilities, how is a brain expected to be organized?

An answer to this question was proposed in mid-century by Canadian psychologist Donald Hebb (1949) in his classic *Organization of Behavior*, who introduced the following concept of a *cell assembly* of the brain's neurons:

> "Any frequently repeated, particular stimulation will lead to the slow development of a 'cell-assembly' a diffuse structure comprising cells... capable of acting briefly as a closed system, delivering facilitation to other such systems and usually having a specific motor facilitation. A series of such events constitutes a 'phase sequence' — the thought process. Each assembly may be aroused by a preceding assembly, by a sensory event, or — normally — by both. The central facilitation from one of these activities on the next is the prototype of 'attention.' "

To better understand what Hebb (and others now) mean by a cell assembly, note that it can be portrayed by way of a social metaphor. We can compare the brain to a city and the individual neurons to its citizens. A particular citizen might be a member of several social assemblies such as a political association, a church, a bowling league, a parent-teacher's group, a hiking club, the junior league, and so on. The members of each social assembly are interconnected because, inevitably, each has a few overlapping members. What's more, shared lists of addresses and telephone numbers allow one organization to activate its own members — or even the members of a like-minded assembly — should an appropriate occasion arise. Members of the hiking club, for instance, could encourage the 4-H club to resist the development of a theme park near their farms. Or the junior league might enlist the support of teachers to close a pornographic bookstore. Just as an individual could be a member of both the hiking club and the league, a single nerve cell would participate in many different assemblies of the brain.

In Hebb's terms, the interconnections of a particular cell assembly form a sort of "three-dimensional fishnet," which "ignites" when a sufficient (threshold) number of its constituent neurons become active. Since an assembly of neurons shares the essential properties of an individual neuron (threshold behavior and all-or-nothing response), one can imagine an *assembly of assemblies*, which Hebb called a "second order assembly," or an *assembly of assemblies of assemblies*, called a third order assembly, and so on up through the organization of the brain.

Human culture

Phase sequence

Complex assemblies

***

***

Assemblies of assemblies

Assemblies of neurons

Neurons

Nerve fibers and synapses

Membrane proteins

Diagram 2.

From this perspective, a human brain is supposed to be hierarchically organized as shown in Diagram 2 above.

Once more we find a nonlinear dynamic hierarchy, to which the above comments concerning the hierarchy of life continue to apply. Out of an immense number of possibilities at each level emerges the atomic or holonic basis for the next higher level. But there is an additional wrinkle.

In life's hierarchy, it is possible to look into the structure at all levels of activity, and watch what transpires. Between the levels of individual neurons and the phase sequence in the brain's hierarchy, unfortunately, this is not possible. Little can be directly measured of a "three-dimensional fishnet" of interconnected neurons. Some thousands of electrodes would be required to be precisely placed at unknown positions, and even if this were possible, it would fatally disturb the dynamics of the brain under investigation.

Again one may ask: Where is the physiological substrate of the mind? As with the hierarchy of life, one wonders whether the question is properly formulated. What *is* mind?

The short answer is that modern science doesn't yet know, and perhaps it never will. Accordingly, one must recognize that science presently provides no limits to the qualitative character of mind. Although individual scientists and philosophers may believe that such constraints exist — as they are fully entitled to do — they cannot credibly argue that such beliefs are the fruits of science.

Hyperemergence of mind?

Although modern science has yet to explain the relationship between brain and mind, one possibility is as follows. Just as life seems to emerge from all levels of the biological hierarchy, mind may be a holistic phenomenon comprising *all* levels of the brain's cognitive hierarchy. This is a qualitatively new sort of emergence, which I shall call *hyperemergence*.

In life's hierarchy, the atomistic entities at each level (proteins, cells, organisms, etc.) arise out of the nonlinear dynamics of the adjacent lower level, but life itself — it seems to me — is of a different nature: it does not merely "pop out" at the highest level, as some suggest. On the contrary, life appears to hyperemerge from many (and perhaps all) levels of biological organization. It is this hyperemergence from many levels of nonlinear dynamic activity which, in my view, makes the phenomenon of life qualitatively different from the emergence of Jupiter's Great Red Spot, a molecule of benzene, or a nerve impulse.

Carrying the same idea over to the brain, one might suppose mind to be a hyperemergent property of the cognitive hierarchy, implying among other properties the capacity for consciousness. From this perspective, both consciousness and thought would be viewed as activities of mind, rather as respiration and reproduction are recognized as activities of life (Hebb 1980).

Thus we are led to a tidy parallel between the concepts of life and mind, but one should not confuse the neatness of a formulation with its validity. Because mind is a famously elusive concept, we are motivated to ask: Does this picture take us far enough?

Since science does not yet provide us with a clear concept of mind, it seems prudent to seek the most general context we can imagine in which to search for it. Thus it is interesting to consider the possibility of interactions between the two dynamic hierarchies displayed above. Are such interactions to be expected?

The involution of brain and body

Few would deny that conscious decisions taken by humans today can influence the character of tomorrow's biosphere (by the clear cutting of a redwood forest, say, or the selective breeding of domesticated animals), but how far back into the history of life do such interactions between life and mind go? Interestingly, an answer was proposed by Edwin Schrödinger (1967) in a book entitled *Mind and Matter*, which today is published together with his classic (1967) *What is Life?*

Following a suggestion of Julian Huxley, Schrödinger sketched ideas that help to dispel some of the gloom related to genetic reductionism. Why is the theory of genetic reductionism gloomy? Because it holds that the many phenomena of life can be entirely understood in terms of a mechanistic struggle between DNA codes for survival. Modifications of our behavior patterns — in this reductionist view — can have no influence on the process of evolution; try as we may, life develops in its preordained way. And since any attempts at self-improvement are lost to the next generation, why even try?

The notion that an individual's learning can alter the genetic code that is passed to its immediate offspring formed the basis for an evolutionary theory introduced by Chevalier de Lamarck early in the nineteenth century and accepted by Charles Darwin as a basis for evolutionary dynamics (Gregory 1987: 418). Although Lamarckism mitigates the pessimism of genetic reductionism, the basis for this theory has been discredited by modern studies. There is no credible evidence that an individual's ordinary behavior can directly modify the structure of its own DNA. None whatsoever. Without violating this scientific fact, however, Schrödinger suggested a version of "feigned Lamarckism" that does permit changes in behavior patterns to alter the course of evolutionary development. How can this be so?

Schrödinger asked his readers to consider a species that is beset by unfavorable factors (several able predators, a harsh environment, no symbiotic arrangements for profit sharing, and so on), which are being managed by producing a very large number of progeny. As one considers the history of life on earth, this is not an unusual situation, merely one in which only a small fraction of the many offspring survive and reproduce. We might say that a species in this situation is ripe for rapid development. Can conscious (or attentive) choice play a role in this evolutionary process?

Let us assume that certain members of this stressed species experience a genetic mutation that would be favored by a particular change in behavior: altering their habitat by moving from the ocean onto land, for example, or climbing into trees to avoid ground based predators. Those descendants who subsequently undergo such supporting mutations are better able to survive and even more likely to select and profit by the new behavior. This is a quintessential example of a *nonlinear* effect: the whole being more than the sum of its parts, making the ultimate outcome of the dynamic process difficult if not impossible to predict from present conditions. A change in behavior favors chance mutations that reinforce the changes in behavior (again a closed causal loop) greatly increasing the survival chances of the mutation in their offspring.

In Schrödinger's words:

> "The most important point is to see that a new character, or modification of a character, acquired by variation, may easily arouse the organism in relation to its environment to an activity that tends to increase the usefulness of that character and hence the 'grip' of selection on it. By possessing the new or changed character the individual may be caused to change its environment — either by actually transforming it or by migration — or it may be caused to change its behaviour towards its environment, all of this in a fashion so as strongly to reinforce the usefulness of the new character and thus to speed up its further selective improvement in the same direction."

If one accepts the possibility that such nonlinear interactions between mutations and elective behaviors have significantly influenced the course of life's history, the evolutionary role of mind becomes particularly important. The introduction of an ability to choose clearly augments an organism's toolbox of useful tactics. (Does this ability need to be conscious? Choice certainly is conscious at the level of *Homo sapiens*, and it probably is not for *Escherichia coli*. Perhaps intermediate species experience a gray scale of consciousness, ranging between these two extremes.) Thus the ability to choose becomes a catalytic factor in the development of life because the rates of change in this process can be greatly increased. In this manner, Schrödinger's feigned Lamarckism makes the evolutionary landscape appear less bleak.

In her recent book *What is Life?*, written in tribute to Schrödinger, evolutionary biologist Lynn Margulis (1995) puts it thus:

> "If we grant our ancestors even a tiny fraction of the free will, consciousness, and culture we humans experience, the increase in complexity on Earth over the last several thousand million years becomes easier to explain: life is the product not only of blind physical forces but also of selection in the sense that organisms choose. All autopoietic beings have two lives, as the country song goes, the life we are given and the life we make."

But who knows? Even this setting may be too narrow to capture the essence of mind. Are there more general formulations to consider?

More general models of mind

Attempts to square observations of human experience with the insights of science are not new; many have attempted to construct more general formulations that would encompass the facts. Here are mentioned two fairly recent attempts that seem to me to be of particular significance.

Popper and Eccles

Essential reading for all who are interested in the mind-body problem is a carefully and imaginatively prepared book entitled *The Self and its Brain* by Karl Popper and John Eccles (1977). This work deftly blends the philosophical insights of Popper with the neurological knowledge of Eccles, a celebrated electrophysiologist, through book-length sections written by each and followed by transcriptions of twelve of their conversations or dialogues. At the outset Popper establishes his central position: "I wish to state clearly and unambiguously that I am convinced that selves exist." Beyond this, his fundamental idea is that reality should be viewed in three different aspects:

World 1.
This is the objective world of the involuted biological and mental hierarchies that is sketched above. In Popper's terms it is the "universe of physical entities" in which the various levels of physical science interact with each other through their appropriate dynamical laws. A reductive materialist would hold that World 1 includes all of reality.

World 2.
Beyond the universe of physical entities, we experience — whether we choose to admit it or not — the psychic reality of an inner life that includes a vast and multicolored quilt of desires, ideas, pains, joys, sorrows, loves, schemes, strivings, and songs that are jumbled together with memories of the past and hopes and fears for the future. This inner reality is called World 2, and of course there are many of them: one for each of us.

World 3.
The world of human cultures in the broadest sense of the term is called World 3, and it includes all "the products of the human mind, such as stories, explanatory myths, tools, scientific theories (whether true or false), scientific problems, social institutions, and works of art." Thus a particular individual (you and I) can experience and interact with only a small fraction of World 3.

Popper notes that a similar, but not identical, perspective goes back to Plato who distinguished between the world of "visible objects" (World 1), the world of "intelligible objects" (World 3), and the "states of the soul" (World 2).

Interactions between Worlds 1, 2, and 3 are rather involved as is indicated by the following considerations: World 3 items are often embodied in World 1 objects. Thus a particular novel might exist as a printed book (coded in the ink that forms the letters on the pages) or on a floppy disk or both, but the World 3 object has an existence that is independent of its World 1 manifestation. World 3 items may also exist without reference to World 1. Examples are the primitive oral traditions that were carried on before the discovery or introduction of written language, in which a story resided in the mind (World 2) of a village elder. World 3 items may exist, unembodied and waiting to be found, without reference to either World 1 or World 2. As an example, Popper cites the properties of the prime numbers before their discovery but after the invention or discovery of the natural numbers. World 2 items are real in the sense that their existence can influence events in World 1. Feelings of fear or love, for example, can make one act in unexpected ways with unintended effects in World 1. A barbarian prince's love for an exotic princess leads to a marriage that brings fresh taste (World 3) into the castle, and begins the construction of new World 1 objects. Unembodied World 3 objects are also real in the same sense. The possibility of making an atomic bomb, for example, led to its construction with World 1 consequences that are not yet fully appreciated. And so on.

Ken Wilber

Even more general than Popper's formulation of the relationships between mind and physical reality is that of Ken Wilber, described in his recent book *Sex, Ecology, Spirituality* (1995), which should be read carefully by students of consciousness. In this model are proposed four aspects or "quadrants" of reality, each of which can be viewed as a dynamic hierarchy. Briefly, two of these four quadrants are: *behavioral* (exterior-individual), corresponding to Popper's World 1 and *intentional* (interior-individual) corresponding to Popper's World 2. The World 3 of Popper, in the formulation of Wilber, corresponds roughly to two additional quadrants: *cultural* (interior-collective), and *social* (exterior-collective).

Wilber suggests that the phenomena of consciousness emerge from inter-actions among all four of these quadrants, a view that I support.

Implications for research in consciousness studies

The above sketches of the elusive nature and hyperimmense intricacy of the human mind carry several implications for the conduct of research in the general area of consciousness studies.

1. It is no longer credible for philosophers to assume the nature of human existence to be entirely limited to its material embodiment, claiming the

support of established scientific knowledge. Present day science, as we have seen, says nothing about such limits. Scientists, of course, can and will believe whatever they please, but the beliefs of scientists should not be confused with the ripe fruits of research.

2. Computer scientists must remain aware — as many are — that their current models of the brain may be vast oversimplifications of real neural systems. Computer functionalism is thus also demoted to the status of a belief.

3. In psychology, it is important to shed the remnants of theoretical behaviorism (as opposed to its experimental aspects), giving significant attention to first person experiments that bring subjective phenomena into focus. In other words, psychologists should say goodbye to "physics envy" and begin to enjoy the status of a mature life science that has confidence in the importance of its own subject matter.

4. In the practice of clinical medicine, the interactive relationship between mind and body should be fully recognized (Weil 1995), and as was proposed three decades ago by Abraham Maslow (1968), psychiatrists should give due consideration to understanding the salient features of healthy minds.

5. Life scientists should avoid overemphasis on molecular biology and its theoretical underpinnings of genetic determinism. Although this experimental program should (and will) continue to be vigorously pursued, the biological community must strive for a balance between the search for genetic causation and the more traditional studies of organic biology.

6. Condensed matter physicists who are becoming interested in biological studies should not let their considerable experience with inanimate matter blind them to novel properties of living systems. As an example of contributions that can be made, a recent book on the brain by Hermann Haken (1996) delves into several of the central issues, suggesting order parameters representing the activity levels of Donald Hebb's cell assemblies.

7. While continuing to explore the yet mysterious dynamics of individual neurons, electrophysiologists are encouraged to devote increased attention to studies of cooperative interactions among many neurons.

8. As the branch of science attempting to integrate human experience, ethnology should give due consideration to the global aspects of cultural configurations (or behavior patterns), striving to understand their formation and development as independent dynamic entities that emerge from atomistic interactions among human minds.

9. Applied mathematicians must pay particular attention to investigations of

nonlinear dynamic hierarchies, attempting to discover the unexpected properties that might emerge. Although this effort is yet in its very early stages, I believe it will play a central role in mathematical research over the coming decades (Scott 1999).

10. Strangely, esthetic experience is given little attention by current students of mind, yet this is one of the most central aspects of the human experience (Santayana 1955). Again such considerations suggest the importance of seeing a human mind as an atom of cultural reality.

Can we anticipate that science — following these lines — will eventually become capable of providing a useful description of the human mind? At this point, one can only guess, but my intuitive feeling is modestly negative. It is difficult for me to see how the relevant variables describing the psychological states and cultural configurations of mental reality can ever be suitably understood and sorted out. The stage upon which humans act is so intricate that one is reminded of George Santayana, the brilliant student and young colleague of William James, who wrote:

> "Reality is more fluid and elusive than reason, and has, as it were, more dimensions than are known even to the latest geometry."

This is not, of course, an argument against trying to extend the traditional tools of science as far as possible. Nonetheless, mathematicians and physical scientists should be concerned about the limits of their methods. Subjectively, I suspect, many are so concerned, refusing to think about the nature of consciousness because they sense the intractability of such problems. There seems no place to begin, leading some to ask if the tools of science need to be modified or augmented in certain ways.

Must science change to comprehend the mind?

In a recent essay, Ken Wilber (1996) has listed and briefly described a dozen current approaches to the study of mind: cognitive science, introspectionism, neuropsychology, individual psychotherapy, social psychology, clinical psychiatry, developmental psychology, psychosomatic medicine, nonordinary states of consciousness, Eastern and contemplative traditions, quantum consciousness, and research in subtle energies. Although encouraged by the range of this activity, he justly laments the fact that each of these efforts appears to be going its own way, with very little interaction among them: "The pieces prevail." What can be done about this balkanization of consciousness research?

In addition to continuing the ongoing work in each of the above activities — a suggestion that most scientists would support — Wilber proposes two additional aspects of modern studies of the mind. First, we should face the possibility that a change in consciousness on the part of the researchers may be needed for an insightful study, and, second, the scientific community should continue to strive for a "genuinely integral" theory of consciousness.

Is this possible? How are such noble goals to be achieved?

Anthropology and the humanities

Interestingly, an answer to a related question was offered a half century ago by the gifted American ethnologist Ruth Benedict in her outgoing address as the first woman president of the American Anthropological Association. Since all scientists who are interested in understanding the human mind should become familiar with this document, I shall quote from it rather liberally (Mead 1973).

While accepting and honoring the status of anthropology as a science, aiming "to arrive at objective, theoretical descriptions of reality," Benedict notes that this is a recent development in the study of mankind. From the Renaissance to the middle of the nineteenth century, the humanities (from *humanitas*, the knowledge of mankind) were at the center of Western intellectual efforts.

> "It was in this field of the humanities that great men for centuries got their cross-cultural insights. It liberated them, it taught them discipline of mind. It dominated the intellectual life of the period. Then about the middle of the last century the new sciences began to take leadership out of the hands of the humanists. Until then science has remained largely a field for amateurs. Its subject matter for generations had been suspect, not only because scientists had questioned facts upheld by contemporary religion, but because the natural sciences dealt with matter and inanimate nature, which stood low in the divine order of the world. They were regarded as enemies of man's higher interests, which were the peculiar field of the humanities."

Anthropology began, she points out, at the time that science was becoming ascendent in Western thought, and it has profited greatly from that tradition, but science and the humanities should not be viewed as mutually exclusive endeavors. "They are supplementary, and modern anthropology handicaps itself in method and insight by neglecting the work of the great humanists." While there are some anthropologists who still exclude "the mind and purposes of man," the great majority of American anthropologists do not, although "they have often not considered sufficiently the difference in training which genuine progress in this field requires. For if anthropology studies the mind of man, along with his institutions, our greatest resource," according to Benedict, "is the humanities."

> "It is my thesis that we can analyze cultural attitudes and behavior more cogently if we know Santayana's *Three Philosophical Poets* and Lovejoy's *Great Chain of Being* and the great works of Shakespearian criticism. Future anthropological work, too, can reach a higher level if we attract, not only students of sociology, but also students of the humanities."

While recognizing that the collection of life histories has been part of anthropological field work, she points out that much of this effort is time consuming and repetitious.

> "The unique value of life histories lies in that fraction of the material which shows what repercussions the experiences of a man's life — either shared or idiosyncratic — have upon him as a human being molded in the environment ... None of the social sciences, not even psychology, has adequate models for such studies. The humanities have. If we are to use life histories for more than items of topical ethnology, we shall have to be willing to do the kind of job on them which has traditionally been done by the great humanists."

Ruth Benedict concluded her farewell address with the following words:

> "My point is that, once anthropologists include the mind of man in their subject matter, the methods of science and the methods of the humanities complement each other. Any commitment to methods which exclude either approach is self-defeating. The humanities criticize the social sciences because they belabor the obvious and are arid; the social sciences criticize the humanities because they are subjective. It is not necessary for the anthropologist to be afraid of either criticism, neither of belaboring the obvious, nor of being subjective. The anthropologist can use both approaches. The adequate study of culture, our own and those on the opposite side of the globe, can press on to fulfillment only as we learn today from the humanities as well as from the sciences."

Is there not a message here for students of consciousness?

References

Elsasser, W.M. 1966. *Atom and Organism: A New Approach to Theoretical Biology.* Princeton: Princeton University Press.

Gregory, R.L. 1987. *The Oxford Companion to the Mind.* Oxford: Oxford University Press.

Haken, H. 1996. *Principles of Brain Functioning: A Synergetic Approach to Brain Activity, Behavior and Cognition,* Berlin: Springer-Verlag, 1996.

Hebb, D.O. 1949. *Organization of Behavior: A Neuropsychological Theory.* New York: John Wiley.

Hebb, D.O. 1980 *Essay on Mind.* Hillsdale, New Jersey: Lawrence Erlbaum Associates.

Margulis, L. and Sagan, D. 1995. *What is Life?* New York: Simon and Schuster.

Maslow, A.W. 1968. *Toward a Psychology of Being,* 2nd edition. New York: Van Nostrand.

Mead, M. (ed.) 1973. *An Anthropologist at Work: Writings of Ruth Benedict.* New York: Avon Books.

Popper, K.R. and Eccles, J.C. 1977. *The Self and Its Brain.* Berlin: Springer-Verlag.

Santayana, G. 1955. *The Sense of Beauty.* New York: Dover (first published in 1896).

Schrödinger, E. 1967. *What is Life?* Cambridge: Cambridge University Press (first published in 1944).

Schrödinger, E. 1967. *Mind and Matter.* Cambridge: Cambridge University Press (first published in 1958).

Scott, A.C. 1995. *Stairway to the Mind: The Controversial New Science of Consciousness.* New York: Springer-Verlag (Copernicus).

Scott, A.C. 1999. *Nonlinear Science: Emergence and Dynamics of Coherent Structures.* Oxford: Oxford University Press.

Weil, A. 1995. "Pharmacology of consciousness: A narrative of conscious experience." In S.R. Hameroff, A.W. Kaszniak, and A.C. Scott, *Toward a Science of Consciousness,* Cambridge: MIT Press, 677–689.

Wilber, K. 1995. *Sex, Ecology, Spirituality: The Spirit of Evolution.* Boston: Shambhala.

Wilber, K. 1996. "How big is our umbrella?" *Noetic Sciences Review,* Winter: 10–17.

CHAPTER *11*

Social Construction and Consciousness

Rom Harré
University of Oxford

Introduction

There does not seem to be *the* 'problem of consciousness', only various conundrums that come to the fore when we reflect on the special character of higher organisms. Roughly one might say that common to many puzzles about consciousness is the thought that human beings, at least, are aware that they are aware of material things, some of the states of their own bodies, and can monitor themselves thinking about these and other matters. In this paper I propose to use the analysis of certain relevant kinds of talk as a way of investigating how far some of the phenomena comprehended under the broad term 'consciousness' are socially constructed. By that I mean the question as to whether they are brought into being, or if already existing, are modified in various ways, by social, that is interpersonal processes and structures. I shall work with the widely shared principle that the main instrument through which such creations and modifications come to be is language.

Analyzing consciousness talk

It is a useful, indeed indispensable part of the opening up of a research programme in psychology to do a little lexicography. Phenomena are made available to people, picked out from the 'hurly burly' of life (as Wittgenstein put it) by perceptual skills that are in part made what they are in the learning of a language. The rules for the use of a word can give us an insight into the domain of its application. Thus the word 'conscious' and its cognates, though late entrants into English, are now well established, so well established that a group of people can be brought from all over the world to study what ever it is that the word 'consciousness' picks out. In doing a lexicographical exercise as a preliminary to defining a research programme we must bear in mind Wittgenstein's reminder that the diverse phenomena that are found within the domain of the words 'conscious' and 'consciousness' may not be unified by a common essence. He thought that the many ways that a common word is used is best pictured as field of family resemblances, structured by an ever shifting network of similarities and differences in the way the words at the focus of an investigation are used. While bearing this point in mind we must be careful not to slip into the post-modernist exaggeration, that there is no firm ground of usage. On the contrary symbol-driven human life is possible only because among the shifting patterns of usage of words there are persisting invariants that serve generations of the users of a language to conduct their everyday lives. We must agree, as Wittgenstein remarked, on a grammar, though we must acknowledge that no grammar lasts for ever.

Several of the everyday uses of the word 'conscious' can be replicated by phrases making use of the words 'aware' and 'attend'. Thus the content of 'I was conscious of a disapproving atmosphere at the meeting' can be rendered by 'I was aware of a disapproving atmosphere at the meeting' while the content of 'I suddenly became conscious of a ticking sound' could be expressed with the phrase 'paid attention to'. This group of words are characteristically used to express a *relation* between a person and an intentional object. Their use presupposes an ontology in which the basic particulars are material things some of which are animated as persons. Examination of a larger slice of 'aware of'/'attend to' discourse would disclose a structure in which a person served as the 'origin' of an array of entities of various sorts, patterned by the 'conscious of' relation. Such structures are typically continuously being transformed around fairly stable invariants, as one takes a walk, has lunch and so on.

But this field of family resemblances includes the abstract noun 'consciousness'. I am of the opinion that the appearance of nouns in the setting up of a research programme in psychology is a danger sign. If psychology is the science of what people *do* then verbs and adverbs ought to carry the burden of descriptive psychology rather than nouns, and especially abstract nouns. Once a word like 'consciousness' is given a central role, then we are strongly tempted to begin to look for a referent for it. 'What is consciousness?' then takes on the air of a serious question, answered by examining it closely, like a question put to a physicist, 'What is heavy water?'. The fact that we cannot answer it readily makes it look as if the question is a hard one which could be answered with a little more effort. But perhaps there is something wrong with the formulation of the question, drawing our thoughts off in a fruitless direction.

Let us return to our linguistic preliminaries. What do we use the word 'consciousness' for? Two uses stand out. One is simply a further candidate for replacement by one of the 'aware of'/'attend to' vocabulary. It is exemplified by such expressions as 'rose to consciousness' or 'drifted into consciousness', roughly equivalent to 'became aware of' or 'noticed'. Then there are uses such as 'lost [regained] consciousness'. Here they seem to refer to the existence of an indefinite range or domain of perception, numerous intentional objects of which someone is aware. Closely allied to this is the use of words like 'awake', said of one who is at that moment aware of the state of the material environment both inside and outside the person's body. To wake up or to regain consciousness is to come to be in such a condition as to be able to become aware of all sorts of things. But it is not just to be aware of this and that state of affairs. It also suggests that a certain enabling condition for being aware of intentional objects, now or once again obtains in the organism itself.

Where we were confronted with an abstract noun, used very broadly, we now have something complex but quite concrete. A person as an embodied being, is in a certain state, a state which is a necessary condition for coming to perceive things, that is to stand in a certain relation to them.

Prescribing consciousness research

To whom should further explorations of consciousness be entrusted? I shall argue that the study of fields of intentional objects should be the domain of discursive psychologists, while the study of the enabling conditions for the existence of such fields is the province of neuropsychology, exploring the state of the brain and nervous system characteristic of those who are awake, paying attention and so on. The first of these suggestions might look very much like a take-over bid by phenomenologists, and to a certain extent that is just what it is. The legitimacy of trying to convey to another person the nature of one's private experience by describing it needs to be defended. The second of these suggestions might look very much like a capitulation to a reductionist programme in psychology, in which seemingly mental state terms are given a new meaning as having a neurophysiological reference. Since that is not my intention I owe the reader at least a sketch of how a phenomenological vocabulary and a neurophysiological vocabulary could be related so that the one does not displace the other.

Let us begin in the phenomenological mode. On what are perceptual domains centred? They seem to be laid out in different orientations to a person. This person is a singularity around which what is perceived is arrayed. To explore the nature of that singularity we enter into the study of selfhood, or at least of one aspect of this multivocal notion. That aspect is the sense each person has of the uniqueness of their location and trajectory through space and time, of being one and only one embodied person.

Here is a problem: do we perceive an ordered world, each from his or her own point of view because we each have an original or native sense of our own singularities? Or do we each have such a sense because we perceive the world in an ordered and *centred* way? To encounter the structure of the perceptual domain of another person, which will include many of the same objects that one can oneself perceive, one can place one's *body* where the other person has been very shortly beforehand. Soon it is enough to imagine what the view from somewhere else would be like. But what guarantees the authenticity of the experience as that of the perceptual domain of someone else? It can be from what they tell us about what they saw, or felt, or heard. But by what devices do we distinguish a description from the point of view of the speaker from a bland, neutral description? The key, I argue, is in our grasp of the grammar of the first person, explicit as in 'I saw the postman go by', or implicit as in 'Can't you hear the phone?'

The expression of consciousness as awareness of something

What sort of display would be an expression characteristic of someone or some creature that was conscious? It might, for instance, be a report of how things looked from the point of view of the speaker. This is done by using the first person singular in the report. The point of view from which the world is being seen, felt, heard etc. is implicitly centred on the body of the speaker.

Using the first person in such a report also accomplishes a more complex social act, namely the taking of responsibility for what has been reported. In saying 'I can see the taxi at last' an anxious member of a travelling party not only indexes the content of the statement with his or her position in space as an embodied being, but also puts his or her character 'on the line', standing behind the report, so to say. If the plume of dust turns out to have been made by a herd of antelope and not a taxi then the reporter is liable to censure, not just for getting it wrong but for raising everyone's hopes falsely. A parrot learns to imitate the sounds of speech and croaks out 'I can see the taxi now'. There isn't one. Do we censure the parrot? Not usually. A parrot does not partake of enough of the human form of life to be liable to praise and blame for its perceptual reports.

That of which a person is conscious, that is, is aware of and/or attends to, has a structure, centred for each person, on his or her body. The fine tuning of the perceptual centring of consciousness, in this sense, will depend on many factors, including whether the person is blind when the field of awareness is tactile and auditory, or perhaps is a patient of Oliver Sachs and suffers from some curious psycho-anaesthesia. People speak and write of the 'structure of consciousness' and most of the time they simply mean the structure of the local environment, as revealed to the visual, auditory, tactile etc. perceptual systems. The discursive expression of that structure, as contrasted say with its expression in a landscape by the use of perspective, is usually revealed in the use of first person constructions, rather than neutral descriptions. Compare 'Look! There goes Sadie' with 'I can see Sadie!' Agentive activities, such as making a shot in billiards, could also reveal the person centred structure of the environment as perceived by the player.

Radically different uses of the first person might persuade us that the structure of consciousness was different for some person, even perhaps for some tribe if the use of an exotic grammar (from our point of view) was widespread. Where does madness end and cultural diversity begin? Only some radically different uses of first person indices would count. And just how far these uses could diverge from the customary ways of speaking is limited. In the case of people displaying multiple personality syndrome we find no evidence in their off-beat grammars of disembodied or diverse locations for perceiving the ordinary furniture of the locality.

Consciousness and other kinds of awareness

So far I have been discussing the grammar of 'aware of' in cases in which that awareness is perceptual. There are other, more cognitive uses of the phrase, such as understanding a meaning and drawing an inference. 'Consciousness' is so multivocal an expression that it turns up in all sorts of contexts, where it is actually doing duty for something other than the perceptual. We find feminists writing of the 'divided consciousness' of women. Examining this usage closely reveals that it does not mean anything thrilling such as 'each and every woman has two centres of awareness somehow located in the one body'. It usually means something quite mundane, that women often find themselves with two sets of (sometimes) incompatible duties; or that women often find themselves having to pay attention to more than one thing at the same time; their take home work on the family computer and the grizzling of a damp and hungry infant. But all these objects competing for attention are located in a single material environment which the person perceives from her singular location as an embodied being. Why use expressions like 'divided consciousness'? One can only surmise that such a word is chosen for its rhetorical impact. It is a striking metaphor, but a far from a transparent terminology for a psychology of gender role differences!

Psychological research programmes

The material embodiment of human beings as persons appears in two different ways in our analysis. A place in the body, somewhere just behind the eyes, serves as the centre of the material environment including one's own body as part of it. However, I have so far not begun to develop an account of other fields of consciousness, in particular memory and imagination. The organisation of recollections and anticipations as the span of a life is patterned around a temporal origin, the 'now' of bodily existence. This too is an indexical, like the first person, and the source of the possibility of tensed statements such as the public expression of thoughts about the past and the future. 'Was' means 'before now', while 'will be' means 'after now'. 'Now' is the moment contemporaneous with an act of speaking. Further research will take us deeper into the study of indexical expressions, locatives of both places and times.

Some state or pattern of states of the body seems to be a necessary requirement for all the modes of awareness that I have touched on. These are the enabling conditions as neural structures and processes. It is important that the right neural phenomena could not be identified without the use of phenomenological criteria, a point to which I will return.

From these two considerations it follows that a *psychological* investigation of some aspect of human life, such as consciousness (perception) or the emotions or reasoning or attitudes or anything else, takes the following form: (1) Since every psychological process or phenomenon is made possible by virtue of a certain condition or state of the brain and nervous systems of those engaged in the activity there is a well defined though ever changing set of questions that can be put to neuroscientists. Following well established tradition I shall call the neurological foundation the 'enabling condition' for the activity. Some enabling conditions exist by nature, so to say, while others are established by training and practice.

(2) Every psychological process or phenomenon is a skilled performance by a person or persons, including perception. A performance is skilled if it is intentional, that is directed to some end and is subject to criteria of correctness, propriety, in short is normatively constrained. Deeper research into the structures of these processes is facilitated by the fact that human beings have various ways of publicly expressing what is directly known privately to each individual. These ways, since they are public, can be studied, analyzed and the principles of their construction discovered. It has been said that perception is not a skilled activity, but there are good reasons for treating it as such. For example, one must learn to identify the type or category to which an object belongs, as well as learning how to discriminate a figure from a ground.

For example playing a musical instrument is a psychological phenomenon, made possible by the changes that have occurred in the brain and nervous system of someone who has acquired the skill. The action of playing is indeed psychological, since it is intentional, the player is trying to play something, and it is normative, that is the performance is subject to a variety of standards in reproducing the score, coordinating one's performance with those of others, phrasing 'musically' and so on. Just in the same way performing an arithmetical calculation, making a decision, displaying an emotion, forming a friendship, seeing a constellation, tasting a fine claret, and so on are all to be construed within the basic framework of enabling conditions and skilled actions In so far as consciousness is a catch-all term for perceptions of various modes and kinds, the study of 'consciousness' too falls within this generic hybrid methodology.

Enabling conditions are somewhat more complex than the brief introductory sketch above would suggest. Not only do they include the neural state of the human organisms involved, but also there are environmental conditions that must also obtain for a skilled performance to be possible. One cannot display one's skills as a mountaineer unless there is some rock face (or artificial surrogate) to climb. One cannot be jealous unless there is someone whose rights to a good are thought by you to be inadequate relative to yours, and so on. One cannot read without some text to follow. In what follows, that is a discussion of consciousness in the discursive frame, the environmental conditions will play a minor though essential part, since it is only in a certain kind of discursive environment that consciousness as we know it, can come into existence.

The grammars of everyday life

Contemporary Anglo-American life, conceived as the joint production of meaningful and normatively constrained patterns of action, of which verbal intercourse is one species, seems to be shaped by four main 'grammars', that is more or less coherent systems of norms and semantic rules.

There is the *Soul or S-grammar*, which makes use of concepts like 'God','soul', 'sin', 'redemption' and so on. This grammar, once universal in the 'West', is now confined to certain rather restricted groups, tribes and regions where it was once dominant. It is still part of working practices of Mormon Utah, for instance. A main feature of S-grammars is the independence of the prime source of activity, the soul, from any necessary relation to the body it 'inhabits'.

There is the *Person or P-grammar*, in which persons are the basic particulars and originating sources of activity. It comprises the tribal dialects and idiolects of everyday life in all those regions of the world where some measure of individualism prevails and where the peculiar blend of Roman and Anglo-Saxon legal traditions are in place. Among some of the specialised dialects of this generic grammar are the idioms of the courtroom, of the shrill claims for rights of the 'entitlement society', and so on. A main feature of P-grammars is the conceptual tie between singular embodiment and personal uniqueness and individuality.

There is the *Organism or O-grammar*: Current Western discourses make use of a third grammar, that in which the basic powerful particulars or active beings are organisms. While it has, so to say, its natural domain of application in discussions about animals it has some important uses in discourse about human beings. The use of this grammar is becoming very widespread in reports of and discussions of the role of a human being's genetic endowment in the pattern of one's life. In so far as one's actions are the product of neural mechanisms of genetic origin one's life is embedded in a discourse in which the concept of 'person' is replaced by that 'organism' in discussions of human beings. Animals are agentive and act teleologically, but the person grammar is extended to them only with difficulty and usually only metaphorically. Animals do not act intentionally in the full sense that would bring into play the grammar of responsibility attributions except in rare cases. Responsibility talk addressed to family pets is surely metaphorical. When addressed to certain primates, such as domesticated chimpanzees it may have a deeper significance, widening the scope of the domain of moral agents. Though babies act for an end they surely do not act for a purpose. If Vygotsky is right, the use a P-grammar with its load of 'responsibility' concepts, for talking about, and usually to, neonates, is part of the necessary conditions for a human organism to mature into a person.

There is the *Molecular or M-grammar*, in which molecules and molecular clusters are the basic particulars and originating sources of activity. Among the dialects shaped by M-grammar are those used to describe human physiology and molecular biology. Discourse framed in this grammar includes such attributions of agency to molecules as the (alleged) power of melatonin to put one to sleep in the sense of a change in the brain rhythms, and excess stomach acid to cause heartburn, in the sense of discharges in the pain receptors. Unlike the P-grammar the M-grammar is strongly hierarchical and displays emergent properties at every level.

Why did top tennis players eat a banana between sets? This query requires an answer couched in M-grammar. But why they no longer seem to do so may need the P-grammar. And so too does an account of the use of cortisone to reduce the inflammation in a cartilage, and so on.

Thus we have a loose cluster of grammars that set the standards of proper discourse for the human domain, the S-, the P-, the O- and the M-grammars. Each has variants, and in certain circumstances they fit together into hierarchies, and, in other circumstances, they complement one another.

Not only does each of these grammars have its associated ontology, or catalogue of sources of activity, but each also comprises taxonomies of dependent particulars, such as action-types in the P-grammar. These give us criteria for partitioning the flow of the activities of persons into meaningful acts. In the O-grammar we have a classificatory resource for identifying behaviour-types as partitions of the activities of pets and some of the wild animals well known to us. The M-grammar allows for the identification of chemical reactions in organ systems, for example the interaction between carotene and cholesterol. Organs, in the M-grammar, are treated as functional partitions of the hierarchical clustering of molecules.

Each grammar has its own distinctive principles of sequence and order among basic and dependent particulars. In P-grammar these include semantic and syntactic rules, moral imperatives and story-lines. Thanks to the work of the ethologists we now see the lives of animals teleologically. This is expressed in the O-grammar in terms of repertoires of actions directed towards maintaining their forms of life, leading to a complex repertoire of means/end principles. But in M-grammar there are only causal laws.

S- and P-grammars differ from O- and M-grammars in the way that responsibility is dealt with. This is particularly important for a philosophy of psychology, since the transition from infancy to maturity of a being that has native agentive powers and acts teleologically, occurs along the dimension of growing responsibility for what it does. Shaver (1985) has proposed an analysis of responsibility dimensions that will do very well as a working grammar for much of the P-grammar of current English language folk psychology[1]. The attribution of responsibility according to Shaver runs as follows:

> A judgement made about the moral accountability of a person of normal capacities, which judgement usually but not always involves a causal connection between the person being judged and some morally disapproved action or event (Shaver, 1985: 66)

The 'causal connection' presupposes the agentive powers of a person, not a Humean regularity of stimulus-type and response-type. Hart (1963), analyzing that variant of the P-grammar that is to be found in English law, cites three necessary conditions for attributions of responsibility.

> That the person understand what is required.
> That the person has deliberated on the matter in hand.
> That the person conforms to the result of the deliberation.

One can see that in the S-grammar the concept of 'sin' depends on very similar conditions obtaining.

Another striking way in which the S- and P-grammars differ from the O- and M-grammars, is in everyday discourse of remembering. Only people (or souls) remember, not their brains nor the molecular structures that ground our recollective capacities. Why is this? To say 'I remember .. ' is to claim some kind of authority, to commit myself to what I assert about the past. How my claims to remember are taken depends on my moral standing in the community, my reliability. It engages my personal qualities. It does not refer to me as an organism.

Playing tennis is another example that requires the P-grammar. The exchange of shots is constrained by conventions of meaning: 'On the line is out'; and of procedure: 'Change ends after four games'. Scores accrue to people and it is people who play shots, good and bad, for which they are responsible, not their bodies nor their racquets.

Finally I draw attention to the grammatical fact that the experiences of falling asleep and of waking, of being in pain and so on, are described in the P-grammar, since it is *persons* who notice what is going on, and its persons who suffer.

How is a phenomenology of experience possible?

The upshot of the discussion so far is that the 'study of consciousness' is a hybrid project, requiring intensive work in the phenomenology of perception, proprioception in all the sense modalities together with a study of acts of recollection, *and* requiring intensive work on the neurophysiology of the conditions which enable acts of perception and recollection. The former are done by people, the latter happen in brains. But if the phenomenological project is to be pursued an age old problem must be solved: how is it possible for there to be a common, public language by the use of which people can discuss how the world appears, how their bodies are, and so on, each from his or her own point of view?

The P-grammar of descriptions and avowals

Many experiences are not shared with others. While we both see the same tennis ball only I feel the pain of my 'tennis elbow'. While we both see the same slice of Tin Roof Fudge Pie only I enjoy the exquisite sensations since you foolishly chose carrot cake. Yet I can discuss the pain of my tennis elbow with my doctor, and I can mortify you with my panegyric on the gustatory delights of a famous 'desert'. But there seems to be an insoluble impasse in philosophy in which the authority of experience clashes with the conditions for sharing a meaning with someone else. In the course of criticising the idea that a language could be established on the basis only of private and personal referents for the teaching the meaning of words, Wittgenstein also provided the means for resolving the impasse.

Wittgenstein's Private Language Argument (PLA)

The shape of the argument

The 'argument' involves three interwoven and mutually supporting strands that are relevant to the distinction between descriptions of states of affairs and avowals of experience. One strand is a demonstration that the general principle that learning the meaning of a word is achieved by a teacher pointing to an exemplar cannot account for how words for private experiences can be learned. There is no public exemplar to which the teacher can point and learner can attend. Meaningful words for sensations and bodily feelings could not have been learned by 'ostension'. Furthermore our experiences, both private and public, are ordered around spatial and temporal 'I-poles', to use Husserl's useful phrase, a feature of experience that contributes massively to the human sense of self. Again there is no public exemplar for learning the words, such as first person pronouns, that we use to express the structured or centred 'shape' of our personal experience. Wittgenstein's demonstration that there must be some other way to learn these important classes of words than by pointing to exemplars, depends upon a commonsense but fundamental observation. The words for discussing publicly the nature and structure of private and personal experience are learned with ease and used without a qualm.

The assumption we have just criticised, about the role of exemplars in learning words, would make no sense in the case of private experiences, without the further assumption that all meaningful words denote *objects*. The second strand of the PLA is an argument to show that feelings are not objects in the sense that the objects that are pointed to in ordinary situations of ostensive learning, say 'potato', are objects. This argument is based on a reflection on the criteria by which judgements of 'same feeling' are made in intrapersonal and in interpersonal comparisons. According to Wittgenstein the concept of 'sameness' for feelings cannot be analyzed along the same lines as we analyze concepts of sameness for such *things* as potatoes.

Judgements of 'sameness' in material contexts are based on criteria of qualitative and numerical identity. Two things are qualitatively identical if they have more or less similar properties. Something is numerically identical, 'still the same' in different circumstances, if its integrity and continuity of existence is uninterrupted. In some of later paragraphs in the exposition of the PLA Wittgenstein shows in some detail that these criteria of identity have no place in language games in which we make such judgements as 'I feel just as bad as I did yesterday' or 'I know just what you are feeling. I felt the same when I had finished my exams'. Yet everyone makes lots of everyday unproblematic judgements of sameness and difference of their own and other people's feelings. Since they do not meet the criteria for 'sameness' and 'difference' of material things, bodily feelings are not objects in the relevant sense. But even if they were their privacy precludes their use as exemplars for denotational learning.

How to resolve this seemingly intractable bouquet of problems? We use feeling words perfectly well, yet it seems that we are never in a position to learn them. We talk about feelings yet they are not at all like the entities of the material world about which we also talk. The impasse comes about because we took two things for granted. We assumed that words are all learned by the teacher pointing to an exemplar of the kind of object talked about while the pupil attends to it. We also assumed that feelings were a special sort of object or entity, for which the usual, thing-related criteria of identity, perhaps ad-justed a little, were appropriate. But feelings are not thing-like. So we have two gaps to fill in understanding how it is possible to discuss our private feelings with others and to reflect on what we felt in the past. How is it that words for feelings do get their proper meanings? And what do we mean by 'same feeling' in both intra and interpersonal contexts?

In a quite similar way an intractable problem arises about that to which the word 'I' refers when I use it of myself in reporting how things are for me.

How could such an expression ever get established in public language if it could be learned only from a public exemplar? There is no public exemplar of the centredness of experience, nor is there any *thing* to which attention could be drawn. My 'self' is no more a thing-like entity than is my pain. And again we can see this by comparing my sense of my own personal identity with my sense of yours. I think you are the same person I saw yesterday mostly by noticing the similarity of certain salient features of your appearance today as yesterday. Of course I might be mistaken. I do not have to use any criterion to judge if I am still the same person I was yesterday, and certainly not one based on bodily appearances. It does not make sense to declare: 'All along I was wrong about the person I am. I have discovered I am you.'

There are subtly different cases of uniqueness of point of view here. I can't have your pains in the way I can't sneeze your sneezes, to borrow another of Wittgenstein's images. To be that instance of pain it has to be your feeling. Thus only you can have it. I can see a herd of cows from your point of view by simply standing where you were a moment ago, but the second term of the relational structure of the seeing of the material environment is uniquely you or uniquely me. But in both cases we slip into seemingly intractable puzzles by taking for granted that it is objects that are in question, where 'the feeling' or 'the self' are assumed to obey the same grammars as 'the colour' and 'the driver'.

Wittgenstein's suggestion that solves the linguistic problem

The suggestion that allows us to transcend the impasse is to be found in the following remarks:

> How do words *refer* to sensations? — There does not seem to be any problem here; don't we talk about sensations every day, and give them names? This question is the same as: how does a human being learn the meaning of the names for sensations? — of the word 'pain' for example. Here is one possibility: words are connected with the primitive, the natural, expressions of the sensation and used in their place. A child has hurt himself and he cries; and then adults talk to him and teach him exclamations and, later, sentences. They teach the children new pain behaviour.
> 'So you are saying that the word "pain" really means crying?' On the contrary: the verbal expression of pain replaces crying and does not describe it. (Wittgenstein, 1953: 244).

There are plenty of language games which have the right combination of natural expressions and alternative verbal expressions. A child picks up a toy and chortles. A footballer writhes in the aftermath of a vigourous tackle. Gaza weeps with disappointment and frustration when he misses the vital shoot out against Argentina. These are natural expressions of how one is feeling. Words for feelings are learned as alternatives to natural ways of expressing feelings. Instead of chortling we learn to say 'I'm delighted'. Instead of weeping some footballers will tell you that they are 'as sick as a parrot'. So here we have the essential move in a resolution of the problem of how it is possible to learn how to use a word for a private feeling in a public context. We learn to use a verbal formula as a substitute for a natural expression. Just the same holds for the centredness of 'consciousness' and the use of the first person. In the same language games we can find the groundings of judgements of 'same and different feeling'. They are not made by a comparison between your feelings and mine, or between my feeling of yesterday and my feeling of today. They are made by attention to parallel patterns in the language games in which our feelings are publicly expressed.

Wittgenstein goes on to develop a thoroughgoing distinction between descriptions of public objects and states of affairs, and avowals of 'how it is with me', the form and content of private experiences. In the former case there is room for evidence, and error. In the latter there is no epistemological gap between the groan and the feeling, nor between the centring of my personal environment on my body and the use I make of 'I' in reporting on that environment from my point of view. The groan expresses the feeling. It does not describe it. Feeling and the disposition or tendency to groan, sigh, rub the spot, weep and so on are integral parts of the same phenomenon. Abstract any of them and the phenomenon disappears. If we have no tendency to groan then whatever the feeling is, it cannot be pain. Expressive ways of using language depend on a pre-existing ethological repertoire of natural expressions of the ways we are feeling, sad, in pain, happy, and so on. This is part of the natural history of humankind (Robinson and Harré, 1997).

The message of this paper is that the same treatment should be given to reflexive expressions like the first person pronouns and verb inflexions as Wittgenstein gave to words for feelings. They are expressions of the centred layout of what we can perceive, of what we can recollect and so on rather than devices used to refer to a mysterious entity within the person. In the Cartesian account of personal identity the inner 'ego' is not only the centre of experience but also a substance of which our experiences are properties. The word 'experience' springs easily to the pen in discussions like this, but it too is fraught with the possibility of bad grammatical analogies, as if the experience of something were a different phenomenon from the thing which we see, feel and so on.

We owe to Wittgenstein an all important insight for a methodology for psychological research, that the ontological distinction between thought (ineffable and meaningful) and language (audible, visible and tangible and meaningful) does not matter in certain key cases, because in the case of avowals, there is a holistic unity. Part of the art of psychological method is to be right in distinguishing those psychological phenomena for which the holistic principle holds and those for which it does not. There is no epistemological gap between a feeling and the expressions of a feeling, in those cases in which there is a natural expression, a part of human ethology, from which the substitution of words for non-verbal modes of expression can take its start. In the case of perception and proprioception the natural expression is to be seen in the way actions are taken — returning a serve, picking up a spoon, scratching an itch and so on. The P-grammar includes the rules for the use of first person indexicals and these are the basis of verbal substitutes for the natural expression of the structure of the environment as we perceive it.

The grammar of the expression of the environment as I perceive it

What is the role of the first person singular in everyday talk? At first glance it might look as if 'I' was a queer kind of name, one that each person could use to refer to him or herself. But already we can see that there is something odd about that suggestion. Unless the person addressed is aware of who is speaking the self-referential function of 'I' is ineffective. So who is 'I' for the moment is discovered, so to say, by knowing who is speaking (or writing). In this way it is quite unlike a proper name. I know who is being referred to when someone uses the words 'John Lennon', even though he is long since dead and gone and only his songs live on. I am addressed by my proper name, but never by 'I'. The pronoun of address is 'you', but that is not a name either. Neither pronoun is used to refer to anybody in the way a proper name can be used to refer to someone.

One common use for the first person singular, in English, is to take responsibility. 'I'll look after the children' is so close to a promise that it would usually be taken to be just another way of promising. However, in order to know where the responsibility lies the interlocutors must know who is speaking. Immediate presence is not necessary. One can make a commitment that is activated only in the future (a will) and one can make promises over the phone. Embodiment is not a necessary condition for this use of 'I'. Commitments could be entered into at a séance.

However there is another use of 'I', often going along with the one just described. 'I' indexes the perceptual content of a report with the spatial position of the speaker. This is common in the everyday life of positioning oneself in space. It is also the core of autobiography. Telling about an event in the first person places the speaker at or near the event in question. 'I watched the planes circle and come in to drop their bombs on the bridge' carries at least the conversational implicature that 'I was there!'. The archetypal autobiographical anecdote has both place and time indexes: 'When I was in Nevada ...' Authority for myself as the author of the story is claimed just by the use of the first person. Compare the fairy tale opening 'Once upon a time there lived a King who had three sons' with the autobiographical 'I was one of three brothers'.

Places are locations in physical space. They are defined by relations between material things. In so far as I have a place in space I have it by virtue of the fact of my embodiment. In so far as the tenses of the verbs in my utterances relate what I am saying to the times of events as past or future, my utterances themselves must be events in the same time frame as those events. In so far as those events are happenings in the material world, so must my utterances be. At least one aspect of myself must be a trajectory of connected locations in space and time.

But there is more. To be a person is to be a singularity, to have just one trajectory in space and time, to be embodied in just one material organism. This is not a ubiquitous fact that students of human life have discovered. It is part of the grammar of the 'person' concept. Strawson (1964) pointed out that it is only as embodied beings that people are routinely identified and reidentified as the singularities they are. They share this metaphysical property with the material things among which they are embodied. As a grammatical remark about people it fits well with the observations I have made above about the indexical force of the first person singular in reports of how the environment strikes me and autobiographical narratives. Personhood is so bounded by the singularity of each human being's embodiment that neither claims to more nor to less than one person per body are permitted to stand. The former exploits the distinction between the use of 'I' to take responsibility and its use to index reports with their spatial and temporal location. If there is a second 'I' in use by this body, then it may be taking responsibility for actions performed by the first 'I' who is then no longer to be blamed for them. The latter is so transparently a ploy if taken contemporaneously that it seems to turn, not on the question of material location as the centre point of perception, but on issues of responsibility. Fascinating though the issue is it is not central to my analysis in here.

In summary then, in order to understand a perceptual report I have to know *where* the speaker is in space. But that spatial position is fixed by the relations that the speaker bears to the things in the material environment. To have a place in such an array a speaker must be embodied, as a thing amongst things. The acts performed by the active person with whom we are engaged are embedded within sequences of events in the material environment, such as the risings and settings of the sun, the ticking of clocks and so on. So a speaker's acts must be carried by events in the material world. To understand a perceptual report fully I must know how the event of making the report and the event reported are related in time. Both must be material events, and this again requires that the speaker be embodied. The general principle that acts must be sustained materially has long been accorded a place in social psychology and ethology in the act-action-behaviour distinction. Behaviours are material phenomena, actions are material phenomena seen as intended by the actor, and acts are the social meanings of actions as they are seen with unfolding social episodes.

The traditional 'mind/body' distinction is no longer required to make sense of the distinction between private and public activities. Instead we are using a distinction between personal and impersonal points of view on the immediate and the distant environment. Singular embodiment, one person per body and one body per person, focuses our attention on that which is localised in space and time. People are many and history is rich in events. The emphasis I have placed in embodiment ought not to obscure the importance of studying cognitive phenomena that are generated in the symbolic interactions of crowds and in the historical unfolding of long term 'conversations'.

If consciousness talk is nothing other than a way of talking about what one perceives from one's own unique point of view, then the 'structure of consciousness' is nothing other than the structure of the field of perceived entities from the point of view of the perceiver. There is a singular but imperceptible 'origin' and a 'pencil' of relations to an ordered array of objects, both within and without the body. A public expression of this private and personal structure is to be found in the indexicals of the P-grammar with which we publicly make available to others 'the environment for me'.

Is consciousness socially contructed?

This sounds like a thrilling question. However, looking more closely at what might be involved it loses its exciting character. The mark of a socially constructed aspect of mind is variation in different cultures, in particular in the different ways languages perform the same or similar functions. Given that everyone's perceptual system, say as described by Gibson (1966), is inherited with certain built-in capacities in what ways could our uses of that system differ?

Fine structure

In addition to the indexical pronouns the grammar of demonstratives also reveals ways that the 'environment-for-me' is structured. English makes do with 'this' and 'that', for things seen, heard and so on near and far from the speaker. The language of the Maya of Yucatan is richer in demonstratives. For instance 'that-seeable-by-you-but-not-by-me' is lexically distinguished from 'that-seeable-by-both-of-us'. In short Maya demonstratives facilitate joint attention to the finer structure of an array of seen objects than does English. In this mundane sense we could say that the difference between Maya conscious-ness and English consciousness is socially constructed, in that the language game of referring to distant objects is learned in social practices, and what is learned during the acquisition of English demonstratives is different from what is learned when acquiring Mayan.

Salience

Even less thrilling is the commonplace that our capacities to differentiate objects in our environment is fine tuned by learning whatever discriminatory criteria are necessary to manage successfully in some local form of life. For instance the ethnobotany of one tribe will differ from that another, so what members of each will pay attention to in their environments will differ.

Further steps in the analysis

There is at least one major issue raised by the treatment offered in this paper
which must remain 'unfinished business'. Eliminating 'consciousness' talk in
favour of more mundane ways of expressing and commenting upon what
people can perceive both inside and outside the envelopes of their bodies, and
interpreting the first person as indexing avowals with the location of the
speaker, presumes that the *distinction* 'speaker-non-speaker' is in place. This
might be the 'I/thou' distinction of some theologians, or it might be the
Kantian double synthesis of 'self-as-perceiver' over against 'object-as-per-
ceived'. Is the maturing infant built to make this distinction or is it created in
Vygotskian psychological symbiosis with beings who have already acquired
it? Infants and chimpanzees, though at first unable to realise that a spot of
paint on their foreheads, visible in a mirror, is on their own faces, soon do
realise this, and try to pick it off. Is the transition due solely to maturation of
the perceptual system or does is it, in some measure socially constructed? I
believe the answer is yet to be found.

Since the P- and O-grammars are both required to delineate a research
programme in the psychology of perception, the question of their relationship
needs to be tackled. I have taken for granted that the criteria by which organs
and organ systems relevant to perception require distinctions drawn in the P-
grammar. Unless the criteria for seeing had been established it would be
impossible to identify eyes as the organs of sight. P-grammar criteria are
taxonomically prior to O-grammar criteria. In short no account of enabling
conditions is possible without an account of the phenomena that they enable.
This point has been made often enough in different terms, for instance by the
use of the phrase 'top/down'. However a robust defence is still required in the
face of reductionist arguments from Davidson (1980) and reductionist *obiter
dicta* from Crick (1994).

Note

1.   I owe notice of Shaver's work to M. A. Spackman.

References

Crick, F. 1994. *The Astonishing Hypothesis: The scientific search for the soul*. New York: Scribner.

Davidson, D. 1980. *Essays on Actions and Events*. Oxford: Clarendon Press.

Gibson, J. J. 1966. *The Senses Considered as Perceptual Systems*. New York: Houghton Miflin.

Hart, H. L. A. 1963. *Law, Liberty and Morality*. Stanford, CA: Stanford University Press.

Robinson, D. N. and Harré, R. 1995. "On the primacy of duties". *Philosophy* 70: 513–532.

Shaver, K. G. 1985. *The Attribution of Blame*. New York: Springer Verlag.

Strawson, P. F. 1964. *Individuals*. London: Methuen.

Vygotsky, L. S. 1962. *Thought and Language*. Cambridge, MA: MIT Press.

Wittgenstein, L. 1953. *Philosophical Investigations*. Trans. G. E. M. Anscombe and G. H. von Wright, Oxford: Blackwell.

CHAPTER 12

Investigating Altered States
on Their Own Terms

State-Specific Sciences

Charles T. Tart[1]
University of California at Davis

Scientific investigation obtains a great deal of its power through specialized and intensive focus on narrowly delineated aspects of reality. The (usually temporary) price of such intense focus may be blindness to other important aspects of reality. This is now obvious in the case of consciousness: *the consciousness of the individual scientist is, far and away, her or his most important instrument*, yet for decades the study of consciousness *per se* was outside of the purview of empirical science (except for studies trying to reduce aspects of consciousness to brain functioning). The last decade has seen a radical change, with the importance of understanding the nature and functioning of consciousness now widely recognized in a variety of disciplines.

A strong root of this resurgence of interest has been the widespread personal experiencing of altered states of consciousness (ASCs). In the 1960s an important source of this was personal experience of both laypersons and scientists with psychedelic drugs. Lately near-death experiences (NDEs) have sparked considerable interest.[2] There has also been an enormous increase in people practicing various meditative disciplines in the West. Such roots of interest illustrate another very important point: *consciousness is not just of academic and scientific interest: consciousness is our very mode of being and the source of the values by which we live our life.* This is often especially true for experiences of ASCs: a brief ASC like an NDE, for example, can alter a person's life and values (for better or worse) far more than years of education or psychotherapy. To apply only reductionist explanations to ASCs is rather like saying that a Picasso painting is due to nothing but putting pigments on canvas. If we do not thoroughly investigate all aspects of consciousness, we suffer from a basic blindness about our lives and values, a blindness that exacts a high penalty.

While there has been some research to date on ASCs, conventional research has not looked much at some primary ASC effects *per se*, viz. feelings of novel and valuable insights into both world and self, *noesis*, experienced by many people in ASCs.[3] Scientists are primarily motivated by a search for understanding, so states promising new insights and understandings were (and are) of interest to parts of the general scientific community, especially to students and younger scientists.

This interest in consciousness became largely dormant during the 1980s, partly as a reaction to the undiscriminating cultural hysteria about psychoactive drug use, and partly because many areas of science were not ready to start investigating consciousness in spite of the strong personal convictions of those who had experienced ASCs. In particular, a proposal for the creation of *state-specific sciences* that I presented in *Science* in 1972 (Tart 1972) turned out to be premature. A major reason for this prematurity was a deep cultural bias, revealed in the approximately one hundred letters to the editor submitted to *Science*, that rationality is *only* possible in our ordinary, "normal," state of consciousness. I believe conditions are now more favorable for this method of studying consciousness on its own terms (in addition to reductionist approaches: see, e.g., McFarlane 1996), so this chapter is an updated presentation of this proposal. Although I focus on ASCs, the discussion herein is applicable to the study of consciousness in general.

I propose that both our understanding of consciousness *per se* and our understanding of reality in general can be advanced by developing sciences that involve the use of essential scientific methods *within* various ASCs, viz. *state-specific sciences*. Such a development is compatible with essential science, although not with some current paradigmatic forms of science.

States of consciousness

A "state" of consciousness, or SoC, may be defined as a usefully distinctive organizational pattern of the components of consciousness. An "altered" state is then a qualitative, as well as perhaps a quantitative, alteration in the overall pattern of mental functioning relative to some SoC chosen as a baseline (usually ordinary consciousness), such that the experiencer feels her consciousness is qualitatively (and often radically) different from the way it functions in the baseline state.

To illustrate, I sometimes ask a class of students if anyone wants to argue that their current experience might actually be a nocturnal dream. After all, it is common for students to dream about being in a classroom. A few people will sometimes want to argue that this might indeed be the case, for some components of their current experience could be experienced in their dreams. But when I ask if they are willing to bet fifty dollars that they will wake up at home in bed in a few minutes, no one takes the bet. Within waking consciousness, it is almost always obvious that the pattern, the gestalt of mental functioning currently being experienced, the current SoC, is clearly different from that remembered as characterizing the ASC of dreaming. In general, across the spectrum of experiential reports, some ASCs are reported to be as different as the states of, for example, water (solid, liquid or gaseous), while the differences between others are more subtle but still of consequence for styles of perception, cognition and functioning.

There is usually an observable induction process (Tart 1975) to destabilize the baseline SoC from which one starts and to guide the formation of the desired ASC. Asking a person to imagine being relaxed and to be non-critical in thinking, for example, is part of the typical process to induce hypnosis. In general, as destabilizing forces reduce the stability of the baseline state, a chaotic-like transition develops, patterning forces affect the components and gestalt of the new ASC, and new stabilizing forces maintain the ASC. But, like most skills, the induction process can be so overlearned and automatized that transition to an ASC can be almost instantaneous.[4] Such fast transitions and habitual familiarity can mean that a person may not consciously recognize that he or she is in an ASC.

While the concept of an ASC can be refined well beyond what is needed in this chapter (see Tart 1975), such as conceptualizing SoCs from a systems theory approach and/or as constituting a *world simulation process*, or a *biological-psychological virtual reality* (BPVR)(Tart 1987, 1991), it is also a common sense concept applied to widespread personal experience. Almost all ordinary people experience the ASC of nocturnal dreaming, for example. Many have experienced the ASCs of alcohol intoxication (not just the mild effects of light drinking on ordinary consciousness) or ASCs induced by other drugs like marijuana. Experiencers of NDEs perceive their consciousness functioning in a drastically altered manner. I also believe that any strong emotional state (rage, depression, ecstasy, etc.) can be usefully conceptualized as an ASC. Other ASCs include those loosely characterized as hypnosis, meditation-induced states, sensory-isolation induced states, mediumistic and possession trance, reverie, shamanic states, guided visualization states, and channeling states.

Kuhnian paradigms and states of consciousness

My concept of SoCs and ASCs as being qualitatively distinct organizations of the patterning of mental (both perceptual and evaluative) functioning, has strong parallels with Thomas Kuhn's (1962) concept of *paradigms* in science. A paradigm is an intellectual achievement that underlies normal science and attracts and guides the enduring work of a number of adherents in their scientific activity. It is a kind of "super theory," a formulation of wide enough scope to bring about the useful organization of most of the major known phenomena of its field. Yet it is sufficiently open-ended in that there still remain important problems to be solved *within* that framework.

Because of their tremendous success, paradigms undergo a change which, in principle, ordinary scientific theories do not undergo. An ordinary scientific theory is *always* subject to further questioning and testing as it is extended. A paradigm undergoes a psychological shift: it becomes a largely implicit framework for most scientists working within it; it becomes the "natural" way of looking at things and doing things. It does not seriously occur to the adherents of a paradigm to question it any more (we ignore, for the moment, what happens during scientific revolutions). Theories become referred to as "laws:" students are almost always taught the "Law" of gravity, not the "theory" of gravity, for example.

A paradigm serves to concentrate the attention of researchers on "sensible" (by the paradigm's logic) problem areas and to prevent them from wasting time on what might be unimportant. On the other hand, by explicitly and implicitly defining some lines of research as "trivial" or "nonsensical," a paradigm acts like a set of blinders. Kuhn has discussed this blinding function as a key factor in the lack of effective communications during paradigm clashes.

The concepts of a paradigm and an SoC have many similarities. Both constitute complex, interlocking sets of procedural rules and theories that enable a person to interact with and interpret experiences within an environment. In both cases, the rules and theories become largely implicit. They are not recognized as tentative working hypotheses; they operate automatically and the person feels she is doing the obvious or natural thing. How the world is "naturally" perceived is especially important. Modern psychological and neurological research has shown that perception is not a simple and "natural" given but highly affected by, semi-arbitrarily constructed by, both nervous system structure and psychological and cultural conditioning. The old saying "Seeing is believing," is only part of the story, for believing is also seeing. Both an SoC or a paradigm can literally control the automatized construction of perceiving and evaluating, such that experience does seem to "obviously" confirm the tenets of the SoC or the paradigm. In Ptolemaic astronomy, the "obvious" retrograde motion of planets is seen as actual movement of the planets; in Copernican astronomy it is obviously an "illusion" caused by the motion of the earth. Experiencing an ASC is thus of considerable interest in essential science because it is analogous to suddenly seeing the world through the construction process of another paradigm.

Paradigm clash

We tend to become emotionally attached to the things which give us pleasure, and a scientist making important progress within a particular paradigm can become emotionally attached to it, as well as being rewarded with peer approval, promotion, publication access to prestigious journals, etc. When data which make no sense in terms of current paradigm are brought to our attention, the usual result is not a reevaluation of the paradigm, but a rejection or misperception of such data. This rejection seems rational to others sharing that paradigm and irrational to others committed to a different paradigm. Einstein's rejection of some of the implications of quantum theory is a well known example, with many colleagues sharing Einstein's "sensible" position, even though his convictions about the nature of reality in this area were eventually undercut by experiments.

In spite of the current resurgence of scientific interest in consciousness, there is still frequent conflict of a paradigmatic sort between those whose approach is based solely on mainstream, usually physicalistic, paradigms and those who also want scientific investigation to progress but who have experienced the alternative paradigmatic points of view that can come from personal experience of various ASCs.

Consider, as a dramatic example, a subject in an experiment involving a deep meditative state producing the unity experience. The subject may tell the investigator that "You and I, all beings, are all one, there are no separate selves!" The investigator "perceives" and is likely to report that her subject showed a "confused sense of identity and distorted thinking processes," or "poor reality contact." The subject is reporting what is "obvious" to him, the investigator is reporting what is "obvious" to her. The investigator's implicit paradigm, based on her scientific training, her cultural background, and her normal SoC, is physicalistic, a world view in which the investigator and subject are discrete physical entities with no energetic or physical connection other than the indirect one of verbal exchange, a "real" condition enormously short of reaching "unity." Her paradigm indicates that a literal interpretation of the subject's statement cannot be true, and therefore *must* be interpreted as mental dysfunction on the part of the subject. The subject, his paradigms radically changed for the moment by being in an ASC, not only reports what is obviously true to him, but perceives the investigator as stuck in a limited state of consciousness, being incapable of perceiving the obvious!

Must the experiencers of ASCs continue to see the mainstream scientists as too often concentrating on the irrelevant, and these scientists see the experiencers as deluded? Or can science deal adequately with ASC (as well as ordinary state) experiences? The thesis I shall now present in detail is that we can deal with important aspects of ASCs using the essence of scientific method, even though a variety of nonessentials, unfortunately overly identified with current science, hinder such an effort.

The nature of knowledge

Basically, science (from the Latin *scire*, to know) deals with knowledge. Knowledge may be defined for our purposes here as an immediately given experiential feeling of congruence between two different kinds of experience, a matching, "I understand." One set of experiences may be regarded as perceptions of the external world, of others, or of oneself; the second set may be regarded as a theory, a scheme, a belief, a system of understanding. I see an object fall, for example (one set of mental experiences) and "know" that it is "caused" by the "force of gravity" (another set of mental experiences comprising my ideas about physics). The feeling of congruence is usually something immediately given in experience, although many refinements have been worked out for judging degrees of congruence.

All knowledge, then, is basically experiential knowledge. Even my so-called objective knowledge of the physical world can be reduced to this: given certain sets of experiences, which I (by habitual assumption) attribute to the external world activating my sensory apparatus, it may be possible for me to compare them with purely internal experiences (memories, previous knowledge about how the hypothesized physical world works) and predict with a high degree of reliability other kinds of subsequent experiences, which I again attribute to the external world.

Because science has been incredibly successful in dealing with the physical world, it has been historically been associated with a philosophy of physicalism, the belief that reality is totally reducible to certain kinds of physical entities. The vast majority of phenomena of ASCs have no known physical manifestations: thus to physicalistic philosophy they are "epiphenomena," not worthy of serious study. But insofar as science deals with knowledge *per se*, it need not restrict itself only to physical kinds of knowledge. To put it another way, the methods of *essential* science are a powerful knowledge gathering and refining tool which can be used more widely than just in studying phenomena of the physical world.

Essential scientific method

I shall discuss the essence of scientific method, what I like to call *essential science*, which is not the same as paradigmatic (which Kuhn also called "normal") science, and show that essential science is compatible with an enlarged study of the important phenomena of ASCs.

As satisfying as the *feeling* of knowing can be, we are often wrong: what seems like congruence at first later does not match, or has no generality. We have learned that our reasoning is often faulty, our observations are often incomplete or mistaken, and that emotional and other nonconscious biasing factors can seriously distort both reasoning and observational processes. Our reliance on authorities, "rationality" or "elegance," while helpful, are not sure criteria for achieving truth. The development of essential scientific method may be seen as a determined effort to systematize the process of acquiring knowledge in such a way as to minimize the various pitfalls of observation and reasoning.

I shall discuss four basic rules of scientific method to which an investigator is committed, namely: (1) observation; (2) logical theory construction; (3) the testing of theory by predicting observable consequences; and (4) full communication linking these various processes. Together these constitute the essential scientific enterprise. I shall consider the wider application of each rule to the study and use of ASCs and indicate how unnecessary physicalistic restrictions may be dropped. Then I will show that all these commitments or rules can be accommodated in the development of state-specific sciences (SSSs).

Observation

The basic processes of essential science are schematized in Figure 1. The arrows represent major information flow routes.

We start with some segment of reality that we want to learn more about and begin making observations, collecting *data*, about what actually happens. It is necessary to realize we can often be insensitive and biased observers, so part of the observational process is a continual commitment to discover our shortcomings and to devise processes and/or instruments that increase the accuracy of our observations: this is represented by the circular "refine" arrow in the observational (and other process) circles in Figure 1.

Although a scientist is committed to observe as well as possible the phenomena of interest, our paradigmatic commitments, our individual and cultural SoCs, make us likely to observe only parts of reality and to ignore or erroneously observe other parts. To date, many important ASC phenomena

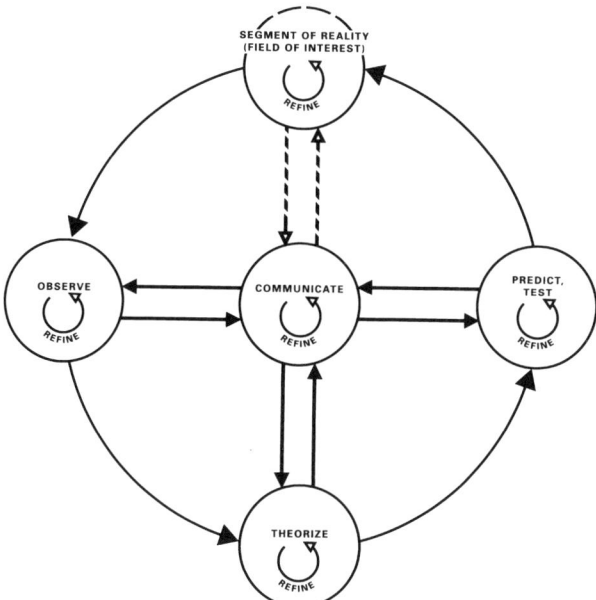

Figure 1

have been observed poorly or not at all because of the physicalistic classification of them as "epiphenomena," thought of as "subjective," "ephemeral"
"unreliable," or "unscientific." Such *a priori* value judgments thus interfere
with observation. Observations of internal processes are probably more difficult to make than those of external physical processes, because of their
inherently greater complexity,[5] but devaluing and not observing them in the
first place is not the way to understanding. *The essence of good science,
however, is that we commit ourselves to observe what there is to be observed,
whether it is difficult or not, whether it fits in with our beliefs and desires or not.*

When the data to be observed are experiences from within and particular
to a specific SoC, then we have *state-specific observations.* They can only be
made by investigators who can function in that specific SoC. Some consequences of this will be discussed later.

There is another observational problem. One of the traditional ideals of
science, the unbiased and isolated observer, whose observations do not affect
the observed, has little place in dealing with many internal phenomena of
SoCs. Not only are the observer's perceptions selective, he may also affect the

things he observes. Rather than increasing errors by pretending to an objectivity we may not have, we must try to understand the characteristics of each
individual observer in order to compensate for them.

A recognition of the frequent factual unreality of the experimenter being
a totally objective and detached observer in the psychological sciences was
starting to become widespread in the 1970s, with studies under the topics of
experimenter bias (Rosenthal 1966) and *demand characteristics* (Orne 1962).
Interest and work in this fell off sharply, however. I suspect that the topic was
too threatening, and so was brushed under the rug rather than really dealt with.
I have done some work in the area (Troffer 1964; Tart 1977) and have always
carried out experiments with the assumption that I am biased and so should try
to be careful to recognize my biases and eliminate sources of bias. A similar
recognition long ago occurred in physics when it was realized that the observed was "altered" by the process of observation at subatomic levels —
more precisely that the observed events did not have definite values until they
interacted with the measuring apparatus — or in relativity theory where the
characteristics/motion of the observer had to be taken into account. When we
deal with ASCs where the observer is the experiencer of the ASC and the
observer's experiences are the data, this factor is of paramount importance.
Not knowing the characteristics of the observer can also confound the process
of consensual validation, which we shall soon consider.

Theorizing

In spite of its primacy, we are not that interested in data *per se*, however. As
discussed earlier, we want to know, to create *theories*, schema, hypotheses —
mental constructs that match and make sense out of the data we have observed. A basic requirement of essential science is that, ideally, our theories
completely account for the data we have observed. In practice we may create
theories that account for that portion of the data we deem of most interest at the
time, but ultimately our theories aim to account for *all* of the "significant"
data. We use some kind of "logic" or system of thought — more precisely
some kind of axiomatic and procedural system of thinking — to create these
theories, and, as with observation, we commit ourselves to improvement, both
looking for potential errors in our logic/system of thought that we can correct
and/or toward expanding the explanatory power of our theories.

A scientist may theorize about his observations as much as he wishes, but the theory he develops must consistently account for all that he has observed, and should have a logical structure that other scientists can comprehend. The requirement to theorize logically and consistently with the data is not as simple as it looks, however. Philosophers long ago demonstrated that *any* logic/system of thought consists of a set of (arbitrary) assumptions and a set of rules for manipulating information, based on these assumptions. Change the assumptions, or change the rules, and there may be entirely different outcomes when the different logics/systems of thought are applied to the same data. In Euclidean geometry, for example, parallel lines remain the same distance apart even when extended to infinity (by assumption alone, as this cannot possibly be tested empirically), but in Riemannian or Lobatschewskian geometry, where there are different assumptions about the nature of space, they either touch or move infinitely far apart when so extended. Problems solved in these three geometries lead to quite different outcomes and all these outcomes have their uses.

A paradigm or an SoC, is a logic/system of thought (or set of logics): each has certain assumptions and rules for working within these assumptions, certain things that are "obviously" true within the logic/system of thought. By changing the paradigm (with its paradigm-specific perceptions and logics) or altering the SoC to an ASC (with its altered, state-specific perceptions and logics), the nature of theory building may change radically. Thus an investigator in SoC#2 might come to very different "logical" conclusions about the nature of the same events that he observed and thought about in SoC#1. An investigator in SoC#1 may comment on the comprehensibility of the second person's ideas from the point of view (paradigm) of SoC#1, but can say nothing about their *inherent* SoC#2 validity. A scientist who could enter either SoC#1 or SoC#2, however, could pronounce on the state-specific comprehensibility of the other's theory, and the adherence of that theory to the rules and logic of SoC#2. Thus, scientists trained in the same SoC may check on the logical validity of each other's theorizing.

It is important to note that the idea of different and arbitrary "logics" or systems of thought is a difficult one that flies in the face of ordinary experience and social norms, for we have a deep belief that there is one ultimate and correct way of reasoning. But the *data* of ASCs to date is that people have experienced a variety of logics. Whether there is some ultimate logic underlying this apparent phenomenological diversity is a question left to future empirical research.

Observable Consequences

Essential science is built on a recognition, however, that a theory being "logical" — conforming to the rules of a system that is based on arbitrary assumptions — is not enough to guarantee progress. We have to avoid the trap of what I like to call the Principle of Limitless Rationalization, a recognition that many of us are smart enough to make a plausible sounding *post hoc* fit between *any* data and some theory, regardless of whether that theory is actually correct in reality. Thus the third step of essential science: the requirement that *a scientific theory must make predictions about new events* which can be observed and *these predictions must be tested*. If your theory predicts, "If A, then B," and you set up A but B doesn't follow, that's too bad for your theory. It doesn't matter if your theory is mathematical, is "elegant," is consistent with currently fashionable and widely accepted theories, and is obviously brilliant and true to you: it's wrong in that it does not predict observables. The theory must either be modified until its predictions get better or it must be replaced with another theory. *In essential science, theory is always secondary to data.* In "normal," paradigmatic science, on the other hand, the paradigmatic framework tends to become predominant and data that doesn't fit is automatically trivialized or overlooked altogether. Paradigms and theories are useful when we use them as appropriate and useful, but when we become attached to them and they function automatically, we are enslaved by them and our vision is constricted.

Ordinarily when we think of empirical validation, we think of validation in terms of testable consequences that produce *physical* effects, but this physicality is not necessary to the essential scientific process. Any known effect, whether interpreted as "physical" or "nonphysical," is ultimately an experience in an observer's mind. All that is essentially required to validate the usefulness of a theory is that it predict that "When certain experiences (observed necessary conditions) have occurred, another specified kind of experience will follow." Thus an essentially scientific theory may be based on data that have no external, physical existence, but are observable as internal data.

Observing the tests of theoretical predictions takes us back to the segment of reality we are interested in (see Figure 1 again), eventually leading to improved understanding. When we begin an area of science we will make relatively crude (in retrospect) observations and have theories that are only gross approximations of reality with moderate support from predictions. Science is not a one time process, however, but a continuous one. The continual operation of this

observe → theorize → test →…..observe → theorize → test…..

cycle ultimately leads to better and better matches between our knowledge and what can be observed.

Communication/Consensual validation

I have described essential science so far as if it were the solitary activity of an individual scientist, but of course science is also a collective process. Any particular individual, no matter how devoted to the ideals of enriching our knowledge through the process of essential science, undoubtedly has her or his own particular biases and shortcomings in observation, theorizing and testing. Thus the fourth element of essential science, *full and honest communication about all the aspects of the processes of observation, theorizing and prediction.* Colleagues check and expand your observations, adding in their own, check and expand the logic of your theories and predictions, test predictions of your theory, etc. Since it is unlikely that all one's colleagues will have biases and shortcomings identical to one's own, a social feedback and correction process works to reduce the effects of biases. As with all other stages of the process, a commitment to improving communications and absolute honesty is essential.

We usually require that observations be *public* in that they must be replicable by any *properly trained* observer. Where the observations are reports of particular internal experiences, the (experienced) conditions that led to the report of certain experiences must be described in sufficient detail that others may duplicate them and consequently have experiences which we judge to be reasonably identical. We assume that experiential data are subject to some sort of natural laws, just as physical data are. That someone else may set up apparently similar conditions but not have the same experiences, suggests that the original investigator gave an incorrect description of the conditions and observations (including the initial observer's relevant characteristics), or that she was not aware of certain essential aspects of the conditions, such as significant individual differences between different observers' styles of mental functioning. Disagreements among observers are stimuli to discover why such disagreement occurs.

The unnecessary physicalistic accretion to this rule of consensual validation is that, physical data being the only "real" data, internal phenomena must
be reduced to physiological or behavioral data to become reliable or they will
be ignored entirely. I believe most physical observations to be more readily
replicable by any *trained* observer (although the training, such as getting a
PhD in physics, may be much more arduous than developing some ASC
abilities!) because physical events can often be expressed in terms of predic-
tive models, a procedure which we have not developed yet for internal events.
In principle, however, consensual validation of internal phenomena by trained
observers is possible. Experienced marijuana users, for example, gave consistent rankings of minimal thresholds for various internal phenomena as a
function of their overall experiential perception of how intoxicated they were
(Tart and Kvetensky 1973). Buddhist meditation tradition has criteria for the
quality of the states reached in meditation (Brown and Engler 1980), criteria
only comprehensible and applicable by those who have attained similar meditative states.

Note too that the emphasis on the public nature of observation in science
has a misleading quality insofar as it implies that any intelligent person can
replicate a scientist's observations. This might have been true early in the
history of science, but nowadays only the highly trained observer can replicate
many observations. I cannot go into a modern physicist's laboratory and
confirm her observations. Indeed, her talk of what she has found in her
experiments (physicists seem to talk about innumerable invisible entities these
days) would probably seem "mystical" (in the pejorative sense of the term) to
me, just as many descriptions of internal states sound "mystical" to those with
a background in the physical sciences.

Given the high complexity of the phenomena associated with ASCs, the
need for replication by *trained* observers is exceptionally important. Since it
generally takes 6 to 10+ years of intensive training to produce a scientist in
most of our conventional sciences, we should not be surprised that there has
been very little reliability of observations from untrained observers of ASC
phenomena or of experiential phenomena in general. Psychology, for example, began in the last century as an introspective discipline, where "trained
observers" intended to isolate and observe the basic elements of the mind, a
sort of mental chemistry model. When different laboratories could not agree in
their basic observations, discouragement set in and psychology moved largely

to behaviorism, throwing away the bulk of the most interesting aspects of mental life, getting a much narrower, but far easier to observe, subject matter.

In retrospect, this failure of early introspective psychology is not hard to understand. A "trained observer" was usually a research assistant with 10 to 20 hours of training, but insofar as we take a 2500 year old tradition (Buddhism) of meditative training seriously, their finding was that almost all people's ordinary minds were (and are) so unstable and biased that it takes something like 5,000 hours of basic training to calm and stabilize the mind so that basic mental phenomena can be reliably observed.[6]

In addition to the fact that state-specific observations are potentially available only to those who can enter the required SoC, a second problem in consensual validation arises from a phenomenon predicted by my concept of ASCs, but not yet empirically investigated, namely, *state-specific communication*. Given that an ASC is an overall qualitative and quantitative shift in the complex functioning of consciousness, such that there are new "logics" and perceptions (which constitute a paradigm shift), it is reasonable to hypothesize that communication may take a different pattern. For two observers, both of whom, we assume, are fluent in communicating with each other in a given SoC, communication about some new observations may seem adequate to them, or may be improved or problematic in specific ways. To an "outside" observer, an observer in a different SoC, the communication between these two observers may seem "nonsensical" or "deteriorated."

Practically all investigations to date by scientists in a state of ordinary consciousness of communication by persons in ASCs have resulted in reports of "deterioration" of communication abilities. In designing their studies, however, these investigators have not taken into account the fact that the patterns and internal logics of communication may have changed. If I am listening to two people speaking in English, and they suddenly begin to intersperse words and phrases in Portuguese, I, as an outside (non-Portuguese speaking) observer, will erroneously perceive a gross "deterioration" in communication. Adequacy of communication between people in the same SoC and across SoCs must be empirically determined.

Thus consensual validation my be restricted by the fact that only observers in the same ASC are able to communicate adequately with each other, and they may not be able to communicate adequately to someone in a different SoC, say normal consciousness.[7]

State-specific sciences

We tend to envision science like this: centered around interest in some particular subject matter, a number of highly selected, and rigorously trained people spend considerable time making detailed observations on the subject matter of interest. To various degrees they have special places (laboratories) or instruments or methodologies to assist them in making finer observations. They speak to one another in a special technical language which they feel conveys precisely the important facts of their field. Using this language, they confirm and extend each other's knowledge of certain data basic to the field. They theorize about their basic data in accordance with the special logic(s) they have been trained in and construct elaborate systems. They validate these by recourse to further observation. These trained people all have a long-term commitment to the constant refinement of observation and extension of theory. Their activity is frequently incomprehensible to laymen. Their work may or may not have some consequences that affect ordinary people's lives.

This general description is equally applicable to a variety of sciences, or areas that could become sciences, whether we called such areas biology, physics, chemistry, psychology, lucid dreaming, understanding of mystical states, or drug-induced alteration of cognitive processes. The particulars of research would look very different, but the essential scientific method potentially running through all is the same.

More formally, I now propose the creation of various state-specific sciences. If such sciences could be created, we would have a group of highly skilled, dedicated, and trained practitioners able to achieve a common SoC (an *altered* state of consciousness, an ASC, remember, in comparison with their ordinary state) and able to agree with one another that they have attained a common state. While in that SoC, they might then investigate various areas of interest, whether these be totally internal phenomena of that given SoC, the interaction of that state with external, physical reality, or the experiences and behavior of people in other SoCs.

The fact that the experimenter should be able to function skillfully in the SoC itself for a state-specific science does not necessarily mean that he would always be the subject/observer. While he might often be the subject, observer, and experimenter simultaneously, it would be quite possible for him to collect data from experimental manipulations of other subjects in the SoC, and either be in SoC himself at the time of data collection (so he would be sensitive to nuances of observers' reports not communicable to people not in that SoC) or be in that SoC himself for data reduction and theorizing.

Illustrations of state-specific sciences

Examples of some observations made and theorizing done by a scientist in a specific ASC would illustrate the nature of a proposed state-specific science. But this is not easy to do because no state-specific sciences have yet been *formally* established.[8] Also, any example that would make good sense to the readers of this chapter (who are, presumably, all in a normal SoC)[9] would not really illustrate the uniqueness of a state-specific science. If parts of it did make sense, it would be an example of a problem that could be approached usefully from both the ASC and our ordinary SoC. Thus it would be too easy to see the entire problem in terms of accepted scientific procedures for normal SoCs and so miss the point about the necessity for developing state-specific sciences.

However there has been significant progress in one area toward laying the foundations of a state-specific science, namely the study of lucid dreaming, and we may already have one highly developed state-specific science which has not been recognized as such.

Lucid dreaming

Lucid dreaming is an ASC that usually begins as an ordinary nocturnal dream (with the usual stage-1 EEG and rapid eye movement [REM] correlates), but at some point the ASC of ordinary dreaming is converted into lucid dreaming by two events. First, the dream thought, "This is a dream." occurs. This is a necessary, but not sufficient, condition for defining a lucid dream, as this dream thought can occur without any further changes in the gestalt quality of consciousness that comprises ordinary dreaming. Then a rapid change in the pattern of consciousness may occur (the induction process is not well understood) that is described by the adjective "lucid," for consciousness is now experienced as having roughly the clarity of one's ordinary waking state — *but one is still sensorily located in the dream world in a perfectly "real" way.* Except for the major sensory change of being located in a quite real dream world (the dreamer feels she is *perceiving* a dream world, usually with as much or more intensity as the ordinary sensory world is perceived, not *imagining* it), the quality of consciousness is very *like*–although not necessarily *identical* with — ordinary consciousness. How is this distinction made? In the same way we discussed at the beginning of this chapter in defining states of consciousness, namely your obvious observation that the pattern of your mental functioning is essentially that of your waking state, not the pattern you recall as constituting your dream state. A lucid dreamer can also test various components of mental functioning, such as checking for continuity and clarity of waking memories, availability of skills (such as "logically" reasoning that it is impossible to be so obviously lucid and conscious while dreaming, but right then you are experiencing the reality that it can happen), etc.

The 1969 publication of my *Altered States of Consciousness* book had the fortunate effect of sensitizing people to the reality of lucid dreaming (it had been almost totally ignored by mainstream dream investigators) by republishing Frederick van Eeden's 1913 article describing and naming this ASC (Tart 1969: 145–158), and considerable attention was then given to the topic. While a lucid dream is a once-in-a-lifetime experience for most people, some have learned to deliberately induce them, if not quite at will at least with at least fair probability of having one on any particular night. Most such investigators have described lucid dreams in ordinary state language to maximize communications, and there is now an extensive literature on this (see, e.g. (Gackenbach 1988; LaBerge 1985). A newsletter (*Lucidity Letter*) that evolved into a journal, *Lucidity*, (now unfortunately defunct for financial reasons) connected investigators so they could share observations, experimental results (what happens when you try X in a lucid dream?), and theories about the nature of lucid dreams. For example, some investigators reported that they could not switch on lights beyond low levels of experienced brightness in their lucid dreams (compared to their memories of waking state light brightness while in the lucid dream) and theorized that there were underlying physiological reasons, involving levels of cortical activation, to explain this. Other investigators practiced switching on lights in their lucid dreams and eventually found they could get bright illumination in their dreams, so the theory of an underlying cortical limit here was rejected.

Investigation of lucid dreams by lucid dreamers is now most strongly represented by a newsletter (*Night Light*) published by one of the pioneering investigators, Stephen LaBerge (information at http://www.lucidity.com) and by the sharing of observations and theories in internet news groups (see, e.g., alt.dreams.lucid). While much of this activity can be seen as the investigation of an ASC from within ordinary consciousness, that is as ordinary state reflection on reports about and memories of lucid dream experiences, there can be state-specific qualities to lucid dreaming (recall the definition above that the SoC in lucid dreaming is very like ordinary consciousness, but not necessarily identical to it). A promising beginning step in investigating this was a study by Bogzaran (1996). She investigated lucid dreamers who had also experienced some of their lucid dreams as a transition state into a more mystical ASC, described as a "multidimensional space." They had great difficulty attempting to describe that state, calling it "ineffable." But when she had them inspect the works of several modern artists (Gordon Onslow Ford, Roberto Matta, Lee Mullican and John Anderson), they found the paintings expressed the multidimensional spaces they had experienced in a way that made sense to them. This may be a step toward an indirect form of state-specific communication, necessary for developing SSSs of lucid dreams, as two lucid dreamers in their lucid dreams are not in direct contact with one another at that time.

Mathematics

I will argue that various branches of pure mathematics constitute at least one, if not several, unrecognized state-specific sciences.[10] I intend this argument to be provocative rather than definitive, in the hope that it will inspire mathematicians to reflect on the SoCs they work in and see how well they fit the concept of state-specific sciences.

The "data" of pure mathematics are entirely experiential, mental in nature. Second, the subject matter of pure mathematics consists of experiential "perceptions"/data as well as theorizing, because mathematicians frequently allude to a sort of quasi-perception of mathematical "forms" ("forms" may be too concrete a word for some mathematics) as a basis for their work. They try to grasp or perceive these forms more and more accurately. Third, mathematicians theorize in terms of various logics, systems of mathematics, and try to apply this correctly. Fourth, predictions from such theories are often tested on other experiential data, mathematical "perceptions" and "intuitions," and the power of the extension of the theories is used as a test of the generality and usefulness of them. Finally there is communication with colleagues about all stages of the process, and these state-specific communications about state-specific observations and state-specific logics are sufficiently well developed among practitioners to allow general agreement among this community of state-specific scientists as to what is and isn't valid.

While one might argue that there is no formal "induction" of an ASC to do mathematical work, recall the observation at the beginning of this paper that with practice induction can be virtually instantaneous and functioning in the ASC so familiar that the person does not notice that she is in an ASC. Indeed more than one SoC may be involved: a mathematician might do her creative work in an ASC, e.g., but switch back to ordinary consciousness for communicating. Some people are naturally talented at entering the appropriate SoC(s) for doing pure mathematics, but most have (also) had the induction procedure of many years duration called getting an advanced degree in mathematics.

Transpersonal psychologist Ken Wilber has expressed a parallel between mathematics and contemplative traditions provocatively as: "Simply because religious experience is apprehended in an 'interior' fashion does not mean it is merely private knowledge, any more than the fact that mathematics and logic are seen inwardly, by the mind's eye, makes them merely private fantasies without public import. Mathematical knowledge is public knowledge to all equally trained mathematicians; just so, contemplative knowledge is public knowledge to all equally trained contemplatives." (Wilber 1984: 20).

If practicing mathematicians will begin making psychological observations of the SoCs they function in, rather than only being absorbed in their work within those states, we may learn a great deal about how state-specific sciences can work. Further, more knowledge *per se* of these mathematically useful SoCs may aid the training of future mathematicians or increase the efficiency of those already utilizing them. It is now up to mathematicians to expand or refute this argument.

Prospects

I believe that an examination of human history and our current situation in a new century provides a strong argument for the necessity of SSSs. Throughout history people have been influenced by spiritual and mystical experiences that are expressed (usually in watered-down and doctrinally edited forms) in the religions that attract large numbers of people. Spiritual and mystical experiences are primary phenomena of various ASCs: because of such experiences, untold numbers of both the noblest and most horrible acts of which people are capable have been committed. Yet in all the time that Western sciences have existed, no concerted attempt has been made to understand these ASC phenomena in essential scientific terms.[11]

It was the belief of many that religions were simply a form of superstition that would be left behind in our "rational" age. Not only has this prediction failed, but our own understanding of the nature of reasoning now makes it clear that it can never be fulfilled. Reason is a tool, and a tool that is wielded in the service of assumptions, beliefs, and needs which are not themselves necessarily subject to reason. There are many logics, not just one correct way of thinking, as discussed earlier. The irrational, and, more importantly, the a-rational, will not disappear from the human situation. Our immense success in the development of the physical sciences has not been particularly successful in formulating better philosophies of life, or increasing our psychological knowledge of ourselves. The sciences we have developed to date are not very human sciences. They tell us *how* to do things, but do not give us much insight on *what* to do or not to do, or *why* to do things.

In the original 1972 presentation of this proposal for establishing state-specific sciences, I noted that "The youth of today and mature scientists in increasing numbers are turning to meditation, oriental religions, and personal use of psychedelic drugs. The phenomena encountered in these ASCs provide more satisfaction and are more relevant to the formulation of philosophies of life and deciding upon appropriate ways of living, than "pure reason" (Needleman 1970). My own impressions are that very large numbers of scientists are now personally exploring ASCs, but few have begun to connect this personal exploration with their scientific activities." While psychedelic drug use is not as central as it was then, the main thrust of this statement is still true.

It is difficult to predict what the chances are of developing state-specific sciences. Our knowledge is still too diffuse and dependent on our normal SoCs. Yet I think it is probable that state-specific sciences can be developed for such SoCs as alcohol intoxication, auto-hypnosis, various meditative states,[12] marijuana intoxication, LSD intoxication, self-remembering, reverie, various emotional states, and biofeedback-induced states (Tart 1969), in addition to lucid dreaming. In all of these SoCs, some volition seems to be retained, so that the observer can indeed carry out experiments on herself or others or both. Some SoCs, in which the wish to experiment during the state may disappear, but in which some experimentation can be carried out if special conditions are prepared before the state is entered, might be ordinary dreaming, hypnagogic states, and high dreams (Tart 1969). Some SoCs, like those associated with NDEs, may simply be too dangerous to deliberately experiment with, although we should try to learn what we can from retrospective reports about them.

The development of SSSs will not be easy. There are important issues which space has not allowed discussion of here, such as (1) distinguishing SSSs from religions, (2) the complementary nature of relationships between various SSSs, with no particular one (including ordinary consciousness science) necessarily having a privileged position with respect to the others, (3) the importance of understanding individual differences in mental functioning to reduce error variance, and (4) sociological and psychological problems for some individuals in experiencing ASCs. These are discussed elsewhere (Tart 1972, 1978).

It is important that the question of the development of SSSs be answered by actual attempts at development, rather than *a priori*, biased ordinary state decisions about what is and isn't possible. As industrialist Henry Ford once said, "Those who think they can and those who think they can't are both right." Considerable scientific adventure lies ahead of us!

Notes

1.   This chapter is adapted by the author from a longer paper (Tart 1998) which is available on the internet at http://www.nscee.edu/unlv/Colleges/Sciences/Consciousness_Studies/ SSS_South_America.html or from the author's web site www.paradigm-sys.com/cttart/, as is the original *Science* paper.

2.   This is most interesting culturally. Many of the Greek founders we trace our rational traditions to were also initiates of one of the prominent mystery religions, the Elusynian mysteries, where inducing something like an NDE as a form of gnosis was central. Because of the enormous advances of modern medicine in resuscitation, it has been estimated that about eight million people have been accidentally "initiated" into the Elusynian mysteries (without preparation, of course) in the last few decades. Most primary research on NDEs is published in the 15 year *old Journal of Near-Death Studies* (Human Sciences Press, 233 Spring St., New York NY 10013–1578).

3.   See (Tart 1971) (text fully available online at http://www.druglibrary.org/schaffer/lsd/ bookmenu.htm) for a comprehensive account of the phenomenology of marijuana intoxication as one example on such ASC effects. A briefer journal version is also available (Tart 1970).

4.   If we could observe our own mental processes well enough we would probably find that "ordinary" consciousness is often a series of rapid and automated transitions between a variety of discrete SoCs, all within the range considered normal, but we need not make that distinction in this chapter.

5.   Because of this, for pedagogical purposes I like to pointedly refer to the physical sciences as the "easy" sciences and the psychological ones as the "hard" sciences.

6.   Personal communication, Shinzen Young, 1985.

7.   A state-specific scientist might find his own work somewhat incomprehensible when he was not in that SoC because of the phenomenon of *state-specific memory*–that is, not enough of his work would transfer to his ordinary SoC to make it comprehensible, even though it would make perfect sense when he was again in the ASC in which he did his scientific work.

8.   "Ordinary consciousness science" is not a good example of a pure state-specific science because many important discoveries have occurred during ASCs, such as reverie, dreaming, meditative-like states and trance states (see Hadamard 1954 e.g.).

9.   When I first proposed the creation of state-specific sciences in 1972, for example, about a hundred letters were submitted to the editor of *Science*. Many (usually from older academics) objected that science was only possible in our ordinary "normal" state, for they believed that all ASCs represented deteriorations in rationality. Younger scientists tended to be enthusiastic about the proposal. The most interesting pair of letters came from one scientist who at first agreed with the older ones that the idea of state-specific sciences was preposterous, but then wrote a second letter to the editor in which he stated that, while he felt embarrassed to write again and was only writing because of his commitment to scientific honesty, he had thought about the state-specific sciences proposal while in an ASC, and it made perfect sense in the altered state! Neither of these letters was published, unfortunately.

10.   I am indebted to Thomas J. McFarlane for this suggestion (see McFarlane 1996) and to Don McCarthy for elaboration of it.

11.   There have been numerous attempts to explain mystical experiences "away" as nothing but psychopathology or abnormal brain functioning, but I find most of these attempts have been more representative of social bias than good science.

12.   In my 1969 Altered States of Consciousness anthology, I proudly announced that I had included two thirds of the English language scientific literature on studies of meditation — which sounded impressive, except that it meant I had included two of the three studies I could find. Since then there has been an enormous increase in studies of meditation (see, e.g., Murphy and Taylor 1996), but they have all been from the "outside," i.e. external observations about the process from an ordinary SoC perspective.

References

Bogzaran, F. 1996. *Abstract Images of the Lucid Mind: Phenomenological Study of Lucid Dreaming and Modern Painting*, Doctoral dissertation: University of Michigan.

Brown, D. P. and J. Engler. 1980. "The stages of mindfulness meditation: A validation study." *Journal of Transpersonal Psychology* 12(143–200).

Gackenbach, J.L.S. 1988. *Conscious Mind, Sleeping Brain: Perspectives on Lucid Dreaming.* New York, Plenum.

Hadamard, J. 1954. *An Essay on the Psychology of Invention in the Mathematical Field.* New York, Dover.

Kuhn, T. 1962. *The structure of scientific revolutions.* Chicago, University of Chicago Press.

LaBerge, S. 1985. *Lucid Dreaming.* Los Angeles, Tarcher.

McFarlane, T. J. 1996. "Integral science: Toward a comprehensive science of inner and outer experience." *Journal of the Western Regional Chapter of the Alternative Natural Philosophy Association* 6(2): 4–15.

Murphy, M. D. S. and E. Taylor. 1996. The Physical and Psychological Effects of Meditation: A Review of Contemporary Research with a Comprehensive Bibliography 1931–1996. ms.

Needleman, J. 1970. *The New Religions.* Garden City, N.Y., Doubleday.

Orne, M. 1962. "On the social psychology of the psychological experiment: with particular reference to demand characteristics and their implications." *American Psychologist* 17: 776–783.

Rosenthal, R. 1966. *Experimenter Effects in Behavioral Research.* New York, Appleton-Century-Crofts.

Tart, C. 1969. *Altered States of Consciousness: A Book of Readings.* New York, John Wiley & Sons, 1969.

Tart, C. 1970. "Marijuana intoxication: Common experiences." *Nature* 226: 701–704.

Tart, C. 1971. *On Being Stoned: A Psychological Study of Marijuana Intoxication.* Palo Alto, California:, Science and Behavior Books; now available at http://www.druglibrary.org/schaffer/lsd/bookmenu.htm.

Tart, C. 1972. "States of consciousness and state-specific sciences." *Science* 176: 1203–1210.

Tart, C. 1975. *States of Consciousness.* New York:, E. P. Dutton.

Tart, C. 1977. "Toward humanistic experimentation in parapsychology: A reply to Dr. Stanford's review." *Journal of the American Society for Psychical Research* 71: 81–102.

Tart, C. 1987. "The world simulation process in waking and dreaming: A systems analysis of structure." *Journal of Mental Imagery* 11: 145–158.

Tart, C. 1991. "Multiple personality, altered states and virtual reality: The world simulation process approach." *Dissociation* 3(222–233).

Tart, C. 1998. "Investigating altered states of consciousness on their own terms: A proposal for the creation of state-specific sciences." *Ciencia e Cultura, Journal of the Brazilian Association for the Advancement of Science* 50(2/3): 103–116.

Tart, C. and E. Kvetensky. 1973. "Marijuana intoxication: Feasibility of experiential scaling of level." *Journal of Altered States of Consciousness* 1: 15–21.

Troffer, S. T., C. 1964. "Experimenter bias in hypnotist performance." *Science* 145: 1330–1331.

Wilber, K. E. 1984. *Quantum Questions: Mystical Writings of the World's Great Physicists.* Boston, Shambhala.

CHAPTER 13

Methods are a Message

John Pickering
Warwick University

Introduction

The welcome return of consciousness to the top of the research agenda presents psychology with a peculiar challenge. This challenge is not immediately apparent if consciousness is considered from the third person perspective, the objective stance of most scientific research. From this viewpoint, it is an aspect the mental lives of *others*, open to observation by anyone and not significantly changed by being observed.

However, and this is the challenge, the most salient aspect of consciousness, *what it's like to be* conscious as Nagel puts it, can only be properly investigated from the first person perspective. This is primordially an experience, part of what Searle calls the 'first-person ontology' of consciousness. Moreover it is private and situated: the state of an individual's *own* mental life at a particular time and place.

There are peculiar difficulties in using first-person data and it could be argued that it actually is not 'data', not, that is, in the usual sense of the objective quantifiable findings reported in most psychological research. If first-person observations are to have a role in psychological science then the consensual replication of experiments will need to be done in a new way. First person observation is also problematic because it is easy to become reflexively entangled in it, as anyone who has attempted to meditate will know.

However, science strives to give as complete an account of the world as possible, without mysterious gaps. Hence if consciousness is to be investigated scientifically, it needs to be considered in *all* its aspects. The first person perspective needs to be included in psychology despite the misgivings of those for whom empiricism and objectivity are the essence of scientific practice. As William James observed: "To be radical, an empiricism must neither admit into its constructions any element that is not directly experienced, nor exclude from them any element that is directly experienced." (James 1912: 42). Good science requires that we "... observe what there is to observe, whether it is difficult or not, whether it fits in with our beliefs and desires or not." (Tart, 1998: 107). Experience of experience itself is certainly direct and is obdurately *there* to observe. Not only that, the *manner* in which it is there is itself obdurately tied to the first person perspective.

Of course, it is possible to limit ourselves to the third person perspective and treat consciousness as part of an external universe towards which an objective stance can be taken. In fact much of psychology proceeds perfectly well in this way, with first person accounts being largely incidental. While this is appropriate for certain purposes, psychology cannot be restricted to this style of inquiry alone, given that its most salient phenomenon is primordially experiential. This is to re-visit the objections made by Husserl, James and Bergson at the turn of the last century that positivism excludes experience from Western science.

However, during this century this exclusion has not been a problem and science has made tremendous progress made in understanding the world objectively. What has been achieved has meant that science is now regarded as a uniquely powerful way to reveal what the world is 'really like'. Its methods are held to be free from social or cultural beliefs and from distortion by what people feel or desire at any given moment. Thus it is no surprise to find objections to treating experience *per se* in psychology. The objection is that to deal with first-person accounts, will threaten the status of psychology as a science and would be a dangerous regress to pre-scientific, and suspect, modes of inquiry.

Here it will be suggested that no such danger exists and that first and third person investigations of consciousness can proceed in mutual co-operation. First-person methods enrich research because they provide data that cannot be got in any other way.

This will not only influence the practice but also the image of psychology since the methods used to investigate a phenomenon give a message about what sort of a thing it is and about the nature of scientific inquiry. If the investigation of consciousness means that new methods are used in psychology, then our view of both consciousness and of psychology may change.

This is the challenge. It is also an opportunity to which, at the turn of the present century, psychologists can respond in the spirit of James and Wundt. For them, psychology was necessarily a pluralist discipline in which subjective and objective aspects of mental life were to be considered in parallel.

What methods do we trust?

There is an imbalance in psychology's methods for investigating consciousness, as they presently stand. This imbalanced is related to Chalmers' distinction between hard and easy problems (e.g. Chalmers 1995). The latter, he suggests, are "... those of explaining the various functional capacities associated with consciousness (reportability, response, monitoring, etc) ... the hard problem is that of explaining how the brain gives rise to (or otherwise relates to) conscious experience ... the problem of 'explaining' the first-person data in terms of third-person data." (Chalmers, personal communication). Psychologists who take psychology as an exclusively objective enterprise are happier dealing with the 'easy' problems using the well-tried methods of conventional scientific inquiry. They might well dismiss the 'hard' problems as metaphysical conundrums best left to philosophers.

Now, of course, the 'easy' problems are hard too. Doing research in cognitive neuroscience is difficult and investigating experience itself may in some ways be easier. No special technology is required, since what happens in the mind is right there to be inspected. To directly encounter what consciousness *is,* all that is needed is to observe experience. Then, hypotheses can be framed about the structure of that experience which may then be systematically tested as findings are obtained, classified and replicated. While such direct phenomenological inquiry is difficult, training will help to make observations reliable and consensual. Moreover, if consciousness is to be investigated fully it is the necessary complement to conventional objective inquiry, since the 'hard' and 'easy' problems overlap. For example, how is it that experience is unified, given that brain activity is spatially and temporally diffuse? To give any sort of satisfactory answer here, we will not only need to study the activity of the brain but also the flow of experience associated with that activity. These two domains of phenomena are complementary aspects of one organic system.

The imbalance appears when we consider the confidence psychology has in the methods appropriate to these two domains. Measuring and recording brain events and external conditions is the business of science. The brass instruments of Leipzig and Wurtzburg and the computerised equipment in today's laboratories are symbols of scientific authority. They produce trustworthy measurements: quantities and how they change. Even though questions have to be answered about validity, accuracy and reliability, we don't usually have much difficulty in understanding what is going on.

Perhaps, then, the 'easy' problems seem easy because it's easy to recognise what is being done. In critical contrast, the historical difficulties encountered with first person methods, such as introspection, has left an abiding mistrust of the direct investigation of experience. Perhaps the 'hard' problems seem hard because it is difficult to understand what is being done in conventional scientific terms.

The *realpolitik* of the academy is significant here. During psychology's struggle to be accepted as a discipline in its own right, instrumentation and quantitative methods were symbols of identity and authority. The method was the message: 'psychology is scientific'. However, having won the struggle, methodological purity has become something of a totem. This is illustrated by the teaching of statistics and experimental design in psychology which, when compared with other sciences, is very much an end rather than a means.

Psychology suffers from a certain rigidity as a consequence. For example, the ethos of experimental control marginalises individual strategies and the experiences that go with them. Control means setting up conditions that separate a single variable from the play of influences that attend every moment of real experience. The control is in the hands of those who design experiments who therefore define what data are to be taken as significant. Those who take part are made passive and anonymous. The experiences of individuals are lost within means and experimental groups. This power to control the meaning of what is going on can be seen in the very language of statistics and experimental design, whose origins lie in agricultural research, quality control and large scale social surveys. Terms like: 'Subjects'; 'Control'; 'Yoked groups'; 'Degrees of freedom'; 'Normal distributions'; 'Standard deviation'; 'Error variance', etc., disclose an underlying concern with power, prediction and conformity to norms.

Indeed, to call the residual sum of squares the 'error' variance, is to devalue the significance of individual behaviour. What is *common* in the mental activity of those participating in experiments is thereby defined as the primary focus; what is individual and idiosyncratic is secondary, merely noise in the data. In order to disclose the 'real' nature of mental life objectively, these extraneous elements must be controlled and averaged out of existence. This is part of Husserl's crisis, the exclusion of experience that decapitates science and philosophy.

Of course, conventional scientific methods have an enduring place in psychology. In fact, they are something of a keel to a subject that has been blown this way and that by controversies over its legitimate subject matter and on how to investigate it. Good design and careful control is vital in a subject where results are easily distorted by subtle biases and assumptions. However, even though there may be unique problems in conducting psychological research, the solution is not to use only one sort of methodology. If academic *realpolitik* means that the experimental ethos becomes a methodological imperative, then it also becomes a limitation. To insist that psychology should only use methods of a certain type would, if taken to extremes, make it virtually impossible to study important aspects of mental life.

It would also bias psychology towards certain types of explanation, which may be far less general than they appear. An example here would be the claim that the computational metaphor is a universal account of cognition (e.g. Newell 1991). This was certainly due in part at least to the feeling that psychology should have a core mechanistic theory. It is now clear, from taking a more organic, systems view, that far from being universal, this metaphor is severely limited (e.g. Edelman 1992; Clark 1999). Thus, we need to be wary of commitment to one type of theory and method. Direct investigation of phenomenal consciousness is clearly useful in addressing the 'hard' problem, even if it is difficult to represent what we are doing in conventional scientific terms.

Also, it may help with some of the unjustified demands made of psychology *qua* science. For historical reasons science has had thrust upon it much of the cultural role, formerly played by religion, of giving meaning to the world and to human existence. It is clear, though, that scientific findings, which are essentially provisional, cannot play the normative role of transcendental beliefs and faith. When science in general is drawn into this role, it becomes open to distortion and misrepresentation. Theodore Roszak, for example, claims:

"Our science, like our technics, is maniacal because it bears the cultural burden of finding meaning where meaning cannot possibly be found. Nevertheless science continues to thrust fanatically into ever denser regions of being, hoping to strike through to some ultimate truth which will vindicate its quest ... the Secret of Life concocted in a test tube ... the Origin of the Universe ... the Mechanism of Intelligence. But all it finds are reductionist caricatures, nihilist know-how." (Roszak, 1972).

We need not go to these extremes to recognise that science is often treated as if it were able to answer any and all questions when it clearly cannot do so. However, claims are sometimes made that science has 'limitless power' (Atkins 1995). Moreover a number of psychologists, biologists and philosophers appear confident that the methods of science as they presently stand, will eventually fully explain consciousness. Among others, the Churchlands, Francis Crick and Richard Dawkins seem to believe that the scientific methods currently used to investigate consciousness could explain it completely. Appeals to experience are dismissed as naive and superficial. The first-person perspective, they claim, is unreliable folk psychology, liable to distortion and hard to replicate. By contrast, scientific methods provide accurate and verifiable facts about the brain and its workings. These will be the answers we want, even if they reduce this or that aspect of common experience to just this or that type of brain activity.

Moreover, and recalling that methods are a message, this reduction is presented as what psychologists *should* want. Given the *realpolitik* of its history, psychology needs to show that it too can do the reductive job for its subject matter that other natural sciences have done for theirs. Thus, physicists suggested that heat was 'just' motion. Biochemists suggested that being alive was 'just' to metabolise. Geneticists suggested that to evolve was 'just' to alter the genome .... and so on. Given this, it is no surprise to find psychologists suggesting that experience is 'just' brain mechanisms since to do so expresses the authority of science. The manner in which the Churchlands, for example, advocate their program of neurophilosophy betokens just this faith in the powers of science. As the easy problems are being solved at such a rate, can solutions to the hard ones be far behind? As the authority of common experience diminishes, so the authority of scientific discourse grows.

It is easy to see, then, why science is sometimes assumed to have the responsibility to explain everything, including human experience, which clearly can't be done at present. It may be that it never can be done, and psychologists need to head off any attempts to saddle them with this task. It is clear, too, that conventional scientific methods have their limits, as most scientists have always recognised. However, we can address these limitations by constantly expanding and refining our practices. Some psychological questions may appear 'hard' because we assume that the methods we presently use are the only way to get a reliable answer to them. If we were to use other methods then perhaps we may take a different view.

To add phenomenological methods to psychological practice will help psychology to resist the role of having to "explain everything" by reduction. These methods are not explanations in the accepted sense of scientific explanations but accounts and descriptions which will help to create the natural history that precedes scientific theories. They may, in the longer term, indeed be the means to find more satisfactory accounts for the structure of human experience, but at present they are a defence against unrealistic expectations placed on psychology.

Psychology's historical need to be identified with the natural sciences has given rise to the belief that the proper way to explain the complexities of experience is to claim that they are 'really' just something else which is simpler. Such cognitive or neuropsychological reduction, like behaviourist reduction before it, will leave psychology at an *impasse*. In attempting to do for mental phenomena what natural science appears to have done for physical and biological ones, psychology is setting itself an impossible task. The formidable technology used to do objective research into mental life does not give the discipline the authority to pronounce on experience itself. Technology may enable us to produce finer and finer descriptions of, say, the spatio-temporal patterns of brain activity, but what will be revealed by doing this? It will be only half the story; a description of the vehicle for consciousness.

What is carried by this vehicle, the dynamic flow of experience, participates with numerous interacting factors in a system that does not stop at the boundaries of the body. This means that consciousness cannot be fully understood from a third-person description of only one part of it, no matter how accurate it may be. Events within the brain are but one such part, and it is as yet unclear what proportion of responsibility they bear for the situated actions of people and other organisms within the larger system as a whole. Recent developments in cognitive science, especially the treatment of cognition as embodied in complex, historical processes and the use of dynamic systems theory, indicate a strong shift towards the whole and away from the parts (e.g. Clark 1999; Port & van Gelder 1995; Hurley 1998; Fogel et al. 1997).

Third person methods are reliable, powerful, but limited. The idea that they can, *on their own,* provide a complete account of experience is a reductive mistake. To understand how human experience is bound up in the systems that support it will also require first-person investigation. The peculiar challenge that consciousness presents is that of changing science's methods and its image.

Postmodern plurality

Changes in science do not arise in a vacuum. The new methods to investigate consciousness that are under consideration here will also reflect the more general postmodern re-appraisal of knowledge and practice. As Vaclav Havel points out, postmodernism means diversity and eclecticism. New meaning is synthesised from practices, views, styles, tastes, theories and images that previously would have been considered too heterogeneous in time, space or cultural *milieu* to have been brought together (Havel 1995).

The core of the postmodern critique is this: no system of ideas and practices has the final word on anything (e.g. Lyotard 1984; Jameson 1991; Harvey 1990). No totalising cultural meta-narrative can be accepted as complete or universal, including those, like science, that have appeared in the three hundred years or so since the Enlightenment. Neither religious nor scientific world views are final truths, nor are their practices exclusive means to finding final truths. They are culturally maintained modes of perception by which we deal with a world that, in a Kantian sense, is not directly knowable.

Hence it is unwise to take a uniform epistemological stance and to proceed as if one particular body of thought and practice can reveal what the world is 'really' like (Clarke 1996, Chapter 1). Science, in this light, is a mode of discourse rather than a way of revealing a world that exists independently of that discourse (Rorty 1979). In the absence of finality, the postmodern predicament is that of having continually to choose, to 'eclect', as Charles Jencks has it (Jencks 1992). This is not a collapse into relativism but a constructive proposal to take cultural practices, including science, forward in the radically pluralist style of William James (1912). Radical pluralism is not merely intellectual liberalism. It is a proposal that multiple perspectives are an intrinsic condition of knowing anything. It proposes that we engage with a multiplicity of views and practices. Science, given its openness and provisionality, is particularly well equipped to do this.

The postmodern critique is not a rejection of science or its methods. In fact, it is not about rejecting anything, except scientism. It is a historical analysis of the nested signification inherent in all cultural practices (e.g. Anderson 1996). That is, the messages carried in any system of discourse and practice are more than their literal or *prima facie* content. The methods used in science, for instance, bring with them a cultural history, rich in implicit values. In Foucault's terms, the archaeology of knowledge, which is the exploration of this history, is a necessary precondition to understanding what any system of discourse produces, including scientific findings.

This has liberating implications for psychology, which is more hampered than other disciplines by the supposed opposition between scientific and non-scientific approaches to understanding the human mind. This unwelcome historical imposition can now be eased. Radical pluralism is a dialogue between a multiplicity of perspectives rather than an effort after a unified view. Going beyond the methodological exclusivity of most psychological research will allow a more realistic and informed interaction between different ways to investigate the mind.

Perhaps above all, the postmodern turn offers psychologists the means to do better science. It is an opportunity to re-incorporate the phenomenological methods that James and Wundt felt were crucial to the science of mental life. These methods with help to map out the territory beyond cognitive or neuro-logical reductionism and shape a discipline in which experience can be treated scientifically without being isolated from its biological and cultural context.

If psychology broadens its methods to include phenomenological traditions and practices, it will be better able to deal with human values (Pickering 1999a). A science that treats experience, feelings and human meaning will help to remedy the damaging separation of fact and value so characteristic of modernist science. As Bohm puts it: 'Postmodern science should not separate matter and consciousness, and should not, therefore, separate facts, meaning and value.' (Bohm 1988).

With this in mind, the next section will briefly discuss some contrasting methods for investigating consciousness. The underlying theme is the message transmitted by these methods, especially to students when they first learn the discipline. It is to be hoped that a more inclusive and humane message will be one outcome of the complementary use of both first and third-person methods.

Investigating consciousness

Positivism and critical realism are the implicit philosophical basis of most psychological investigation. Despite their impact elsewhere, phenomenological traditions, the works of Husserl, Heidegger or Merleau-Ponty, for example, have had relatively little influence on Anglo-American psychology. If they are dealt with at all, it is primarily as philosophers who treat consciousness as part of the existential conundrum of the human condition. Their discursive writings do not immediately suggest empirical work. The stylistic gulf separating, say, Merleau-Ponty's *Phenomonology of Perception* and the treatment of perception in most Anglo-American psychology illustrates the difficulty of bringing phenomenological traditions to bear on mainstream psychological research.

The postmodern turn towards a plurality of views and practices, although no panacea, may help to bridge this divide. In fact, bridges across the divide have been in place for decades, although these are not directly concerned with phenomenological investigation. In social psychology, for example, the paradigm shift of the 1970's towards discourse, ethnomethodological research and social construction, has now matured into a well-organised and productive research programme within which qualitative methods are central (e.g. Richardson 1996; Bannister et al. 1994).

Qualitative methods and phenomenological investigations both aim to deal systematically with the accounts that people offer for the meaning of their actions and their experience. They provide observations, at an appropriate level, of human activity, reasons and experiences as they occur in real situations. While systematic, they nonetheless aim to preserve the naturalism and values of the world as experienced. The objective, as for phenomenological inquiry, is to protect the world of human meaning from reductive misrepresentation. Bruner, although he is not concerned with phenomenological traditions or qualitative methods *per se*, makes a very similar point. He claims that the original impulse behind the cognitive revolution, to account for the human encounter with a world made meaningful by culture, has been misdirected by an over-commitment to an internal, mechanistic metaphor for mental life (Bruner, 1990).

Phenomenological inquiry and qualitative methods both satisfy the requirement made by critical social scientists for methods that to do justice to what people actually say about what they do, about their experiences and about the reasons behind their actions. This requirement enhances the power of the subject to contribute to the meaning of scientific research. It opposes the tendency of positivistic investigations to explain away qualitative, personalised accounts as 'really just' the surface manifestations of underlying cognitive or neurological mechanisms. In that exercise, the control of what the data mean, about what is 'really' going on, is firmly in the grip of the experimenter.

Qualitative methods are typically used in research into human social interaction and the meanings given to that interaction by the people participating in it. Along with these methods there comes a new attitude to theory making, which is grounded in participatory observation and often includes the attitudes and identity of the investigator. Qualitative methods include ethnography, the analysis of discourse, narratives, protocols and conversations, structured interviews and textual/archival studies. A recent conference on qualitative methodologies described them as the means " ...to paint social portraits that are diverse, multifold, and shaped by a variety of historically placed and culturally influenced lived experiences."

The contrast with conventional scientific practices, which are nothing like the 'painting of social portraits' is clear and the use of qualitative methods is a strongly contested matter. Advocates of such methods object to the privileged status given to conventional science's assumptions, methods and findings. They claim that even if quantitative methods are as accurate and rigorous as ingenuity can make them, if they do not address human mental life at the right grain, they maybe quite irrelevant to what is 'really' going on.

What 'really' means here is the nub. For critical social scientists, psychological reality consists primarily of interactions within the culturally-formed world and the accounts, reasons and feelings that people report about them. The accompanying cognitive or neurological activity, for all that it makes these interactions possible, is nonetheless secondary and scientific accounts of that activity are contestable: "Scientific knowledge is not determined by 'the actual character of the physical world' but instead by the social relations, beliefs and value systems that pertain within scientific communities." (Woolgar 1996: 19).

Opponents of qualitative methods object that, say, brain activity is obviously 'really' there and that observing it objectively is more than mere social agreement. Morgan, a redoubtable defender of the quantitative ethos, is quite clear about why qualitative methods should be opposed, although, unlike some opponents, he does not in fact feel that they are either inaccurate or inconclusive. His objection is that they are *unscientific* and hence should not

"...be given the authority of science." (Morgan 1998). The scientific identity of psychology, along with the status and funding that goes with it, should not be threatened by the inclusion of first-person accounts. It is not that such accounts are either unreliable or unrealistic, it is that they just do not look the part. In this struggle to define and control the discipline, supporters of qualitative methods object to the hegemony of the quantitative approach, claiming that it diminishes and distorts the treatment of human psychological life (Valsiner 1991). Opponents object that qualitative methods diminish the scientific status of psychology.

However, with the turn towards plurality, there can be progress beyond mere opposition. For example, a productive *rapprochement* is emerging based on complementary roles for qualitative and quantitative methods. The role of the latter is in theory *testing* while the former are for theory *generation* (Burt & Oaksford 1999). In the investigation of consciousness there seems to be just this sort of role waiting for qualitative methods, once they are adapted to fit the shorter timescales and more tightly focused activities dealt with in cognitive science.

Work has begun to appear bringing cognitive science and phenomenological traditions closer together (e.g. Varela, Thompson & Rosch 1990; Marcel 1988; Varela & Shear 1999). Even the work of a psychologist as strongly committed to ecological realism as James Gibson is now being compared with the ontological concerns of philosophers such as Heidegger (Still & Good 1998). Merleau-Ponty's concern with the role of the body in perception also has much in common with Gibson's ecological approach and with the trend towards embodied treatment of cognition noted above. Thus, phenomenological investigations and qualitative methods are not so far removed from conventional scientific research. Indeed they appear to be a means to change and enhance psychological practice.

Research that combines qualitative and quantitative methodologies is a form of epistemological triangulation with which to map the new territory opened up by the vigorous research programme on consciousness. For example, in trying to find the neural correlates of consciousness a natural step is to try to match experience to brain activity. Descriptions of both are hard to come by. Recording of brain activity is intrusive and reporting on experience often interferes with it.

These problems are not insoluble. For example, binocular rivalry or multistable figures like the Necker cube or the Rubin vase-face, offer the possibility of correlating brain activity to well-defined changes in visual experience. Logothetis and his colleagues have trained monkeys to 'report', by pulling levers, which of two alternative experiences they are having. These reports are then matched to single unit recordings being made at the same time. The findings have changed previous models of multistability, especially in the case of binocular rivalry. Rather than the mutual inhibition of monocularly driven neurones, it now seems more likely that changes in experiences are linked to mutually inhibiting populations of binocular units, probably located in the temporal cortex (Logothetis 1998).

Techniques for recording brain activity such as PET scans and the various forms of magnetic resonance imaging are now being used in experiments where the conscious state of the brain is an independent variable. For instance, Alkire et al. made PET scans of subjects while they were hearing word lists from which they later recalled or recognised words (Alkire et al. 1996). Lists were presented both when subjects were conscious and when they were anaesthetised. While subjects had no recall of words presented when they had been unconscious, forced-choice recognition tests showed that learning had occurred. Moreover, comparing brain activity during conscious and unconscious learning revealed reliable differences. Specifically, activity in the thalamic nuclei appeared to be higher during the presentation of words that were subsequently available for conscious recall.

Studies like these are creating a new role for conscious states and reports about them in psychological research. Instead of being merely adjuncts to objective data, they are beginning to be used as independent variables. Events in the subjective realm, like the change from one interpretation of a bi-stable figure to another, can now be linked to brain activity in ways which makes their role in research more quantitative and discriminative.

The contrast here with the controversies surrounding the use of qualitative and quantitative methods is striking. There is no struggle for which type of data is to be given explanatory primacy. Objective and subjective investigations of mental phenomena are being integrated into a broader research paradigm. In areas where subjective experience is of the essence, the parallel use of third and first person methods is natural research strategy.

Research on the perception of time is another such area. Much of it deals with how people and animals estimate, compare, remember and otherwise process intervals of time as defined by external events and timing devices. A great deal has been learned about the structure of temporal experience, for

example the perception of simultaneity and succession and about what length-
ens or shortens the estimation of intervals. The assumption is often made here
that some aspect of neural activity performs a similar function to periodic
devices such as the pendulums or oscillating crystals in clocks. The processing
of time then becomes equivalent to comparing the occurrence of external
events with the activity of this internal clock, which at its most literal would be
some form of counting of the number of periods through which it had passed.

The balance of research into time perception is in favour of quantitative
models of how the internal clock is read. Qualitative treatments of temporal
experience itself, the feeling of how time is passing, get relatively less attention, most of it coming from psychologists in countries with stronger phenomenological traditions than those in the Anglo-American world. The balance of
work presented in the proceedings of a recent conference on time perception
illustrates this very well (Macar et al. 1992).

Now however, research is appearing which strikes a different balance
between the objective and the experiential approaches to time. Varela, for
example, has extended his programme of neurophenomenology to include the
treatment of the psychological moment, or 'present-time consciousness' as he
terms it (Varela 1999). Gallagher too sees the investigation of the experience
time as an illustration of a closer relationship between phenomenology and
cognitive science (Gallagher 1997).

Wider implications of phenomenological investigation

Engaging with phenomenology connects psychology with important changes
to the wider scientific world picture, especially those associated with dynamic
system theory. These changes promote a view of cognition as embodied in
historical organic systems (Prigogine 1996; Clark 1999). Embodiment and
historicity are central to the positions of Husserl, Bergson and Merleau-Ponty,
who are likely to be cited both in research on the subjective experience of time
and on autopoietic systems and other far-from-equilibrium phenomena (e.g.
Prigogine & Stengers 1984).

Prigogine, for instance, explicitly attributes his interest in dissipative
systems to the influence of Bergson, for whom the essence of time lies in the
experience of duration, not the *measurement* of it. This experience of time
cannot be spatialised and counted as one might measure the distance along a

line or the number of times a pendulum has travelled back and forth. Time is both the medium for mental life and the trace of its activity, which for Bergson was an aspect of all living systems. Time in this experiential sense only exists within living systems and although it has direction it does not necessarily flow uniformly.

Now human experience may run in only one direction and vary in pace, but in classical physics, time is uniform and reversible. This meant that for committed classical physicists (Einstein was one famous example) our compelling experience of time as something which passes is merely an illusion. To take the experience of time seriously, scientists appear to need a special explanation. Bergson suggested that experience was associated with an immaterial force, the *elan vital*, running counter to the tendency of matter to follow predictable paths and eventually to fall into inert disorder. This notion, however, came to be seen as a romantic rather than a scientific one and contributed to Bergson's virtual eclipse during most of this century.

The systems view is sometimes presented as a way to achieve what Bergson proposed without the need for a mysterious new force in nature (e.g. Laszlo 1996: 8). Physical laws as they are presently understood can deal with the emergence of higher levels of organisation and can provide a scientific account of organic systems. These autopoietic systems, so long as there is sufficient energy and information flowing through them, preserve their own integrity, becoming more complex and ordered in the process (Maturana & Varela 1992). Cognition in this view participates in an evolutionary process from which emerges sentience, intentionality and, when amplified by symbolic resources, human consciousness (e.g. Deacon 1997).

As psychology engages with the first-person perspective and systems thinking, it is drawn into ontological and epistemological issues. Recently, in the spirit of radical pluralism, these have tended to cross traditional cultural boundaries. For example, bridges are now being built between Western scientific traditions for studying the mind and prescientific traditions such as Buddhism (Pickering 1997, 1995; Hayward & Varela 1992). Studies of time perception have been undertaken from a Buddhist standpoint (Novak 1996) and the Buddhist ontological doctrine of *Paticca Samuppáda*, commonly translated as 'dependent origination,' has been interpreted in systems terms (Macy 1991). While interest in Buddhism is not new, what is perhaps new is the confidence that a more informed methodological synthesis is now possible (e.g. Wallace 1999).

Other traditions offer other practices, like meditation, which has long been recognised as a powerful way to study the mind. It has been part of Hindu and Buddhist cultures for thousands of years. In the Western academic world, however, it is rarely taught. If it is, it is more likely to be encountered in courses on personal development or psychological health. However, meditative practices are a productive complement to the methodological ethos that presently dominates psychology. Nothing will be taken away from experimental rigour by including them in psychological research practices. In the study of consciousness, meditative techniques can provide a much needed reacquaintance with the phenomenon itself.

Clearly, there needs to be a great deal of caution here. Superficial resemblances between Western science and Eastern systems of thought are all too easy to find. Many treatments of meditation clearly do no justice whatsoever to the traditions to which they belong. We cannot therefore expect to adopt some practices and immediately derive from them the results obtained by those skilled at using them. However, we can learn something even from an initial contact. As the extract from an email exchange below indicates, Charles Tart finds that acquaintance with authentic traditions of meditation has helped him to see why Western attempts to employ first-person methods failed:

> "I believe one of the main reasons (why introspection failed) is that we assumed almost any normal person could become a "trained observer" of basic mental processes with a few hours of training. Now my own studies of Buddhist meditation, where the estimate is about 5,000 hours of training before most people could quiet their mind enough to begin to adequately observe basic mental processes .... have convinced me that ordinary consciousness is quite undifferentiated and unskilful at observing its own manifestations — ... But, we *can* learn to become much more discriminative observers of our own mental processes. Western psychology gave up far too early trying to become a science with mental events as primary data — we simply weren't trained."

To use meditation and phenomenological techniques in psychology would not in fact be as radical a departure as it might first appear. Such things influenced the founders of the discipline. For example, Freud acknowledged both Schopenhauer and Eduard von Hartmann as important contributors to the concept of an active unconscious. Hartmann relied heavily on phenomenological methods (see e.g. Hartmann 1884) while Schopenhauer was among the first major philosophers in the West to take informed notice of Eastern thoughts. Meditative techniques, and other practices from prescientific traditions, can, with proper caution, be approached as methodological resources in their own right and not as historical curios that science will somehow explain away.

The aim here has been to suggest a move beyond a single methodological stance. The challenge of investigating consciousness is that it cannot be a complete scientific project without qualitative data and first person accounts. The tools are there. The growing literature on qualitative methods provides a model of how to integrate first-person data into psychology. These methods will need modification before they can be more closely integrated with cognitive science, but this is beginning to happen and a new research agenda is taking shape.

If this agenda changes the identity of psychology, the change is unlikely to be damaging in the way that opponents of qualitative methods fear. Nothing in the adoption of first-person data excludes or diminishes what third-person data reveals. Psychology has enduring features in common with the other more established sciences. However, because of the internal logic of its subject matter, it also has compelling reasons to develop a distinctive balance of quantitative and qualitative methods.

Conclusion

The return of consciousness is a chance to broaden psychology's methods and thereby to change the message they convey about the nature of psychology as a science. A more eclectic methodological and theoretical mix is already taking shape and we are beginning to see richer psychological research that no longer limit us to a single style of discourse. Hunt's recent synthesis of cognitive, ecological and transpersonal approaches is a splendid example of such radical pluralism (Hunt 1997). Pluralism sends a message about both psychology and about consciousness. The message is that the reductive ethos of the natural sciences needs to be complemented by first-person methods and a dual-aspect view of the mind body relationship (cf. Velmans 2000).

The theoretical developments needed to do this are already available. Systems theory in particular provides the theoretical means to go beyond the treatment of consciousness as merely a cognitive mechanism in the brain. Qualitative methods and phenomenological investigation, in conjunction with quantitative methods already in use, provide the practical means to investigate consciousness in a way that does justice to both its objective as well as its subjective aspects.

Opening up psychology to phenomenological investigation will mean broadening the psychological curriculum. One rather controversial proposal from Charles Tart calls for a State Specific Science, in which altered states of consciousness are to be investigated by taking the given experience as primary rather than as a departure from normal 'reality' (e.g. Tart 1972; 1998). Some of these states, such as drug induced hallucinations and near-death experiences are very dangerous and cannot be part of the undergraduate curriculum. Less risky forms of personal investigation could be and would provide a sharp and critical alternative to psychological methods as they presently stand.

Individual experience is virtually invisible when depersonalised subjects carry out tasks set by experimenters. Although the manner in which the task is carried out may be fundamentally different because of individual strategies, experimental control consigns the consequent variation to the *oubliette* of error variance. It is a matter of emphasis. If the model of psychological research is to frame universal theories, then individual differences are indeed noise. If instead we seek a science of mental life that can also address personal and cultural differences in cognitive skills and the different experiences that accompany them, then such differences are also a signal (see e.g. Neisser 1997; Cole 1996)

To capture such a signal requires appropriate methods, some of which, such as meditation, may need to be sought outside the conventional scientific canon. While first person methods have been part of psychology's history, in more recent times there has been a great deal of interaction with pre-scientific traditions for investigating mental life and this interaction is in line with changes in the broader scientific worldview (e.g. Griffin 1988; Clarke 1996). However, practices which have been systematically developed over thousands of years cannot simply be bolted on to Western psychological science. There needs to be careful consideration of how they might fit with conventional methods. Nonetheless sensitive use of such techniques will be an effective addition to psychology's resources.

Developments like this have significance well beyond mere methodology. The separation of facts and values in science, an echo of the Enlightenment, is incompatible with the ethos of most meditative practices. In Buddhism, for example, the separation of fact and value is not made. Knowledge of the mind is intrinsically valued since the point in getting it is to live more skilfully. By contrast if one were to ask Western cognitive scientists: "What is this research for? What does it tell us about how we should act?" the answer might be: "It is not actually *for* anything. The objective is to discover what the mind is really like. What *should* then follow is not the concern of cognitive science itself."

It is part of the postmodern critique that knowledge is intrinsically valued. Even the mere act of making an observations can have deep ethical consequences. For example, many of those who have been able to observe the earth from space have become ecological activists — often against the grain of their previous political views. Just observing the earth from space brings home in a particularly powerful way that the biosphere is a single interdependent system. If psychologists limit their methods to the third person perspective, it will restrict the encounter with the most central phenomenon of human mental life. Opening up psychology to methods that allow the experience of the psychologist to become part of their field of inquiry will yield a very different form of knowledge. What this inquiry reveals will be intrinsically valued. To know the mind better is to be better able to understand one's own experience and one's own actions.

Science is occasionally demonised as driven by the urge for control and domination. The reduction of mental life to mere cognitive mechanisms appears all too clearly to be part of this ethos. If the mind is treated as machine-like then the possibilities for controlling it will be increased. Here 'control' means the control of the mind of one person by another. As it is the fate of scientific discoveries to be used, whatever scientists had intended, scientific investigations of consciousness must be treated with considerable care (Pickering 1999b).

By contrast, if psychology employs more first-person methods then it will promote a different picture. Mental control, meaning that of one's own mind, will be discovered to be very difficult. Such a discovery weakens the image of psychology as the scientific means to oppressive technologised intervention in human affairs.

The methods used to investigate consciousness bear many messages, not least of which being that psychology needs to deal in first-person, qualitative data. It is not a devaluation to recognise that psychology is a special case among the sciences. Quite the reverse, it is the way to create a more complete and inclusive science of mental life.

References

Alkire, M., Haier, R., Fallon, J. & Barker, S. 1996. PET Imaging of Conscious and Unconscious Verbal Memory. *Journal of Consciousness Studies*, 3(5/6): 448–462.

Anderson, W. (Ed.) 1996. *The Fontana Post-modernism Reader*. London: Fontana.

Atkins, P.W. 1995. The limitless power of science. In Cornwell, J. (Ed.) *Nature's Imagination: The Frontiers of Scientific Vision*. London: Oxford University Press.

Bannister, P., Burman, E., Parker, I. Taylor, M. & Tindall, C. 1994. *Qualitative Methods in Psychology: a research guide*. Buckingham: Open University Press.

Bohm, D. 1988. Postmodern Science and a Postmodern World. In Griffin, D. R. (Ed.) *The Reenchantment of Science, Postmodern Proposals*. Albany: State University of New York Press.

Bruner, J. 1990. *Acts of Meaning*. Harvard University Press.

Burt, K. & Oaksford, M. 1999. Qualitative Methods: Beyond Beliefs and Desires. *The Psychologist*. 12(7): 332–335.

Chalmers, D. 1995. Facing up to the problem of consciousness. *Journal of Consciousness Studies*, vol. 2 (3): 200–219.

Clark, A. 1999. An embodied cognitive science? *Trends in Cognitive Sciences*. 3(9): 345–351.

Clarke, C. 1996. *Reality Through the Looking Glass: Science and Awareness in the Postmodern World*. Edinburgh: Floris Books.

Cole, M. 1996. *Cultural psychology: a once and future discipline*. Harvard University Press.

Deacon, T. 1997. *The Symbolic Species*. London: Penguin.

Edelman, G. 1992. *Bright Air, Brilliant Fire*. New York: Basic Books.

Fogel, A., Lyra, M. & Valsiner, J. (Eds.) 1997. *Dynamics and Indeterminism in Developmental and Social Processes*. Edited by Fogel, A., Lyra, M. & Valsiner, J. New Jersey, Erlbaum.

Gallagher, S. 1997. Mutual Enlightenment: Recent Phenomenology in Cognitive Science. *Journal of Consciousness Studies*, 4(3): 95–214.

Griffin, D. R. 1988. Introduction. In *The Reenchantment of Science: Postmodern Proposals*, edited by Griffin, D.R. Albany: State University of New York Press.

Hartmann, E. von. 1884. *Philosophy of the Unconscious*. London, Trübner.

Harvey, D. 1990. *The Condition of Postmodernity*. Oxford: Blackwell.

Havel, V. 1995. Self Transcendence. In *Resurgence*, No. 169, March, pages 12–14. (ISSN: 0034–5970). This is the text of an address given on receiving the Liberty Medal in Philadelphia on July 4th. 1994. Reproduced in part on pages 208–215 of Anderson, W. (Ed.) *The Fontana Post-modernism Reader*. London: Fontana.

Hayward, J. & Varela, F. (Eds.) 1992. *Gentle Bridges*. Boston: Shambala.

Hunt, H. 1995. *On the Nature of Consciousness: cognitive, phenomenological and transpersonal perspectives*. Yale University Press.

Hurley, S. 1998. *Consciousness in Action*. Harvard University Press.

James, W. 1912. *Essays in Radical Empiricism*. London: University of Nebraska Press.

Jameson, F. 1991. *Postmodernism, or the Cultural Logic of Late Capitalism*, Durham, Duke University Press.

Jencks, C. 1992. The Postmodern Agenda. In *The Postmodern Reader,* edited by Jencks, C., London: Academy Editions.

Laszlo, E. 1996. *The Systems View of the World.* Creskill, NJ.: Hampton Press.

Logothetis, N. 1998. Single units and conscious vision. *Philosophical Transactions of The Royal Society of London, Series B-Biological Sciences,* 353(1377): 1801- 1818

Lyotard, J-F. 1984. *The postmodern condition: a report on knowledge.* Trans. by Geoff Bennington and Brian Massumi. Manchester: Manchester University Press.

Macar, F., Pouthas, V. & Friedman, W. 1992. *Time, Action and Cognition.* Dordrecht: Kluwer Academic.

Macy, J. 1991. *Mutual Causality in Buddhism and General Systems Theory: the dharma of natural systems.* Albany: State University of New York Press.

Marcel, A. 1988. Phenomenal Experience and Functionalism. In *Consciousness in Contemporary Science,* edited by Marcel, A. & Bisiach, E. Oxford University Press.

Maturana, H. & Varela, F. 1992. *The Tree of Knowledge.* Boston: Shambala.

Morgan, M. 1998. Qualitaitive Research: Science or Pseudo Science? (pages 481–483) and Postscript (page 488)*The Psychologist: Bulletin of the British Psychology Society,* Vol. 11, No. 10.

Neisser, U. 1997. Concepts and self-concepts. In *The Conceptual Self in Context: culture, experience, self-understanding.* Edited by Neisser, U. & Jopling, D., Cambridge University Press.

Newell, A. 1991. *Unified Theories of Cognition.* Cambridge University Press.

Novak, P. 1996. Buddhist Meditation and the Consciousness of Time. *Journal of Consciousness Studies,* 3(3): 267–277.

Pickering, J. 1995. Buddhism & Cognitivism. *Asian Philosophy,* 5(1): 23–38.

Pickering, J. (Ed.) 1997. *The Authority of Experience.* London: Curzon Press.

Pickering, J. 1999a. Consciousness and Psychological Science. *British Journal of Psychology,* 90(4): 611–624.

Pickering, J. 1999b. Ethics are Intrinsic to Consciousness Science. *Journal of Consciousness Studies,* 6(6/7): 202–206.

Port, R. & Van Gelder, T. 1995. *Mind as Motion.* MIT Press.

Prigogine, I. & Stengers, I. 1984. *Order out of Chaos.* London: Flamingo.

Prigogine, I. 1996. The Heraclitus of Modern Science. *Journal of Consciousness Studies,* 3(4): 374–378.

Richardson, J. 1996. *Handbook of Qualitative Research Methods.* Leicester: BPS Books.

Rorty, R. 1979. *Philosophy and the Mirror of Nature.* Princeton University Press.

Roszak, T. 1972. *Where the Wasteland Ends: politics and transcendence in post industrial society.* New York: Doubleday.

Still, A. & Good, J. 1998. The Ontology of Mutualism. *Ecological Psychology,* 10(1): 39–63.

Tart, C. 1972. States of consciousness and state-specific sciences. *Science,* 176:1203–1210.

Tart, C. 1998. Investigating altered states of consciousness on their own terms:A proposal for the creation of state-specific sciences. *Ciência e Cultura: Journal of the Brazilian Association for the Advancement on Science.* Vol 50(2/3):103–116.

Valsiner, J. 1991. Construction of the Mental. *Theory and Psychology,* 1(4): 477–494.

Varela, F. & Shear, J. (Eds.) 1999. *The View From Within.* Exeter: Imprint Academic.

Varela, F. 1999. Present-Time Consciousness. *Journal of Consciousnes Studies,* 6(2/3): 111–140.

Varela, F., Thompson, E. & Rosch, E. 1991. *The Embodied Mind.* Boston: MIT Press.

Velmans, M. 2000. *Understanding Consciousness.* London: Routledge.

Wallace, B. 1999. The Buddhist Tradition of Samatha: methods for refining and examining consciousness. *Journal of Consciousness Studies,* 6(2/3): 175–187.

Woolgar, S. 1996. Psychology, Qualitative Methods and the Idea of Science. In *Handbook of Qualitative Research Methods,* edited by Richardson, J. Leicester: BPS Publications.

CHAPTER *14*

An Integral Approach to Consciousness Research

A Proposal for Integrating First, Second and Third Person Accounts of Consciousness

Ken Wilber
Boulder

Roger Walsh
University of California at Irvine

Introduction

As this book demonstrates, there has recently been something of an explosion of interest in the development of a "science of consciousness," and yet there are at present approximately a dozen major but conflicting schools of consciousness theory and research. The approach to consciousness studies suggested in this chapter assumes that each of these schools has something irreplaceably important to offer, and thus what is required is a general model sophisticated enough to incorporate the essentials of each of them. These schools include the following:

1. *Cognitive science*, which tends to view consciousness as anchored in functional schemas of the brain/mind, either in a simple representational fashion, such as Jackendoff's (1987) "computational mind," or in the more complex emergent/connectionist models, which view consciousness as an

emergent of hierarchically integrated networks. The emergent/connectionist is perhaps the dominant model of cognitive science at this point, and is nicely summarized in Alwyn Scott's *Stairway to the Mind*, the "stairway" being the hierarchy of emergents summating in consciousness.

2. *Introspectionism* maintains that consciousness is best understood in terms of intentionality, anchored in first-person accounts — the inspection and interpretation of immediate awareness and lived experience — and not merely in third- person or objectivist accounts, no matter how "scientific" they might appear. Without denying their significant differences, this broad category includes everything from philosophical intentionality to introspective psychology, existentialism, and phenomenology.

3. *Neuropsychology* views consciousness as anchored in neural systems. Unlike cognitive science, which is often based on computer science and is consequently vague about how consciousness is actually related to organic brain structures, neuropsychology is a more biologically based approach and views consciousness as intrinsically residing in organic neural systems of sufficient complexity.

4. *Individual psychotherapy* uses introspective and interpretive psychology to treat psychological distress. It thus tends to view consciousness as primarily anchored in an individual organism's adaptive capacities. Most major schools of psychotherapy embody a theory of consciousness precisely because they must account for a human being's need to create meaning and signification, the disruption of which results in painful symptoms of mental and emotional distress. In its more avant-garde forms, such as the Jungian, this approach postulates collective structures of intentionality (and thus consciousness), the fragmentation of which contributes to psychopathology.

5. *Social psychology* views consciousness as embedded in networks of cultural meaning, or, alternatively, as being largely a byproduct of the social system itself. This includes approaches as varied as ecological, Marxist, constructivist, and cultural hermeneutics, all of which maintain that the nexus of consciousness is not located merely or even principally in the individual.

6. *Clinical psychiatry* focuses on psychopathology. For a half century, psychiatry was largely anchored in a Freudian metapsychology, but the field increasingly views consciousness in strictly neurophysiological and biological terms, verging on a clinical identity theory: consciousness is the neuronal system, so that a presenting problem in the former is actually an imbalance in the latter, correctable with medication.

7. *Developmental psychology* views consciousness not as a single, static entity but as a developmentally unfolding process with a substantially different architecture at each of its stages of growth. Thus an understanding of consciousness demands investigating the architecture at each of its levels of unfolding. In its more avant-garde forms, this approach includes higher stages of exceptional development and wellbeing, and the study of gifted, extraordinary, and supranormal capacities, viewed as higher developmental potentials latent in all humans. This includes higher stages of cognitive, affective, somatic, moral, and spiritual development.

8. *Psychosomatic medicine* views consciousness as strongly and intrinsically interactive with organic bodily processes, evidenced in such fields as psychoneuroimmunology and biofeedback. In its more avant-garde forms, this approach includes consciousness and 'miraculous healing,' the effects of prayer on recovery, light/sound and healing, spontaneous remission, and so on. It also includes any of the approaches that investigate the effects of intentionality on healing, from art therapy to visualization to psychotherapy and meditation.

9. *Nonordinary states of consciousness*, from dreams to psychedelics, constitute a field of study that, its advocates believe, is crucial to a grasp of consciousness in general. Although some of the effects of psychedelics — to take a controversial example — are undoubtedly due to "toxic side-effects," the consensus of research opinion is that they also act as "nonspecific amplifiers of experience," and thus they can be instrumental in disclosing and amplifying aspects of consciousness that might otherwise go unstudied (Grof 1998).

10. *Eastern and contemplative traditions* maintain that ordinary consciousness is but a narrow and restricted version of deeper or higher modes of awareness, and that specific injunctions (yoga, meditation) are necessary to evoke these higher and exceptional potentials. Moreover, they all maintain that the essentials of consciousness itself can only be grasped in these higher, postformal, and nondual states of consciousness (Feuerstein 1998; Walsh 1999).

11. What might be called the *quantum consciousness* approaches view consciousness as being intrinsically capable of interacting with, and altering, the physical world, generally through quantum interactions, both in the human body at the intracellular level (e.g., microtubules), and in the material world at large (psi). This approach also includes attempts to plug consciousness into the physical world according to various avant-garde physical theories (e.g., boot-strapping, hyperspace, strings).

12. *Subtle energies* research postulates subtler types of bioenergies beyond the four recognized forces of physics (strong and weak nuclear, electromagnetic, gravitational), and that these subtler energies play an intrinsic role in consciousness and its activity. Known in the traditions by such terms as *prana, ki,* and *chi* — and said to be responsible for the effectiveness of acupuncture, to give only one example — these energies are often held to be the "missing link" between intentional mind and physical body. For the Great Chain theorists, both East and West, this bioenergy acts as a two-way conveyor belt, transferring the impact of matter to the mind and imposing the intentionality of the mind on matter.

13. Evolutionary psychology and its close relative sociobiology see behavior and consciousness in functional terms as expressions of evolutionary pressures. From this perspective, consciousness and its various forms and expressions exist because of, and are to be understood in terms of, the evolutionary advantage they confer (Wright 1994; Barkow, Cosmides & Tooby 1992). This is in some ways opposite to the stance of *consciousness inessentialism* which argues that animals, including humans, might survive and flourish just as well without conscious awareness.

The approach to consciousness described in this paper involves a model that explicitly draws on the strengths of each of those approaches, and attempts to incorporate and integrate their essential features. But in order to understand this model, a little background information is required. What follows is a very brief summary of an approach developed at length in a dozen books, including *Transformations of Consciousness, A Brief History of Everything,* and *The Eye of Spirit,* which the interested reader can consult for detailed arguments and extensive references.

The four corners of the kosmos

Figure 1 is a schematic summary of "the four quadrants" of existence: intentional, behavioral, cultural, and social. These four quadrants are a summary of a data search across various developmental and evolutionary fields, including over two hundred developmental sequences recognized by various branches of knowledge — ranging from stellar physics to molecular biology, from anthropology to linguistics, from developmental psychology to ethical orien-

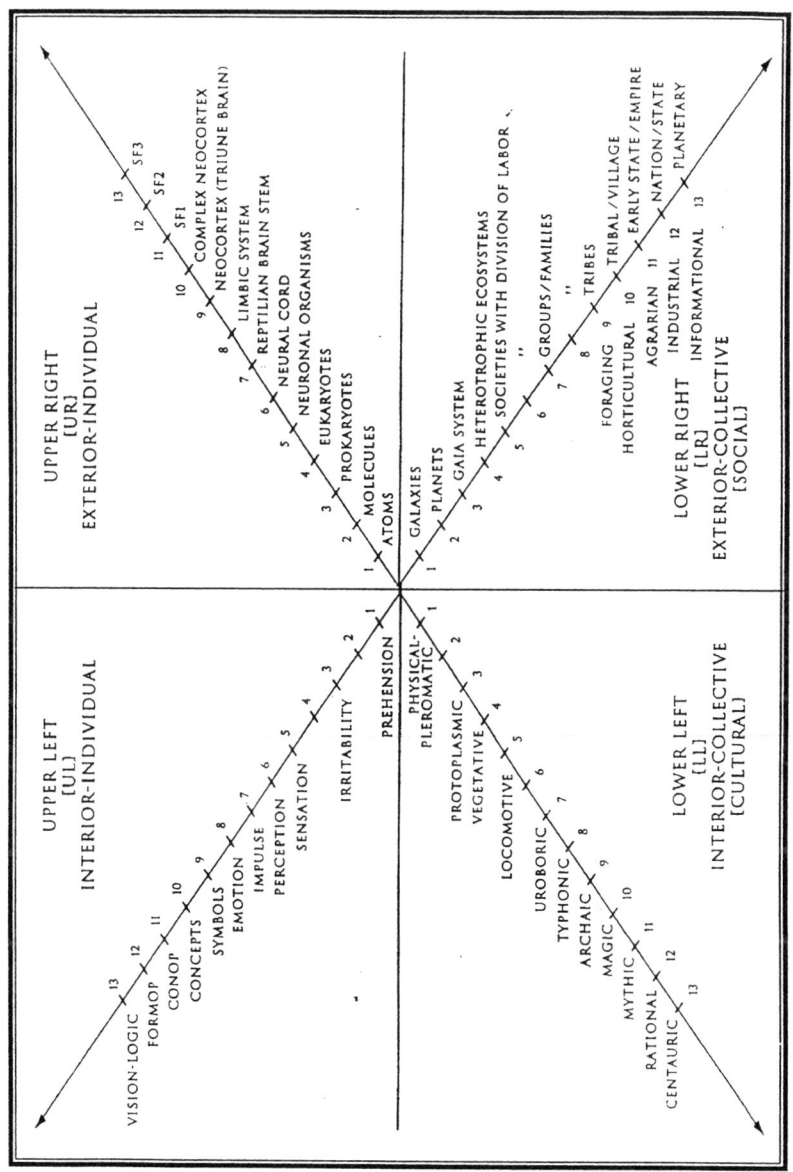

Figure 1

tations, from cultural hermeneutics to contemplative endeavors. They include both Eastern and Western disciplines, as well as premodern, modern, and postmodern sources (Wilber 1995, 1996).

These various developmental sequences all fell into one of four major classes — the four quadrants — and within those four quadrants there was substantial agreement as to the various stages or levels in each. Figure 1 is a simple summary of this data search; it thus represents an a posteriori conclusion, not an a priori assumption.

Of course people can differ about the details of such a diagram, and Figure 1 is not intended to be cast in stone. It is presented here as a reasonable summary that helps carry the present discussion. Likewise, each of the quadrants might more accurately be constructed as a branching tree, and not a simple straight line, indicating the rich variation within each grade and clade (each level and type). Each quadrant includes both hierarchies (or clear gradations) and heterarchies (or pluralistic and equivalent unfoldings within a given grade). Figure 1, again, is nothing but a simple schematic summary to help further the discussion.

Upper right (exterior-individual/behavioral) quadrant

This quadrant is perhaps the most familiar. It is the standard hierarchy presented by modern evolutionary science: atoms to molecules to cells to organisms, each of which "transcends but includes" its predecessor in an irreversible fashion: cells contain molecules, but not vice versa; molecules contain atoms, but not vice versa, and so on — the "not vice versa" constitutes the irreversible hierarchy of time's evolutionary arrow. (SF1, SF2, and SF3 refer to higher structure-functions of the human brain, which we will explain in a moment.)

Each of these individual units, in other words, is what Koestler called a "holon," a whole that is simultaneously part of some other whole (a whole atom is part of a whole molecule, a whole molecule is part of a whole cell, etc.). The Upper Right quadrant is simply a summary of the scientific research on the evolution of individual holons.

Lower right (exterior-collective/social) quadrant

But individual holons always exist in communities of similar holons. In fact, the very existence of individual holons in many ways depends upon communities of other holons that, if nothing else, provide the background fields in which individual holons can exist. Erich Jantsch (1980), in his pioneering book *The Self-Organizing Universe*, pointed out that every "micro" event (individual holon) exists embedded in a corresponding "macro" event (a community or collective of similarly structured holons). These communities, collectives, or societies are summarized in the Lower Right quadrant, and they, too, simply represent the results of generally uncontested scientific research.

Thus, for example, Jantsch points out that when atoms were the most complex individual holons in existence, galaxies were the most complex collective structures; with molecules, planets; with procaryotes, the Gaia system; with limbic systems, groups and families; and so forth.[1] Jantsch made the fascinating observation that while individual holons generally get bigger (because they transcend and include their predecessors: molecules are bigger than the atoms they contain), the collective usually gets smaller (planets are smaller than galaxies; families are smaller than planets, etc.). The reason is that as an individual holon gets more complex (possesses more depth), the number of holons that can reach that depth become less and less, and thus the collective becomes smaller and smaller (e.g., there will always be fewer molecules than atoms, and thus the collective of molecules — planets — will always be smaller than the collective of atoms — galaxies). This entire trend can be summarized as: evolution produces greater depth, less span (Wilber 1995).

Those are the two "Right Hand" quadrants. What both of those quadrants have in common is that they represent holons that all possess simple location — they can all be seen with the senses or their extensions; they are all empirical phenomena; they exist in the sensorimotor worldspace. They are, in other words, objective and interobjective realities; they are what individual and communal holons look like from the outside, in an exterior and objectifying fashion.

Upper left (interior-individual/intentional) quadrant

But various types of evidence suggest that every exterior has an interior. If we likewise do a data search among the evolutionary trends of interior apprehension, we also find a largely uncontested hierarchy of emergent properties summarized in the Upper Left quadrant: prehension to irritability to sensation to perception to impulse to image to symbol to concept to rule (concrete operations or "conop") to formal operations ("formop") and synthesizing reason ("vision-logic"). The higher levels correspond with structure-functions in the brain labeled SF1, SF2, and SF3 in the Upper Right. The existence of most of those emergent properties are largely uncontested by specialists in the field, and the holons listed in the Upper Left represent a simple summary of some of the major evolutionary capacities of interior apprehension. (There is still some heated discussion over the nature of "emergence," but the existence and evolutionary order of most of the various capacities themselves, from sensation to perception to image and concept, are generally uncontested.)

There is, however, rather endless debate about just how "far down" you can push prehension (or any form of rudimentary consciousness). Whitehead (1929/1959) pushes it all the way down, to the atoms of existence (actual occasions), while most scientists find this a bit much. Teilhard de Chardin's (1964) conclusion seems to be the most sensible: "Refracted rearwards along the course of evolution, consciousness displays itself qualitatively as a spectrum of shifting shades whose lower terms are lost in the night."

Lower left (interior-collective/cultural) quadrant

As always, every individual holon exists in a community (i.e., every agency is actually agency-in-communion). If we look at the collective forms of individual consciousness, we find a communally-shared sensitivity (from flocks of geese to human zeitgeist) including various worldspaces or worldviews. These various cultural or communal interiors are summarized in the Lower Left quadrant.

Moreover, cultural worldviews evolve and those who have carefully investigated this historical evolution include researchers from Jean Gebser to Michel Foucault to Jurgen Habermas. This research is detailed in *Up from Eden* and summarized in the Lower Left quadrant in Figure 1. "Uroboros" means reptilian (or brain-stem based); "typhonic" means emotional-sexual (limbic-system based); archaic, magic, mythic, and rational are fairly self-explanatory (they are four of the most significant of the human cultural worldviews to evolve thus far), "Centauric" means a bodymind integration and cognitive synthesizing activity which some researchers, including Gebser (1985) and Habermas (1990), see starting to emerge at this time.

The four quadrant grid

Thus, the upper half of Figure 1 refers to individual holons, the lower half, to their collective forms. The right half refers to the exterior or objective aspects of holons, and the left half, to their interior or subjective forms. This gives us a grid of exterior-individual (or behavioral), interior-individual (or intentional), exterior-collective (or social), and interior-collective (or cultural) — a grid of subjective, objective, intersubjective, and interobjective realities.

Unfortunately, as we will see, because many researchers specialize in one quadrant only, they tend to ignore or, even worse, deny the existence of the other quadrants. Materialist or Right-Hand theorists, for example, tend to deny substantial existence to interior, Left-Hand, and conscious intentionality. We will see many examples of this type of quadrant partiality, a reductionism that we will henceforth thoroughly bracket. In saying that the holons presented in each quadrant are largely uncontested, we mean specifically by those who actually study that quadrant in its own terms.

Once we put these four quadrants together, a surprising set of further conclusions rather startlingly announce themselves. These conclusions seem crucial to grasping the overall nature of consciousness.

The contours of consciousness

Quadrants and their languages

Begin with the fact that each of the quadrants is described in a different type of language. The Upper Left is described in "I" language; the Lower Left is described in "we" language; and the two Right Hand quadrants, since they are both objective, are described in "it" language. These are essentially Sir Karl Popper's (1974) "three worlds" (subjective, cultural, and objective); Plato's (1956) the Good (as the ground of morals, the "we" of the Lower Left), the True (objective truth or it-propositions, the Right Hand), and the Beautiful (the aesthetic beauty in the I of each beholder, the Upper Left); Habermas' (1984–5) three validity claims (subjective truthfulness of I, cultural justness of we, and objective truth of its). Historically of great importance, these are also the three major domains of Kant's (1951, 1990) three critiques: science or its (Critique of Pure Reason), morals or we (Critique of Practical Reason), and art and self-expression of the I (Critique of Judgment).

In short, the Upper Left is described in *first-person,* the Lower Left in *second-person,* and the Right Hand in *third-person* language. Each major approach to consciousness tends to emphasize only one of those voices. The first-person, I-language, phenomenological approaches include #2, 4, 9, 10, and 12. The second-person, we-language, intersubjective accounts include #5 (which itself is a catch-all category for hermeneutics, cultural studies, and *verstehen* sociology). And third-person, it-language, objectivist accounts include #1, 3, 6, 11 and 13. One of our major conclusions is that an integral theory of consciousness would explicitly include all three types of accounts: a 1–2–3 of consciousness studies.

Quadrants and their validity claims

Equally important, each of the quadrants has a different "type of truth" or validity claim — different types of knowledge with different types of evidence and validation procedures. Thus, propositions in the Upper Right are said to be true if they match a specific fact or objective state of affairs: a statement is true if the map matches the territory — so-called objective truth (representational truth and the correspondence theory of truth).

In the Upper Left quadrant, on the other hand, a statement is valid, not if it represents an objective state of affairs, but if it authentically expresses a subjective reality. The validity criterion here is not just truth but truthfulness or sincerity — not "Does the map match the territory?" but "Can the map-maker be trusted?" I must trust you to report your interior status truthfully, because there is no other way for me to get to know your interior, and thus no other way for me to investigate your subjective consciousness.[2]

In the Lower Right quadrant of interobjective realities, the validity claim is concerned with how individual holons fit together into interlocking systems. Truth in this quadrant concerns the elucidating of the networks of mutually reciprocal systems within systems of complex interaction. The validity claim, in other words, is grounded in interobjective fit, or simply functional fit.

In the Lower Left quadrant, on the other hand, we are concerned not simply with how objects fit together in physical space, but how subjects fit together in cultural space. The validity claim here concerns the way that my subjective consciousness fits with your subjective consciousness, and how we together decide upon those cultural practices that allow us to inhabit the same

cultural space. The validity claim, in other words, concerns the appropriateness or justness of our statements and actions (ethics in the broadest sense).
Not just, "Is it true?", but "Is it good, right, appropriate, just?" And if you and
I are to inhabit the same cultural space, we must implicitly or explicitly ask
and to some degree answer those intersubjective questions. We must find
ways, not simply to access objective truth or subjective truthfulness, but to
reach mutual understanding in a shared intersubjective space. Not that we
have to agree with each other, but that we can recognize each other, the
opposite of which is, quite simply, war. These validity claims and their
different languages are summarized in Figure 2.

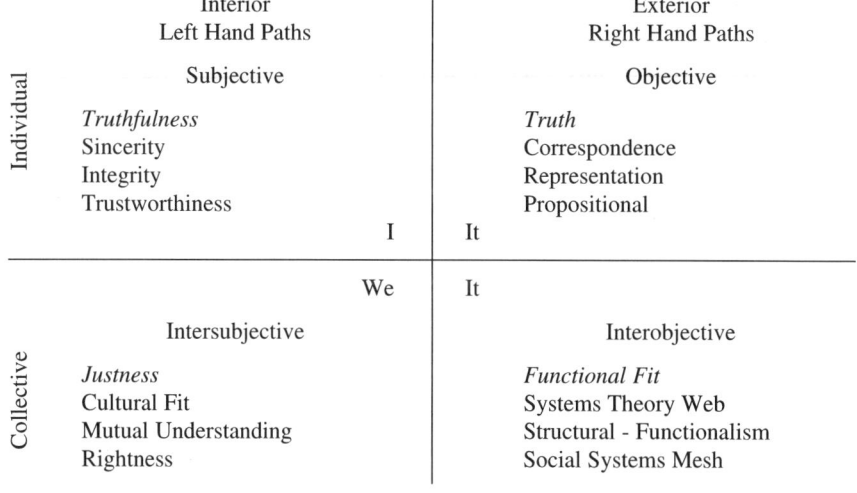

Figure 2

Common elements of knowledge acquisition: The three strands

If we now look carefully at each of these four validity claims or "types of truth" and attempt to discern what all of them have in common — that is, what all authentic knowledge claims have in common — we seem to find the following (Wilber 1996, 1997):

Each valid mode of knowing consists of an injunction, an apprehension, and a confirmation. The injunction is always of the form, "If you want to know this, do this." This injunction, exemplar, or paradigm is, as Kuhn (1970) pointed out, an actual practice, not a mere concept.

In other words, the injunction or exemplar brings forth a particular data domain — a particular experience, apprehension, or evidence (the second strand of all valid knowledge). This apprehension, data, or evidence is then tested in the circle of those who have completed the first two strands. Bad data or bad evidence is rebuffed, and this potential falsifiability is the crucial third component of all genuine validity claims; it most certainly is not restricted to empirical or sensory claims alone: there is sensory experience, mental experience, and spiritual experience, and any specific claim in each of those domains can potentially be falsified by further data in those domains. For example, the meaning of Hamlet is not about the joys of war: that is a bad interpretation and can be falsified by virtually any community of adequate interpreters.

Thus, each holon seems to have at least four facets (intentional, behavioral, cultural, and social), each of which is accessed by a different type of truth or validity claim (objective truth, subjective truthfulness, intersubjective justness, and interobjective functional fit). And all of those four validity claims follow the three strands of valid knowledge acquisition: injunction, apprehension, confirmation/rejection (or exemplar, evidence, falsifiability).

Notice that assessing the Left Hand quadrants depends significantly upon interpretation, whereas the Right Hand quadrants are all primarily empirical events. Objective exteriors can be seen, but all subjectivity requires interpretation.

Thus, it appears that the two Right Hand validity claims (objective truth and functional fit) are grounded in empirical observation (and some sort of correspondence theory of truth); whereas the two Left Hand validity claims (subjective truthfulness and intersubjective meaning) require extensive interpretation or hermeneutics (and some sort of coherence theory of truth). And we can begin to see why the human knowledge quest has almost always divided into these two broad camps: empirical vs. hermeneutic, positivistic vs. interpretive, scientific vs. intuitive, analytic vs. transcendental, Anglo-Saxon and Continental, Right Hand and Left Hand. The correct point is, of course, that both are indispensable.

The interdependence of the quadrants

Most fascinating of all, perhaps, is that each quadrant has correlates in all the others. That is, since every holon apparently has these four facets (intentional, behavioral, cultural, and social), each of these facets has a very specific correlation with all the others. These can readily be seen in Figure 1. For example, wherever we find a holon with a limbic system, we likely find that it has an interior capacity for impulse/emotion, it lives in the collective of a group, herd, or family, and it shares an emotional-sexual worldview. Apparently each quadrant causes, and is caused by, the others, in a circular and nonreducible fashion, which is precisely why all four types of truth (and all four validity claims) are necessary to access the various dimensions of any holon.

The further reaches of human nature

We need one last piece of background information. Figure 1 summarizes the four main strands of evolutionary unfolding to date. But who is to say this extraordinary unfolding has to stop with the formal or rational stage? Why not higher stages? "The mental man has not been Nature's best effort or highest reach....We have to exceed our present consciousness and surpass our present status of Nature," claimed Aurobindo (1970). Who can believably say that this amazing current of evolution simply came to a crashing halt once it produced you and me?

Several of the theories summarized in the Introduction are predicated on the fact that consciousness evolution seems to show evidence of higher (postformal, or transpersonal) stages of growth. There appear to be, in other words, several higher stages in the Upper Left quadrant. (Alexander and Langer 1990; 1984; Kohlberg and Ryncarz 1990).

The school of transpersonal psychology, in particular, has begun to investigate these higher stages (Walsh & Vaughan 1993). Substantial cross-cultural evidence strongly suggests that there are at least four broad stages of postformal consciousness development — that is, development that goes beyond but includes the formal operational level: the psychic, the subtle, the causal, and the nondual. Since each quadrant has correlates in the others, we anticipate different brain states associated with these postformal states, as well as different micro-communities or "*sanghas*." See Wilber (1995, 1997) for further discussion.

The precise definitions of those four postformal stages need not concern us; interested readers can consult the appropriate authorities, for example, in Walsh and Vaughan (1993). The point is simply that there now exists a substantial amount of rather compelling evidence that interior consciousness can continue the evolutionary process of transcend and include, transcend and include, so that even rationality itself is transcended (but included!) in postformal stages of awareness, stages that increasingly take on characteristics that might best be described as spiritual or mystical. But this is a "mysticism" thoroughly grounded in genuine experience and verifiable by all those who have successfully followed the requisite set of conscious experiments, injunctions, and exemplars (Wilber 1995).

In Zen, for example, we have the injunction known as *shikan-taza* (or sitting meditation). The mastery of this exemplar or paradigm opens one to various *kensho* or *satori* experiences (direct apprehensions of the spiritual data brought forth by the injunction), experiences which are then thoroughly tested by the community of those who have completed the first two strands. Bad, partial, or inaccurate apprehensions are thoroughly rebuffed and rejected by the community of the adequate (falsifiability). Zen, in other words, aggressively follows the three strands of all valid knowledge acquisition, which is probably why it has gained such a solid and "no-nonsense" reputation in spiritual studies.[3]

It is from these types of experimental, phenomenological, Left-Hand paths of knowledge acquisition that transpersonal researchers have concluded that there exist at least four higher stages of postformal development available as structural potentials of their own bodymind. If, with reference to the Upper Left quadrant, we add these four higher and postformal stages to the standard stages given in Figure 1, we arrive at: the Great Chain of Being, precisely as traditionally outlined by philosopher-sages from Plotinus to Aurobindo to Asanga to Chih-I to Lady Tsogyal. Figure 3 is a short summary of the Great Chain as given by perhaps its two most gifted exponents, Plotinus (1992) and

The Great Chain of Being and Consciousness	
PLOTINUS	AUROBINDO
Absolute One (Godhead)	Satchitananda/Supermind (Godhead)
Nous (Intuitive Mind) [subtle]	Intuitive Mind/Overmind
Soul/World-Soul [psychic]	Illumined World-Mind
Creative Reason [vision-logic]	Higher-mind/Network-mind
Logical Faculty [formop]	Logical mind
Concepts and Opinions	Concrete mind [conop]
Images	Lower mind [preop]
Pleasure/pain (emotions)	Vital-emotional; impulse
Perception	Perception
Sensation	Sensation
Vegetative life function	Vegetative
Matter	Matter (physical)

Figure 3

Sri Aurobindo, (1970) showing the stunning similarity of the Great Chain wherever it appeared, East or West, North or South (a truly "multicultural" map if ever there was one). Again, the exact details need not detain us; interested readers can consult other works for a finer discussion (Smith 1976; Lovejoy 1964; Wilber et al. 1986). The point is simply that the interior dimensions of the human being seem to be composed of a spectrum of consciousness, running from sensation to perception to impulse to image to symbol to concept to rule to formal to vision-logic to psychic to subtle to causal to nondual states. In simplified form, this spectrum appears to range from subconscious to self-conscious to superconscious; from prepersonal to personal to transpersonal; from instinctual to mental to spiritual; from preformal to formal to postformal; from instinct to ego to God. Thus, you can perhaps start to see why an "all-quadrant, all-level" approach may be the minimum degree of sophistication necessary to secure a genuinely integral theory of consciousness.

Consciousness distributed

If we now return to the thirteen theories outlined in the Introduction, we can perhaps start to see why all of them have proven so durable: they are each accessing one or more of the forty plus quadrant-levels of existence, and thus each is telling us something very important (but partial) about consciousness. This is why all of those approaches may be important for an integral view of consciousness. An "all-level, all-quadrant" approach finds important truths in each of them, and in very specific ways.

But it is not simply that we have a given phenomenon called "conscious-ness" and that these various approaches are each giving us a different view of the beast. Rather, it appears that consciousness actually exists "distributed" across all four quadrants with all of their various levels and dimensions. There is no one quadrant (and certainly no one level) to which we can point and say, there is consciousness. Consciousness is in no way localized in that fashion.

Thus, the first step toward a genuine theory of consciousness is the realization that consciousness is not located in the organism. Rather, con-sciousness is a four-quadrant affair, and it exists, if it exists at all, distributed across all four quadrants, anchored equally in each. Neither consciousness, personality, individual agency, nor psychopathology can be located simply or solely in the individual organism. The subjective domain (Upper Left) is always already embedded in intersubjective (Lower Left), objective (Upper Right), and interobjective (Lower Right) realities, all of which are partly constitutive of subjective agency and its pathologies.

It is true that the Upper Left quadrant is the locus of consciousness as it appears in an individual, but that's the point: as it appears in an individual. Yet consciousness on the whole is anchored in all of the quadrants — intentional, behavioral, cultural, and social. If you "erase" any quadrant, they all disap-pear, because each is intrinsically necessary for the existence of the others.

Thus, it is quite true that consciousness is anchored in the physical brain (as maintained by theories 1, 3, 6, 8). But consciousness is also and equally anchored in interior intentionality (as maintained by theories 2, 4, 7, 10, 11), an intentionality that cannot be explained in physicalist or empiricist terms nor disclosed by their methods or their validity claims.

By the same token, neither can consciousness be finally located in the individual (whether of the Upper Left or Upper Right or both together), because consciousness is also anchored in cultural meaning (the intersubjec-tive chains of cultural signifieds), without which individuated consciousness does not develop. Without this background of cultural practices and meanings (Lower Left), my individual intentions do not and cannot even develop, as the occasional cases of "wolf boy" demonstrate. In precisely the same way that there is no private language, there is no individual consciousness. You cannot generate meaning in a vacuum, nor with a physical brain alone, but only in an intersubjective circle of mutual recognition. Physical brains raised in the wild ("wolf boy") generate neither personal autonomy nor linguistic competence, from which it plainly follows, the physical brain per se is not the autonomous seat of consciousness.

Likewise, consciousness is also embedded in, and distributed across, the material social systems in which it finds itself. Not just chains of cultural signifieds, but chains of social signifiers, determine the specific contours of any particular manifestation of consciousness, and without the material conditions of the social system, both individuated consciousness and personal integrity fail to emerge.

In short, consciousness is not located merely in the physical brain, nor in the physical organism, nor in the ecological system, nor in the cultural context, nor does it emerge from any of those domains. Rather, it is anchored in, and distributed across, all of those domains with all of their available levels. The Upper Left quadrant is simply the functional locus of a distributed phenomenon.

In particular, consciousness cannot be pinned down with "simple location" (which means, any type of location in the sensorimotor worldspace, whether that location actually be simple or dispersed or systems oriented). Consciousness is distributed, not just in spaces of extension (Right Hand), but also in spaces of intention (Left Hand), and attempts to reduce one to the other have consistently and spectacularly failed. Consciousness is not located inside the brain, nor outside the brain either, because both of those are physical boundaries with simple location, and yet a good part of consciousness exists not merely in physical space but in emotional spaces, mental spaces, and spiritual spaces, none of which have simple location, and yet all of which are as real (or more real) than simple physical space (they are Left Hand, not Right Hand, occasions).

The Right Hand reductionists attempt to reduce intentional spaces to extensional spaces and then "locate" consciousness in a hierarchical network of physically extended emergents (atoms to molecules to cells to nervous system to brain), and that will never, never work. It gives us, more or less, only half the story (the Right Hand half).

David Chalmers (1995) recently caused a sensation by having his essay "The Puzzle of Conscious Experience" published by *Scientific American*, bastion of physicalist science. Chalmers's stunning conclusion was that subjective consciousness continues to defy all objectivist explanations. "Toward this end, I propose that conscious experience be considered a fundamental feature, irreducible to anything more basic. The idea may seem strange at first, but consistency seems to demand it" (p. 83). It never ceases to amaze how Anglo-Saxon philosophers greet the reinvention of the wheel with such fuss.

But Chalmers makes a series of excellent points. The first is the irreducibility of consciousness, which has to be "added" to the physical world in order to give a complete account of the universe.

This simple attempt to reintroduce both Left and Right Hand domains to the Kosmos has been considered quite bold, a testament to the power of reductionism against which so obvious a statement seems radical. Chalmers moves toward a formulation: "Perhaps information has two basic aspects: a physical one and an experiential one.... Wherever we find conscious experience, it exists as one aspect of an information state, the other aspect of which is embedded in a physical process in the brain" (p. 85). That is, each state has an interior/intentional and exterior/physical aspect. But perhaps all holons have not just those two, but rather four, fundamental and irreducible aspects. So every "information state" actually and simultaneously has an intentional, behavioral, cultural, and social aspect; and moreover, each of those aspects has at least ten basic levels — much closer to a theory of everything, if such even makes any sense.

Chalmers goes on to point out that all of the physicalist and reductionist approaches to consciousness, including Daniel Dennett's (1991) and Francis Crick's, only solve what Chalmers calls "the easy problems" (such as objective integration in brain processes) leaving the central mystery of consciousness untouched. He is quite right, of course.

Chalmers says that "the hard problem" is "the question of how physical processes in the brain give rise to subjective experience" — that is, how physical and mental interact. This is still the Cartesian question, and it is no closer to being solved today than it was in Descartes' time — precisely because the brain (and every Right Hand event) has simple location, whereas intentionality (and every Left Hand event) does not.

For example, in the simple hierarchy: physical matter, sensation, perception, impulse, image, symbol, concept..., there is an explanatory gap between matter and sensation that has not yet been satisfactorily bridged — not by neuroscience, nor cognitive science, nor neuropsychology, nor phenomenology, nor systems theory. As David Joravsky (1982) put it in his review of

Richard Gregory's (1982) *Mind in Science*. "How is sensation related to neural activity? Unfortunately, we do not know." The reason, he says, is that there is "an irreducible gap between physics and sensation which physiology cannot bridge" — what he calls "an impassible gulf between our two realms." Between, that is, the Left and Right halves of the Kosmos.

But, of course, it is not actually an impassible gulf: you see the physical world right now, so the gulf is bridged. The question is, how? And the answer, we believe, only discloses itself to postformal awareness. The "impassible gulf" is simply another name for the subject/object dualism, which is the hallmark, not of Descartes's error, but of all manifestation, which Descartes simply happened to spot with unusual clarity. It is still with us, this gap, and it remains the mystery hidden in the heart of *samsara*, a mystery that absolutely refuses to yield its secrets to anything less than postformal and nondual consciousness development (we will return to this in a moment).

In the meantime, one thing seems certain: the attempt to solve this dilemma by any sort of reductionism — attempting to reduce Left to Right or Right to Left, or any quadrant to any other, or any level to any other — is doomed to failure, simply because the four quadrants are apparently very real aspects of the human holon, aspects that aggressively resist being erased or reduced. Such reductionisms, to borrow Joravsky's phrase, "create mysteries or nonsense, or both together."

And that is precisely why some kind of "all-quadrant, all-level" approach to consciousness is likely the only viable approach to a genuinely integral theory of consciousness. We can now look briefly at what might be involved in the methodology of such an approach.

Methodology of an integral approach

The methodology of an integral study of consciousness would apparently require at least three broad wings. The first is a commitment to interdisciplinary study and thinking. In our time of massive information overload this is obviously no small requirement and none of us will master it. However, all of us can try to seek out and be open to ideas and information outside our own particular base (quadrant-level).

This allows us to begin the second requirement: the simultaneous tracking of the various levels and lines in each of the quadrants, then noting their correlations, each to all the others, and in no way trying to reduce any to the others.

The third is our own interior transformation and development. This is one crucial reason why the Left Hand dimensions of immediate consciousness have been so intensely ignored and aggressively devalued by most "scientific" researchers. Any Right Hand path of knowledge can be engaged without a demand for interior transformation (or change in level of consciousness); one merely learns a new translation (within the same level of consciousness). More specifically, most researchers have already, in the process of growing up, transformed to rationality (formop or vision-logic), and no higher transformations are required for empiric-analytic or systems theory investigations.

But the Left Hand paths, at the point that they begin to go postformal, demand a transformation of consciousness in the researchers themselves. You can master quantum physics without transforming consciousness; but you cannot in any fashion master Zen without doing so.

But if you have not transformed to (or at least strongly glimpsed) the causal and nondual realms (transpersonal and postformal), you will not be able to see the referents of most of Plotinus's sentences, or those of other transpersonal philosophies (Walsh 1989). They will make no sense to you. You will think Plotinus is "seeing things" — and he is, and so could you and I, if we both transform to those postformal worldspaces, whereupon the referents of Plotinus's sentences, referents that exist in the causal and nondual worldspaces, become plain as day. And that transformation is an absolutely unavoidable part of the paradigm (the injunction) of an integral approach to consciousness.

So those three wings — interdisciplinary study, nonreductionistic "simul-tracking" of all quadrants, and the transformation of researchers themselves — may all be essential for an integral approach to consciousness. Thus, an integral theory of consciousness is not merely an eclecticism of the dozen major approaches summarized above, but rather a tightly integrated approach that follows intrinsically from the holonic nature of the Kosmos.

The methodology of an integral approach to consciousness is obviously complex, but it follows some of the simple guidelines we have already outlined: three strands, four validity claims, ten or more levels of each. To briefly review:

The three strands operative in all valid knowledge are injunction, apprehension, confirmation (or exemplar, evidence, confirmation/rejection; or instrumental, data, fallibilism). These three strands appear to operate in the generation of all valid knowledge — on any level, in any quadrant. But each quadrant has a different architecture and thus a different type of validity claim through which the three strands operate: propositional truth (Upper Right), subjective truthfulness (Upper Left), cultural meaning (Lower Left), and functional fit (Lower Right).

Further, there are at least ten major levels of development in each of those quadrants and thus the knowledge quest takes on different forms as we move through those various levels in each quadrant. The three strands and four claims are still fully operating in each case, but the specific contours vary.

Meditation: An opportunity for integral research

There has recently been an explosion of meditation research and a recent review listed well over 1000 publications (Murphy & Donovan 1997). However, this research has is limitations. Most subjects have been relative beginners who have not accessed higher states and stages, many parameters have been only vaguely related to the goals of meditation (i.e., transpersonal development), many researchers have not themselves done sufficient practice to understand the significance of advanced experiences, and there has been little integration across quadrants. (Notable partial exceptions can be found in Alexander et al. 1990; Wilber et al. 1986). However, the opportunity for more multilevel, multiquadrant integrative research is available. What might such a program look like?

One place to begin would be in the Upper Left quadrant with a careful examination of the phenomenology of advanced experiences. This could include both the content analysis of classic texts, such as Daniel Brown (1986) has begun, and with interviews of contemporary practitioners: paper and pencil measures such as the Profile of Meditative Experiences and interpretative techniques such as the Rorschach (Brown & Engler 1986). The result would be a detailed phenomenology of meditative experience.

At least some of these experience will reflect higher states and stages. As such they will be comprehensible to researchers only to the extent that the researchers themselves have transformed to, or at the very least glimpsed, these levels. Otherwise the phenomenology of these higher stages, as well as the psychologies and philosophies derived from them, will remain what Immanuel Kant called "empty concepts" (Walsh 1989). Therefore, undertaking a contemplative discipline of some kind will be a necessary prerequisite for researchers studying these areas.

These subjective findings could be correlated with objective Upper Right quadrant parameters. These include both psychometric scales (Alexander et al. 1990) biology, e.g., electroencephalography, brain imaging (MRI & PET), and biochemistry (Shapiro & Walsh 1984; West 1987). At the specific moment of any particular meditative experience, what are the physiological correlates?

On the collective side, it would be fascinating to see the social forms and institutions (Lower Right quadrant) that practitioners prefer, create and feel supported by. Considerable information is available from classical texts, which suggest lifestyles and institutions of simplicity, quiet, nonmaterialism, service, and a *sangha* (community of practitioners). How these institutions will manifest in the contemporary information age is a viable object of research. Conversely, what social institutions are conducive to meditative development?

To complete the integral picture we will want to investigate the culture (Lower Left quadrant) that accompanies these postformal experiences, biology and social structures. What worldviews and ethical systems arise? What shared understanding of reality emerges, and how does it affect experience, behavior and social institutions? Conversely, what are the effects of intersubjective structures — different languages, worldviews, moral systems — on meditative experiences?

And of course we will want to examine development across time in all four quadrants. How do gradually deepening experiences and insights interact with behavior, culture and society?

An integral, all-quadrant, multilevel (both personal and transpersonal) developmental approach such as this is demanding and will obviously require that researchers have interdisciplinary skills and contemplative training. But the rewards will be a far richer understanding of this area than any we have had to date.

Let us now quickly run through the major schools of consciousness studies outlined in the Introduction and indicate exactly some of the implications of an integral approach in each case.

An all-quadrant, all-level approach

The emergent/connectionist cognitive science models (such as Alwyn Scott's *Stairway to the Mind*) apply the three strands of knowledge acquisition to the Upper Right quadrant, the objective aspects of individual holons. Statements are thus guided by the validity claim of propositional truth tied to empirically observable events, which means that in this approach the three strands will acknowledge only those holons that register in the sensorimotor worldspace (i.e., holons with simple location, empirically observable by the senses or their extensions). Nonetheless, all holons without exception are holarchic, or composed of hierarchical holons within holons indefinitely, and so this emergent/connectionist approach will apply the three strands to objective, exterior, hierarchical systems as they appear in the individual, objective organism (the Upper Right quadrant).

All of this is fine, right up to the point where these approaches overstep their epistemic warrant and try to account for the other quadrants solely in terms of their own. In the case of the emergent/connectionist theories, this means that they will present a valid Upper Right hierarchy (atoms to molecules to cells to neural pathways to reptilian stem to limbic system to neocortex). But then consciousness is somehow supposed to miraculously jump out at the top level (the Left Hand dimensions are often treated as a monolithic and monological single entity, and then this "consciousness" is simply added on top of the Right Hand hierarchy, instead of seeing that there are levels of consciousness which exist as the interior or Left Hand dimension of every step in the Right Hand hierarchy).

So in an integral theory of consciousness, we would certainly include the Upper Right hierarchy and those aspects of the emergent/connectionist and evolutionary psychology models that legitimately reflect that territory; but where those theories overstep their epistemic warrant (and are thus reduced to reductionism), we should perhaps move on.

The introspective/interpretative approaches give us the interior contours of individual consciousness: the three strands legitimately applied to the interior of individual holons under the auspices of truthfulness. This exploration and elucidation of the Upper Left quadrant is an important facet of an integral approach to consciousness. It is perhaps best exemplified in the first-person, phenomenological, and interpretive accounts of consciousness that can be found from depth psychology to phenomenology to meditation and contemplation, all of which, at their most authentic, are guided by injunction, apprehension, and confirmation, thus legitimately grounding their knowledge claims in reproducible evidence.

Eastern and nonordinary state models point out that there are more things in the Upper Left quadrant than are dreamt of in our philosophy, not to mention our conventional psychologies. The three strands of all valid knowledge are here applied to states that are largely nonverbal, postformal, and transpersonal.

Those approaches are quite right: no theory of consciousness can hope to be complete that ignores the higher or postformal dimensions of consciousness itself. Moreover, this demands that, at some point, researchers interested in these levels and their implications must transform their own consciousness in order to be adequate to the evidence. This is not a loss of objectivity but rather the prerequisite for data accumulation, just as we do not say that learning to use a microscope is the loss of one's objectivity — it is simply the learning of the injunctive strand. In this case, the data is postformal, and so therefore is the injunction.

Advocates of subtle energies *(prana,* bioenergy) bring a piece of the puzzle to this investigation. However, they often seem to believe that these subtle energies are the central or even sole aspect of consciousness, whereas these energies may be merely one of the lower dimensions in the overall spectrum itself. For the Great Chain theorists, East and West, *prana* is simply the link between the material body and the mental domain. Moreover, the whole point of a four-quadrant analysis is that what the great wisdom traditions tended to represent as disembodied, transcendental, and nonmaterial modes actually have correlates in the material domain (every Left Hand occasion has a Right Hand correlate), and thus it is much more accurate to speak of the physical bodymind, the emotional bodymind, the mental bodymind, and so on. This simultaneously allows transcendental occasions and firmly grounds them. And in this conception, *prana* is simply the emotional bodymind in general, with correlates in all four quadrants (subjective: proto-emotions; objective: limbic system; intersubjective: magical; interobjective: tribal). What is not helpful, however, is to claim that these energies alone hold the key to consciousness.

Psi studies (telepathy, precognition, psychokinesis, clairvoyance) have been some of the more controversial aspects of consciousness research. This controversy may be resolving in light of recent advances. These advances include increasingly tight experimental designs, replicable findings across laboratories (e.g. the Ganzfield studies), and statistical meta-analyses which have revealed surprisingly highly significant findings (Radin 1997).

None of the intentional and Left Hand dimensions of consciousness follow the physical rules of simple location, and we don't need psi events to tell us that. Thus, an integral theory of consciousness would take seriously at least the possibility of psi phenomena, without blowing their possible existence all out of proportion; they are, at best, a small slice of a very big pie.

Of the thirteen major approaches listed in the introduction, the quantum approaches are the ones that appear to lack substantial evidence at this time. To date the theoretical conclusions (such as that intentionality collapses the Schrödinger wave function) are based on extremely speculative notions that most physicists themselves find quite dubious (Wilber 1996).

A central problem with these quantum approaches is that they are trying to solve the subject/object dualism on a level at which it cannot be solved. That problem is (dis)solved only in postformal development, and no amount of formal propositions will come anywhere near the solution. Nonetheless, this line of research might help to elucidate some of the interactions between biological intentionality and matter.

All of those approaches center on the individual. But the cultural approaches to consciousness point out that individual consciousness does not, and cannot, arise on its own. All subjective events are always already intersubjective events. There is no private language; there is no autonomous consciousness. The very words we are both now sharing were not invented by us, do not come solely from my consciousness or from yours. Rather, we simply find ourselves in a vast intersubjective worldspace in which we live and move and have our being. This cultural worldspace (the Lower Left quadrant) has a hand in the very structure, shape, feel, and tone of our consciousness, and no theory of consciousness is complete that ignores this crucial dimension.

In these cultural hermeneutic approaches, the three strands are applied to the intersubjective circle itself, the deep semantics of the worlds of meaning in which we collectively exist. These cultural worldspaces evolve and develop (archaic to magic to mythic to mental, etc.), and the three strands applied to those worldspaces, under the auspices of mutual understanding and appropriateness, reveal those cultural contours of consciousness, which is exactly the course these important approaches take. This, too, is a crucial component of an integral theory of consciousness.[4]

As for the social sciences: the materialities of communication, the techno-economic base, and the social system in the objective sense reach deep into the contours of consciousness to mold the final product. The three strands, under the auspices of propositional truth and functional fit, expose these social determinants at each of their levels, which is exactly the appropriate research agenda of the empirical social sciences.

A narrow Marxist approach, of course, has long been discredited (precisely because it oversteps its warrant, reducing all quadrants to the Lower Right). However, the moment of truth in historical materialism is that the modes of material production (e.g., foraging, horticultural, agrarian, industrial, informational) have a profound and constitutive influence on the actual contents of individual consciousness, and thus an understanding of these social determinants is absolutely crucial for an integral theory of consciousness.

Summary and Conclusion

This outline, abbreviated as it is, nonetheless indicates the broad contours of the methodology of an integral theory of consciousness, and indicates the inadequacy of less comprehensive approaches. The integral aspect enters in simultaneously tracking each level and quadrant in its own terms and then noting the correlations between them. This is a methodology of contemporaneously tracking the various levels and lines in each of the quadrants and then correlating their overall relations, each to all the others, and in no way trying to reduce any to the others.

This "simultracking" requires a judicious and balanced use of all four validity claims (truth, truthfulness, cultural meaning, functional fit) Each of these is redeemed under the warrant of the three strands of valid knowledge acquisition (injunction, apprehension, confirmation) carried out across the dozen or more levels in each of the quadrants — which means, in shorthand fashion, the investigation of sensory experience, mental experience, and spiritual experience: the eye of flesh, the eye of mind, and the eye of contemplation: all-level, all-quadrant.

And this means that, where appropriate, researchers will have to engage various injunctions that transform their own consciousness, if they are to be adequate to the postformal data. If we do not do this, then we will not know this. We will be the Churchmen refusing Galileo's injunction: look through this telescope and tell me what you see.

Thus, an integral approach to consciousness might include the following agendas:

1. Continue research on the various particular approaches. Each of the thirteen approaches almost certainly has some sort of important (if limited) truth to contribute.

2. Confront the simple fact that, in some cases, a change in consciousness on the part of the researchers themselves is mandatory for the investigation of consciousness itself.

3. Continue to grope our way toward a genuinely integral theory of consciousness itself. This includes the actual methodology of "simultracking" the various phenomena in each level-quadrant and noting their actual interrelations (the "simultracking" of events in "all-quadrant, all-level" space).

Thus, each of the thirteen approaches finds an important and indispensable place, not as an eclecticism, but as an intrinsic aspect of the holonic Kosmos. Put simply, an integral theory would attempt to seamlessly include and integrate first-, second-, and third-person approaches. The analysis presented here suggests that every first-person experience is embedded in second-person structures with third-person correlates, and all can, and should, be investigated simultaneously. Subjective awareness is correlated with objective forms, and both arise only in the clearing created by intersubjective structures, such that all three domains (or more specifically, all four quadrants) are mutually caused and causing: the 1–2–3 of consciousness studies.

The methodologies that purport to give us a "theory of consciousness," but which investigate only one quadrant (not to mention only one level in one quadrant) are clearly not giving us an adequate account of consciousness at all.

However, an "all-quadrant, all-level" approach holds a chance of an authentic and integral theory of consciousness, if such indeed exists.

Notes

1.   See Jantsch (1980) for an extended discussion of this theme. Jantsch correlates "micro-evolution" (of individual holons) with "macroevolution" (their collective/social forms), pointing out the coevolutionary interactions between individual and social.

2. This becomes extremely important in individual psychotherapy and depth psychology, because those disciplines have fundamentally exposed the ways in which I might be untruthful to myself about my own interior status. "Repression" and other defences are deceptions, concealment, or lies about the contours of my own interior space, and "therapy" (or at least insight oriented therapy) is essentially learning ways to be more honest and truthful when interpreting my interior texts. Therapy is the sustained application of the validity criterion of truthfulness to one's own estate.

3. Of course, not everybody who takes up Zen — or any contemplative endeavor — ends up fully mastering the discipline, just as not everybody who takes up quantum physics ends up fully comprehending it. But those who do succeed — in both contemplation and physics, and indeed, in any legitimate knowledge quest — constitute the circle of competence against which validity claims are struck, and Zen is no exception in this regard.

4. The fact that we all exist in cultural worldspaces that are governed largely by interpretive and not merely empirical realities, and the fact that these cultural interpretations are partially constructed and relative, has been blown all out of proportion by the postmodern poststructuralists, who in effect claim this quadrant is the only quadrant in existence. They thus attempt to reduce all truth and all validity claims to nothing but arbitrary cultural construction driven only by power or prejudice or race or gender. This cultural constructivist stance thus lands itself in a welter of performative self-contradictions: it claims that it is true that there is no such thing as truth; it claims that it is universally the case that only relativities are real; it claims that it is the unbiased truth that all truth is biased; and thus, in all ways, it exempts its own truth claims from the restrictions it places on everybody else's. Whenever the other quadrants are denied reality, they in effect sneak back into one's system in the form of internal self-contradictions — the banished and denied validity claims reassert themselves in internal ruptures (Wilber 1995, 1997).

    Thus the extreme cultural constructivists implicitly claim objective and universal truth for their own stance, a stance which explicitly denies the existence of both universality and truth. Hence John Searle (1995) had to beat this approach back in his wonderful *The Construction of Social Reality*, as opposed to "the social construction of reality," the idea being that cultural realities are constructed on a base of correspondence truth which grounds the construction itself, without which no construction at all could get under way in the first place. Once again, we can accept the partial truths of a given quadrant — many cultural meanings are indeed constructed and relative — without going overboard and attempting to reduce all other quadrants and all other truths to that partial glimpse.

References

Alexander, C., Langer, E., Newman, R., Chandler, H. & Davies, J. 1989. Transcendental Meditation, mindfulness and longevity: An experimental study with the elderly. *Journal of Personality and Social Psychology*, 57, 950–964.

Alexander, C., Rainforth, M. & Gelderloos, P. 1991. Tanscendental Meditation, self actualization, and psychological health: A conceptual overview and statistical meta-analysis. *Journal of Social Behavior and Personality* 6, 189–247.

Alexander, F., French, T. & Bacon, C. 1946. *Psychoanalytic therapy: Principles and application.* New Jersey: Ronald Press.

Allport, G. 1964. The fruits of eclecticism: Bitter or sweet? *Acta Psychologica, 23,* 27–44.

Arlow, J. 1995. Psychoanalysis. In R. Corsini & D. Wedding (Eds.), *Current Psychotherapies* (5th ed., pp. 15–50). Itasca, IL: F.E. Peacock.

Barkow, J.H., Cosmides, L. & Tooky, J. 1992. The adapted mind: Evolutionary psychology and the generation of culture. Oxford: Oxford University Press.

Boss, M. 1963. *A psychiatrist discovers India.* New York: Basic Books.

Brown, D., Forte, M., & Dysart, M. 1984. Differences in visual sensitivity among mindfulness meditators and non-meditators. *Perceptual and Motor Skills, 58,* 727–733.

Byrom, T. 1976. *The dhammapada: The sayings of the Buddha.* New York: Vintage.

Chan, W. (Ed.). 1963. *A sourcebook in Chinese philosophy.* Princeton, NJ: Princeton University Press.

Creel, H. 1953. *Chinese thought from Confucius to Mao Tse-tung.* Chicago: University of Chicago Press.

Engler, J. 1983. Vicissitudes of the self according to psychoanalysis and Buddhism: A spectrum model of objects relations development. *Psychoanalysis and Contemporary Thought 6,* 29–72.

Feng, G. & English, J. (Trans.). 1974. *Chuang Tsu: Inner Chapters.* New York: Vintage.

Feuerstein, G. 1996. *The Shambhala guide to yoga.* Boston: Shambhala.

Freud, S. 1962. *A general introduction to psychoanalysis* (J. Riviere , Trans.). Garden City, N.J.: Garden City Publishing. (Original work published 1935).

Freud, S. 1933/1965. *New introduction lectures* (J. Strachey, Trans.). New York: Norton.

Gabbard, G. 1995. Psychoanalysis. In H. Kaplan & B. Saddock (Eds.), *Comprehensive textbook of psychiatry, 6th ed., Vol. 1.* (pp. 431–478). Baltimore, M.D.: Williams & Wilkins.

Gampopa 1971. *The jewel ornament of liberation* (H.Guenther, Trans.). Boston: Shambhala.

Goldstein, J. 1983. *The experience of insight.* Boston, MA.: Shambhala Press.

Goleman, D. 1988. *The meditative mind.* Los Angeles: J.P. Tarcher

Goleman, D. 1995. *Emotional intelligence.* N.Y.: Bantam

Grof, S. 1998. *The cosmic game.* Albany, N.Y.:SUNY Press.

Ishiyama, F. 1988. Current status of Morita Therapy research. *International Bulletin of Morita Therapy 1,* 58–83.

Jackendoff, R. 1987. Consciousness and the computational mind. Cambridge, Mass: MIT Press.

James, W. 1910/1950. *The principles of psychology.* New York: Dover.

James, W. 1958. *The varieties of religious experience.* New York: New American Library.

James, W. 1960. *William James on psychical research.* G. Murphy & R. Ballou, (Eds.). New York: Viking.

Jung, C. 1955. *Mysterium conjunctionis: Collected works of Carl Jung (Vol. 14).* Princeton, N.J.: Princeton University Press.

Jung, C. 1968. *The psychology of the child archetype, in collected works of C.J. Jung (Vol. 9, Part I), Bollingen Series XX (2nd ed.).* Princeton, N.J.: Princeton University.

Jung, C. 1973. *Letters.* Adler, G. (Ed.). Princeton, NJ: Princeton University Press.

Kabat-Zinn, J. 1990. *Full catastrophe living.* New York: Delacorte.

Kabat-Zinn, J., Wheeler, E., Light, T., Skillings, A., Scharf, M., Cropley, T., Hosmer, D. & Bernhard, J. 1998. Influence of a mindfulness meditation-based stress reduction intervention on rates of skin clearing in patients with moderate to severe psoriasis undergoing phototherapy (UVB) and photochemotherapy (PUVA). *Psychosomatic Medicine* 60, 625–632.

Kegan, R. 1982. *The evolving self.* Cambridge, MA.: Harvard University Press.

Kohlberg, L. 1981. *Essays on moral development: Vol. I. The philosophy of moral development.* New York: Harper and Row.

Kornfield, J. 1993. *A path with heart.* New York, N.Y.: Bantam Books.

Kornfield, J. 1995. *Living dharma teachings of twelve Buddhist masters.* Boston: Shambhala.

Kristeller, J. & Hallett, B. 1999. An exploratory study of a meditation-based intervention for binge eating disorder. *Journal of Health Psychology.* (In press).

LaBerge, S. 1985. *Lucid dreaming.* Los Angeles: J.P. Tarcher.

Lau, D. (Trans.) 1979. *Confucius: The analects.* New York: Penguin

Lazarus, A. 1995. Multimodal therapy. In R. Corsini & D. Wedding (eds.) *Current psychotherapies* (5th. Ed., pp. 322–355). Itasca, IL.: Peacock.

Maslow, A. 1967. Self-actualization and beyond. In J. Bugental (Ed.). *Challenges of humanistic psychology* (pp 279–286). New York: McGraw-Hill.

Maslow, A. 1968. *Towards a psychology of being (2nd ed.).* Princeton: Van Nostrand.

Maslow, A. 1970. *Religions, values and peak experiences.* New York: Viking.

Maslow, A. 1971. *The farther reaches of human nature.* New York: Viking.

Murphy, M. & Donovan, S. 1997. *The physical and psychological effects of meditation.* Sausalito, CA: Institute of Noetic Sciences.

Myers, D. 1992. *The pursuit of happiness.* New York: Avon.

Needleman, J. 1984. *The heart of philosophy.* New York: Bantam.

Nisagadatta, Sri 1973. *I am that: Conversations with Sri Nisargadatta Maharaj, Vol. 1.* (M. Friedman, Trans.). Bombay: Chetana.

Nyanaponika 1976. *Abhidharma studies.* Kandy, Sri Lanka: Buddhist Publication Society.

Ornish, D. 1990. *Dr. Dean Ornish's program for reversing heart disease.* New York: Ballantine Books.

Perls, F. 1969. *Gestalt therapy verbatim.* Lafayette, CA: Real People Press.

Perry, W. (Ed.) 1981. *The treasury of traditional wisdom.* Pates Middlesex, UK: Perennial Books.

Prabhavananda, S. & Isherwood, C. (Trans.). 1972. *The song of God: Bhagavad Gita* (3rd ed.). Hollywood: Vedanta Society.

Prabhavananda, S. & Isherwood, C. (Trans.) 1978. *Shankara's crest-jewel of discrimination.* Hollywood: Vedanta Press.

Raskin, N. & Rogers, C. 1995. Person-centered therapy. In R. Corsini & D. Wedding (Eds.), *Current psychotherapies* (5th ed., pp. 128–161). Itasca: IL: F.E. Peacock.

Reynolds, D. 1981. Naikan psychotherapy. In R. J. Corsini (Ed.), *Handbook of innovative psychotherapies* (pp 544–553). New York: John Wiley.

Rogers, C. 1959. A theory of therapy, personality and interpersonal relationships as developed in the client centered framework. In S. Koch (Ed.), *Psychology: The study of a science* (Vol 3., pp. 184–256). New York: McGraw Hill.

Schumacher, E. 1973. *Small is beautiful: Economics as if people mattered.* New York: Harper and Row.

Sengstan 1975. *Verses on the faith mind* (R. Clarke, Trans.). Sharon Springs, NY: Zen Center.

Shapiro, D.H. 1980. *Meditation: Self regulation strategy and altered state of consciousness*. New York: Aldine.

Shapiro, D. & Astin, J. 1998. *Control therapy*. N.Y.: John Wiley

Shapiro, D. & Walsh, R. (Eds.). 1984. *Meditation: Classic and contemporary perspectives*. New York: Aldine.

Shapiro, S., Schwartz, G & Bonner, G. 1999. Effects of mindfulness-based stress reduction on medical and premedical students. *Journal of Behavioral Medicine 21*, 581–599.

Shearer, P. (Trans.). 1982. *Effortless being: The Yoga Sutras of Patanjali*. London: Wildwood House.

Tart, C. 1986. *Waking up: Overcoming the obstacles to human potential*. Boston: New Science Library/Shambhala.

Walsh, R. 1989. Can Western philosophers understand Asian philosophies? *Crosscurrents, XXXIX*, 281–299 (Reprinted in J. Ogilvy (Ed.) *Revisioning Philosophy*. Albany, N.Y.: SUNY Press).

Walsh, R. 1990. *The spirit of shamanism*. Los Angeles: J. Tarcher.

Walsh, R. 1999. *Essential spirituality: The seven central practices to awaken heart and mind*. New York: John Wiley.

Walsh, R. & Shapiro, D.H. (Eds.). 1983. *Beyond health and normality: Explorations of exceptional psychological wellbeing*. New York: Van Nostrand Reinhold.

Walsh, R. & Vaughan, F. (Eds.). 1993. *Paths beyond ego: The transpersonal vision*. Los Angeles: J. Tarcher.

West, M. (Ed.). 1987. *The psychology of meditation*. Oxford: Clarenden Press.

Whitmont, E. 1969. *The symbolic quest*. Princeton: Princeton University Press.

Wilber, K. 1980. *The Atman project*. Wheaton, IL: Quest.

Wilber, K. 1981. *No boundary*. Boston, MA: New Science Library/ Shambhala.

Wilber, K. 1995. *Sex, ecology, spirituality*. Boston: Shambhala.

Wilber, K. 1996. *A brief history of everything*. Boston, MA: Shambhala.

Wilber, K. 1997. *The eye of spirit*. Boston: Shambhala.

Wilber, K. 1999a. *One taste: The journals of Ken Wilber*. Boston: Shambhala.

Wilber, K. 1999b. *The collected works of Ken Wilber (5 Vols.)*. Boston: Shambhala.

Wilber, K., Engler, J. & Brown, D. (Eds.). 1986. *Transformations of consciousness: Conventional and contemplative perspectives on development*. Boston: New Science Library/Shambhala.

Yalom, I. 1980. *Existential psychotherapy*. New York: Basic Books.

Yu-Lan, Fung. 1948. *A short history of Chinese philosophy*. (D. Bodde, trans.). N.Y.: Free Press/MacMillan.

CHAPTER 15

A Psychologist's Map
of Consciousness Studies

Max Velmans

In ordinary life, first-person accounts of our mental life and actions in terms of what we think, desire, feel, believe, and experience with our senses provide useful explanations of what is going on. Indeed, for most everyday purposes, such accounts are more useful than the more theoretically driven accounts offered by cognitive psychology, neuropsychology and other sciences of the mind. They also provide an initial point of departure for a science of consciousness. In themselves, however, they no more *exhaust* the scope of a science of consciousness than everyday descriptions of the physical world exhaust the scope of physics. As in physics, a science of consciousness aims for more precise knowledge, deeper understanding, and to discover *general* truths that can be applied to individual situations (thereby providing a measure of prediction and control). As in any communal science this requires the development of a systematic investigative methodology.

How can one investigate phenomenal consciousness? The authors in this text are agreed that one cannot do so simply by investigating something *other* than phenomenal consciousness — even something that relates as closely to it as its neural causes and correlates. As in other areas of science, causes and correlates are not ontological identities.[1] That said, there is nothing to prevent a systematic enquiry into how phenomenal consciousness *relates* to brain processes and to the embedding physical and social world.

This enables one to create a form of "consciousness science" that is already well known and well accepted in psychological research. Psychophysics for example has traditionally investigated how changes in simple dimensions of external physical stimuli (such as intensity and frequency) are translated by perceptual systems into changes in experience. Cognitive psychology investigates the ways in which mental processes operate and how some of these processes (selective attention, working memory, and so on) relate to and support current experience. Neuropsychology tracks the changes in the brain that cause or correlate with normal and disordered forms of experience (see Farthing 1992, and readings in Velmans 1996a; Cohen & Schooler 1997).

Overall this provides a two-pronged approach to consciousness studies in which traditional third-person methods for investigating the brain and physical world are combined with first-person methods for investigating subjective experience with the aim of finding "bridging laws" which relate such first- and third-person data to each other. These traditional routes to the investigation of experience require no *a priori* commitment to philosophical reductionism (of first- to third-person data). On the contrary, first-person approaches provide data that cannot be obtained from a third-person perspective — for example what it is like to have a given conscious experience or to be in a given conscious state. And third-person approaches provide data that cannot be obtained from a first-person perspective — for example data about what is going on in the brain while one is having a given experience. As I have argued in Velmans (1991a) "first-person and third person perspectives are complementary and mutually irreducible. A complete psychology requires both."

There are of course many different ways in which first- and third person investigations can complement each other. In some situations the relation of first- to third-person data may be very precise. Ordinary conscious states are always *of* something, so it is plausible to suppose that both they and their neural correlates are representational states. It is also plausible to suppose that given conscious states and their neural correlates encode identical information (about what they represent) although this information may be formatted in very different ways. Consequently, at the interface of consciousness with its neural correlates it may be possible to specify the relation of first- to third-person information with mathematical precision; for example, it may be possible to specify the topology of phenomenal space, the topology of correlated neural representational space, and the mapping of one on to the other.[2]

First- and third-person investigations can also be "complementary" in the more general senses indicated in Part 1:A of this book. The aetiology of conscious mental states can be investigated both in first-person terms and via third-person methods such as the non-invasive imaging techniques described by Fenwick (Chapter 2) which provide real-time information about operations of the brain that correlate with given experiences. Shevrin (Chapter 3) demonstrates how a combination of first- and third-person approaches can also be mutually supportive in the discovery of *unconscious* mental states. In other situations the complementary use of first- and third-person information pits interpretations based on first-person data *against* that obtained via third-person techniques. Here the aim is to find interpretations that most fully account for *all* the data. Sometimes, third-person data can show first-person theories about the mental states that cause behaviour to be wrong (as in the celebrated studies of folk-psychological beliefs by Nisbett and Wilson 1977). Conversely, Solms (Chapter 4), demonstrates how first-person psychoanalytic investigation of right hemisphere syndrome (a combination of anosognosia, neglect, and defective spatial cognition), can reveal flaws in standard third-person, neurophysiological accounts.

Difficulties in the development of more sophisticated first-person methods

In the study of consciousness, both first- and third-person methods clearly have a role to play. However, given the traditional commitment to "objective" third-person methods in western science, it is not surprising that these have become far more sophisticated than the so-called "introspective" techniques. Neural imaging studies illustrate this point nicely. As Pickering (Chapter 13) observes, they typically employ impressive machinery with multicoloured displays producing data that can only be analysed with sophisticated statistical techniques. By contrast, the conscious activities and reports required of subjects in neural imaging studies are usually very simple. For example, in studies that investigate the transition from a preconscious to a conscious visual state, subjects might be asked to attend to a simple visual stimulus and to report whether or not they see it. In studies that investigate the processes supporting visual imagery, subjects might be asked to report when they have a visual image (of some object) and so on. In such situations, subjects are asked to enter into or are placed into a given mental state, but the *investigation* of that state is largely up to the experimenter (using entirely third-person techniques) rather than the subject.

In the early psychological laboratories of Wundt, Titchener and their followers, it was hoped that first-person methods could be developed that are, in their own way, as sophisticated as third-person methods. Although the history of psychological science has shown that this is not easy to achieve, this project was never entirely abandoned, even during the behaviourist years (see Stevens, Chapter 5). With the re-emergence of consciousness studies the development of better first-person methods has once again become serious scientific business.[3]

What are the residual problems? As the chapters in Part 3 of this book demonstrate, there is more than one map that can be drawn of the consciousness studies terrain — depending on one's direction of approach and the depth and breadth of one's focus. Given this, it is not surprising that both the analysis of problems and the suggested solutions differ. In Chapter 10, Scott (a mathematician) treats consciousness as an emergent property of complex biological systems that can only be analysed in its full complexity. In Chapter 11, Harré views the problems of consciousness from the perspective of linguistic philosophy and consequently focuses on the need to distinguish the language and methodology one uses to describe persons from that required to describe brains. Once distinguished, one can relate these to each other. Tart (Chapter 12), by contrast, approaches the problems of consciousness from the perspective of an investigator of altered conscious states. Consequently, he focuses on the need to *enter into* a given conscious state in order to understand it fully, which opens up the possibility that investigators of consciousness may need to develop a series of "state-specific sciences." Advocating a postmodern turn in psychology, Pickering (Chapter 13) views the problems of consciousness as symptomatic of more general problems faced by an overly restrictive psychological science. For him, phenomenological methods and systems thinking need to supplement cognitive and neurological methods to provide a complete science of the mind. Taking a multidisciplinary approach, Wilber & Walsh (Chapter 14) draw a map of the consciousness studies terrain that is as large as the cosmos itself, including its evolution, its microcosm and macrocosm, its individual and social (relational) aspects, and its inner and outer manifestations. This map includes all that we are or can be conscious of. As they make clear, consciousness studies may be divided into distinct *domains*. Ultimately, all domains support each other (being parts of the whole), but investigative techniques, and the methods of attaining agreement and settling disagreement need to be tailored to the given domain that one wishes to explore. I have noted in the Introduction (Chapter 1), that one must choose the map that is most useful for one's purposes for oneself. My own tentative map approaches the terrain with the traditional concerns of an experimental psychologist. Viewed this way, what are the difficulties that first-person methods face? The problems are of three kinds:

1. Epistemological problems: How can one obtain public, objective knowledge about private, subjective experiences?
2. Methodological problems: Given that one cannot attach measuring instruments directly up to experiences, what psychological "instruments" and procedures are appropriate to their study?
3. The relation of the observer to the observed: The more closely coupled an observer is with an observed, the greater the potential influence of the act of observation on the nature of the observed ("observer effects"). Given this, how can one develop introspective and phenomenological methods where the observer *is* the observed?

Epistemological problems[4]

Although the private, subjective nature of conscious experience is widely thought to preclude its scientific investigation. I will argue that this is not where the real problems lie. Rather, the epistemological problems posed by the study of subjective experience are largely artefactual, arising from a misconceived, dualist, splitting of the world which we have inherited from Descartes. This implicit dualism is clearly shown in the model of perception shown in Figure 1. In fact there are *two* splits in this model: (1) the observer (on the right of the diagram is clearly separate from the observed (the light on the left of the diagram) and (2) public, objective "physical phenomena" in the external world or in the brain (in the lower part of the diagram) are clearly separated from private, subjective psychological phenomena "in the mind" (represented by the cloud in the upper part of the diagram).

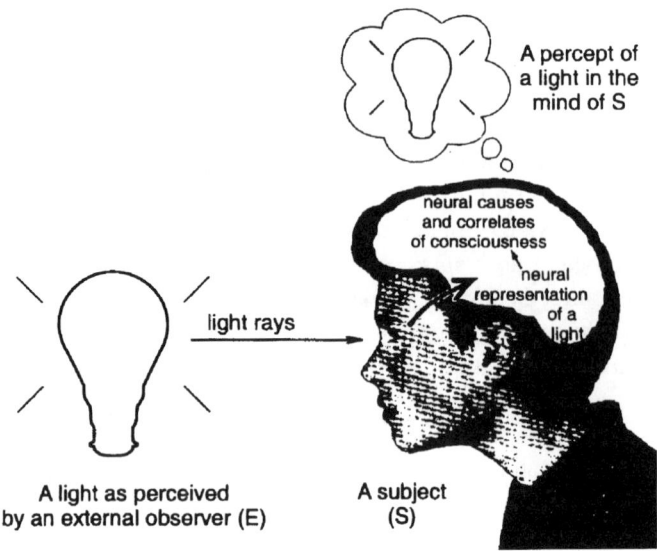

A percept of
a light in the
mind of S

neural causes
and correlates
of consciousness

neural
representation
of a
light

light rays

A light as perceived
by an external observer (E)

A subject
(S)

How we make sense of this in conventional studies of perception

Following usual procedures, a subject (S) is asked to focus on the light and
report on or respond to what she experiences, while the experimenter (E)
controls the stimulus and tries to observe what is going on in the subject's
brain. E has observational access to the stimulus and to S's brain states, but has
no access to what S experiences. In principle, other experimenters can also
observe the stimulus and S's brain states. Consequently, what E has access to
is thought of as "public" and "objective." However, E does not have access to
S's experiences, making them "private" and "subjective" and a problem for
science. This apparently radical difference in the epistemic *status* of the data
accessible to E and S is enshrined in the words commonly used to describe
what they perceive. That is, E makes *observations*, whereas S merely has
subjective experiences.

Although this way of looking at things is adequate as a working model for
many studies it actually misdescribes the *phenomenology* of conscious experience — and, consequently misconstrues the problems a study of conscious
experience must face. A more accurate model of the way events in the world
are experienced by subjects is shown in the reflexive model of perception in
Figure 2.

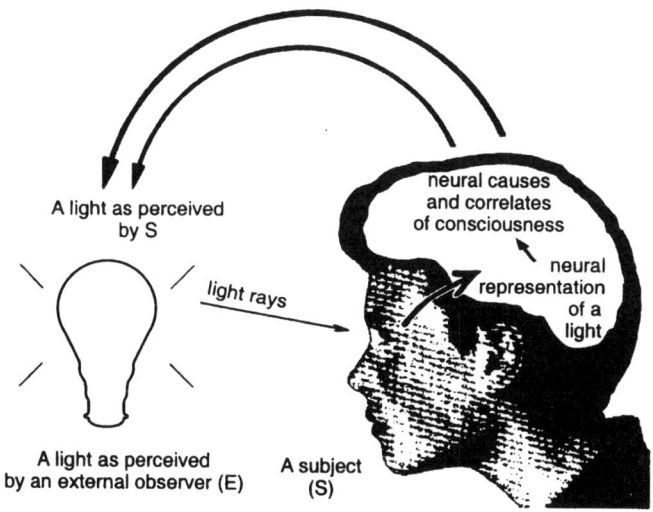

Figure 2

This reflexive model accepts conventional wisdom about the physical and neurophysiological causes of perception — for example, that there really is a physical stimulus in the room that our experience of it *represents*. But it gives a different account of the nature of the resulting experience. According to this non-dualist view, when S attends to the light in a room she does not have an experience *of* a light "in her head or brain," with its attendant problems for science. She just sees a light in a room. Indeed, what the subject experiences is very similar to what the experimenter experiences when he gazes at the light (she just sees the light from a different angle) — in spite of the different terms they use to describe what they perceive (a "physical stimulus" versus a "sensation of light"). If so, there can be no actual difference in the subjective versus objective status of the light *phenomenology* "experienced" by S and "observed" by E. I have developed the case for this and analysed its consequences elsewhere (Velmans 1993a, 1996b, 2000). However, one can easily grasp the essential similarities between S's "experiences" and E's "observations" from the fact that *the roles of S and E are interchangeable*.

A thought experiment — "changing places"

What makes one human being a "subject" and another an "experimenter"? Their different roles are defined largely by *differences in their interests* in the experiment, reflected in differences in what they are required to do. The subject is required to focus only on her *own* experiences (of the light), which she needs to respond to or report on in an appropriate way. The experimenter is interested primarily in the *subject's* experiences, and in how these depend on the light stimulus or brain states that he can "observe."

To exchange roles, S and E merely have to turn their heads, so that E focuses exclusively on the light and describes what he experiences, while S focuses her attention not just on the light (which she now thinks of as a "stimulus") but also on events she can observe in E's brain, and on E's reports of what he experiences. In this situation, E becomes the "subject" and S becomes the "experimenter." Following current conventions, S would now be entitled to think of her observations (of the light and E's brain) as "public and objective" and to regard E's experiences of the light as "private and subjective."

Notice that this outcome, where the epistemic status of the experienced light switches from "subjective" to "objective" as S switches from being a "subject" to an "experimenter" is absurd, as the phenomenology of the light remains the same, viewed from the perspective of either S or E, whether it is *thought of* an "observed stimulus" or an "experience." Nothing has changed in the character of the light that E and S can observe other than the focus of their interest. That is, in terms of *phenomenology* there is no difference between "observed phenomena" and "experiences." This raises a fundamental question: If the phenomenology of the light remains the same whether it is thought of a "physical stimulus" or an "experience," is the phenomenon *private and subjective* or is it *public and objective*?

All experiences are private and subjective

I do not have direct access to your experiences and you do not have direct access to mine. For example I cannot experience your pain, your thoughts, your colour qualia, the way your body feels to you, the way the sky looks to you, the way I look to you, etc. I can only have my own experiences (however well I empathise). The privacy and subjectivity of each individual's experience is well accepted in philosophy of mind. It seems to be a fundamental given of how we are situated in the world.

In dualism, "experiences" are private and subjective, while "physical phenomena" are public and objective as noted above. However, according to the reflexive model there is no *phenomenal* difference between physical phenomena and our experiences *of* them. When we turn our attention to the external world, physical phenomena just *are* what we experience. If so, there is a sense in which physical phenomena are "private and subjective" just like the other things we experience. For example, I cannot experience your phenomenal mountain or your phenomenal tree. I only have access to my own phenomenal mountain and tree. Similarly, I only have access to my own phenomenal light stimulus and my own observations of its physical properties (in terms of meter readings of its intensity, frequency, and so on). That is, *we each live in our own private, phenomenal world*. Few, I suspect, would disagree.

Public access to observed entities and events; public phenomena in the sense of similar, shared, private experiences

What are the implications of this for science? If we each live in our own private, phenomenal world then each "observation" is, in a sense, private. This was evident to the father of operationalism, the physicist P.W. Bridgman (1936), who concluded that, in the final analysis, "science is only my private science". However, this is clearly not the whole story. When an entity or event is placed beyond the body surface (as the entities and events studied by Physics usually are) it can be perceived by any member of the public suitably located in space and time. Under these circumstances such entities or events are "public" in the sense that there is *public access* to the observed entity or event *itself*.

This distinction between the *phenomenon* perceived by a given observer and the entity or event *itself* is important. In the reflexive model, perceived phenomena *represent* things-themselves, but are not identical to them. The light perceived by E and S, for example, can be described in terms of its perceived brightness and colour. But, in terms of physics, the stimulus is better described as electromagnetism with a given mix of energies and frequencies. As with all visually observed phenomena, the phenomenal light only *becomes*

a phenomenal light once the stimulus interacts with an appropriately structured visual system — and the result of this observed — observer interaction is
a light as-experienced which is private to the observer in the way described
above. However, if the stimulus itself is beyond the body surface and has an
independent existence, it remains there *to be* observed whether it is observed
(at a given moment) or not. That is why the stimulus itself is *publicly
accessible* in spite of the fact that each observation/experience of it is private
to a given observer.

To the extent that observed entities and events are subject to similar
perceptual and cognitive processing in different human beings, it is also
reasonable to assume a degree of *commonality* in the way such things are
experienced. While each experience remains private, it may be a private
experience that others share. For example, unless observers are suffering from
red/green colour blindness, we normally take it for granted that they perceive
electromagnetic stimuli with wavelength 700 nanometers (nm) as red and
those of 500 nm as green. Given the privacy of light phenomenology there is
no way to be certain that others experience "red" and "green" as we do
ourselves (the classical problem of "other minds"). But in normal life, and in
the practice of science, we adopt the working assumption that the same
stimulus, observed by similar observers, will produce similar observations or
experiences. Thus, while experienced entities and events (phenomena) remain
private to each observer, if their perceptual, cognitive and other observing
apparatus is similar, we assume that their experiences (of a given stimulus) are
similar. Consequently, experienced phenomena may be "public" in the special
sense that other observers have similar or shared experiences.

Being clear about what is private and what is public

The consequences of this non-dualist analysis can be summarised as follows:
- There is only *private* access to individual observed or experienced *phenomena*.
- There can be *public* access to the entities and events which serve as the
  stimuli for such phenomena (the entities and events which the phenomena
  represent). This applies, for example, to the entities and events studied by
  physics.
- If the perceptual, cognitive and other observing apparatus of different

observers is similar, we assume that their experiences (of a given stimulus) are similar. In this special sense, experienced phenomena may be *public* in so far as they are *similar or shared private experiences.*

From subjectivity to intersubjectivity

This reanalysis of private versus public phenomena also provides a natural way to think about the relation between *subjectivity* and *intersubjectivity*. Each (private) observation or experience is necessarily *subjective*, in that it is always the observation or experience of a *given* observer, viewed and described from his or her individual perspective. However, once that experience is shared with another observer it can become *inter*-subjective. That is, through the sharing of a similar experience, subjective views and descriptions of that experience potentially converge, enabling intersubjective agreement about what has been experienced.

How different observers establish intersubjectivity through negotiating agreed descriptions of shared experiences is a complex process that involves far more than shared experience. One also needs a shared language, shared cognitive structures, a shared world-view or scientific paradigm, shared training and expertise and so on. In the process of establishing intersubjectivity, interacting observers can also influence each other's experience and shared understanding of experience in more subtle, interpersonal and social ways to create a shared perspective. This adoption of a shared perspective, from which *we* see each other and the world is sometimes referred to as "the second person perspective" (see for example, Wilber & Walsh Chapter 14). We return to this briefly below (in the discussion of "observer effects"). All we need to note for now is that, to the extent that an experience or observation can be *generally* shared (by a community of observers), it can form part of the database of a communal science.

Different meanings of the term "objective" that are used in science

According to the analysis above, phenomena in science can be "objective" in the sense of *intersubjective*. Note, however, that intersubjectivity requires the *presence* of subjectivity rather than its absence. Observation statements (descriptions of observations) can also be "objective" in the sense of being dispassionate, accurate, truthful, and so on. Scientific method can also be "objective" in the sense that it follows well-specified, repeatable procedures (perhaps using standard measuring instruments). However, if the analysis above is correct, one cannot make observations without engaging the experiences and cognitions of a conscious subject (unobserved meter readings are not "observations"). If so, science cannot be "objective" in the sense of being *observer-free*.

Intra-subjective and inter-subjective repeatability

According to the reflexive model, there is no phenomenal difference between *observations* and *experiences*. Each observation results from an interaction of an observer with an observed. Consequently, each observation is *observer-dependent* and *unique*. This applies even to observations made by the same observer, of the same entity or event, under the same observation conditions, *at different times* — although, under these circumstances, the observer may have no doubt that he/she is making *repeated* observations of the same entity or event.

   If the conditions of observation are sufficiently standardised an observation may be *repeatable* within a community of (suitably trained) observers, in which case intersubjectivity can be established by collective *agreement*. Once again, though, it is important to note that different observers cannot have an *identical* experience. Even if they observe the same event, at the same location, at the same time, they each have their own, unique experience. *Inter*subjective repeatability resembles *intra*subjective repeatability in that it merely requires observations to be sufficiently similar to be taken for "tokens" of the same "type." This applies particularly to observations in science, where repeatability typically requires intersubjective agreement amongst scientists observing similar events at *different* times and in *different* geographical locations.

Consequences of the above analysis for a science of consciousness

The above provides an account of the empirical method, i.e. of what scientists actually do when they test their theories, establish *intersubjectivity*, *repeat-*

ability and so on which accepts that observed, physical phenomena just *are* the entities and events that scientists experience. Although I have focused on physical events, this analysis applies also to the investigation of events that are usually thought of as "mental" or "psychological." Although the methodologies appropriate to the study of physical and mental phenomena may be very different, the same *epistemic* criteria can be applied to their scientific investigation. Physical phenomena and mental (psychological) phenomena are just different kinds of phenomena which observers experience (whether they are experimenters or subjects). $S_{1 \text{ to } n}$ might, for example, all report that a given increase in light intensity produces a just noticeable difference in brightness, an experience/observation that is intersubjective and repeatable. Alternatively, $S_{1 \text{ to } n}$ might all report that a given anaesthetic removes pain or, if they stare at a red light spot, that a green after-image appears, making such phenomena similarly public, intersubjective, and repeatable.

This closure of psychological with physical phenomena is self-evident in situations where the same phenomenon can be thought of as either "physical" or "psychological" depending on one's interest in it. At first glance, for example, a visual illusion of the kind shown in Figure 3, might seem to present difficulties, for the reason that physical and psychological descriptions of this phenomenon conflict.

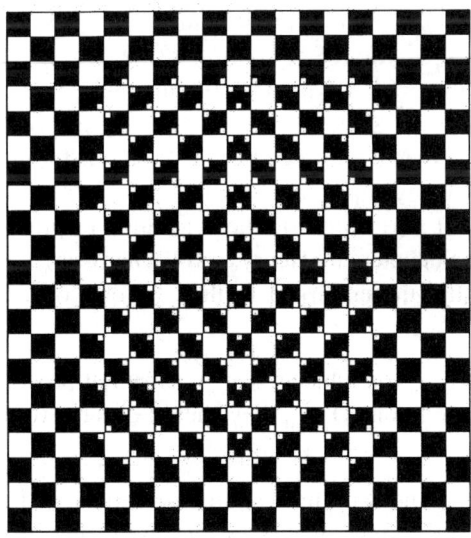

Figure 3

Physically, the figure consists entirely of squares, joined in straight lines, while subjectively, most of the central lines in the figure seem to be bent. However, the physical and psychological descriptions result from two different observation procedures. To obtain the physical description, an experimenter E typically places a straight edge against each line, thereby obscuring the cues responsible for the illusion and providing a fixed reference against which the curvature of each line can be judged. To confirm that the lines are actually straight, other experimenters ($E_{1 \text{ to } n}$) can repeat this procedure. In so far as they each observe the line to be straight under these conditions, their observations are public, intersubjective and repeatable.

But, the fact that the lines *appear* to be bent (once the straight edge is removed) is similarly public, intersubjective and repeatable (amongst subjects $S_{1 \text{ to } n}$). Consequently, the illusion can be investigated using relatively conventional scientific procedures, in spite of the fact that the *illusion* is unambiguously *mental*. One can, for example, simply move the straight edge outside the figure making it seem parallel to the bent central lines — thereby obtaining a measure of the angle of the illusion.

The empirical method

In short, once the *empirical method* is stripped of its dualist trappings, it applies as much to the science of consciousness as it does to the science of physics, and it applies both to western phenomenological methods, focused on ordinary conscious states (reviewed in the chapters by Stevens, Depraz, Varella & Vermersch, and Pickering) and to methods for investigating altered states, such as those developed in the east (see chapters by Fontana, Tart, and Wilber & Walsh). It also applies to the evaluation of processes for changing experience (see the chapters by Henry, and Richardson).

Stated formally, the empirical method follows one, fundamental principle:

If observers $E_{1 \text{ to } n}$ (or subjects $S_{1 \text{ to } n}$), carry out procedures $P_{1 \text{ to } n}$, under observation conditions $O_{1 \text{ to } n}$, they should observe (or experience) result R

(assuming that $E_{1 \text{ to } n}$ and $S_{1 \text{ to } n}$ have similar perceptual and cognitive systems, that $P_{1 \text{ to } n}$ are the procedures which specify the nature of the experiment or investigation, and that $O_{1 \text{ to } n}$ includes *all* relevant background conditions, including those internal to the observer, such as their attentiveness, the paradigm within which they are trained to make observations and so on).

Or, informally:

> *If you carry out these procedures you will observe or experience these results.*[5]

Complicating factors: symmetries and asymmetries of access[6]

Investigations of consciousness do, of course, face domain-specific problems, which are different to those typically encountered in investigations of the external world. These differences arise partly from differences in the questions of interest, partly from differences amongst some of the phenomena studied and partly from systematic differences in the typical *access* an observer has to the observed.

For experimental purposes, the entities and events studied by physics are located *external* to the observers. Placed this way, such entities and events afford *public access* (see above) and different observers establish intersubjectivity, repeatability and so on by using similar exteroceptive systems and equipment to observe them. E and S in Figure 2, for example, might observe the light via their visual systems, supplemented by similar instruments that measure its intensity, frequency and other physical properties. When S and E (and any other observer suitably place in space and time) use similar means to access information about a given entity or event we may say that they have *symmetrical access* to the observed (in this case, to the stimulus light itself). If the event of interest is located on the surface of or within S's body, or within S's brain, as would be the case in the study of physiology or neurophysiology, it remains external to E. Thus placed, it can still afford public, symmetrical access to a community of other, suitably placed external observers ($E_{1 \text{ to } n}$). Consequently, such events can be investigated by the same "external" means employed in other areas of natural science.

In the study of consciousness, however, what the *subject* observes or experiences is of primary interest and, if one compares the information *about* S available *to S* with the information *about S* available *to E* (and other external observers), various forms of *asymmetry* arise. If the event of interest is located on the surface of or within S's body, she may be able to observe or experience that event through interoceptive as well as exteroceptive systems. For example, if she stabs her finger with a pin she might not only be able to see the pin go in, but also to experience a pain in her finger consequent on skin damage. Under these circumstances, she has two sources of information about the event taking place in her skin, while E retains only exteroceptive (visual) information about this event, as before. Likewise, if one stimulates S's brain with a microelectrode, she might, like E, be able to observe the electrical stimulation (with an "autocerebroscope"[7]). But, in addition, she might be able to experience the effects of such stimulation in the form of a consequent visual, auditory, tactile or other experience. In such situations, observers E and S have *asymmetrical access* to the observed.

Crucially, E and S (and any other observers) have *asymmetrical access* to each other's *experiences* of an observed (asymmetrical access to each other's observed phenomena). That is, they know what it is like to have their own experiences, but they can only access the experiences of others indirectly via their verbal descriptions or non-verbal behaviour. This applies to *all* observed phenomena, for example, it applies even if the observed is a simple physical stimulus, such as the light in Figure 2. As E does not have direct access to S's experience of the light and vice-versa, there is no way for E and S to be *certain* that they have a similar experience (whatever they might claim). E might nevertheless *infer* that S's experience is similar to his own on the assumption that S has similar perceptual apparatus, operating under similar observation arrangements, and on the basis of S's similar observation reports. S normally makes similar assumptions about E. It is important to note that this has not impeded the development of physics and other natural sciences, which simply ignore the problem of "other minds" (uncertainty about what other observers actually experience). They just take it for granted that if *observation reports* are the same, then the corresponding *observations* are the same. The success of natural science testifies to the pragmatic value of this approach.

Given this, it seems justifiable to apply the same pragmatic criteria to the observations of subjects in studies of consciousness (i.e. to their "subjective reports"). If, given a standard stimulus and standardised observation conditions, different subjects give similar reports of what they experience, then (barring any evidence to the contrary) it is reasonable to assume that they have similar experiences. Ironically, psychologists have often agonised over the merits of observation reports *when produced by subjects*, although like other scientists, they take them for granted *when produced by experimenters*, on the grounds that the observations of subjects are "private and subjective," while those of experimenters are "public and objective." As experimenters do not have access to each other's experiences any more than they have access to the experiences of subjects, this is a fallacy, as we have seen. Provided that the observation conditions are sufficiently standardised, the observations reported by subjects can be made public, intersubjective, and repeatable amongst a community of subjects in much the same way that observations can be made public, intersubjective and repeatable amongst a community of experimenters. This provides an epistemic basis for a science of consciousness that includes its phenomenology.

In sum, asymmetries of access complicate, but do not prevent the investigation of experience. In Figure 2, E has access, in principle, to the events and processes in S's visual system, but not to S's experience. While S focuses exclusively on the light, she has access to her experience, but not to the antecedent processing in her visual system. Under these circumstances, the information available to S *complements* the information available to E. As noted earlier, to obtain a complete account of visual perception one needs to utilise *both* sources of information.

Methodological problems

It goes without saying that the empirical method, formulated in this way, provides only basic, *epistemic* conditions for the study of consciousness. One also requires *methodologies* appropriate to the subject matter — and the methodologies required to study conscious appearances are generally very different from those used in physics. There are many ways in which the phenomena we usually think of as physical or psychological differ from each other and amongst themselves (in terms of their relative permanence, stability, measurability, controllability, describability, complexity, variability, dependence on the observational arrangements, and so on). Even where the *same* phenomenon is the subject of both psychological and physical investigation (as might be the case with the light in Figure 2 above) the *interests* of psychologists and physicists differ, requiring different investigative techniques. A physicist, for example, is typically interested in the nature of the light as such, characterised for example in terms of the quantum mechanical properties of its constituent photons. Psychologists are more interested in how such physical energies are translated by the visual system into phenomenal appearances, for example in the ability of the visual system to translate changes in light intensity and frequency into discriminable changes in brightness and colour. Unlike entities and events *themselves*, one cannot hook measuring instruments up to conscious appearances. For example, an instrument that measures the intensity of the light in Figure 2 (in lumens) cannot measure its experienced brightness. Given this, one needs some method of systematising subjective judgements and consequent reports, for example, by recording minimal, discriminable differences in brightness, in the ways typically used in psychophysical experiments. [8]

The need to translate observations into observation reports also occurs, of course, in natural science, although here, reports are often made precise through the use of measuring instruments (which can be hooked up to the observed entities and events themselves). In some cases, a mental phenomenon can also be "measured", in spite of the fact that the only observer with access to that phenomenon is the subject. It is standard practice, for example, to measure the size of a visual illusion by requiring subjects to adjust the dimensions of an external, comparison stimulus so that it matches the dimensions of the illusion (see, e.g., the discussion of the illusion shown in Figure 3 above).

That said, not all phenomena of interest to consciousness studies are easy to measure or even to communicate in an unambiguous way. Some experiences are difficult to translate into words, and therefore into subjective reports. Images, for example, generally lack the clarity, vividness and relative permanence of events as experienced out in the world, which may make them difficult to describe with accuracy and precision. Consequently, indirect measures of imagery such as its effects on memory, learning, perception and so on are common in imagery research.[9] Difficulties may also arise because one does not have a vocabulary adequate to communicate some experience unambiguously. Most human beings know what it is to love or be angry, but the many nuances of such experience are more difficult to describe (the differences in the feeling of the love of wild places, love of one's child, love of one's lover, love of the truth, love of life, compassionate love, and so on). Investigators typically deal with such situations by developing new typologies and descriptive systems (as with the typologies developed for the chemical sense modalities, taste and smell). The way experiences are categorised into types and the extent to which given categories are differentiated in ordinary language are also, in part, culture-specific. English, for example, has a highly differentiated colour terminology (consequent on the development of pigments and dyes) whereas the language of the Dani tribesmen of New Guinea has only two colour terms ("mola" for warm, light colours and "mili" for dark, cold ones). In such situations, investigators can bypass linguistic differences by using non-verbal responses — measuring, say, colour discrimination or memory by requiring subjects to visually match target colours with comparison colours on a colour chart.

These brief points about methodological problems and some of the ways that they are commonly addressed will be familiar to those trained in psychological research. Psychology and its sister disciplines have developed many different methodologies for investigating sensation, perception, emotion, thinking, and many other areas that deal directly or indirectly with how phenomena are experienced. However, as the chapters in this book demonstrate, there is much more to be said about this subject and still much to be done.

The relation of the observer to the observed

Observations in science or in ordinary life are, to varying degrees, dependent on the *relation* of the observer to the observed. The very act of observation can affect the nature of the observed although the strength of this effect depends on the strength of the observer/observed coupling. As Norbert Wiener (the father of cybernetics) pointed out, in classical physics the observer and the observed are, in general, "loosely coupled" and the effects are relatively small (although one still has to take account of the effect of one's measuring equipment on what is being measured). In psychology, when the observed is another human being, the observer and observed are often "closely coupled" which can produce a range of "experimenter effects." In traditional experimental psychology, as in physics, care is taken to control for such effects. Experimenters might place themselves in a different room to the subject, take care to be non-invasive, give non-leading instructions, and so on.

However, in consciousness studies the effect of relationship on experience can itself be a topic of considerable interest. By what process of mutual influence, for example, do we make the transition from first- to second-person perspectives? How does the private, subjective, phenomenal world (which "I" inhabit) become the shared, intersubjective world (which "we" inhabit)? And how does the intersubjective world of "we" have enduring effects on the private world of "me." As Pickering, and Wilber & Walsh (this volume) make clear, individual experience is also shaped by its broader social and cultural context. This provides another rich field of study, as the full effects of such embeddings are not well understood. Individual relationships also vary in their "quality" with potentially potent effects on the participants. Henry (Chapter 7), for example, reviews evidence that the quality of relationship between therapist and client is a major determinant of change in clients' experience. And, Richardson (Chapter 8) examines ways in which different forms of intersubjectivity established in clinical practice contribute to a "therapeutic relationship." A detached versus an engaged clinician-client relationship, for example, may have very different consequences for what can be revealed or expressed in therapeutic encounters, which can have powerful effects on health outcome and well being. But what *determines* the quality of relatedness? How, for example, can one move from isolation to communication, intersubjectivity, empathy, and intimacy?

The relation of the observer to the observed is most intimate, of course, in situations where the observer *is* the observed, for example, in the use of introspective and phenomenological methods where subjects become the primary investigators of their own mental processes and states. In this situation "observer effects" seem to be unavoidable. The very act of directing one's attention to one's own mental states affects those states, for the simple reason that the direction and quality of attention itself defines a state of mind. Once one adds the problems of self-description, self-analysis, and self-interpretation (of mental states) it is little wonder that Stevens (Chapter 5) concludes that only relatively concrete, data-driven, sensory states can provide conscious contents that are sufficiently stable and intersubjectively repeatable to provide data for a systematic, introspective science.

However, other authors suggest that it is possible for the mind to become sufficiently stable to attain a deeper first-person knowledge of its own nature, uncovering states and processes that can be confirmed by an appropriately trained research community. Such investigative techniques often encourage a dispassionate, focused but open attitude to whatever emerges in experience (noticing whatever emerges without grasping, avoiding, judging, and so on). Depraz et al. (Chapter 6), for example, give a detailed description of a first-person investigative method that requires a "phase of suspension of habitual thought and judgement", a "phase of conversion of attention from the exterior

to the interior" and a "phase of letting go or receptivity towards the experience." Various readings in *The View From Within* (see note 3) illustrate how
this method (augmented by other techniques) can be applied in practice. For
example, an investigation of intuition by Petitmengen-Peugeot (1999) revealed the states of mind preparatory to having creative insights in a sufficiently detailed form to provide a basis for making predictions about how to
facilitate such states. And Varela (1999) demonstrates how a detailed phenomenological exploration of the experience of time can provide first-person
accounts that can be related to sophisticated models of the brain's temporal
processing. Needless to say, the application of such subtle introspective
methods requires careful training (a common situation in science) — in this
instance, training in how to enter into an appropriately receptive state of mind.
This may be an example of the "state-specific sciences" suggested by Tart, as
only those researchers who can enter into the appropriate states of mind can
confirm or disconfirm the findings. It is important to note however that the
utility and productiveness of such research methods can be assessed in the
normal way, in terms of whether they enable prediction, control, provide a
more integrated understanding of the phenomena under investigation, and so
on. For example, Petitmengen-Peugeot's findings on states conducive to
creativity can be evaluated in terms of whether others trained to enter into such
states really do become more creative. And Varela's findings on the phenomenology of experienced time may be supported (or not) by triangulating
evidence about temporal processing in the brain.

It should be clear that in the application of such phenomenological
methods, changing the state of mind of the observer becomes an unavoidable
part of the investigation. Conversely, another traditional purpose of self-
investigation is to *effect* change, for example in the therapeutic and clinical
situations reviewed in the chapters by Henry and Richardson. In discovering
its own nature, the mind changes its nature. This process too, may follow
discoverable, systematic principles — and it may be that in this, consciousness
studies in western science has a good deal to learn from traditional first-person
investigative methodologies that have been developed over the millennia with
aim of inducing such changes, particularly in the east (as suggested by
Fontana, Chapter 9).

Conclusions

There are many maps that can be drawn of consciousness studies. But from the perspective of psychological science, the difficulties posed by the study of consciousness may be categorised into epistemological problems, methodological problems, and problems that follow from the potential effects of the observer on the observed.

It has traditionally been thought that one cannot make consciousness studies into an "objective" science on the grounds that one cannot obtain public, objective knowledge about private, subjective experiences. However, all science relies on the experiences/observations of scientists. Scientists can be "objective" in the sense of being dispassionate, employ procedures that are "objective" in the sense of being well specified and repeatable, and develop "objective knowledge" in the sense of *intersubjective* knowledge. But no observations in science are "objective" in the sense of being observer-free. Nor does science *require* "observer-free observations." The heart of science is the *empirical method* which, simply put, is *if you follow these procedures you will observe or experience these results*. This applies as much to a science of consciousness as it does to physics.

No science of consciousness can be complete without first-person methods. Although existing first-person methods can be combined with third-person methods in a variety of useful, complementary ways, there is a clear need to develop more sophisticated first-person methods, particularly for those aspects of experience that are relatively complex, impermanent, unstable, or variable, or are difficult to describe, measure, or control. As with any area of investigation, the investigative tools and procedures need to be tailored to the phenomena under study. While there is a great deal of methodological development to be done, particularly in less well-articulated domains of experience, such development is standard practice in psychological science.

Within consciousness studies, there are many situations where the very act of observation can change the observed. These "observer effects" take two forms: The way an external observer relates to an experiencing subject can alter his or her experience ("experimenter effects"). With introspective methods where the observer *is* the observed, the act of introspection *already* produces a change in the operations of the mind.

Depending on one's purposes, there are two basic ways of dealing with such effects: one can attempt to *minimise* them, or study and *harness* them.

Techniques for minimising observer effects in the study of other people all hinge on 'removing' the observer (in some sense) from the observation — either literally, by placing the observer in a separate room, or metaphorically, by being non-invasive, giving non-directive instructions, etcetera. While self-observation techniques cannot remove the observer, they often encourage a dispassionate, focused, but open attitude to whatever emerges in experience (noticing whatever emerges without grasping, avoiding, judging, and so on).

For other purposes, the way that relationship changes experience is itself of primary interest. The experiences of individual observers are embedded in interpersonal, social and cultural contexts, requiring continuous re-negotiation of the borders between the first-person space of "I" and the second-person space of "we". The transitions between subjectivity and intersubjectivity are complex and not fully understood. The effects of different forms of self-investigation on the contents of consciousness are similarly obscure. Such observer/observed interactions become particularly important when the deeper purpose of the investigation is to transform experience rather than to describe it, analyse it or theorise about it. *How* different forms of engagement with others or oneself might facilitate such change is an important topic for research.

It has to be said that the methodological problems are sometimes complex and the solutions sometimes controversial, particularly in the use of introspective and phenomenological methods where subjects become the primary investigators of themselves. But this does not alter the fact that the *phenomena* of consciousness provide data that are potentially public, intersubjective and repeatable. Consequently, the need to use and develop methodologies appropriate to the study of such phenomena does not place them beyond science. Rather, it is part of science.

Notes

1.   If consciousness could be demonstrated to be *nothing more than* a state or function of the brain it would be possible to study consciousness by studies of the brain alone. I have summarised some of the fallacies of such reductionism in Velmans (1998) and reviewed these in depth in Velmans (2000), so I will not repeat this analysis here.

2.   Following this theoretical approach, phenomenal and neural-state "spaces" are dual aspects of a form of mental information, and their very different phenomenal and neural formats arise from the different first- versus third-person perspectives from which that information is viewed. In some respects (but not others) this is analogous to wave-particle complementarity in quantum mechanics where the wave- or particle-like nature of

photons depends entirely on the measuring arrangements, and where a complete description of photons requires both wave and particle accounts. A more detailed analysis of such "psychological complementarity", is given in Velmans (1991a, Section 9.3, 1991b, Sections 8 and 9, 1993a, 1996c, and 2000, Chapter 11). Some aspects of this position have also been adopted by Chalmers (1995) and MacLennan (1996) (see the commentary on Chalmers in Velmans, 1995).

3.   See readings in Pope & Singer (1978), the *View From Within* an entire issue of *The Journal of Consciousness Studies*, 6, 2/3, 1999, and the on-line course and discussions of "The Investigation of Conscious Emotion: Combining first- and third-person methodologies." Sponsored by the University of Arizona at Tucson and the *Journal of Consciousness Studies*, February to March, 1999.

4.   The following analysis of epistemological problems is largely taken from Velmans (1999).

5.   It is interesting to note that Tart, and Wilber & Walsh (this volume) arrive at a very similar conclusion.

6.   The following analysis is taken largely from Velmans (2000), Chapter 8.

7.   A hypothetical machine for viewing activity in one's own brain, e.g. via a T.V. monitor attached to sensors which detect electrical, magnetic or other activity.

8.   To clarify the epistemic issues, I have so far focused only on very simple cases of conscious experience (simple visual percepts, pains and so on) which are relatively easy to study and control. Under normal conditions, for example, visual perception appears to be so tightly guided by the information picked up by the retina that the resulting experience gives every appearance of being a "direct perception" of what is out-there in the world. Consequently, given similar stimuli, presented under similar viewing conditions, with similar expectations, experimental instructions and so on, different subjects are likely to agree that they see the same thing. By contrast, experienced thoughts, emotions and images are largely determined by endogenous factors, and even when they are influenced by events in the external world, they generally represent some inner response *to* external events, rather than representing the events themselves. This makes them heavily dependent on individual differences in heredity, personal history, momentary fluctuations in attention and interest, and on other endogenous factors, making them less easy to reproduce under controlled conditions. Other experiences may be rare or even unique to the individuals involved. While these factors complicate investigation they do not prevent it. Psychologists simply include such complicating factors within their research — investigating the effects of heredity, learning, and attention on thinking and emotion, making use of single case studies where needed and so on. In some studies investigators harness subjects' ability to control their own experience. A common method of studying imagery for example is to ask subjects to generate a given image, and then to perform some task that reveals something about its nature or use. When a given experience is very difficult to reproduce at will, it can be investigated when it occurs naturally, as in studies of dreaming during REM sleep. As in natural science, the accuracy of reports can become suspect when stimuli or experiences are near the limits of detectability, for example, when a weak signal is embedded in noise — in which case estimation procedures have to be developed, such as those suggested by signal detection theory. One also has to be mindful of the well-known effects of the act of observation on

the nature of the observed. Such "experimenter effects" have been extensively investigated in psychology (along with the means by which they can be minimised), but they can be particularly powerful when the observer *is* the observed, for example, when a subject studies (rather than simply reports on) her own conscious experience. In such cases one either has to attempt to limit such influences (cf Ericsson & Simon, 1984) or to harness them, for example in situations where focused self-observation is intended to transform conscious states rather than to describe them (see below).

9.   A useful review of current methods for investigating imagery is given by Richardson (1999).

References

Bridgman, P.W. 1936. *The Nature of Physical Theory*. Princeton, NJ: Princeton University Press.

Chalmers, D. 1995. "Facing up to the problem of consciousness". *Journal of Consciousness Studies* 2(3): 200–219.

Cohen, J.D. and Schooler, J.W. (eds). 1997. *Scientific Approaches to Consciousness*. Hillsdale, N.J.: Lawrence Erlbaum Associates.

Ericsson, K.A. and Simon, H. 1984. *Protocol Analysis: verbal reports as data*. Cambridge, Mass.: MIT Press.

Farthing, J.W. 1992. *The Psychology of Consciousness*. Englewood Cliffs, NJ: Prentice-Hall.

MacLennan, B. 1996. The elements of consciousness and their neurodynamic correlates. *Journal of Consciousness Studies* 3 (5/6): 409–424.

Nisbett, R.E., and Wilson, T.D. 1977. "Telling more than we can know: Verbal reports on mental processes". *Psychological Review* 75: 522–536.

Petitmengen-Peugeot, C.1999. "The intuitive experience". *Journal of Consciousness Studies* 6(2/3): 43–77.

Pope, K.S and Singer, J.L. (eds). 1978. *The Stream of Consciousness: Scientific investigations into the flow of experience*. NY: Plenum Press.

Richardson, A. 1999. "Subjective experience: Its conceptual status, methods of investigation, and psychological significance. *The Journal of Psychology* 133(4): 469–485.

Varela, F.J. 1999. "Present-time consciousness". *Journal of Consciousness Studies* 6(2/3): 111–140.

Velmans, M. 1991a. "Is human information processing conscious?" *Behavioral and Brain Sciences* 14(4): 651–669.

Velmans, M. 1991b. "Consciousness from a first-person perspective". *Behavioral and Brain Sciences* 14(4): 702–726.

Velmans, M. 1993a. "A reflexive science of consciousness". In *Experimental and Theoretical Studies of Consciousness*, Ciba Foundation Symposium No.174, Chichester: Wiley.

Velmans, M. 1993b. "Consciousness, causality and complementarity". *Behavioral and Brain Sciences* 16(2): 409–416.

Velmans, M. 1995. "The relation of consciousness to the material world". *Journal of Consciousness Studies* 2(3): 255–265.

Velmans, M (ed). 1996a. *The Science of Consciousness: Psychological, Neuropsychological and Clinical Reviews*. London: Routledge.

Velmans, M. 1996b. "What and where are conscious experiences?" In M. Velmans (ed), *The Science of Consciousness: Psychological, Neuropsychological and Clinical Reviews*. London: Routledge.

Velmans, M. 1996c. "Consciousness and the "causal paradox"." *Behavioral and Brain Sciences* 19(3): 537–542.

Velmans, M. 1998. "Goodbye to reductionism". In S.Hameroff, A.Kaszniak and A.Scott (eds), *Towards a Science of Consciousness II: The Second Tucson Discussions and Debates*. Cambridge, Mass.: MIT Press.

Velmans, M. 1999. "Intersubjective science". *Journal of Consciousness Studies* 6(2/3): 299–306.

Velmans, M. 2000. *Understanding Consciousness*. London: Routledge.

Name Index

Subject Index

In the series ADVANCES IN CONSCIOUSNESS RESEARCH (AiCR) the following titles
have been published thus far or are scheduled for publication:

1. GLOBUS, Gordon G.: *The Postmodern Brain*. 1995.
2. ELLIS, Ralph D.: *Questioning Consciousness. The interplay of imagery, cognition, and emotion in the human brain*. 1995.
3. JIBU, Mari and Kunio YASUE: *Quantum Brain Dynamics and Consciousness. An introduction*. 1995.
4. HARDCASTLE, Valerie Gray: *Locating Consciousness*. 1995.
5. STUBENBERG, Leopold: *Consciousness and Qualia*. 1998.
6. GENNARO, Rocco J.: *Consciousness and Self-Consciousness. A defense of the higher-order thought theory of consciousness*. 1996.
7. MAC CORMAC, Earl and Maxim I. STAMENOV (eds): *Fractals of Brain, Fractals of Mind. In search of a symmetry bond*. 1996.
8. GROSSENBACHER, Peter G. (ed.): *Finding Consciousness in the Brain. A neuro-cognitive approach*. n.y.p.
9. Ó NUALLÁIN, Seán, Paul MC KEVITT and Eoghan MAC AOGÁIN (eds): *Two Sciences of Mind. Readings in cognitive science and consciousness*. 1997.
10. NEWTON, Natika: *Foundations of Understanding*. 1996.
11. PYLKKÖ, Pauli: *The Aconceptual Mind. Heideggerian themes in holistic naturalism*. 1998.
12. STAMENOV, Maxim I. (ed.): *Language Structure, Discourse and the Access to Consciousness*. 1997.
13. VELMANS, Max (ed.): *Investigating Phenomenal Consciousness. Methodologies and Maps*. 2000.
14. SHEETS-JOHNSTONE, Maxine: *The Primacy of Movement*. 1999.
15. CHALLIS, Bradford H. and Boris M. VELICHKOVSKY (eds.): *Stratification in Cognition and Consciousness*. 1999.
16. ELLIS, Ralph D. and Natika NEWTON (eds.): *The Caldron of Consciousness. Motivation, affect and self-organization – An anthology*. 2000.
17. HUTTO, Daniel D.: *The Presence of Mind*. 1999.
18. PALMER, Gary B. and Debra J. OCCHI (eds.): *Languages of Sentiment. Cultural constructions of emotional substrates*. 1999.
19. DAUTENHAHN, Kerstin (ed.): *Human Cognition and Social Agent Technology*. 2000.
20. KUNZENDORF, Robert G. and Benjamin WALLACE (eds.): *Individual Differences in Conscious Experience*. 2000.
21. HUTTO, Daniel D.: *Beyond Physicalism*. 2000.
22. ROSSETTI, Yves and Antti REVONSUO (eds.): *Beyond Dissociation. Interaction between dissociated implicit and explicit processing*. 2000.
23. ZAHAVI, Dan (ed.): *Exploring the Self. Philosophical and psychopathological perspectives on self-experience*. 2000.
24. ROVEE-COLLIER, Carolyn, Harlene HAYNE and Michael COLOMBO: *The Development of Implicit and Explicit Memory*. 2000.
25. BACHMANN, Talis: *Microgenetic Approach to the Conscious Mind*. n.y.p.
26. Ó NUALLÁIN, Seán (ed.): *Spatial Cognition. Selected papers from Mind III, Annual Conference of the Cognitive Science Society of Ireland, 1998*. n.y.p.

27. McMILLAN, John and Grant R. GILLETT: *Consciousness and Intentionality.* n.y.p.
28. ZACHAR, Peter: *Psychological Concepts and Biological Psychiatry. A philosophical analysis.* n.y.p.
29. VAN LOOCKE, Philip (ed.): *The Physical Nature of Consciousness.* n.y.p.